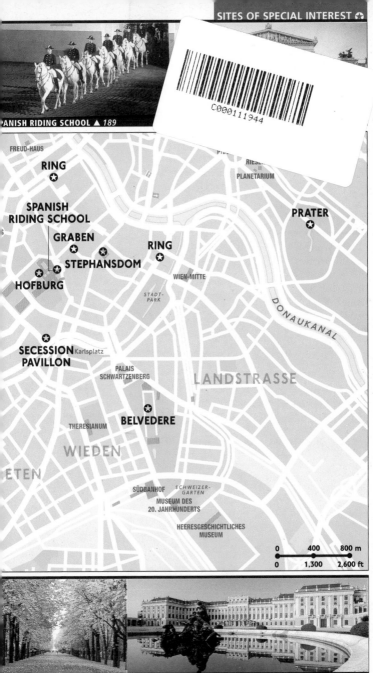

ANISH RIDING SCHOOL ▲ 189

FREUD-HAUS

RING ✿

PLANETARIUM

RIESE

PIE

SPANISH RIDING SCHOOL

PRATER ✿

GRABEN ✿

RING ✿ ✿

STEPHANSDOM ✿ ✿

WIEN-MITTE

HOFBURG ✿ ✿

STADT-PARK

DONAUKANAL

SECESSION PAVILLON ✿ Karlsplatz

PALAIS SCHWARTZENBERG

LANDSTRASSE

BELVEDERE ✿

THERESIANUM

WIEDEN

ETEN

SÜDBAHNHOF

SCHWEIZER-GARTEN

MUSEUM DES 20. JAHRHUNDERTS

HEERESGESCHICHTLICHES MUSEUM

| 0 | 400 | 800 m |
| 0 | 1,300 | 2,600 ft |

E PRATER ▲ 267 SCHÖNBRUNN ▲ 275

THE RING
By tram, on foot or by hackney carriage, take a tour along the Ring, the boulevard that encircles the old town.
SECESSION PAVILION
Enter in the spirit of the Secessionist movement, led by Gustav Klimt in the early 20th century. The pavilion stands as the movement's manifesto.
THE BELVEDERE
The two Belvedere palaces, the Upper Belvedere and Lower Belvedere, are both masterpieces of Viennese Baroque secular architecture.
THE PRATER
Enjoy a leisurely walk in the Prater, the favorite park of the Viennese, famous for its fun fair and its Ferris wheel.
SCHÖNBRUNN
Marvel at the elegance of the palace beloved of the Habsburgs.

VIENNA

EVERYMAN GUIDES

● Encyclopedia section

■ **NATURE** The natural heritage: species and habitats characteristic to the area covered by the guide, annotated and illustrated by naturalist authors and artists.

HISTORY AND LANGUAGE The impact of international historical events on local history, from the arrival of the first inhabitants, with key dates appearing in a timeline above the text.

ARTS AND TRADITIONS Customs and traditions and their continuing role in contemporary life.

ARCHITECTURE The architectural heritage, focusing on style and topology, a look at rural and urban buildings, major civil, religious and military monuments.

AS SEEN BY PAINTERS A selection of paintings of the city or country by different artists and schools, arranged chronologically or thematically.

AS SEEN BY WRITERS An anthology of texts focusing on the city or country, taken from works of all periods and countries, arranged thematically.

▲ Itineraries

Each itinerary begins with a map of the area to be explored.

✪ **SPECIAL INTEREST** These sites are not to be missed. They are highlighted in gray boxes in the margins.

★ **EDITOR'S CHOICE** Sites singled out by the editor for special attention.

INSETS On richly illustrated double pages, these insets turn the spotlight on subjects deserving more in-depth treatment.

◆ Practical information

All the travel information you will need before you go and when you get there.

USEFUL ADDRESSES A selection of the best hotels and restaurants compiled by an expert.

PLACES TO VISIT A handy table of addresses and opening hours.

APPENDICES Bibliography, list of illustrations and general index.

MAP SECTION Maps of all the areas covered by the guide, followed by an index; these maps are marked out with letters and figures making it easy for the reader to pinpoint a town, region or site.

Each map in the map section is designated by a letter. In the itineraries, all the sites of interest are given a map reference (for example: **B** A1).

● ▲ ◆
The above symbols within the text provide cross-references to a place or a theme discussed elsewhere in the guide.

The itinerary map shows the main sites, the editor's choices and the places of special interest.

The mini-map pinpoints the itinerary within the wider area covered by the guide.

At the beginning of each itinerary, the distance, the suggested means of travel and the time it will take to cover the area are indicated beneath the maps:
🚶 On foot
🚢 By boat
🕐 Duration

✪ This symbol indicates places of special interest.

★ The star symbol indicates sites singled out by the editor for special attention.

3

● **Encyclopedia section**

▲ Itineraries in Vienna

◆ Practical information

THE CITY CENTER ▲ 129
The historic and artistic faces of Vienna, and city life: from narrow pedestrianized streets to the great shopping areas of Kärntnerstrasse, and from the Baroque palaces of Annagasse to the smart restaurants of the Fleischmarkt.

THE HOFBURG ▲ 173
From Michaelerplatz, a step back into the city's imperial history, with the Hofburg (Imperial Palace) and its treasures: the chapel, the fabulously rich library, and the stables, where the Spanish Riding School is now based.

THE RING ▲ 197
This circular thoroughfare is lined with public buildings and neo-classical private palaces dating from the late 19th century, when the Viennese aristocracy and high finance were at their apogee. Very near the Burggarten is the Kunsthistorisches Museum, where masterpieces of Italian and Flemish painting are on display.

FROM SECESSION TO MUSIKVEREINSGEBÄUDE ▲ 231
A proclamation of Art Nouveau, the Secession Pavilion and the elegant residential buildings on Wienziele attest to the creativity of the early 20th century. Two unmissable monuments in this district of Vienna are the famous Karlsplatz station and the Karlskirche, the most typically Baroque of all Viennese churches.

FROM THERASIANUM TO ZENTRALFRIEDHOF ▲ 243
South of the Ring, the sumptuous summer residences of the aristocracy are remarkable for their beauty, number and variety. The Schwarzenberg Palace, the Lower Belvedere and its Museum of Baroque Art, with their fairytale atmosphere, are surrounded by splendid parks.

FROM THE PRATER TO THE DANUBE ▲ 263
Very near the working class area of Leopoldstadt, the Prater, with its famous Ferris wheel, is a favorite place for Viennese people, who come there to walk and relax. Further north the former orangery of Augarten Park now houses the Augarten china factory.

FROM SCHÖNBRUNN TO THE STEINHOF ▲ 273
In the Schönbrunn, the Viennese palace modeled on Versailles, there is much to see, including the apartments of Franz-Joseph and Sissi and many salons, and the park with botanical garden, tropical greenhouses and Tyrolien chalets. Nearby is the Kirche am Steinhof, Otto Wagner's finest achievement.

FROM JOSEFSTADT TO KLOSTERNEUBURG ▲ 289
From Alsergrund, the medical district, to "Red Vienna", the worker's city, this itinerary ends by following in the footsteps of the great composers, which lead to the pretty villages of Heiligenstadt, Nussdorf and Grinzing, set in the midst of vineyards and endowned with pleasure gardens.

● Encyclopedia section

■ **NATURE**
Philippe J. Dubois,
assisted by Andreas Ranner
and Pierre Crisol
■ **HISTORY**
Jean-Louis Poitevin,
Jean-Claude Klotchkoff,
François de Lannoy
■ **ARTS AND TRADITIONS**
Jean-François Frémont
(music),
Jean-Louis Poitevin
■ **ARCHITECTURE**
Jean-Louis Gaillemin,
Dominique Fernandes
■ **VIENNA AS SEEN BY PAINTERS**
Jean-Louis Gaillemin
■ **VIENNA AS SEEN BY WRITERS**
Jean-Louis Poitevin

▲ Itineraries in Vienna

Jean-Claude Klotchkoff,
Pierre de Lagarde
(History of Art musem),
Jean-Louis Gaillemin
(Klimt, Schiele, Gerstl, Kokoschka)

◆ Practical information

Catherine Polsterer, Veronika Vollmer

EVERYMAN GUIDES
Published by Everyman Publishers Plc

First published 1994
Further editions, revised and updated:
July 1997 and September 2000

© 2000 Everyman Publishers Plc

Originally published in France by
Nouveaux-Loisirs, a subsidiary of
Editions Gallimard, Paris, 1993
© 1993 Editions Nouveaux-Loisirs.

Vienna – ISBN 1-84159-010-X

TRANSLATED BY
Antony Roberts

EDITED AND TYPESET BY
Book Creation Services Ltd, London

WE WOULD ALSO LIKE TO THANK
Christian Brandsätter, Ferdinand
Fellinger (Historischesmuseum der Stadt
Wien), Edwin Hofbauer (Österreichische
Nationalbibliothek), Traudl and Eric
Lessing, Andreas Ranner
(Österreichische Gesellschaft für
Vogelkunde), Richard Schmitz and
Sonia Schmitz.

VIENNA
■ **EDITOR**
Patrick Jézéquel and
Pierre de Laubier
■ **LAYOUT**
Yann Le Duc, Annie Civiard (Practical
information) and Olivier Brunot
■ **PICTURE RESEARCH**
Catherine Boncenne

■ **ILLUSTRATIONS**
NATURE: Jean Chevallier,
François Desbordes, Jean-Michel Kacédan,
Alban Larousse, Catherine Lachaux,
Claire Felloni, Pascal Robin, John Wilkinson
ARCHITECTURE : Michel Aubois,
Michel Simier, Maurice Pommier,
Cent Alantar, Philippe Biard, Hugh Dixon,
Frédéric Hillion
ITINERARIES: Vincent Brunot, Jean-Philippe
Chabot, Jean-Marc Lanus
MAPS : Vincent Brunot, Jean-Yves Duhoo,
Caroline Picard (colorist)
COMPUTER GRAPHICS: Paul Coulbois,
Cyrille Mallié

■ **LOCAL CORRESPONDENT**
Catherine Polsterer

■ **PHOTOGRAPHY**
Philippe Bénet, Matthias Cremer, Renata
Holzbachovà, Kathrin Leithner

Printed in Italy by Editoriale Lloyd

EVERYMAN GUIDES
Gloucester Mansions, 140a Shaftesbury Avenue,
London WC2H 8HD
guides@everyman.uk.com

Encyclopedia section

The Ring at the beginning of the
20th century, with the State Opera
to the right.

The ferris wheel at the Prater in the 1930's.
It was later made famous by Carol Reed's film,
The Third Man (1949).

The Graben c. 1900. The Fountain of St Leopold is in the foreground, with the Plague Column (Pestsäule) beyond.

Nature

The park at Schönbrunn ▲ 284 has plenty of broad open spaces, perfectly adapted for birds foraging for worms and field insects.

From the tiniest shady square to the magnificent Schönbrunn Park, Vienna's green areas shelter a surprising variety of wild creatures. The city is still a favorable environment for woodland bird species such as the tawny owl, the stock dove and various woodpeckers (including the rare Syrian woodpecker, Vienna being the westernmost point of its range). There are forest trees everywhere, such as beech and moss-capped oak. Even the shy pine marten may sometimes be seen at Schönbrunn.

A panoply of species, most of them common to the forests of Central Europe, make Schönbrunn a true woodland park.

CARRION AND HOODED CROW
Vienna is one of the points in Central Europe where these two sub-species appear to co-exist. The carrion crow is thought to be expanding its territory eastward, at the expense of its close relative.

NORWAY MAPLE. The broad leaves of this maple resemble those of the plane tree.

SYCAMORE A smooth-trunked tree which can grow to heights of 100 feet.

LIME TREE. Delicious honey can be made from lime blossom.

HORSE CHESTNUT Some of Vienna's parks have chestnut avenues that are hundeds of years old.

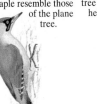

GREEN WOODPECKER This large woodpecker often feeds on the ground.

MIDDLE SPOTTED WOODPECKER. This is rare in cities but is common in Vienna.

GREAT SPOTTED WOODPECKER. This is common in Vienna's parks and gardens.

NUTHATCH The nuthatch is easily identified by its "tuit, tuit, tuit" call.

BLACKBIRD The blackbird can be seen foraging everywhere in the grass parks of Vienna.

BLACKCAP This migratory species reappears in Vienna's parks in April.

RED SQUIRREL The red squirrels at Schönbrunn are so confident and inquisitive that one can almost touch them.

17

THE WIENERWALD

PINE MARTEN. The pine marten's usual diet consists of rodents and small birds, but it will also eat berries and wild fruit.

BEECH TREE

The Wienerwald (Vienna Forest), a good example of Central European woodland, stretches all the way from the gates of the city to the foothills of the Alps. A dominant tree species is the beech, which favors humid, well-ventilated soil. The oak family is also strongly represented, with several trees many centuries old, and also the Norwegian pine, which often grows in companionship with the oak. Red deer, fallow deer and wild boar abound in the Wienerwald, where they still occupy the old imperial game preserves, while woodpeckers and flycatchers (both red-breasted and white-collared) are the commonest birds.

EUROPEAN RED DEER
The more distant and protected areas of the forest shelter large numbers of deer.

Female

Male

Male

RED-BREASTED AND COLLARED FLYCATCHERS
These two species of flycatcher, characteristic inhabitants of the great forests of Central Europe, are strongly represented in the Wienerwald. They appear in the older beech and oak plantations in about mid-May.

WOOD WARBLER
This bird is very common in the groves of older trees.

RAMSON
The undergrowth of the Wienerwald is carpeted with this plant in May.

SPOTTED SALAMANDER
This reptile is found in wet areas of the woods, especially at dusk.

EURASIAN WILD BOAR
This shy creature steers well clear of human beings.

THE DANUBE

In former times, the Danube at Vienna was a maze of branch streams and side-channels, much prone to flooding. This explains the Viennese preoccupation with the movements of the river.

The first attempt to regulate the river was made after a flood in 1501, but this came to nothing since the Danube continued to overflow its banks. The canal acquired its present appearance during the 18th century, when a dam was erected draining several major side channels. A terrific flood in 1787 demolished many new dikes. In the late 19th and especially in the 20th century, permanent regulatory measures were undertaken: these were completed in 1972, with the creation of the 13-mile New Danube Canal and the Donauinsel Island. Wild fauna settled on this artificial island, and the site is now heavily populated with ducks throughout the winter.

GREAT CORMORANT
The cormorant is on the increase throughout Europe; it winters on the banks of the Danube and is often seen in the center of Vienna.

BLACK-THROATED DIVER
Like its cousin the red-throated diver, this bird is a rare visitor to the Danube in winter; most divers spend winter in coastal waters.

Although it is artificial and surrounded by buildings, the canalized Danube attracts large numbers of water birds in winter on account of its abundant food sources.

male   female

POCHARD
A few hundred of this diving duck visit the Vienna area from November to March.

CARP
Carp thrive in all the Danube's quieter backwaters, living on mollusks, worms and vegetable debris.

female

male

TUFTED DUCK
This winter-visiting diving duck lives on the tiny mussels which thrive in Vienna's waterways.

CATFISH
A transplant from North America, the catfish competes successfully with indigenous fish species.

GREEN TOAD
This can be found right in the heart of Vienna.

EUROPEAN KINGFISHER
The concrete banks of the river do not suit this bird as a nesting site, but it can easily spend all winter along the Danube Canal.

Winter   Summer

BLACK-HEADED GULL
The black-headed gull enlivens the river with its swooping, graceful flight.

THE LOBAU

Downstream
from Vienna, the
Danube meanders past a
labyrinth of small backwaters. In
the cool, dank soil in this area, willows, field
maples and elms have grown up; there are also
extensive plantations of poplars. Some branches of the
Danube are also covered in reedbeds. These calm waters are
convenient spawning grounds for many species of fish.

The Lobau is made up of riverside woodlands
penetrated by still backwaters, more or less
directly connected to the main stream.

EUROPEAN BEAVER
This species was on the
brink of extinction and has
now been successfully
reintroduced both here and
in other regions of Europe.

male   female

ICTERINE WARBLER
The grating,
mimicking cry of this
warbler echoes
among the willows
along the river.

RIVER WARBLER
The song of this
brown-colored
oriental species
resembles the sound
of an elderly sewing
machine.

REED BUNTING
The smallest patch of
swamp is colonized by
the humidity-loving
reed bunting.

GOLDEN ORIOLE
The song of the oriole
can be heard in the
tallest poplars and
willows.

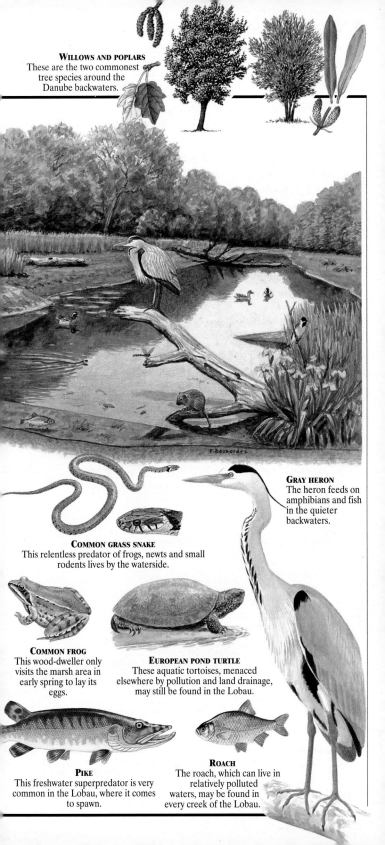

WILLOWS AND POPLARS
These are the two commonest tree species around the Danube backwaters.

GRAY HERON
The heron feeds on amphibians and fish in the quieter backwaters.

COMMON GRASS SNAKE
This relentless predator of frogs, newts and small rodents lives by the waterside.

COMMON FROG
This wood-dweller only visits the marsh area in early spring to lay its eggs.

EUROPEAN POND TURTLE
These aquatic tortoises, menaced elsewhere by pollution and land drainage, may still be found in the Lobau.

PIKE
This freshwater superpredator is very common in the Lobau, where it comes to spawn.

ROACH
The roach, which can live in relatively polluted waters, may be found in every creek of the Lobau.

NEUSIEDLERSEE AND SEEWINKEL

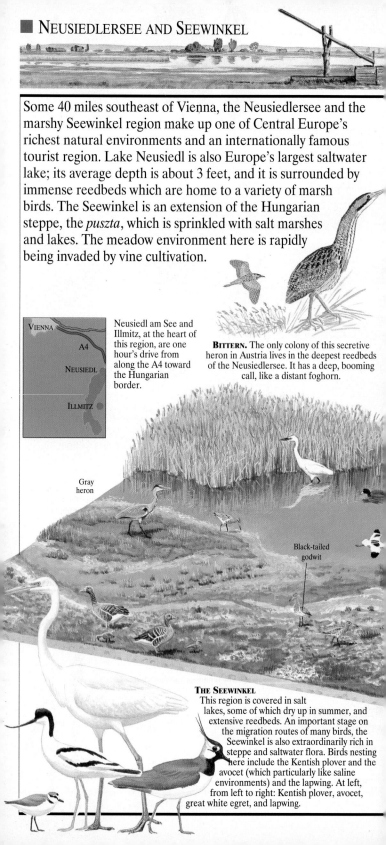

Some 40 miles southeast of Vienna, the Neusiedlersee and the marshy Seewinkel region make up one of Central Europe's richest natural environments and an internationally famous tourist region. Lake Neusiedl is also Europe's largest saltwater lake; its average depth is about 3 feet, and it is surrounded by immense reedbeds which are home to a variety of marsh birds. The Seewinkel is an extension of the Hungarian steppe, the *puszta*, which is sprinkled with salt marshes and lakes. The meadow environment here is rapidly being invaded by vine cultivation.

Neusiedl am See and Illmitz, at the heart of this region, are one hour's drive from along the A4 toward the Hungarian border.

BITTERN. The only colony of this secretive heron in Austria lives in the deepest reedbeds of the Neusiedlersee. It has a deep, booming call, like a distant foghorn.

Gray heron

Black-tailed godwit

THE SEEWINKEL
This region is covered in salt lakes, some of which dry up in summer, and extensive reedbeds. An important stage on the migration routes of many birds, the Seewinkel is also extraordinarily rich in steppe and saltwater flora. Birds nesting here include the Kentish plover and the avocet (which particularly like saline environments) and the lapwing. At left, from left to right: Kentish plover, avocet, great white egret, and lapwing.

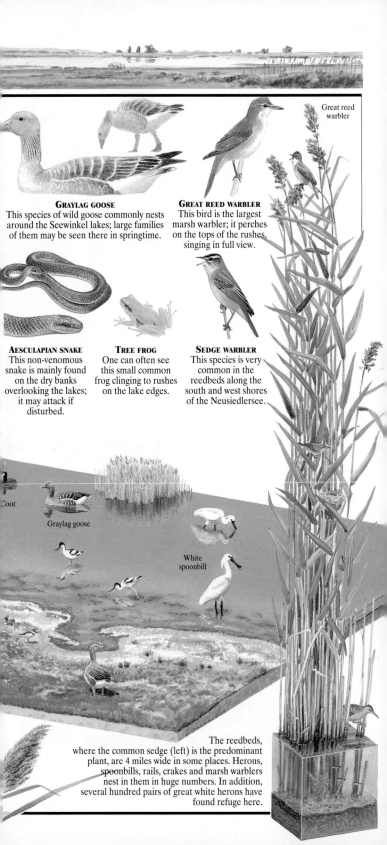

GRAYLAG GOOSE
This species of wild goose commonly nests around the Seewinkel lakes; large families of them may be seen there in springtime.

GREAT REED WARBLER
This bird is the largest marsh warbler; it perches on the tops of the rushes, singing in full view.

Great reed warbler

AESCULAPIAN SNAKE
This non-venomous snake is mainly found on the dry banks overlooking the lakes; it may attack if disturbed.

TREE FROG
One can often see this small common frog clinging to rushes on the lake edges.

SEDGE WARBLER
This species is very common in the reedbeds along the south and west shores of the Neusiedlersee.

Coot

Graylag goose

White spoonbill

The reedbeds, where the common sedge (left) is the predominant plant, are 4 miles wide in some places. Herons, spoonbills, rails, crakes and marsh warblers nest in them in huge numbers. In addition, several hundred pairs of great white herons have found refuge here.

■ VINEYARDS OF VIENNA

The Austrian capital has given its name to a wine growing area of around 1800 acres owned by some two hundred and fifty different wine growers, whose vines cover the slopes overlooking the Danube. Wineries line the main streets of the surrounding villages; at the official closing of the grape harvest on November 11, the growers invite guests to try the year's new vintage (*Heuriger*).

"HEURIGEN" ● *68.* Some of the *Heurigen* have become full-blown wine restaurants.

Viennese wine is considered drinkable at every stage of its vinification, as *Most*, *Sturm* or *Heuriger*. *Gespritzt* (white wine mixed with sparkling water) is also popular.

The principal grape varieties are the Grüner Veltliner (top of the page) and the Neuburger, in addition to one or two indigenous vines (above, the Blaue Portugiese). Much the commonest is the Grüner Veltliner, which yields a light, fruity wine. As a rule, the Viennese prefer Riesling ● *69*, which is more elegant, or Chardonnay, which is more woody.

"WIENER TRILOGIE"
One of the few Viennese red wines, this is a blend of cabernet sauvignon, pinot noir and the local fruity Zweigelt grapes.

SCHWARZENBERGPLATZ These vine stalks are a symbolic reminder that the vineyards reached right into the center of town in former days.

History and language

History of Vienna

The Venus of Willendorf,
30,000–25,000 BC
(Hallstatt civilization).

334–30 BC *Conquest of the Persian Empire by Alexander the Great.* **264–122 BC** *Roman conquest of the Mediterranean Basin.*	Vienna was founded at the meeting of two great highways: one which crossed Europe following the Danube, and the other which linked the Baltic to Italy. From 500 to 15 BC the site of Vienna was a small town occupied by a Celtic tribe, the Vendi.

VINDOBONA UNDER THE ROMANS

31 BC
Battle of Actium.

AD 29
Octavius founds Imperial Rome.

AD 395
Partition of the Roman Empire (Western and Eastern).

At the close of the 1st century AD, the Romans made Vienna (Vindobona, then Flaviana Castra) a frontier fortress to watch the Danube upstream from Carnuntum, capital of Pannonia. In 180, following the invasions of the Quadi and the Marcomanni, Vindobona was destroyed. In 213 the city gained the status of a municipality and began a period of prosperity; at the end of the same century, Emperor Probus authorized the legionaries stationed at Vindobona to cultivate their own vines.

Hercules, pre-4th-century vase. The Hoher Markt (right).

THE GREAT INVASIONS. In 365 the Barbarians finally succeeded in crossing the Danube. In 400 Vindobona was destroyed again. In the 6th century it was occupied by the Lombards, then by the Avars; between 630 and 660, the Avars founded the Slavic kingdom of Samo. In 795 Charlemagne defeated the Avars, forced their submission and joined Ostmark (the Eastern Marches) to his empire. In 881, the Moravians under Prince Svatopluk (870–94) invaded the town, which by then bore the Slavic name of Wiena. The Hungarians were defeated by Otto I at the battle of Lechfeld (955); Otto received the imperial crown in 962 and founded the Germanic Holy Roman Empire. In 974 Emperor Otto II fortified the Eastern Marches of Bavaria.

476
Western Roman Empire collapses.

800
Charlemagne crowned Emperor of the West.

"WIENNE" UNDER THE BABENBERGS

863
Preaching by the Byzantine monks Cyril and Methodus.

962
Coronation of Otto I, first Holy Roman Emperor.

1054
Greek Schism.

1099
The crusaders take Jerusalem.

In 976 Otto II named Leopold of Babenberg hereditary Margrave (*Mark-Graf*, or Lord of the Marches) of Ostmark. In 996, the name Ostarrichi first appears, and in 1030 Wienne. At that time Wienne was the second largest town north of the Alps, after Cologne. The Babenbergs enlarged their landholdings (bordering the Leitha by 1043) and made Vienna their capital and place of residence in 1135. The first Romanesque church of St Stephen was consecrated in 1147. In 1156 Emperor Frederick I Barbarossa gave Henry Jasormigott the title of Duke of Austria, and the latter left his castle, Leopoldberg, to establish his court just outside the walls at Am Hof. From 1160, Henry set about rebuilding St Stephen's. In 1192 the King of England, Richard Coeur de Lion, was arrested at Erdberg and his eventual ransom was used to build new walls

> "Bella gerant alii, tu felix Austria nube."
> "Let others make war:
> thou, happy Austria, makest marriages."
>
> Matthias Corvinus

for Vienna, which were completed in 1200. More building went on around the Kärntnerstrasse, the Kohlmarkt and the Graben. In 1221 Leopold IV granted municipal and commercial privileges to Vienna, notably the monopoly of trade with Hungary. In 1246 Frederick II the Warlike, last Duke of Babenberg, was killed at the victorious battle of the Leitha against the Hungarians. Ottokar II of Bohemia and Bela IV of Hungary both claimed his throne, causing the great interregnum in the Holy Roman Empire.

1270
Seventh and last crusade: death of St Louis at Tunis.

1357
The Ottomans gain their first foothold in Europe.

VIENNA AS THE SEAT OF THE HOLY ROMAN EMPIRE

From 1250 to 1273, the popes and the Germans engaged in a ferocious struggle, and Austria passed into the hands of Ottokar II of Bohemia, who built the Hofburg.

THE HABSBURGS. The interregnum came to an end in 1273, when Rudolph von Habsburg (1218–91), the overlord of German Switzerland, was elected King of the Romans because "he bore a grudge against no man". Rudolph immediately claimed Austria and demanded the homage of Ottokar II. He finally succeeded when, in 1278, Ottokar died at the Battle of Marchfield, after having seized Vienna in 1276. In 1282 Rudolph I gave Austria and Styria as fiefs to his sons Albert I and Rudolph II; but the Viennese rebelled against Rudolph when he tried to take away their privileges, forcing him to grant them a municipal charter: henceforth the city was administered by its own mayor. The Habsburgs went on to complete the Schweizertrakt of the Hofburg, begun by Ottokar II, and encouraged the development of the aristocratic quarter (Herrenviertel). In 1298 Albert I von Habsburg was elected King of the Romans. From 1303 to 1340, the dynasty built the choir of St Stephen's (1330–9), the Church of the Augustines (from 1330 onward), the Church of Maria Stiegen and a new St Stephen's Cathedral. The founder of the cathedral, Duke Rudolph IV, created a university in 1365 to rival that of Prague, founded in 1348. After clashes between the Christian and Jewish communities, the Jewish quarter was demolished in 1421. In 1433 the spire of St Stephen's Cathedral was completed. In 1437 Duke Albert V of Austria (1401–39) became King of Bohemia and Hungary and was subsequently elected Emperor, as Albert II. The title remained with the Habsburgs until 1806 (except for the years 1742–5). In 1462, following a quarrel between Frederick III (1443–93) and his brother Albert, the people laid siege to the sovereign and his family in the Hofburg for two months. Vienna became a bishopric in 1469. In 1485 Matthias Corvinus, King of Hungary, occupied the city after a four-month siege. He died in the Hofburg in 1490; Archduke Maximilian, the "last chevalier", then retook Vienna. He became Holy Roman Emperor Maximilian I (1493–1519); Philip, his son, married Jeanne of Castile, daughter of Ferdinand and Isabella, the heiress to Castile and Aragon. Maximilian himself founded the choir of the court in 1498. In 1515, the cathedral was the scene of the wedding of Maximilian I's grandson

Rudolph II (1552–1612).

1378
The Great Schism in the West.

1440
Invention of the printing press at Gutenberg.

1453
The fall of Constantinople.

Maximilian I (1459–1519) by Dürer.

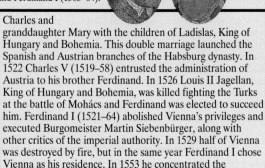

Charles V (1500–58)
and Ferdinand I (1503–64).

1517
Luther begins to preach reform.

1520–66
Reign of Suleyman the Magnificent: height of the Ottoman Empire.

Prince Eugène (1663–1736).

1535
Calvin publishes his "Institutes of the Christian Religion".

1545–63
The Council of Trent heralds the start of the Counter-Reformation.

Maximilian II (1527–76) and his family.

1555
The Peace of Augsburg: victory of Lutheranism in Germany.

1571
The Holy League triumphs over the Turks at Lepanto.

1689–1725
Peter the Great builds Russia into a great power.

Charles and granddaughter Mary with the children of Ladislas, King of Hungary and Bohemia. This double marriage launched the Spanish and Austrian branches of the Habsburg dynasty. In 1522 Charles V (1519–58) entrusted the administration of Austria to his brother Ferdinand. In 1526 Louis II Jagellan, King of Hungary and Bohemia, was killed fighting the Turks at the battle of Mohács and Ferdinand was elected to succeed him. Ferdinand I (1521–64) abolished Vienna's privileges and executed Burgomeister Martin Siebenbürger, along with other critics of the imperial authority. In 1529 half of Vienna was destroyed by fire, but in the same year Ferdinand I chose Vienna as his residence. In 1553 he concentrated the administration of all his subject states (Alsace, Southern Germany, Austria, Hungary and Bohemia) in the city.

THE TURKS. In 1529 Sultan Suleyman I's army was at the gates of Vienna, but the resistance of the Count of Salm and persistent heavy rain saved the city from this first siege. Ferdinand I, King of the Romans since 1531, became Emperor in 1558, succeeding his brother Charles V. The completion of the city wall (1560) took up most of the available resources, so there are few Renaissance buildings in Vienna. Ferdinand's son Maximilian II was a Protestant; after 1570 close to 80 percent of the Viennese had converted to the new religion. He founded the Spanish Riding School in 1572; his successor Rudolph II (1570–1612) left Vienna and moved to Prague in 1582.

TRIUMPH OF THE COUNTER-REFORMATION. In the first half of the 17th century, Catholic monastic orders installed themselves in Vienna at the behest of Cardinal Khlesl to fight heresy: the Carmelites and the Hospitallers of the Brotherhood of Grace moved into Leopoldstadt, the Paulaner installed themselves on the Wieden, and the Augustines built their Church of Saint Roch on the Landstrasse. The flowering of the first wave of Viennese Baroque architecture, created by Italian architects and artists, was a manifestation of the Counter-Reformation, which produced the churches of the Franciscans, Dominicans, Capuchins and Jesuits, in addition to the Baroque Scots monastery. Ferdinand II (1619–37) was a highly effective adversary of Protestantism; it was he who gave Leopoldstadt to the Jewish community in 1625 (they were to be expelled again in 1670). From 1618 to 1648 the Thirty Years' War ravaged Germany and Bohemia; in 1619 the Czechs rebelled and threatened Vienna. Then at the battle of the White Mountain near Prague in 1620, the Catholics defeated the Protestants and confirmed the power of the Habsburgs. The Protestants were driven from Bohemia and Moravia; the Counter-Reformation had triumphed. However the Peace of Westphalia (1648) confirmed the partial failure of religious universalism by establishing the principle of *cuius regio, eius religio* (whoever is king, that is the religion). The Emperor, though master of his own fief, was forced to recognize Germanic liberties in the rest of the Holy Roman Empire, which by then had fragmented into a series of

principalities. The plague epidemic of 1679 preceded the second siege of Vienna by the Grand Vizier Kara Mustafa (1683). The arrival of the King of Poland, John Sobieski, and Charles, Duke of Lorraine, finally relieved the defenders, who were commanded by the Count of Starhemberg. Charles of Lorraine and Max-Emmanuel of Bavaria undertook the reconquest of Hungary: Buda and Pest were liberated in 1686 and the Peace of Karlowitz followed. In 1699, the Turks evacuated Hungary.

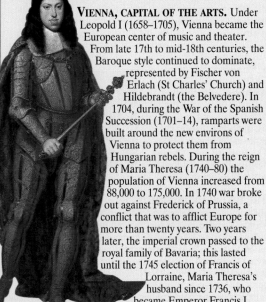

VIENNA, CAPITAL OF THE ARTS. Under Leopold I (1658–1705), Vienna became the European center of music and theater. From late 17th to mid-18th centuries, the Baroque style continued to dominate, represented by Fischer von Erlach (St Charles' Church) and Hildebrandt (the Belvedere). In 1704, during the War of the Spanish Succession (1701–14), ramparts were built around the new environs of Vienna to protect them from Hungarian rebels. During the reign of Maria Theresa (1740–80) the population of Vienna increased from 88,000 to 175,000. In 1740 war broke out against Frederick of Prussia, a conflict that was to afflict Europe for more than twenty years. Two years later, the imperial crown passed to the royal family of Bavaria; this lasted until the 1745 election of Francis of Lorraine, Maria Theresa's husband since 1736, who became Emperor Francis I (1745–65). The Schönbrunn Palace was completed in 1769. After 1750, the Baroque style gave way to Rococo. The collapse of the 1756 alliances (hastened by the new relationship between Austria and France) led to the 1770 marriage of the Empress' daughter Marie-Antoinette with the future Louis XVI of France. Joseph II (1780–90) began to centralize the Austrian monarchy. The principal reforms, or "Josephism", were established by the Edict of Toleration (1781), the abolition of serfdom (1781), the suppression of many monasteries, and a trend toward "Germanization".

The Church of St Charles; Leopold I (1640–1705) (left); the Battle of Wagram (1809) (above).

1762–96
Reign of Catherine II in Russia.

1773
Suppression of the Jesuits (founded in 1534).

1783
American Independence confirmed by the Treaty of Versailles.

1804
Beginning of the Serbian revolt against the occupying Turks.

1805
Battle of Trafalgar.

1809
Napoleon annexes the Papal States.

1825
The first railway is built in England.

1835
Industry starts to use steam power.

The people of Vienna assisting the French wounded, 19th-century engraving.

31

Francis I
(1768–1835).

The Austrian Empire

Prince von
Metternich
Winneburg
(1773–1859); right, a
Vienna café scene.

1862
*Bismarck's accession
to power.*

1871
*Proclamation of the
German Empire.*

Franz-Joseph
(1830–1916).

In 1797 Bonaparte marched on Vienna but preliminary
negotiations at Leoben halted the advance. The subsequent
Treaties of Campo Formio and Lunéville deprived the
Habsburgs of their authority in Italy and their possessions in
the Low Countries (Belgium). Eclipsed by the influence of
Napoleon, Francis II (1792–1832) renounced the title of Holy
Roman Emperor. In 1805 the Napoleonic armies took Vienna
and retained control of it until 1806. The Holy Roman
Empire was dissolved in the same year, with Francis II taking
the title of Emperor Francis I of Austria. In 1810, Napoleon
married Archduchess Marie-Louise, putting a seal on his
control of Austrian affairs; but already the continental
blockade had begun to paralyze commerce and the war effort
was creating terrific inflation. In 1813 Napoleon was defeated
at Leipzig; he evacuated
Germany, and in 1814 the
Austrians and their allies
occupied the French capital.
After the peace concluded at
Paris, Napoleon went into
exile on the island of Elba.
The Holy Alliance between
Austria, Prussia and Russia
was then established at the Congress of Vienna.

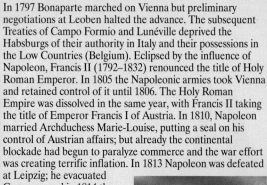

The Biedermeier era. The period between 1815 and
1848, under the government of Prince Metternich, was
Vienna's golden age. As the city grew more industrialized, its
cultural life was distinguished by a bourgeois lifestyle known
as "Biedermeier". At this time the first neo-classical buildings
were constructed in Vienna; the bastions, which had been
dismantled by the French in 1809, were converted into
gardens (Volksgarten and Burggarten). By 1817 the old
ramparts had become a public promenade. Vienna flourished
again as a capital of music, poetry and literature. The
Biedermeier epoch came to an end with the bombardment of
Vienna by Prince Windischgrätz in 1848, the Year of
Revolutions. In that year Ferdinand I (1835–48), brother of
Francis I, was forced to abdicate in favor of his nephew,
Franz-Joseph I. The simultaneous Hungarian revolution was
crushed with the help of Russian forces.

The reign of Franz-Joseph (1848–1916). In 1849
Austria, which had lost none of its power and influence as a
result of the revolution, thwarted a concerted Prussian
attempt to unify Germany (the retreat of Olmütz). Ten years
later war broke out in Italy; disastrous Austrian reverses at
Magenta and Solferino were followed by the loss of
Lombardy and Milan. Now the German question returned to
the forefront. The defeat at Sadowa (Königgrätz) in 1866 had
serious repercussions, with the loss of the Veneto and
Austria's withdrawal from the Germanic Confederation,
thenceforward dominated by Prussia. In 1867, the Empire was
transformed by the installation of an Austro-Hungarian
double monarchy, which enabled Franz-Joseph to reconcile
Austria with Hungary. By 1850 Vienna had expanded as far as
Gürtel and had a total of eight districts, with 431,000

> "And at the very moment when the Führer's motor escort began its parade through the ancient city of the Habsburgs, all the church bells began to ring out in obscene jubilation."
>
> George Clare

inhabitants. In 1857 the Emperor ordered the destruction of the ramparts and their replacement by the Ring, and later the Danube flood of 1862 led to the construction of the Donaukanal (1870–5). The State Opera was completed in 1869; its inaugural performance was *Don Giovanni* by Mozart. The Vienna World's Fair of 1873 was a huge success, despite the fact that it was held in the midst of a stock market crash and a cholera epidemic. The metro system was constructed between 1894 and 1900. In 1891 the 11th to 19th districts were incorporated into the city, and in 1904 the 20th and 21st districts on the other side of the Danube were absorbed.

Scene from the 1848 Revolution.

1912–13
The Balkan Wars.

1933
Hitler becomes Chancellor of the Third Reich.

1945
Conference at Yalta and destruction of Hiroshima.

VIENNA, CAPITAL OF AUSTRIA

By 1910 Vienna, with a population of two million, was the fourth largest city in Europe after London, Paris and Berlin. It had residents of the many nationalities (a dozen in all) which made up the Austro-Hungarian Empire. In 1914 Archduke Franz-Ferdinand, heir apparent to Franz-Joseph, was assassinated at Sarajevo; Austria declared war on Serbia, after which the conflict spread to the rest of Europe. Charles I, Franz-Joseph's nephew, succeeded him in 1916. After an unsuccessful attempt to sue for peace in 1917, Austria found itself, in 1918, on the defeated side. After October in that year, the Empire was broken up with the tacit approval of the Allies. In 1919, the Treaty of Saint-Germain reduced Austria to the Ostmark established by Charlemagne and forbade its union with Germany. Vienna became the capital of a republic of 6 million people living in an area of 52,000 square miles, whereas before it had ruled 52 million in an area of 435,000 square miles. A Socialist government dominated municipal affairs in Vienna until 1934, grappling with the economic crisis that followed World War One. A new social policy was introduced; by 1927 Socialists and Christian Democrats were fighting pitched battles in the streets. After riots in 1934, Chancellor Dollfuss set up an authoritarian regime and sought a rapprochement with Mussolini's Italy. By 1938 Austria had aligned itself with Germany (the "Anschluss"). By the end of World War Two, when Soviet troops entered Vienna in 1945, the city had been heavily bombed. After the war Austria was divided into four zones and occupied by the Allies. Vienna, in the Soviet zone, was consigned to a four-power administration. In 1955, by the Belvedere Treaty, Austria regained its sovereignty and became a neutral state. Today Vienna contains the headquarters of several United Nations agencies, as well as OPEC; it has also hosted a series of disarmament conferences. In 1986 Kurt Waldheim, UN Secretary General, became President of the Austrian Republic, but did not seek a second term in 1991.

1968
Prague Spring.

1989
Fall of the Berlin Wall: end of the Cold War.

1990
War in Yugoslavia.

Kurt von Schuschnigg (1897–1977).

Viennese in front of a cinema destroyed in the 1940's.

1991
Breakup of the Soviet Union.

1993
Partition of Czechoslovakia.

THE TURKS AT THE GATES OF VIENNA

John Sobieski ● *31*,
King of Poland, relieves Vienna.

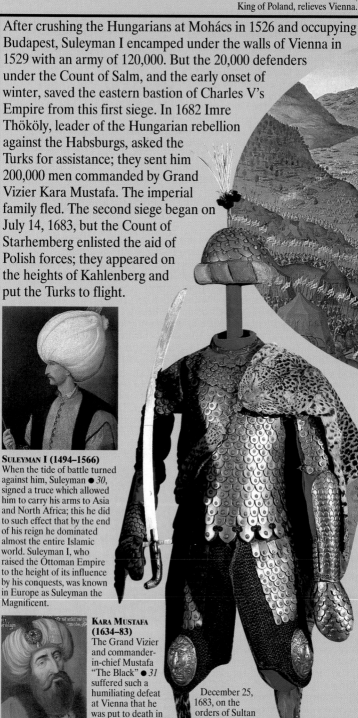

After crushing the Hungarians at Mohács in 1526 and occupying Budapest, Suleyman I encamped under the walls of Vienna in 1529 with an army of 120,000. But the 20,000 defenders under the Count of Salm, and the early onset of winter, saved the eastern bastion of Charles V's Empire from this first siege. In 1682 Imre Thököly, leader of the Hungarian rebellion against the Habsburgs, asked the Turks for assistance; they sent him 200,000 men commanded by Grand Vizier Kara Mustafa. The imperial family fled. The second siege began on July 14, 1683, but the Count of Starhemberg enlisted the aid of Polish forces; they appeared on the heights of Kahlenberg and put the Turks to flight.

SULEYMAN I (1494–1566)
When the tide of battle turned against him, Suleyman ● *30*, signed a truce which allowed him to carry his arms to Asia and North Africa; this he did to such effect that by the end of his reign he dominated almost the entire Islamic world. Suleyman I, who raised the Ottoman Empire to the height of its influence by his conquests, was known in Europe as Suleyman the Magnificent.

KARA MUSTAFA (1634–83)
The Grand Vizier and commander-in-chief Mustafa "The Black" ● *31* suffered such a humiliating defeat at Vienna that he was put to death in Belgrade on December 25, 1683, on the orders of Sultan Mehmet IV.

THE TURKS DRIVEN FROM EUROPE

In 1683 Leopold I took advantage of the unexpected triumph at Vienna to send Duke Charles of Lorraine into battle against the Turks. Charles reconquered all of Hungary and pushed his campaign to Belgrade (1688), after liberating Budapest in 1686. In 1697, Prince Eugène of Savoy ▲ *247* defeated the Ottomans at Zenta; this allowed him to impose the Peace of Karlowitz (1699), whereby the Turks ceded Hungary entirely. In a subsequent campaign Prince Eugène won a decisive victory at Belgrade.

A SERIOUS ENEMY

The Ottoman forces, which used classic weapons and light cavalry, were capable of sustaining long sieges with artillery powerful enough to breach the strongest ramparts. The bell of St Stephen's Cathedral in Vienna, known as the Pummerin ▲ *134*, was cast of metal from cannons captured from the Turks.

● MARIA THERESA AND JOSEPH II

SCHÖNBRUNN ▲ *274*. The imperial couple and their sixteen children conducted their private family life amid the Rococo décor commissioned by Maria Theresa.

When Crown Prince Leopold died in 1716, Emperor Charles VI von Habsburg had no male heir. He nominated his eldest daughter, Maria Theresa, to be his heir, so that the younger (Caroline) branch of his family could retain the throne. Backed by the Pragmatic Sanction, the edict by which he regulated his succession, Charles VI pleaded his cause with all the great courts of Europe: these, in exchange for considerable financial and territorial advantages, eventually recognized Maria Theresa as the heir to the throne. Everything was called back into question after the Emperor's death in 1740; this sparked off the War of Austrian Succession (1740–8), in which a young woman of twenty-three successfully defended her cause against most of the rest of Europe.

MARIA THERESA (1717–80) ▲ *158, 260* Maria Theresa secured the throne of Hungary in 1740 and in 1745, she engineered her husband Francis of Lorraine's election to the imperial throne. The Treaty of Aix-la-Chapelle (1748) restored peace, and the Empress undertook a series of reforms. Reducing the power of the aristocrats, she established Vienna as the capital of a centralized state. Her administrators were trained at the School of the Theresanium ▲ *244*. The professions of justice, education and medicine were overhauled, new factories built, industry was protected by high import tariffs and roads were improved.

FRANCIS I (1708–65) Maria Theresa distanced her husband from real power. Francis I was a poor adviser and soldier, much happier with his science specimens than with affairs of state.

JOSEPH II ▲ 292 AND CATHERINE OF RUSSIA

On the death of his father, Archduke Joseph joined his mother as co-regent. When she died in 1780, he succeeded her, continuing her work of centralization, reinforcing the role of the administration and police force, and encouraging industry and the arts.

JOSEPH II (1741–90)

"Josephism" ▲ 291 severely curtailed the power of the Roman Catholic Church in the Habsburg states by abolishing the religious orders and confiscating church property. By his Edict

THE SEVEN YEARS' WAR ▲ 260

In 1756 Austria took up arms to recapture Silesia from Prussia, thus starting a war which embroiled all of Europe. Thanks to the wily diplomacy of Count Kaunitz, the Empress contrived to upset the previous system of alliances. She became reconciled with France, Austria's traditional enemy, after her former British allies made a pact with the Prussians; she also obtained the support of Sweden, of some of the German princes and of Russia. The Prussians were eventually crushed at Kunersdorf in 1759, and the Treaty of Paris, signed in 1763, brought peace to a Europe which had been bled dry by warfare.

of Toleration (1781) Joseph also granted freedom of worship to all other religions in Vienna.

"The Emperor Joseph II working the soil in the Moravian village of Slavikowitz."

THE COLLAPSE OF THE HOLY ROMAN EMPIRE

At the ball in the Redoutensäle.

Archduke Charles ▲ *261* defeated the French at Aspern (1809).

In 1792 a general war began against Revolution France, but in 1797 Napoleon advanced northward as far as Leoben. The Treaties of Campo Formio (1797) and Lunéville (1801) confirmed the defeat of the Habsburgs. In 1804 Napoleon's coronation compromised the authority of the Habsburg emperor in Germany, and the creation of the Confederation of the Rhine, followed by the Treaty of Pressburg (1805) sounded the death knell of the Holy Roman Empire. In 1804 Francis II renounced the title of Holy Roman Emperor and became Francis I, Emperor of Austria.

THE RETURN OF THE EMPEROR
This fresco in the Museum of Art History ▲ *208* shows the return of Francis I to Vienna in 1809, after its occupation by Napoleon. Since he was opposed to revolutionary ideas, Francis joined the coalition against France. But his policies did not bear fruit until 1813, with the defeat of Napoleon at Leipzig and the evacuation of Germany ● *32*.

The Congress of Vienna continued throughout 1814 and 1815.

"THE CONGRESS DOESN'T WORK, IT DANCES." (PRINCE DE LIGNE)

At the ball in the Redoutensäle, a ballroom and banquet hall in Josefsplatz, 6,000 people turned up instead of 3,000, because the doormen resold the invitations as soon as they were handed in. A total of 1,500 vermeil spoons vanished with the departing guests.

TALLEYRAND (1754–1833) ▲ *147*
A powerful presence at the Congress of Vienna, France's Minister for Foreign Affairs tried to curb the demands of the Allies but Napoleon's return in March 1815 ruined his efforts.

The Czar of Russia, Alexander I ▲ *180*, bragged that he had danced for forty consecutive nights while the Congress was in progress. The party ended with the formation of the Holy Alliance between Russia, Prussia and Austria.

● THE REVOLUTION OF 1848

A caricature showing Metternich in flight during the revolution.

The period preceding the 1848 revolution, known as the Vormärz, was an era of prosperity and cultural expansion for Vienna, which saw the construction of the first neo-classical buildings and the start of the industrial revolution. A steamship company opened on the Danube in 1823, gas was first used in 1828 and the country's first railway line was built in 1837. The Vormärz and the Biedermeier epoch came to a definitive end on March 13, 1848, when a huge demonstration took place in front of the Landhaus (the diet or parliament of Lower Austria). The crowd demanded reforms; the armed forces opened fire and killed some of their number, which led to a general uprising.

The Viennese plundered the arsenal and murdered the Minister of War, Count Latour (above). Prince Metternich, who had been chancellor since 1815, fled the city.

The execution of the parliamentary deputy Robert Blum on November 9, 1848. Blum had taken part in the October uprising.

THE UNIVERSITY GUARDS
The university was one of the main battle areas during the revolution; the students formed an "academic legion" of their own.

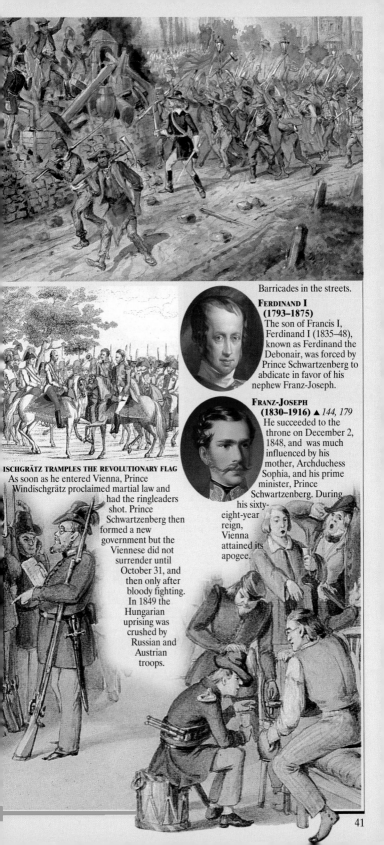

Barricades in the streets.

**FERDINAND I
(1793–1875)**
The son of Francis I,
Ferdinand I (1835–48),
known as Ferdinand the
Debonair, was forced by
Prince Schwartzenberg to
abdicate in favor of his
nephew Franz-Joseph.

**FRANZ-JOSEPH
(1830–1916)** ▲ *144, 179*
He succeeded to the
throne on December 2,
1848, and was much
influenced by his
mother, Archduchess
Sophia, and his prime
minister, Prince
Schwartzenberg. During
his sixty-
eight-year
reign,
Vienna
attained its
apogee.

ISCHGRÄTZ TRAMPLES THE REVOLUTIONARY FLAG
As soon as he entered Vienna, Prince
Windischgrätz proclaimed martial law and
had the ringleaders
shot. Prince
Schwartzenberg then
formed a new
government but the
Viennese did not
surrender until
October 31, and
then only after
bloody fighting.
In 1849 the
Hungarian
uprising was
crushed by
Russian and
Austrian
troops.

● THE DESTRUCTION OF VIENNA

THE SCHILLING
The coinage put into circulation in 1924
was reestablished after the war.

With the fall of the Habsburgs in 1918, the empire collapsed and a republic was proclaimed. The 1920's brought a serious economic crisis; the Socialists, who were in a minority in the country, dominated political life in Vienna. At the 1930 elections, the Nazi party was moderately successful, and then Chancellor Dollfuss, who was hostile to Hitler's ambitions, was assassinated in 1934. The country found itself squeezed

by Nazi Germany; in March 1938 "Anschluss" (union) was proclaimed in Vienna, and Hitler entered the city in triumph. Austria subsequently entered World War Two on the German side. In 1945, the Soviets attacked the German troops who had retreated to Vienna by bombarding the city. After this, Austria was occupied by the Allies for a decade.

Vienna's situation became more difficult after 1944. Apart from the Allied bombings, which had begun in 1943, the city was seriously short of food, relying on a fast-developing black market. In August 1944, the theaters and public areas were closed and the working week lengthened to sixty hours. In October a mass recruitment (*Volksturm*) of all males between 16 and 60 years old was proclaimed. At the same time Vienna became a refuge for deserters and opponents of the Nazi regime. Finally, in 1945, Austrian patriots assisted in the liberation of the city.

"THE THIRD MAN" ▲ *192, 267*
This 1949 film starring Orson Welles remains a record of post-war Vienna in ruins.

THE REINSTALLATION OF THE PUMMERIN
The cathedral ▲ *132*, renovated section by section, was finally restored to use in 1948. At the end of the 1950's the spire was rebuilt and the recast Pummerin ● *35*, ▲ *134* was hoisted onto the unfinished North Tower.

DESTRUCTION AND HUMAN LOSS
The bombings killed 12,000 people and wrecked 20 percent of the buildings in Vienna; a further 270,000 Viennese were made homeless. In 1945, Vienna's recorded death rate was the highest in Europe.

"FOUR MEN IN A JEEP"
Military policemen from the four occupying powers (America, Russia, Britain and France) driving around the city in the same vehicle, an incident which was immortalized on film.

THE RUINED CATHEDRAL
The entire roof of St Stephen's collapsed, while the towers were burning.

POSTER FOR SUBSCRIPTIONS
The post-war period was devoted to raising the nation from its ruins. The reconstruction of the cathedral, which had burned down in 1945, took more than ten years. The Opera ▲ *223* reopened in 1955, a few months after the Treaty which restored Austria's sovereignty.

Germans from the north, arriving in Vienna for the first time, take it for granted that the language spoken here will be identical to their own, so they are rather taken aback to find that the Viennese do indeed speak German, but in a completely different manner. The consonants are run together, the vowels have a chanted quality; the language sounds sweeter, livelier, more cheerful. In this unexpected music, the northerner tends to perceive a betrayal of what he considers to be the pure, authentic German language. Such tiny variations and differences, which do not affect the linguistic structures, make it clear that we are listening to a dialect. German is a language which has grown from a mosaic of dialects and patois, such as Swabian or Bavarian; not until

"The cook, the cellarmaster, and the Croatian canvas-seller in Vienna" *(Die Köchinn, der Vullnermeister und der croatische Leinwandhändler in Wien)*. Watercolor by J. Opitz from the collection "Viennese Types" (c. 1810).

Three Jews in discussion.

"Obviously the Slovenes, the Galicians, the Ruthenes from Poland, the Jews in caftans from Boryslaw, the cattle dealers from the Bacska, the Muslims of Sarajevo, the chestnut-sellers from Mostar, all sing the Emperor's anthem. But the students of Brno and Eger, the dentists, chemists, waiters, barbers and photographers from Linz, Graz, Knittelfeld, the men with goitres from our Alpine valleys, all sing the *Wacht am Rhein*. Gentlemen, this allegiance of Nibelungen Teutons will be the death of Austria."

Joseph Roth,
*The Crypt of the
Capuchins*

Coachmen and boatmen on a craft going up the Danube. Watercolor by J. Opitz.

Luther and the Gutenberg press was there any kind of uniformity to it. While all the dialects of the north eventually bowed to the model imposed by Prussia, the southern countries, Bavaria and the different regions of Austria, held out stoutly, with a view to affirming their individuality. All language conveys and expresses both a character and an outlook on life. Hence, in a manner of speaking, the Viennese are the equivalent of the Geordies of the UK's Tyneside.

VIENNESE GERMAN: A GALAXY OF SOURCES

When Vienna was an imperial capital, all the languages of the empire were spoken there; Viennese popular speech owes many of its characteristics to this influence. The court itself was not averse to using the local dialect. On the other hand, Viennese slang was evolved less in the salons of the aristocracy than in the streets; until recently it accurately reflected the complex mosaic of this most cosmopolitan of cities. Social classes and castes, provincials and foreigners came to live in particular quarters and made their contributions to the development of the language. Vienna is definitely not a German city, in the sense that at least two-thirds of its population hail from non-German-speaking origins. There were, first of all, the Turks who remained behind after the siege of the city. Then there were always plenty of Slavs and Hungarians. Even today, Vienna attracts these ethnic groups, as it does Slovenes, Croats and Czechs. Viennese German was shaped by such immigrants. Therefore the task of finding the origins of certain words and expressions can often be extremely complicated. For example, the name for the delicious Viennese pancakes, *Palatschinken*, comes from the Hungarian, but the Hungarians got it from the Romanians, who had themselves slightly altered it from the old Latin word for cake, *placenta*. Again in the food line, the Viennese word for "maize" originates in the Balkans, but was first filtered through Serbo-Croat before alighting in Vienna as *kukuruz*. The apricot, *aprikose* in German, became *marille* in Vienna. This word comes from Latin, via Italian. Finally, the word for "tomatoes" comes from India by way of French; in Vienna they are called *paradeiser*, because the new fruit was compared to the golden apple of Paradise, *pomodoro* in Italian, shortened to *paradise* in Austria. Mostly it is cooking terms which show the traces of the various ethnic influences, but other, rarer examples confirm the wealth of the mixtures which have shaped this language and with it the soul of Vienna.

FRENCH AND THE VIENNESE DIALECT. Although the French share no frontier with the Austrians, France has played a prominent role in Austria's history. Even more surprising is the contribution of the French language to Viennese. For example, card games are very much colored by French. The

"Where could she hail from? Vienna? Never. And since she was smiling... German? Perhaps, given the correctness of her pronunciation. On the other hand, those dark eyes full of promise, that black hair... Now he knew it: she was Italian. Catching Thérèse's distracted eye, the young man burst out laughing and reassured her. He knew now she was from Vienna, her accent betrayed her in spite of herself, but as for her race, he could have sworn there was southern blood in her veins."

Arthur Schnitzler,
Thérèse

"Die Kleine Poste" (the little post office).

"What makes the difference between the Austrian and the German is the language they share."
Karl Kraus

● THE DIALECT OF VIENNA

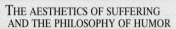

Sleeve of a record
by Karl Ambros
(1979).

Along with classical music, jazz, rock and *Schrammelmusik*, the Viennese "chanson" is sung by a few local celebrities (Falco, below, has been internationally famous for ten years or more) and contributes to the survival of the Viennese dialect.

word *coupiern* (*couper*) is used for "cut"; *trèfle*, *coeur*, *carreau* and *pique* (meaning club, heart, diamond and spade) are borrowed directly. Many words adopted in Viennese from French have also made their way into English usage. Dressmaking has borrowed *fasson* from *façon* meaning fashion and *frack* from *froc*, a dress; in the newspaper world, the Viennese talk of the *journal* and the *presse*. The kitchen features prominently, as one might expect, with *consommé*, *kotelett*, *petits fours* and *meringues*. The Viennese use the word *flair* just as both French and English speakers do; likewise the word *bordell* (chaos), which came to Vienna from old French by way of Dutch, and the inevitable *rendez-vous*, which was formerly a military command.

THE AESTHETICS OF SUFFERING AND THE PHILOSOPHY OF HUMOR

The Viennese dialect has its peculiarities, which are shared by all Viennese, and to them the city owes much of its rich flavor. The Viennese have a certain relish for pleasure blended with fatalism, irony and insolence. This mixture of optimism and despair, with the latter carefully distilled so as not to be quite unbearable, may be found in the writing of Karl Kraus and in the contemporary poetry of H.C. Artman or E. Janal. It is the constant receptiveness of the Viennese language to all influences which has enabled it to dance around the quicksand of linguistic standardization. Viennese is a spoken tongue: anyone attempting to formalize it or transcribe it is doomed to failure. Some words are easy to transcribe: I in English, which is *Ich* in German, becomes *I* again in Viennese. Once you get into complete sentences, things become more complicated. Nowadays, linguistic standardization has produced irreversible effects elsewhere, and yet the dialect of Vienna still remains an inexhaustible living archive of the city, or rather of its citizens' unconscious; a treasure chest in which all can delve for their lost roots, or find the strength to reaffirm their uniqueness as inhabitants of Vienna. "A rhythmical philosophy, laced with humor" is how Peter Wehle has described the Viennese way of speaking. It shows, if nothing else, that a single language can give expression to many different facets of the human soul, and in that sense they speak a language very different from ordinary German in Vienna.

"He spoke the nasal German of the high officials and minor nobility of Austria...it was a gentle tongue, though it could also be precise, tender and malicious."

Joseph Roth,
The Radetsky March

"THE GOLDEN CROWN"
Originally called "Das Elephantenhaus"; since 1690 "Zur Goldenen Krone". Notice the Fountain of St Leopold ▲ *138* on the Graben in this pre-1866 photo.

Arts and traditions

In the 18th century, Vienna reached an important point in its musical history. The removal of the Turkish threat allowed the city to regain its former prosperity and, in the first fifty years of the century, to endow itself with churches and Baroque palaces. Its musical life, already rich, developed fast around a group of Italian composers and performers (Bononcini, Caldara, Conti, Metastasio and Porpora). The Viennese appetite for opera was insatiable, and the city became one of the centers of musical classicism as exemplified by Gluck, Haydn and Mozart.

WOLFGANG AMADEUS MOZART (1756–91) ▲ *106, 147*
Mozart was writing musical notes before he could shape the letters of the alphabet. At the age of six he performed at Schönbrunn ▲ *281*; in 1768 he returned to Vienna to compose his first "opera buffa" (*La finta semplice*) and his first "Singspiel" (*Bastien and Bastienne*). In 1773, during a third stay in the city, he heard Haydn's Quartets and under their influence composed six of his own, which confirmed his independence of the Italian style.

CHRISTOPH WILLIBALD GLUCK (1714–87)
Gluck was the son of a gamekeeper; at the end of his life he was one of the richest and most famous operatic composers of his time. From 1755 he was musical director at the court of Vienna; thereafter he toured Europe with his many operas, which he adapted to the tastes of the various capitals. At sixty years old, acclaimed all over Europe, Gluck achieved his crowning triumph in Paris, invited by his former pupil Marie-Antoinette. In 1779 he returned to Vienna, where he died of apoplexy in 1787

"TOO MUCH GENIUS TO PLEASE"

In 1782, breaking with Collaredo, the archbishop of Salzburg, Mozart moved to Vienna ▲ 227 in spite of the warning given to him: "After a while the Viennese always crave something new." His fame grew until 1785, but ultimately the Viennese did not comprehend his genius. After 1786 Mozart's star was on the wane and his family began to suffer increasing financial difficulties. All the same, he composed nearly all his greatest masterpieces in Vienna (*The Marriage of Figaro, Don Giovanni* and *The Magic Flute*). He was the first musician who dared to free himself from the position of a domestic.

THREE PRINCES

Haydn spent thirty years in the service of Paul Antony, Nicolas the Magnificent and Nicolas II Esterházy ▲ 162.

LUCK THE REFORMER

After his training in Italy, Gluck set out to establish Italian opera as a serious art. In the end, however, he laid the groundwork for the German opera which began with Mozart and ended with Wagner and the post-Romantics.

JOSEPH HAYDN (1732–1809)

Haydn's career began with the cathedral choir ▲ 152, 162 after which he remained for thirty years in the service of the Esterházy family. His frequent visits to Vienna kept him in contact with the musical life of the city; in 1785 he established a close friendship with Mozart, based on mutual admiration.

ghibisig _fan_

Classicism's swan song was dominated by two titanic figures: Haydn and Mozart. Two other personalities, Beethoven and Schubert, confirmed Vienna's musical preeminence in the first two decades of the 19th century. A new wind was blowing through the world of the arts, yet these composers personified the enduring fascination of Vienna for artists. Beethoven, though not Vienna-born, could never leave the place once he had adopted it as his home; Schubert was a true Viennese who lived there all his life.

FRANZ SCHUBERT (1797–1828)
At the age of twelve, Schubert was composing works for his family quartet, but his true genius was for *Lieder*. His six hundred *Lieder*, nearly all of them masterpieces, demonstrate a sure sense of drama that goes right to the heart of the subject.

Schubert's musical training was much more serious than legend has it. As a boy he sang in the imperial chapel choir and worked with Antonio Salieri. But his fame hardly spread beyond the circle of friends who gathered to hear his latest works (the

schubertiades ▲ 227). Since he had no regular income, Schubert shared his friends' lodgings and was an habitué of the cafés and *Heurigen* ● 68. From 1822 onward his health began to fail, but he produced a lot of work in his last years.

He died with the name of Beethoven on his lips and was buried near the master ▲ 262.

> "After Beethoven, I truly wonder if there is anything left to do."
> Franz Schubert

Beethoven

JOHANNES BRAHMS (1833–97)
Having come to Vienna to "drink the wine Beethoven drank", Brahms remained for the rest of his life and gave the city a musical luster which it had lost through its obsession with the waltz ● 56. His daring classicism delighted the Viennese; Brahms, the most classical of the German Romantics, stands midway between Beethoven and Schubert ▲ 262. The one taught him Germanic rigor, the other Viennese charm.

A TORMENTED GIANT
A hirsute, miserly, short-tempered man, Beethoven was stone deaf from 1819 onwards ▲ 298; nevertheless in his music he created the coherence that was lacking in his life. He came to Vienna for the first time in 1792. By the end of his life he had written nine symphonies, all of them masterpieces of emotional expression so complete that both Wagner and Debussy considered it impossible to write others after him. After the unexpected triumph of his opera *Fidelio* in 1814, Beethoven engrossed himself in the creation of sixteen quartets, the last five of which bore no relation to the other written works of this genre and showed extraordinary genius.

LUDWIG VAN BEETHOVEN (1770–1827)
Born in Bonn, Beethoven narrowly missed taking lessons with Mozart in 1787; in the end Haydn brought him to Vienna. In his early career he was supported by noble families.

51

The admirers of Richard Wagner, Anton Bruckner (for whom the discovery of *Tannhäuser* was a revelation), Gustav Mahler and Hugo Wolf, were succeeded by the three members of the "Vienna School". This title

ANTON BRUCKNER (1824–96)

was given to the group Arnold Schönberg formed with his two most famous disciples, Alban Berg and Anton von Webern, and refers to the teachings of Schönberg at Vienna between 1904 and 1924. The three were not only close friends, but also closely aligned in their work.

BRUCKNER: "HALF GENIUS, HALF CRETIN" (MAHLER)

Bruckner first heard Wagner at Linz, near his birthplace. In 1868 he was appointed court organist and a teacher at the conservatory of Vienna. His life in the city was much like that Brahms but the two avoided each other. Bruckner's social gaffes are legendary: one of the worst was when he slipped some money to Hans Richter, after the maestro had conducted one of his eleven symphonies.

A GREAT CONDUCTOR

Mahler was the greatest conductor of his time, lavishing care on scenery and staging, and selecting singers for their ability to fill particular rôles. From 1897 he directed the Vienna Opera for ten years, before departing for New York. There he fell sick and asked to be taken home to Vienna, where he died five days after his return.

HUGO WOLF (1860–1903)
Expelled from the conservatory and highly unpopular because of his pro-Wagner articles and attacks on Brahms in the *Wiener Salonblatt*, Wolf failed in all his attempts to gain recognition. After 1888 he found success with his *Lieder* (three hundred in all) which led him to compare his work with Schubert's.

GUSTAV MAHLER (1860–1911) ● 54
Mahler was Wolf's fellow-disciple, sharing his apartment and his admiration for Wagner. Wagner thought it impossible for anyone to write a symphony after Beethoven; but Mahler applied Wagner's own aesthetic dictum to his work: for him, to write a symphony was "to build a world, using all the technical resources available to a musician". As the last true Romantic (along with Richard Strauss), Mahler joined the Secessionist coteries ● *86*, ▲ *232* and defended the early works of Schönberg.

> "The symphony should be like the universe, all-embracing."
>
> Gustav Mahler

Arnold Schönberg, by Egon Schiele ▲ 252.

ARNOLD SCHÖNBERG (1874–1951)

At an early stage, Schönberg was influenced by the writings of Brahms and the chromatics of Wagner and Richard Strauss; later, he distanced himself from the traditional musical language. He dedicated his famous treatise on harmony, *Harmonielehre*, to his friend Mahler.

Großer Musikvereinssaal

Montag, 31. März, ½8 Uhr abends

Großes Orchester-Konzert

Arnold

Schönberg

Dirigent

Das Orchester des Wiener Konzertvereines
Gesang: A. Boruttau, Margarete Bum, Maria Freund
Schönberg: Kammersymphonie. Mahler: Kindertotenlieder
Werke von Alban Berg, Anton v. Webern u. A. v. Zemlinsky
Wagner: Tristan-Vorspiel

Karten bei Kehlendorfer

ngerstraße 3 und an der Konzertkassa Canov

GESELLSCHAFT FÜR GRAPHISCHE INDUSTRIE WIEN VI.

THE VIENNA SCHOOL

With Schönberg, music ceased to be a "figurative" art. In 1908 he eliminated all precedence of one sound over another; then he perfected dodecaphonics, a way of organizing the twelve semi-tones in a series governed by the absence of any functional relationship between sounds, without the possibility of repeating one of them before all the others have been heard. Dodecaphonics proved to be one of the crucial stages in the development of 20th-century music.

ANTON VON WEBERN (1883–1945)

He worked with Schönberg until 1908. Passing through Germany and Prague before the war, he later rejoined his master in Vienna. His works are characterized by brevity, abstraction and dodecaphonic rigor. He retired after 1933 and was killed accidentally by an American bullet near Salzburg.

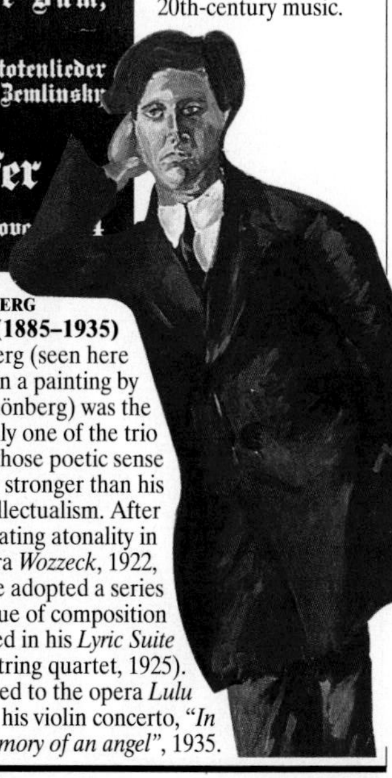

ALBAN BERG (1885–1935)

Berg (seen here in a painting by Schönberg) was the only one of the trio whose poetic sense proved stronger than his intellectualism. After investigating atonality in the opera *Wozzeck*, 1922, he adopted a series technique of composition (first used in his *Lyric Suite* for string quartet, 1925). This led to the opera *Lulu* and his violin concerto, *"In memory of an angel"*, 1935.

53

*The concert in celebration of the marriage
of Joseph II and Isabella of Parma.*
Painting by Martin Meytens (1695–1770) ● 98.

Vienna is a city steeped in tradition, where life still revolves around music and most of the great Viennese musical institutions are very much alive. The most famous is the Vienna Boys' Choir (*Wiener Sängerknaben*), whose origins go back to the 12th century and which was attached to the Hofmusikkapelle, created by Maximilian I. The collapse of the monarchy forced the municipal authorities to reorganize the choir around concert tours. After World War Two, the choir school moved to the Augarten Palace, where it is to this day. One hundred and fifty children attend it, receiving comprehensive musical and vocal training in addition to a general education. The choir sings mass at the Hofburgkapelle on Sundays and feast days, except in July and August.

CHOIRS OF VIENNA
The two principal amateur choirs, the *Singakademie* and the *Sing Verein*, which date back to the great days of Romanticism, still dominate Viennese choral life. The former performs at the Konzerthaus and the latter at the Musikvereinsgebäude.

"WIENER PHILHARMONIC"
In 1842 the Prussian conductor Otto Nicolai decided to give two symphony concerts every year with the orchestra of the Vienna State Opera. The word "philharmonic" was used for the first time to describe the second of these concerts; until the departure of Nicolai in 1847, these events were a regular feature of musical life in Vienna. They were organized by the Opera musicians themselves, who shared the profits. The Philharmonic attained its final form in 1860 with the election of Otto Dessoff, who spent the next fifteen years turning it into a Music Society (the Musikverein) housed in the Music Society Building (the Musikvereinsgebäude ▲ 242, ◆ 326) which recently acquired a new auditorium with 2,000 seats and perfect acoustics.

CELEBRATED CONDUCTORS
The world's greatest conductors came one after another to the Wiener Philharmonic, among them Hans Richter, Gustav Mahler ● 52, ▲ 232, 301 (right) and many guest conductors. In 1908 Felix Weingartner began his nineteen-year reign, which was followed by that of Wilhelm Furtwängler, who presided over the most outstanding period in the orchestra's history.

ОQUE MUSIC. In 1952 the *Concentus Musicus*, created by Nicolaus Harnoncourt d instrumentalists from the Wiener Symphoniker, initiated a fresh approach to - and 18th-century music. A Viennese tradition formed in Harnoncourt's wake, with the *Musica Antica, Capella Academica* and *Clemencic Consort.*

CHAMBER MUSIC

Chamber music is very much a part of life in Vienna. Young instrumentalists come from all over the world to deepen their knowledge of the styles of the different Viennese composers, notably Haydn, Mozart and Beethoven, whose traditions of performance have been handed down intact from the 18th century. In the last few decades, many new ensembles have emerged, most of them short-lived despite enormous success. The Alban Berg Quartet, founded in 1971 and supported by the Alban Berg Foundation, is today one of the world's most renowned ensembles.

More recently, younger groups such as the Hagen and Artis quartets have been acclaimed as the foremost of their generation.

THE WALTZ

The terms *walzen* (to turn around) or *walzerisch tanzen* (to dance turning round) appeared in the mid-18th century, when used to describe the final set of the *Ländler* (a popular dance in triple time derived from the court minuet). First the aristocracy, then the bourgeoisie were attracted by the new dance, which was found to be far less rigid than the minuet. The Congress of Vienna (1814–15) was accompanied by a frenetic round of balls and waltzing, after which the craze spread like wildfire all over Europe. The waltz was soon accepted in society everywhere; it reached its apogee after the 1848 revolution, with the reign of Johann Strauss the Younger, the "Waltz King" (1825–99).

STRAUSS AND LANNER
In 1819, Johann Strauss the Elder (1804–49) joined the orchestra of Joseph Lanner (1801–43). Their relationship quickly soured after Lanner published some of Strauss' compositions under his own name. Strauss formed his own orchestra, the Strauss Kapelle, and in 1829 signed a contract to play in the *Zum Sperl*, the smartest café in Vienna. Liszt, Wagner and Chopin came to hear the

Strauss repertoire, which quickly became symbolic of the Viennese style. In addition to waltzes, Strauss churned out galops, polkas and quadrilles by the score. After 1883 the Strauss Kapelle toured all over Europe with its waltz melodies.

When dancing the waltz, one leads with the left foot. To complicate matters, the Viennese also dance what they call the *Linkerwalzer*, a reverse waltz with the right foot leading.

STRAUSS AND SON
Rivalry between the two Johann Strausses, father and son, began with the triumph of the son's new orchestra. In 1848 the father celebrated the victory of the Austrian forces over the Italian rebels with his *Radetzky March*; at the same time the son was composing *Barricadenlieder* and a *Revolution March*. On the death of his father, the younger Strauss ▲ *227* took over the Strauss Kapelle and continued its seasonal concerts and international engagements.

THE GLISSADE
The swing which gives the waltz its special impetus is produced by anticipating the second step and holding back on the third.

The proliferation of ballrooms with slippery parquet dance floors instead of hardened clay led to the evolution of the glissaded step, as opposed to the skipped step; this in turn reduced the breadth of the movements involved.

FRENETIC COMPOSITION
Johann Strauss composed 200 waltzes, 140 polkas, 70 quadrilles and 50 marches. In 1863 he handed his orchestra over to his brothers and devoted himself to operettas ● *60*, ▲ *140*. Josef Strauss died in 1870 leaving Eduard to run the orchestra alone. It was dissolved in 1901.

57

● THE BALLS

JOINING THE DANCE
Colonel Willy von Vestenbrugg-Ellmayer taught young Viennese how to dance in the early 1900's. His method was as strict as the one used by the trainers at the imperial stables: he tolerated no error.

Kaiser Walzer

The ball, a tradition for many centuries in the courts of Europe, is still a popular feature of Viennese life. The ball season, from mid-January to mid-February, exactly corresponds to the period of Carnival preceding Lent. Right from its beginnings in the 19th century, the waltz was danced as often in the emperor's palace as in the dance halls of the workers and the bourgeoisie; the latter, modeled on the great ballrooms of Paris, were introduced to Vienna by the Strauss family.

WIENER OPERNBALL

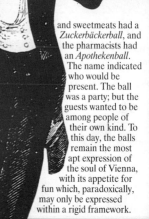

THE INSTITUTIONAL WALTZ

The balls of Vienna did not escape class divisions; they may even have deepened them. Every region of Austria would hold its own ball; so too would every profession. Balls were even given by such esoteric groups as the "Association of Workers and Employees of the Administrative Section of the Conservative Party". The wholesalers and retailers of sweets and sweetmeats had a *Zuckerbäckerball*, and the pharmacists had an *Apothekenball*. The name indicated who would be present. The ball was a party; but the guests wanted to be among people of their own kind. To this day, the balls remain the most apt expression of the soul of Vienna, with its appetite for fun which, paradoxically, may only be expressed within a rigid framework.

58

THE EMPEROR'S BALL

The ball season opens on December 31 with the *Kaiserball* at the Hofburg ▲ 175. The most famous ball is the one at the State Opera – the *Opernball* ▲ 223 (above) – created for the court in 1877. Nowadays, the Austrian aristocracy has opened its doors to the internationally wealthy, but tradition is still strictly observed. The daughters of rich and titled Austrian families make their debuts at the *Opernball*.

TRADITIONS

Costume balls are rare in Vienna. Evening clothes for men and long dresses for women are the norm; the national costume – the *Tracht* and the *Dirndl* ● 64 – may also be worn, but guests are expected to show that they know and respect the rules of etiquette. Above: the Police Ball, the Hunters' Ball and the *Opernball*. At the Hunters' Ball – the *Jägerball* – the atmosphere is more relaxed.

● THEATER IN VIENNA

The curtain of the former
Josephstadt Theater (below);
the Staatsoper (right) ▲ 223.

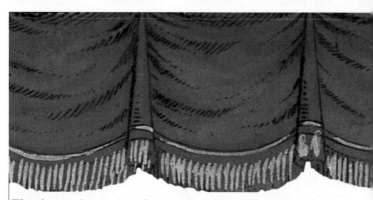

The theater has a more important role in Vienna than in any
other city. Ever since the Baroque period and the emergence of
popular theaters the Viennese have tended to view dramatic
fiction as more credible than the current events
described by newpapers. Satire, romantic comedy and
social criticism are the main ingredients of a
theatrical tradition which has always had a
popular dimension, and has renewed itself by
drawing on this source. An example of this is the
archetypal Viennese anti-hero Hans Wurst, a
peasant who first appeared in the 18th century and
who is still present in 20th-century plays.

THE OPERETTA
Franz von Suppé, Johann
Strauss the Younger ● 57, ▲ 140, 227,
Karl Millöcker, Carl Zeller, Karl-Michael
Ziehrer and Franz Lehár ▲ 299 were the
principal creators of this genre, which
blended French humor and Viennese wit.

NESTROY'S "DER TALISMAN"
The plays of contemporary Austrian writers such
as Bernhard, Handke and Horváth are regularly
staged abroad, but the great 19th-century classics
by Raimund, Nestroy and
Grillparzer have yet to
be revived.

The Burgtheater does not confine itself to a classical repertoire but features some controversial modern works: in 1988 there was uproar over the Thomas Bernhard play *Heroes' Square*.

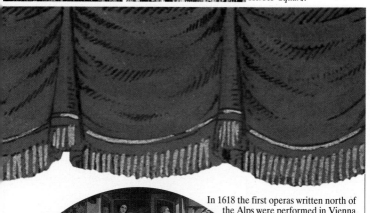

In 1618 the first operas written north of the Alps were performed in Vienna. The Baroque era fostered the idea of a work of art uniting all the arts, as later conceived by Richard Wagner ▲ *224*: at that time music was inconceivable without ballet, given its roots in carnival traditions.

Vienna has produced several playwrights and composers of genius. Lunettes of the operas *Der Freischütz* by Weber (above) and *The Magic Flute* by Mozart ● *48,* ▲ *147, 281* (left) designed by Moritz von Schwind are shown.

THE BURGTHEATER. Founded by Maria Theresa in 1741, the original Burgtheater was on St Michael's Square. On Joseph II's birthday ● *37,* ▲ *291* February 12, 1797, Haydn ● *49,* ▲ *152, 162, 164* conducted a choir and orchestra there in the first performance of the anthem which was to become the Emperor's Hymn, later adopted as Austria's national anthem.

The present Burgtheater on the Ring ▲ *204,* opposite the City Hall, was opened on October 14, 1888, with an inaugural performance of Franz Grillparzer's ● *62,* ▲ *147 Esther*. In addition to a group of statues by Carl Kundmann (*Apollo and the Muses of Tragedy and Comedy*) above the portal, the wings of the theater contain Art Nouveau frescoes by Franz Matsch and the brothers Gustav ▲ *227, 234, 250* and Ernst Klimt.

THE BIEDERMEIER STYLE

Between 1815 and 1848 ● *40* there was peace
throughout Europe. In Austria, the start of the
Industrial Revolution was accompanied by a new style
of living that became known as the Biedermeier style.

Biedermeier, the "worthy Meier" (an
imaginary hero), personified a return to
bourgeois values. Everyone from the
emperor to the man in the
street decorated his home
with deliberate simplicity. It
was an era of domestic
contentment, when families
played music together.
People frequented the
guinguettes (taverns) at
the Prater and in the
Weinerwald. The Theater
an der Wien (1831–45) was packed out
for Grillparzer's dramas and the
boulevard plays of Nestroy and Raimund.

UNCLUTTERED COMFORT
The Biedermeier style, the forerunner of modern design, produced a number of functional, quietly elegant domestic objects and decorative features. Simple desks and chairs like these were as much in demand at the emperor's court as in ordinary Viennese bourgeois households.

A VIENNESE INTERIOR
The bourgeois comfort and simplicity of this erior are characteristic the Biedermeier style. is a long way from the grandiose "antique" décor in favor at the beginning of the 19th century.

"WIENER ZIMMER" (1837)
The Biedermeier style of painting glorified genre scenes of bourgeois family life. The painter Ferdinand Georg Waldmüller ● *100* is considered the master of Biedermeier style.

● TRADITIONAL AUSTRIAN COSTUME

Viennese fashion has always been influenced by local costumes, combined with a taste for what was stylish in Paris. During the Secession era, the School of Applied Arts opened a fashion department; its best-known member was Emilie Flöge, Gustav Klimt's muse, who designed all her own clothes. In 1909 the stylist Gertrud Pesendorfer created the modern *Dirndl* from old patterns, and after World War One there was a general revival of interest in traditional costumes.

The Vienna School of Fashion is based in Schloss Hetzendorf (Hietzing, 13th District ▲ *286*).

EVERYDAY "DIRNDL" AND PARTY "DIRNDL"
The color, shape and embroidery of the *Dirndl* vary, from region to region. The one worn at Bozn, in Italy's Southern Tyrol (left), is blue and red, with black facings.

The woman's garment called a *Dirndl* consists of a *Dirndlbluse*, a short blouse cut off under the bosom; the *Dirndl* itself, which is a skirt sewn to a bodice worn over the *Dirndlbluse*; and an apron to protect the skirt.

64

The women wear black deerskin shoes decorated with silver buckles and fringes. The men wear ankle boots. Hats and head coverings vary from region to region.

MATERIALS AND MOTIFS

The *Dirndl* is often made entirely of cotton, though the bodice can be linen or velvet. The patterns of the skirts tend to be garlands of little flowers, or geometrical motifs forming stripes, or else simple stripes.

In Vienna, traditional costumes *(Trachten)* are now only worn on special occasions: weddings, shooting parties, hunters' balls *(Jägerball ● 59)*, and the Salzburg Festival. They are also worn by waiters in some restaurants.

The skirts are embroidered; the socks and stockings ● *72* are of lace.

WINTER "DIRNDL"

In winter, women prefer to wear the bodice, a woolen brocade skirt and a silk taffeta apron.

Men wear scarves, thick stockings and generously ruffled shirts.

HUNTING COSTUME

This includes leather trousers, short for boys and long for men, and a knitted jacket of loden or linen, which is usually brown or gray-green in color.

● THE CAFÉS

"In the cafés are people who want to be alone, but who, to be so, need company." Alfred Polgar

An Armenian immigrant named Johann Diobato was Vienna's first coffee-maker. In 1685 he obtained the right to prepare and serve "the Turkish beverage in the form of coffee" from the Imperial Aulic Council. Within a very short time many other coffeehouses had opened: people went to them to read the first newspapers and to play the game of billiards, which had hitherto been restricted to the aristocracy. Some cafés became the haunts of chess and card players; others were known for their musical programs. Johann Strauss the Elder, for example, began his career in the cafés. From its earliest origins, the Viennese café has always been much more than an establishment in which assorted coffees and drinks are served. Its cosy, comfortable atmosphere has made it a regular meeting place for artists, journalists and politicians.

The *Café Central* (above) ▲ *160*.

The *Sacher Hotel* (below) ▲ *140*.

"THE FIRST CAFÉ IN VIENNA"
Legend has it that a Polish spy named Kolschitzky, shown here in Moorish costume in a painting by Franz Schams (1862), stole sacks of coffee beans from the Turks. The beans were at first thought to be camel fodder. The Pole, who knew the secret of coffee-roasting, is said by some to have opened Vienna's first café.

The *kleiner Schwarzer* (small black coffee), the *Melange* (coffee with hot milk), the *Kapuziner* (black coffee with a little cream), or the *Einspänner* (black coffee with whipped cream) invariably come with a glass of water, a croissant (*Kipfel*, another souvenir of the Turkish siege) and a newspaper. All cafés serve pastries, most of them topped with a helping of whipped cream.

ROUND TABLES

Viennese cafés were at their most popular at the beginning of the 20th century, when they became the focus of intellectual life in the city. Every group had its appointed café. At the *Café Central* one was sure to see Karl Krauss, Peter Altenberg (the man with the hat at the top of the page, seen here at the *Griensteidl*), Egon Friedell and Alfred Polgar.

Herman Bahr, Arthur Schnitzler and Hugo von Hofmannsthal usually met at the *Café Griensteidl*. In the 1920's, Robert Musil, Hermann Broch, Franz Werfel and Joseph Roth frequented the *Herrenhof*, while Gustav Klimt, Egon Schiele and Oskar Kokoschka had their tables at the *Museum*. Otto Wagner and Adolf Loos, the Art Nouveau architects, also spent many hours here: Loos designed the interior in 1899.

"THE PASSION FOR NEWSPAPERS"

A cartoon from the Biedermeier era ● *62*. Reading the newspapers, smoking and talking have always been the principal occupations of café-goers. In Vienna, the rooms are quiet and spacious, and you can spend a whole day for the price of a *kleiner Schwarzer*.

THE "HEURIGEN"

The vineyards of Nussdorf and Heiligenstadt on the hillsides of Nussberg produce a Riesling wine of very high quality ● 72.

The arrival of each year's new wine *(Heuriger)*, announced by the hanging of a pine branch over the door, is a cause for celebration in the *Heurigen (guingettes* or small taverns) of Vienna's suburbs. This wine, typical of the Vienna region, is a light, white wine that should be served chilled. It is made from a blend of grapes from the vineyards of the Wienerwald along the hillsides of Kahlenberg, Bisamberg and Nussberg that surround the city. The cultivation of vines in "Germania" (as well as in Gaul and Spain) was first authorized by the Roman Emperor Probus in the 3rd century, with a view to supplying the legions garrisoning those countries with their own sources of wine.

As well as wine, the *Heurigen* serve country dishes such as lentils and bacon, roast pork, local ham and pastries.

The new wine *(Heuriger)* is served in quarter-liter bottles and is often a blend of the best produce of the Vienna region.

The Viennese taste the new wine in a festive atmosphere, shaded by birches and hazels in courtyards and gardens that often have fine views across the Danube Valley.

Today, the vines are cultivated by about seven hundred winegrowing families in the ring of villages ■ 26 (Nussdorf, Heiligenstadt, Grinzing, Sievering and Neustift) that surround Vienna.

"In the Wienerwald, the violets were flowering blue and the couples were trysting. In our favorite café we joked, laughed, and played chess, teetotum and the tarot."

Joseph Roth

"SCHRAMMELMUSIK"
The *guinguettes* are famous for their typical *Schrammelmusik*. Joseph Schrammel (1850–93) gave this music its distinctive form by putting together a quartet of two violins, a guitar and a small clarinet (later replaced by an accordion). To the repertoire of older songs, some of them dating from the 18th century, Schrammel added compositions of his own. His *Wien bleibt Wien!* remains a favorite popular Viennese melody.

THE BEST WINES
The winegrowing villages produce more than 792,500 gallons of wine a year, the most popular of which are the Sylvaner of Grinzing, the Riesling of Nussberg, the muscats of Sooss and the red wines from Vöslau which include the *Goldeck von Schlumberg*.

At the emperor's table, etiquette required that the emperor should be served first; he immediately began to eat. Franz-Joseph was said to be so frugal that he finished his food before most of the guests could begin, so the luckless young officers who were placed at the bottom of his table got nothing to eat. For this reason they went afterward to dine at the *Sacher Hotel*, where they enjoyed a *Tafelspitz* ("table end") cut of beef. The *Sacher* still serves the best beef in town.

1. MAIN INGREDIENTS FOR EIGHT PEOPLE: 3 lb 5 oz tender rump steak, 6¼ pints water, 2 onions, 2 carrots, half a celery root, sprig of parsley, 2 bay leaves, 10 peppercorns, 4 juniper berries, 1–1½ teaspoons lovage seeds.

2. Rinse the meat and place in a pan of boiling water. Cook for 30 minutes, then add the peeled vegetables, the celery, parsley and bay leaves made into a bouquet garni, and the spices. Partially cover and simmer for another 1½ hours on a low flame. Pierce the meat with a knife: if the blade comes out cleanly, the meat is ready.

3. GARNISH: 2 lb 3 oz potatoes, 1 diced onion, salt, pepper, oil, lump of butter, pinch of cumin.

4. Boil the potatoes in their skins, allow to cool and peel. Sauté the onions in a pan with a few spoonfuls of oil. Cut the potatoes into thin rounds and place in the pan, add salt and pepper to taste, and fry until golden. Add a little butter and some cumin to refine the taste before serving.

5. APPLE AND HORSERADISH SAUCE: 4 peeled apples, ½ pint white wine, 1–1½ teaspoons sugar, finely chopped horseradish.

6. Peel the apples, remove seeds and dice.

> "In regard to 'garnishes', as the Germans of the Reich call them, I could wish next time that what you call horseradish were not steeped for quite so long. It shouldn't be allowed to lose its aroma in the milk."
>
> Joseph Roth

7. Soften the apples by simmering them in the white wine and sugar, strain off the wine, then reduce to a purée.

8. Put back a little wine for better consistency if necessary. Add the finely chopped horseradish.

10. Drain the bread well and chop finely, blend with the hard-boiled eggs.

9. CHIVE SAUCE: 2 hard-boiled eggs, 3 slices white bread soaked in milk, 2 egg yolks, ⅓ oz salt, ½–¾ teaspoon sugar, 1–1½ teaspoons vinegar or juice of half a lemon, chopped chives, 5 oz oil.

12. Beat the mixture to a mayonnaise, adding the oil very slowly. Add chives and season to taste with salt and lemon juice.

11. Add the egg yolks, salt, sugar and vinegar or lemon juice, mixing well.

13. Cut the boiled beef into slices about ½ inch thick (on the bias). Garnish with the vegetables from the stock chopped into small pieces; then moisten with a little stock. Serve the potatoes and horseradish sauce either in separate dishes or directly on the plates if you prefer. Serve the chive sauce separately.

● Specialties

Glassworks. The *Lobmeyr* glassworks was founded in Vienna in 1823. Horejce (design above) and Loos (wine service below) designed patterns here. *Lobmeyr* manufactured the chandeliers for the Kennedy Center (1971), for the Metropolitan Opera (1966), and for the Vienna Opera (1955).

Porcelain
The factory, which moved to the Augarten Palace in 1923, was founded in 1718. Right, Augarten's most famous product, the *Maria-Theresia* pattern.

Sparkling wine
Johann-Kattus (1857) is based at the oldest house in Vienna, on the Am Hof.

Bread
There are said to be as many different types of bread in Vienna as there are days in the year. For breakfast, and for making sandwiches, the Viennese favor the *Semmel*, a small, round, white roll.

Stockings
Since 1946 *Wolford* has built its reputation on quality, softness and durability.

Confectionery. Vienna produces *bonbons* (miniature chocolates) by the boxful. The *Altman & Kühne* confectionery

shop was designed by Otto Wagner; its wrapping paper design dates from the 1900's. *Demel* is famous for its pastries.

Coffee. *Julius Meinl*, a coffee-exporting house since 1862, is now a large chain of grocery stores.

Architecture

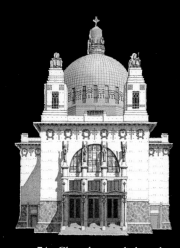

Following the high Gothic period, religious architecture in the rigidly Catholic capital of the Habsburgs quickly fell under the influence of the Counter-Reformation. In the late 16th century Vienna welcomed a host of Italian architects who brought with them the latest Baroque styles. The Austrians Johann Bernhard Fischer von Erlach (1656–1726) and his son Josef Emanuel (1693–1742) and the German Johann Lukas von Hildebrandt (1668–1745) developed the new "theater of stone".

FRANZISKANERKIRCHE (1603 AND 1611) ▲ *149*
The Franciscan Church of St Jerome brings together the Southern German Renaissance style and vestiges of Gothic in one of the more singular oddities of Viennese architecture.

SALVATORKAPELLE (1520–30) ▲ *172*
The portal of the Chapel of the Saviour, a rare example of the Renaissance style in Vienna, has features that are typically Italian.

KARLSKIRCHE (1715–37) ▲ *238*. Designed by J. B. Fischer von Erlach, the Church of St Charles with its twin campaniles inspired by the columns of Trajan and Marcus Aurelius is an extraordinary example of the imperial Baroque style. Its grandiose façade could be that of a building in Rome. It was commissioned by Charles VI in honor of St Charles Borromeo to celebrate the end of the plague of 1713 and is triumphal in tone, with an elliptical floor plan and a dome of the kind already used with the Peterskirche. Its dramatic power was intended to express "the glory of Vienna, the modern Rome".

RUPRECHTSKIRCHE (740) ▲ *154*
The Church of St Rupert is the oldest in
Vienna. Its Romanesque nave was built
between 1130 and 1170; the choir,
belltower and doorway date from the 14th
and 15th centuries.

CARMELITENKIRCHE (1623) ▲ 269
The Carmelite Church of St Joseph offers a less
conventional version of the classic Roman
façade, not unlike the one chosen by the
Dominicans for their church. The three levels of
the façade, narrowing from base to summit,
create a strong vertical tension. This is
emphasized by the lines of the pilasters and by
the various decorative elements, which also
accentuate each projecting angle of the
composition. The relative economy of
decorative effects lends a certain austerity to
the structure.

DOMINIKANERKIRCHE (1631–34) ▲ 152
The Church of the Dominicans, a project
shared by the architects Spatz, Biasino and
Canevale, was closely copied from the Church
of Gesù in Rome. The façade (1666–74) is in
the same vein: its broad lower story is
succeeded by a narrower one, flanked by
upside-down corbels and topped with a
triangular pediment.

PETERSKIRCHE (1703–53) ▲ *139*
The Church of St Peter was designed by
Johann Lukas von Hildebrandt, working
from an initial plan by
Gabriele Montani. The
portal, by Andrea
Altomonte, was put in fifty
years later. The building
has great energy, with a
dome rising over a
narrow but fluid
façade framed
by two soaring
towers.

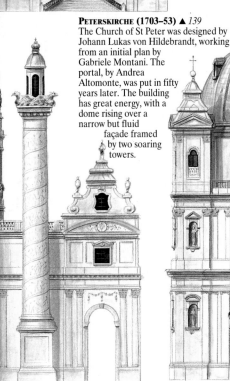

The churches within the original city walls are usually part of groups of buildings and are often situated in courtyards, or *Höfe*. There are very few planned perspectives to set off the diverse façades and belltowers. Almost as if they were torn between the Italian dome and the Gothic spire, the Viennese architects resorted to a wealth of combinations, spawning a number of charming hybrids such as the basic "onion" and "pumpkin" shapes.

The belltowers of Vienna add a note of fantasy to some of the city's otherwise pretentious and conventional Italianate façades.

ANNAKIRCHE ▲ *146* **AND STIFTSKIRCHE** *(Mariahilfer Strasse 24).* The Baroque churches of St Anne (1630–1715) and the Abbey (1739) are both powerful and graceful.

EVANGELISCHE KIRCHE *(Dorotheergasse 16)* ▲ *138* The belltower (1887) of the Protestant Reform Church is a clever pastiche adding a flourish to the church built by Nigelli in 1784.

SERVITENKIRCHE (1651–77) ▲ *293* The clocktowers of the Church of the Servites, rebuilt in 1754 to a design by F. S. Rosenstingls, emphasize the straightforward Baroque style of the façade.

SCHOTTENKIRCHE (12th–17th century) ▲ *163* Between 1643 and 1648, the Italians Silvestro Carlone and Andrea Felice d'Allio gave the venerable Scottish church ▲ *163* the Baroque features it has today. The bulb-domed main belltower, isolated behind the chevet, provides a pleasant counterpoint to the simple lines of the façade and the two towers on either side.

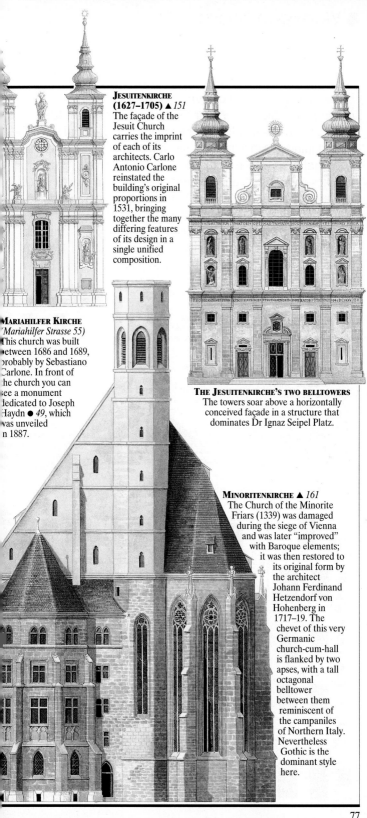

JESUITENKIRCHE (1627–1705) ▲ *151*
The façade of the Jesuit Church carries the imprint of each of its architects. Carlo Antonio Carlone reinstated the building's original proportions in 1531, bringing together the many differing features of its design in a single unified composition.

MARIAHILFER KIRCHE
(Mariahilfer Strasse 55)
This church was built between 1686 and 1689, probably by Sebastiano Carlone. In front of the church you can see a monument dedicated to Joseph Haydn ● *49*, which was unveiled in 1887.

THE JESUITENKIRCHE'S TWO BELLTOWERS
The towers soar above a horizontally conceived façade in a structure that dominates Dr Ignaz Seipel Platz.

MINORITENKIRCHE ▲ *161*
The Church of the Minorite Friars (1339) was damaged during the siege of Vienna and was later "improved" with Baroque elements; it was then restored to its original form by the architect Johann Ferdinand Hetzendorf von Hohenberg in 1717–19. The chevet of this very Germanic church-cum-hall is flanked by two apses, with a tall octagonal belltower between them reminiscent of the campaniles of Northern Italy. Nevertheless Gothic is the dominant style here.

In Vienna, houses of the bourgeois are often almost indistinguishable in style from aristocratic mansions. Rich bourgeois tradespeople and craftsmen copied and adapted the formal and figurative repertoires of the palaces in four- to six-floor buildings, which were often inhabited by several different families and mostly concentrated along the narrow streets of the inner city (Innere Stadt). As tastes changed, the oldest bourgeois houses dating from the 15th and 16th centuries were successively revamped to suit the Baroque, neo-classical and Biedermeier fashions; the bright colors of their façades contrast strongly with pure white or gray-beige ornamentation.

THE BOW WINDOW
(Naglergasse)
Projections such as these are a familiar feature of 17th- and 18th-century Viennese buildings.

CORNER BUILDING ▲ *139*
(Naglergasse 13–15)
Large bourgeois houses, mostly dating from the 15th and 16th centuries, overlook Naglerstrasse, a street that runs along the old Roman ramparts. This 15th-century building was given a classical façade in 1700 and, during the 18th century, further ornamented with a colored relief of the coronation of the Virgin.

DREIMÄDLERHAUS (1803)
▲ *166 Schreyvogelgasse 10*
The "House of the Three Maidens" is an example of bourgeois Viennese neo-classical style

"ZUM BLAUEN KARPFEN" ▲ 146 *(Annagasse 11)* "The Blue Carp" is an 18th-century building altered in 1814 by the architect Ehmann, who turned it into a subtle neo-classical composition incorporating arabesque motifs and cameo figures.

BIEDERMEIER REFINEMENT ● 62 A powerful frieze by the sculptor J. Klieber does not detract from the extraordinary delicacy of the colors on this façade. It is an example of the classic Biedermeier style which took Vienna by storm in the early 19th century.

BAROQUE WINDOW ▲ 168 *(Kurrentgasse 12)* An ogee arch lends further dynamism to the already lively colors.

BIEDERMEIER WINDOW *(Nestroyplatz)* A tracery of friezes and balustrades punctuates the formality of the design.

KURRENTGASSE 6–8 The buildings along this narrow thoroughfare form a classic 18th-century urban ensemble. The first floor is characterized by continuous reliefs; above, the four floors gradually diminish in height, with identical and regular bay windows on each level. Nos. 6 to 8 offer a variation on the basic five-tier design. The details of the distribution and the choice of decorative motifs – the double bays and pediments, for example – give variety to the rhythms of the façades.

● BAROQUE PALACES

The palaces of the many great magnates who converged on Vienna to attend the court, or to serve in the government or army, were built around the Hofburg, the imperial residence. The façades of these noble residences influenced the style of public buildings, which were constructed to look like palaces, with pediments sporting the imperial two-headed eagle. These great houses were usually adorned with sculptures whose purpose was to emphasize the contrasts between the other architectural features. There were gods and giants, caryatids and Atlantes, together with symbols of glory and trophies of war. Neo-classicism was to bring a calmer note to the palaces of Vienna, though there was another brief period of exuberance during the era of the Ring.

Heraldic eagle on the façade of the Arsenal.

THE STATE CHANCELLERY (HOFBURG) (1726–30) ▲ *175* Wing designed by J. B. Fischer von Erlach.

THE ARSENAL (1731) ▲ *258*. A building constructed by Anton Ospel. The rich statuary by Lorenzo Mattielli offsets the otherwise extreme regularity of the composition.

THE OLD UNIVERSITY (1735–55) ▲ *151* The Aula (Main Hall) of the university was built in an eclectic European style in which Baroque principles began to be supplanted by neo-classical ones.

THE TRAUTSON PALACE (1702–5) Oedtl built this palace to plans by J. B. Fischer von Erlach. The clear structure of the wings, together with the exaggerated importance of the central part, echoes the 16th-century Palladian style.

THE BELVEDERE (1714–22). The original concept of the twin Belvedere Palaces, which are connected by a garden, came from the close collaboration between the architect, Johann Lukas von Hildebrandt, and his client, Prince Eugène of Savoy. The Lower Belvedere (above, left-hand page) served as a summer residence; the more ceremonial Upper Belvedere (this page, above) was used for balls and receptions.

PORTAL OF THE LOBKOWITZ PALACE
Added in 1710 by J. B. Fischer von Erlach to the palace built by Tencala, this portal copies the high altar of the Church of the Franciscans at Salzburg.

THE KINSKY PALACE (FORMERLY THE DAUN PALACE) (1713–16) ▲ *164*. The opulence of this palace's stunning façade, constructed by Hildebrandt, is only a prelude to its highly original interior.

CARYATIDS
Young girls sculpted by Franz Anton Zauner at the Pallavicini Palace.

THE BATTHYANY-SCHÖNBORN PALACE (1698–1706) ▲ *165*
is palace, designed by J. B. Fischer von Erlach, is based on originals
Bernini in Rome. Its façade was modified in the 19th century when the central coping of its attic story was removed.

THE PALLAVICINI PALACE (1783–4) ▲ *192*
In this neo-classical construction, Ferdinand von Hohenberg simplified the flamboyant rhythms of the traditional façade.

BELVEDERE ATLANTES
One of the four giant
statues supporting
the heavy arches of
the upper palace
Sala Terena of
Belvedere ▲ 256.

It was a common
feature of the
architecture of antiquity to
include the representation of the
captive foe, thereby seemingly neutralizing
his power. As the capital of an empire which
had to be tightly controlled if it were not to
unravel, Vienna understandably overdid the
symbolism of such stone captives in its
government buildings, usually showing Turks
metamorphosed into Atlantes. These
Baroque figures were also designed to stress the
tectonic points in architectural structures. As a
rule they were positioned at ground-floor level
but from time to time they appear on upper-
storey façades in rather more relaxed attitudes.

THE BELVEDERE

This was the summer residence of Prince Eugène of Savoy (1663–1736) ● *35*, ▲ *247*, a great military commander and diplomat who won several victories over the Turks. The upper palace was built by Johan Lukas von Hildebrandt in 1772.

MONUMENT TO A GENERAL'S GLORY

The superabundance here of Atlantes and "tamers of wild horses" is an acknowledgment of the power of Prince Eugène. These giant figures are bent double beneath the weight of the arches of the Sala Terena on the garden side of the building; they seem more graceful as part of the staircase, where the decor shows the exploits of Alexander the Great. All of them carry weapons, as if to stress their underlying message.

THE NEO-CLASSICAL EPOCH

During the 19th century, the imitators of Greek antiquity preferred reflective good taste to displays of muscular strength in sculpture.

ATTITUDES

During the 18th century, sculptors took liberties with the theme of Atlas. Some of their Atlantes are allowed to forsake their tasks in order to contemplate with a certain irony the comings and goings in the world beyond the palace gates.

PRINCE EUGÈNE'S WINTER PALACE ▲ *147*

Both in the country and in town, Prince Eugène was partial to muscular Titans as embodiments of his victories. Here they accompany the visitor up the staircase, from a dark and severe ground floor to a brighter, more human *piano nobile*.

● THE RINGSTRASSE

THE BURGTHEATER (1874–88) ▲ *204*
Detail of the dome over the main hall
and the balustrade above the façade.
This theater was constructed by
Gottfried Semper and Karl von
Hasenauer.

Since it was suffering from lack of space, Vienna decided to demolish its old fortifications in 1860. In place of the ramparts majestic boulevards were created, along with sites for the palaces and temples of the new bourgeoisie: the Stock Exchange, the City Hall, the Parliament, the universities, museums, Fine Arts Academy and State Opera. The joyous eclectism of the Ringstrasse, which looks like an adult construction set in which architects including Otto Wagner strove to outshine one another, was criticized by purists like Adolf Loos, who called the area a "Potemkin City", symbolic of the impotence and hypocrisy of industrial society.

The Museum of Art History
and the Natural History
Museum ▲ *207* were built by
Gottfried Semper and Karl
von Hasenauer in the form
of two half-Renaissance,
half-Baroque palaces, facing
each other across the Maria-
Theresien-Platz.

**THE RATHAUS
(1872–3)** ▲ *205*
Friedrich von
Schmidt's City Hall is
a symbol of municipal
freedom directly
confronting the old
town. It aimed to
rival the lavishness of
the imperial court.

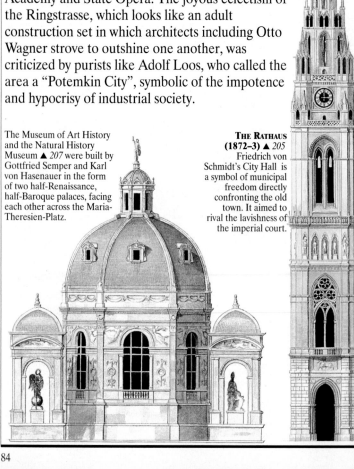

ATHENEBRUNNEN BY THE PARLIAMENT BUILDING (1874–83)

Theophil von Hansen designed the Parliament in neo-Grecian style in homage to the land where democracy was born. The white-marble Athena Fountain, surrounded by allegories of the virtues and of the great rivers of the empire, has a gilded helmet and shield. This statue, designed by Hansen and completed by Carl Kundmann in 1902, is modeled on the gold and ivory statue of Athena by Phidias at the Parthenon in Athens.

THE TODESCO PALACE (1861–4) ▲ 223

Built on the Kärtnerstrasse in front of the Opera by Ludwig von Förster and Theophil von Hansen, the Todesco Palace was one of the first buildings of its kind to be built for a bourgeois businessman. Its neo-Renaissance style was intended to evoke the splendor of the Medicis.

A RESIDENTIAL BUILDING

On the corner of Grillparzerstrasse ▲ 203 and Rathausstrasse, this apartment block demonstrates the skill of turn-of-the-century architects in concealing floors in order to achieve the tripartite pattern of Italian Renaissance palaces. A rustic overlay links the first three floors, while the attic windows are camouflaged in the ornamented cornices.

THE VOTIVKIRCHE ▲ 203

Drawing on the great 13th-century cathedrals of France for inspiration Heinrich von Ferstel could not resist introducing a certain rationalist emphasis on the basic elements of Gothic architecture, particularly in the design of the graceful main façade.

The Vienna Secession (1897–1907) was an association formed by artists to break with academic art conventions. In architecture it was dominated by Otto Wagner (1841–1918), who began the transition from the neo-Renaissance eclecticism of the Ring epoch to a form of rigorous but ornamental Art Nouveau (known in Vienna as Jugendstil, 1894–1914) which was rimmed with steel, covered in ceramic, and embellished with aluminum and copper ornaments. Well before 1900, Secessionist architecture had developed the kinds of straight lines that were later to fuel French Art Deco. Josef Hoffmann (1870–1956) set his cubist outlines within lavish corner designs, and delighted in reversing the values of classical proportion on decorated structures. Adolf Loos (1870–1933), a dandy and a provocateur, pushed his own style of iconoclastic purism to the brink of the surreal.

THE ANKERHAUS (1893–5) ▲ *138*
This house on the Graben by Otto Wagner contrasts the light metal structure of its ground floor and mezzanine and the glass of its terraces, with the stone of its rich façade.

THE SCHÜTZENHAUS (1906–7)
The Lock House, also by Otto Wagner, is all that remains of the Kaiserbad dam installation, part of a scheme for regulating the Danube which (like the Metro) was a major feature of Vien in 1900. A plinth of granite, plaques of white marble attached with rivets, and blue porcelain tiles combin to form a frieze which goes well with the Schützenhaus' technic function. The building very elegant, given its utilitarian purpose.

**LEOPOLDKIRCHE
(1905–7) ▲ 288**
…icily sumptuous church of St Leopold
…was a neo-Byzantine version of the
…Karlskirche ▲ 238 and a triumphant
…con on the hill above the new Steinhof
lunatic asylum.

**THE KARL LUEGER MEMORIAL CHURCH
(1908–10) ▲ 262.** This building is a much more
eclectic, academic version of the one at the
Steinhof. It is dedicated to the memory of Karl
Lueger ▲ 227, a populist mayor during the last
years of the empire.

…ECESSION (1897–8) ▲ 222, 232. Although he went on to pay tribute
…o the extravagant international Art Nouveau style, Joseph Maria
…Olbrich (1867–1908) produced his best work in the Secession Pavilion,
…shrine to the various artists of the Secession movement. The archaic
…igor and oriental lavishness of this edifice evoke the palace of a
…alome figure dressed by Klimt ▲ 227, 250 and Koloman Moser
▲ 235. Outrageous in its useless luxury, the empty dome covered in
triumphal laurel leaves was intended to echo that of
the Karlskirche on the far side of the Wien.

**THE HOUSE OF
DR VOJCSIL (1900–1)**
Designed by
O. Schöntha, this
house displays the
Jugendstil trend of
affixing Mannerist
ornaments to
classical structures.

**KARLSPLATZ METRO
STATION (1898–9)**
▲ 223, 240

A classic
Jugendstil
creation by Otto Wagner.
The technical concept
was revolutionary, with
prefabricated metal
elements covered in
colored ceramic panels.

**THE MEDALLION
HOUSE ▲ 237**
Otto Wagner
constructed three
rental apartment
blocks (1898–9),
including the
Medallion House.
Its floral motifs
evoke the pages of
the review *Ver
Sacrum*, as do
those of its
neighbor, the
Majolikahaus.

Tubular heating vent ▲ 228

During the period of artistic renewal that took place between 1890 and 1900, Otto Wagner proposed a novel architectural concept which took account of modern techniques and extolled the individual freedom of the artist, outside the mainstream styles of history. Wagner stripped his buildings of all decorative formalism, and instead accentuated surface effects. Sculpted motifs were replaced by flat ornamentation, producing a more highly colored, dark-on-light result with lines whose sole purpose was to stress decorative perfection. The first building of this type on the Ringstrasse, the Postsparkasse (Post Office Savings Bank, 1904–6) perfectly illustrates Wagner's theory, which was to become one of the fundamental tenets of the modern movement.

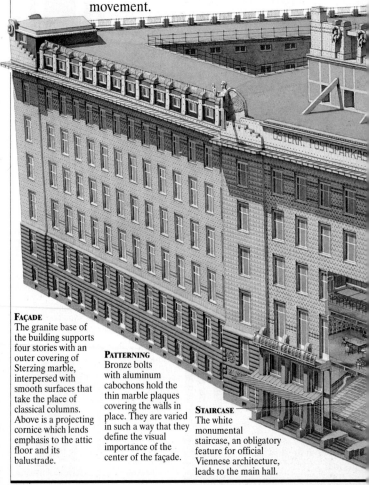

FAÇADE
The granite base of the building supports four stories with an outer covering of Sterzing marble, interspersed with smooth surfaces that take the place of classical columns. Above is a projecting cornice which lends emphasis to the attic floor and its balustrade.

PATTERNING
Bronze bolts with aluminum cabochons hold the thin marble plaques covering the walls in place. They are varied in such a way that they define the visual importance of the center of the façade.

STAIRCASE
The white monumental staircase, an obligatory feature for official Viennese architecture, leads to the main hall.

FLOOR PLAN. A regular polygon whose symmetry exalts functional character and mastery of the latest modern building techniques.

WINGED VICTORIES
These cast aluminum figures were designed by Othmar Schimkowitz.

The systematic division of the floor plan into parallel cells reveals the use of a metal framework.

SCULPTURE
While rejecting merely decorative features, Wagner was very partial to monumental sculpture – for example, these figures which punctuate the upper parts of his building.

MATERIALS
Otto Wagner had a clear preference for industrial materials that looked artificial – steel, glass and cement, for example – and was extremely interested in metal-framed constructions. The features that show are used as decor and as pretexts for abstract geometrical compositions in which the architect skillfully creates a range of material effects with mat, shiny, smooth or grainy surfaces.

THE MAIN HALL
The marriage of form and technological necessity is expressed here without any stylistic go-between. The hall's functional purpose is immediately made clear, with structures and technical installations transformed into furnishings which illustrate Wagner's dictum "Necessity is the only criterion for Art".

VAULTING OF THE MAIN HALL
The system of construction used for the Main Hall is drawn from naval architecture (with tie-beams and narrow columns of fluted metal), and comes together to remarkable effect in a thin, curved layer of glass and steel, a technical tour de force. It allows light to flood into the hall.

● MODERN HOUSES

THE WITTGENSTEIN HOUSE (1926–8) *(Kundmanngasse 19)*
Paul Engelmann and Ludwig Wittgenstein invested a large
amount of money in this beautifully conceived and executed
minimalist construction.

After the bourgeois neo-classicism of the
Biedermeier epoch, the Industrial Revolutio[n]
produced a horde of newly rich Viennese wh[o]
built large Italianate villas on the hills
surrounding the city. Otto Wagner, who beg[an]
by designing luxurious houses of this sort,
adopted Secessionist principles. Adolf Loos carried this purism t[o]
its logical conclusion without, however,
attaining Wittgenstein's degree of
philosophical rigor, and Josef
Hoffmann used wit and subtle
classical allusions to redefine
the Biedermeier style.

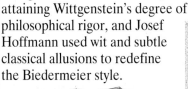

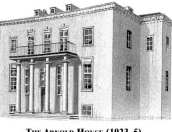

THE ARNOLD HOUSE (1923–5)
Lois Welzenbache applied the elongated
classicism of his master, Hoffmann, but added
a traditional Biedermeier façade.

VILLA SKYWA-PRIMAVESI (1913–15)
In this street façade Hoffmann
plays with the proportions
and outline of classical
composition.

FLOORPLAN OF THE VILLA WAGNER I (1886–8)
(Hüttelbergstrasse 26)
A terrace site, two wings with columns, and majestic flights of steps
leading in – Wagner's first villa exhibits Palladian influences redefined
in the light of turn-of-the-century symbolism.

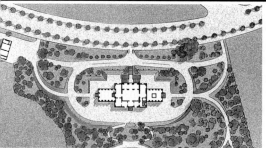

**VILLA WAGNER II
DOORWAY.** Leopold
Forstner's Warrior
Athena over the
doorway marries with
the rest of the design
because of its stylistic
character and formal
three-part casing.

The greatest single source of inspiration was Arnold Böcklin's
Seaside Villa, which effectively took Viennese
architecture beyond the limits of the
Italian model.

VILLA WAGNER II (1912–13)
(Hüttelbergstrasse 28)
The disciplined geometrical use of ornament
and archaic coloring are part of the architect's
evolution toward a form of monumental
austerity, encompassing both the Secessionist
and Weiner styles.

THE HOFFMANN HOUSE (1930–2)
Built specially for the Werkbund exhibition,
this project for a working man's home
blends economy of materials, comfort and
functional effectiveness; the handling of
space, particularly that of the glassed-in
entrance, is remarkable.

**HAUS MOLLER
(1927–8)**
Designed by Adolf
Loos a year after
Tristan Tzara's
house in
Montmartre.
The façade is
anthropomorphic, its ironic
mask surreptitiously reintroducing
the ornamentation and axial emphasis
so admired by the architect's modernist
disciples.

VILLA AST (1909–11) *(Steinfeldgasse 2)*
In this last of the Hohewarte houses,
Josef Hoffmann expresses his view of
classicism in the form of solid, foursquare
buildings. Even so, his ornamental
details go directly against the grain of
traditional values.

THE MOLL HOUSE (1906–17)
(Steinfeldgasse 8). It blends well with the neo-
Biedermeier buildings that surround it.

After the breakup of the empire and the proclamation of the Austrian Republic in 1918, Vienna ceased to be an international capital. The serious economic downturn which ensued caused wholesale migrations and a huge increase in the population of Vienna, which created a severe shortage of housing. In 1919 the socialist triumph at the municipal elections transformed the city, which by then was a "state within a state", into a testing ground for a workers' democracy. The great working-class building projects *(Hof)*, constructed between 1919 and 1933, are an impressive reminder of the ambitions of socialist Vienna, in both the sociopolitical and the architectural spheres.

KARL-SEITZ-HOF
(1926–7) ▲ *297*
This refined complex by Hubert Gessner is built around a monumental semicircle.

KARL-MARX-HOF
(1927–30) ▲ *295*
This majestic structure by Karl Ehn (more than a half mile long, containing 1,600 apartments), extends around six central towers built over 40-foot arches. The ensemble has the look of a great triumphal archway.

RESIDENTIAL COMPLEX (1924–5) (PHILLIPSGASSE 8)
With an astounding strap-work façade, stone harps at the corners, triangular bow windows and a variety of apertures, this building by Siegfried Theiss and Hans Jaksch seems to be an attempt to enliven the monotony of the urban environment.

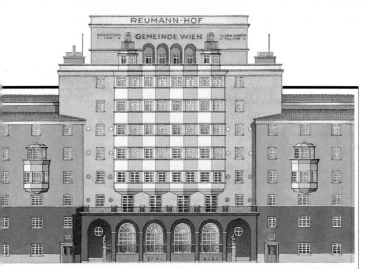

REUMANNHOF (1924–6) ▲ *297*
In order to give his massive Reumannhof a palatial appearance, Gessner grouped large numbers of bow windows in the central part of the building, in the ground-floor arcades, and at the attic levels.

DOOR AT KLOSEHOF (1924). This has all the elegance of Hoffmann's classic modernism ▲ *235*.

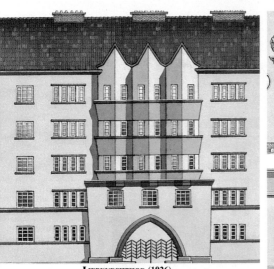

LIEBKNECHTHOF (1926)
In this building Karl Krist's expressionist and constructivist instincts subtly modify the historical elements, such as the ogival arch and the gabled turrets of bow windows, inspired by Gothic antecedents.

DOOR AT SANDLEITENHOF (1924–8)
Hoppe, Schönthal, Matuschek, Theiss, Jaksch, Krauss and Tölk: a litany of architects for a complex in which everyday motifs are handled with superb imagination.

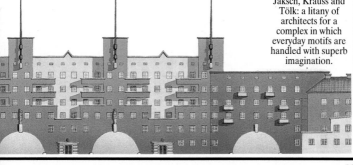

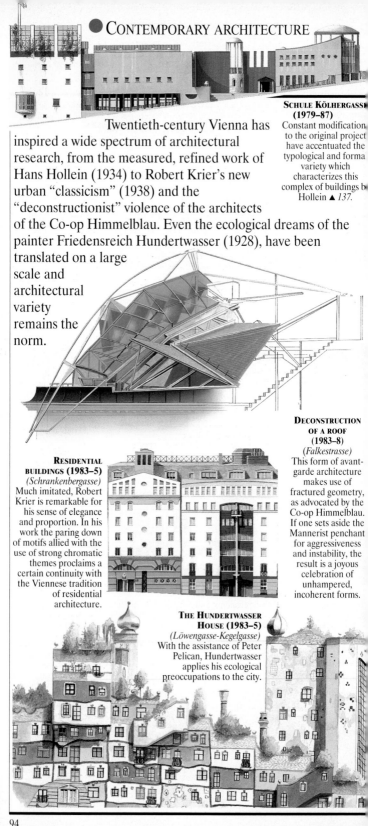

CONTEMPORARY ARCHITECTURE

Twentieth-century Vienna has inspired a wide spectrum of architectural research, from the measured, refined work of Hans Hollein (1934) to Robert Krier's new urban "classicism" (1938) and the "deconstructionist" violence of the architects of the Co-op Himmelblau. Even the ecological dreams of the painter Friedensreich Hundertwasser (1928), have been translated on a large scale and architectural variety remains the norm.

SCHULE KÖLHERGASSE (1979–87)
Constant modification to the original project have accentuated the typological and forma variety which characterizes this complex of buildings b Hollein ▲ 137.

DECONSTRUCTION OF A ROOF (1983–8)
(Falkestrasse)
This form of avant-garde architecture makes use of fractured geometry, as advocated by the Co-op Himmelblau. If one sets aside the Mannerist penchant for aggressiveness and instability, the result is a joyous celebration of unhampered, incoherent forms.

RESIDENTIAL BUILDINGS (1983–5)
(Schrankenbergasse)
Much imitated, Robert Krier is remarkable for his sense of elegance and proportion. In his work the paring down of motifs allied with the use of strong chromatic themes proclaims a certain continuity with the Viennese tradition of residential architecture.

THE HUNDERTWASSER HOUSE (1983–5)
(Löwengasse-Kegelgasse)
With the assistance of Peter Pelican, Hundertwasser applies his ecological preoccupations to the city.

Vienna as seen
by painters

As the pupil and sometime copyist of his uncle Antonio Canal, otherwise known as Canaletto, Bernardo Belloto (1720–80) suffered for many years from unfair comparison with his master. Yet he was wise enough to leave Venice at an early age and travel through the rest of Italy, after which he went to Dresden at the invitation of the Elector of Saxony, the then king of Poland Augustus III. Enchanted by the Elbe Valley, Belloto began painting the romantic canvases which established his reputation at the courts of Munich, Vienna and Warsaw. He was invited to Vienna by Empress Maria Theresa, where he produced a series of portraits of the city in which detail and charm were matched with genuine poetry. In his *View of Vienna from the Upper Belvedere* (above, 1722) Belloto depicts the overlapping gardens of the Salesian monastery and the Belvedere, along with the Belvedere's orangery and the gardens of the Schwartzenberg Palace. The domes of the churches of St Charles and of the Salesians frame the composition, and in the distance is the old city, a thicket of towers dominated by the spire of St Stephen's; beyond is the undulating Wienerwald. In this picture Belloto contrasts the wordly atmosphere of the Belvedere with the romantic garden of the Schwarzenbergs. The *Freyung at Vienna* (opposite) shows a square in the old town. Side by side with bourgeois buildings stand (on the left) the Harrach, Kinsky and Batthyány-Schönborn palaces, while the people milling around the street stalls are drawn from all social classes.

‎ 'But all the same I am the guardian at the art museum, and a state
official,' he said. 'In the evening, after six o'clock has struck, I lock up
‎ not criminals but works of art: I turn the key on Rubens and Belloto.' "

Old Masters

Some painters owe their posthumous reputations less to artistic talent than to the quality of their contemporary observation: among these are Longhi in Venice, Van Mour in Constantinople, and Martin van Meytens (or Mytens) in Vienna. Meytens (1695–1770) was of Dutch origin but was raised in Stockholm, where his father was court painter. After studying in Holland and England, he settled in Paris where, as the protégé of the Duke of Orléans, he painted the French king's portrait and forty miniature portraits for Peter the Great. After visiting the courts of Dresden and Vienna, Meytens traveled to Italy to study the Venetians before returning to the imperial capital. There, in 1730, he was appointed official court painter and, twenty-nine years later, became Director of the Fine Arts Academy. Today the interest in his work lies mainly in the glimpse of 18th-century dress and, in his badly composed larger canvases, the rich period detail. An example is the series of paintings commissioned by Maria Theresa ● 36 for the marriage of her son, the future Joseph II, to Isabella of Parma, in 1760. The painting at the top depicts the wedding procession on its way to the Augustinian Church; the one to the left shows a concert given at the Burgtheater before the imperial family on the same occasion.

The hills of the Wienerwald ■ 18 have always been a favorite walking place for the Viennese; for painters, their attraction lay in the romantic views they afforded of the city and the villages around it. These included Nussdorf, Grinzing and, as here, Mödling (1848 and 1849, above) as depicted by Ferdinand Georg Waldmüller (1793–1865). An advocate of realism who was hostile to academic art, Waldmüller left one of the most complete visual descriptions of Viennese society during the Biedermeier epoch ● 62. His court portraits, and scenes of rural life, portray a society that is still patriarchal at the dawn of industrialization. His landscapes, which are particularly famous, are bathed in a hard light which breaks up the silhouettes of the trees and lends an unearthly sharpness to perspectives. Instead of including scenes of Italy like so many other neo-classical landscape painters, he took care to paint his landscapes realistically, preferring to attack them from close up, thus circumventing the tyranny of "good composition". An example is his view of the Prater (opposite), where at that time the meadow was still mown by locals. In his most poignant landscapes Waldmüller conveyed a sense of the hard existence that lay behind the peasants' colorful traditional costumes.

"The rendezvous took place at noon the next day, at the sign of the blue stag. This was a Grinzing tavern where, in summer, they used to come with sausage and ham to drink the new wine; and so they dined under the acacia, among the barrels with their sixteen hoops."

Paul Morand

Self-portrait by
Rudolf von Alt.

he best-known members of the Alt family were Franz and Rudolf, the sons of Jacob Alt of Frankfurt. An itinerant landscape painter, Jacob painted watercolors of every part of the empire, including several of Vienna (below, 1817). Rudolf, the "Viennese Canaletto", carried the same genre to new heights before concentrating on interiors; he eventually earned his keep supplying the imperial nobility with albums of their residences. The studio below (main picture) is that of Hans Makart, a neo-Renaissance artist who painted portraits of Ringstrasse ladies.

After a period of
rapid economic
expansion, by 1900
Vienna was suffering
from social unrest.
The avant-garde
showed little interest,
but naturalist painter
Joseph Engelhart
(1864–1941) set
about portraying
contemporary Vienna
in paintings such as
*An Evening at the
Sophienbad* (right).
(The Sophienbad
was popular with the
middle class during
the winter season.)
A more attentive
observer than
Engelhart, Carl Moll
(1861–1945) ▲ 255
viewed social reality
with the rational view
of the Dutch painters
(above, the *Muttel
Fabrik*).

Vienna as seen
by writers

FIRST IMPRESSIONS

A SMALL TOWN

William Lithgow (1582–1645?) passed through Vienna during his travels across Europe, but was disappointed to find that it did not live up to its reputation.

❝Being arrived at Vienne, I found the Towne, and the flying fame of it fa different, either for greatnesse, strength, or wealth; for the Towne rising upon moderat height circular, is but of small compasse without, not passing two Englis miles.

The suburbs round about, being twice as great as the Towne; and the strength of it is no way comparable to a hundred Cities that I have seene, neither is it for wealth so much to be admired, being depraved of Seas, shipping, and navigation, having onely the needfull prosperity of dry land Townes.❞

WILLIAM LITHGOW, *RARE ADVENTURES AND PAINFULL PEREGRINATIONS*, 1614–32, PUB. JAMES MACLEHOSE & SONS, GLASGOW, 1906

A CHRISTIAN WELCOME

Peter Tolstoi (1645–1729), the Russian ambassador to Vienna, was very impressed to see the care given in a hospital which he visited in 1698.

❝I was at a *shpital* (Ger. *Spital*), that is, a hospital or a house for the ill. This hospital is built outside the city of Vienna in a suburb, on the other side of a tributary of the river Danube; in this hospital is a very long room, and in this room, opposite the doors, a man's bones are placed beneath glass in an icon-case, arranged into a likeness [of a man] and held together with brass wire. These are the bones of the man who first began to build this hospital. In this same room around the walls are placed many beds of fine joiner's work, and around each bed is placed a green curtain, and on each bedstead is placed good bedding. They are covered with white sheets, and on each bed is a good blanket. On these beds lie the sick, and by the head of each sick person is a tankard with a drink, and the tankards are all pewter; each sick person also has a white towel. This hospital is just being built by the imperial treasury. Alongside of this hospital is a good pharmacy for the drugs for those sick people, and doctors are attached to it; and the druggists and chemists in this pharmacy are assigned to it, and all are kept at the emperor's expense. In the middle of that long room in which the sick people lie is a *kaplica*, that is, a small church, where the Roman monks conduct a Mass for the sick daily early in the morning. And here they have set the tables on which the sick eat; and on the other side of this long room is a small garden, and placed i it are grapes, and this is why they built it: when a sick person begins to recover fron his illness, he may stroll in this garden because of its coolness. They accept into thi hospital the sick of every rank without cost; they only inquire if the sick person ha no means of his own, and these they accept into this hospital, and they rest and are treated with great care; they also admit into this hospital traveling foreigners wh fall ill, and they keep these sick people in this place until they are completely cured and when they are completely healthy, they are free to go wherever they wish without paying; no one takes anything from anyone in this hospital, and they d this because of the Christian faith and for the saving of souls.❞

THE TRAVEL DIARY OF PETER TOLSTOI, 1697 TRANS. MAX J. OKENFUSS PUB. NORTHERN ILLINOIS UNIVERSITY PRESS, 198

VIENNESE APARTMENTS

Lady Mary Wortley Montagu (1689–1762) was the wife of the British ambassador to Constantinople, so spent much time overseas. She soon became known in society for her eloquent and incisive letters, which were first published in 1837 after her death. The following letter, to her sister the Countess of Mar, was written on September 8, 1716, and describes the living accommodation available in Vienna at the time.

"This town, which has the honour of being the emperor's residence, did not at all answer my ideas of it, being much less than I expected to find it; the streets are very close, and so narrow, one cannot observe the fine fronts of the palaces, though many of them very well deserve observation, being truly magnificent, all built of fine white stone, and excessive high, the town being so much too little for the number of the people that desire to live in it, the builders seem to have projected to repair that misfortune, by clapping one town on the top of another, most of the houses being of five, and some of them six stories. You may easily imagine, that the streets being so narrow, the upper rooms are extremely dark; and, what is an inconveniency much more intolerable, in my opinion, there is no house that has so few as five or six families in it. The apartments of the greatest ladies, and even of the ministers of state, are divided but by a partition from that of a tailor or a shoemaker; and I know nobody that has above two floors in any house, one for their own use, and one higher for their servants. Those that have houses of their own, let out the rest of them to whoever will take them; thus the great stairs (which are all of stone) are as common and as dirty as the street. 'Tis true, when you have once travelled through them, nothing can be more surprisingly magnificent than the apartments. They are commonly a *suite* of eight or ten large rooms, all inlaid, the doors and windows richly carved and gilt, and the furniture such as is seldom seen in the palaces of sovereign princes in other countries – the hangings the finest tapestry of Brussels, prodigious large looking-glasses in silver frames, fine japan tables, beds, chairs, canopies, and window curtains of the richest Genoa damask or velvet, almost covered with gold lace or embroidery. The whole made gay by pictures, and vast jars of japan china, and in almost every room large lustres of rock crystal.**"**

THE LETTERS AND WORKS OF LADY MARY WORTLEY MONTAGU,
EVERYMAN'S LIBRARY, LONDON 1993

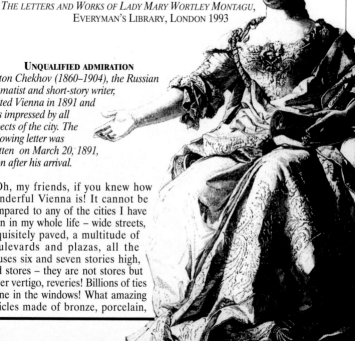

UNQUALIFIED ADMIRATION

Anton Chekhov (1860–1904), the Russian dramatist and short-story writer, visited Vienna in 1891 and was impressed by all aspects of the city. The following letter was written on March 20, 1891, soon after his arrival.

"Oh, my friends, if you knew how wonderful Vienna is! It cannot be compared to any of the cities I have seen in my whole life – wide streets, exquisitely paved, a multitude of boulevards and plazas, all the houses six and seven stories high, and stores – they are not stores but sheer vertigo, reveries! Billions of ties alone in the windows! What amazing articles made of bronze, porcelain, leather! Enormous churches, yet they do not oppress you by their bulk, but care[s] the eyes because they seem to be woven of lace. The Cathedral of St Stephen an[d] the *Votivkirche* are especially admirable. They are not edifices but tea biscuits. Th[e] Parliament, the City Hall, the University, are magnificent. Everything [is] magnificent, and only today and yesterday I understood fully that architecture [is] really an art. And here art is offered not piecemeal, as with us, but it stretches [in] belts for miles. Many monuments. In every side street, without fail, a bookshop. [In] their windows you notice Russian books too, but alas, they are not by Albov [or] Barantzevich or Chekhov, but by all kinds of anonymous authors writing an[d] printing abroad. I saw Renan and *The Secrets of the Winter Palace*, etc. Odd[ly] enough, here everyone may read and say whatever he pleases.

Know, ye natives, what manner of cabs are here, deuce take them. No buggies, but only brand-new, pretty carriages drawn by one or, more frequently, two horses. Th[e] horses are wonderful. On the box sit dandies in short coats and top hats, reading newspapers. Civility and courtesy.

Dinners are good. There is no vodka, they drink beer and tolerable wine. One thin[g] is objectionable: they charge for bread. Before handing you the check they ask, *Wieviel Brödchen?* i.e. how many rolls did you gobble? And they charge for each roll.

The women are beautiful and elegant. And in general everything is deucedly elegant.**"**

LETTERS OF ANTON CHEKHO[V]
PUB. VIKING PRESS, NEW YORK, 197[?]

SIGHTSEEING

Djuna Barnes (1892–1982), the American novelist, illustrator and short-story writer, is best remembered for her novel, "Nightwood", published in 1936 with a preface by T. S. Eliot. It describes a nightmare world of troubled characters and has, according to Elio[t] "a quality of horror and doom very nearly related to that of Elizabethan tragedy".

"He took her first to Vienna. To reassure himself he showed her all the historic buildings. He kept saying to himself that sooner or later, in this garden or that palace, she would suddenly be moved as he was moved. Yet it seemed to him that he too was a sightseer. He tried to explain to her what Vienna had been before the war; what it must have been before he was born; yet his memory was confused and hazy, and he found himself repeating what he had read, for it was what he knew best. With methodic anxiety he took her over the city. He said, 'You are a *Baronin* now.' He spoke to her in German as she ate the heavy *Schnitzel* and dumplings, clasping her hand about the thick handle of the beer mug. He said: '*Das Leben ist ewig, darinliegt seine Schonheit.*' They walked before the Imperial Palace in a fine hot sun that fell about the clipped hedges and the statues warm and clear. He went into the *Kammergarten* with her and talked, and on into the *Gloriette*, and sat on first one bench, and then another. Brought up short, he realized that he had been hurrying from one to the other as if they were orchestra chairs, as if he himself were trying not to miss anything; now, at the extremity of the garden, he was aware that he had been anxious to see every tree, every statue at a different angle."

Djuna Barnes, *Nightwood*, 1936,
Pub. Faber & Faber, London, 1958

MUSIC

STREET MUSICIANS

Dr Charles Burney (1726–1814) was an organist, musical historian and minor composer who wrote accounts of his travels in Europe collecting material for his master work, a four-volume "General History of Music" published in 1776–89. Here he describes the music heard in the streets and lodging houses of Vienna.

"[One] night two of the poor scholars of this city sung, in the court of the inn where I lodged, duets in *falsetto*, *soprano* and *contralto*, very well in tune, and with feeling and taste. I sent to enquire whether they were taught music at the Jesuits' college, and was answered in the affirmative. Though the number of poor scholars, at different colleges, amounts to a hundred and twenty, yet there are at present but seventeen that are taught music.

After this there was a band of these singers, who performed through the streets a kind of glee, in three and four parts: this whole country is certainly very musical. I frequently heard the soldiers upon guard, and sentinels, as well as common people, sing in parts. The music school at the Jesuits' College, in every Roman Catholic town, accounts in some measure for this faculty; yet other causes may be assigned, and, among these, it should be remembered, that there is scarce a church or convent in Vienna, which has not every

morning its *mass in music*: that is, a great portion of the church service of the day, set in parts, and performed with voices, accompanied by at least three or four violins, a tenor and bass, besides the organ; and as the churches here are daily crowded, this music, though not of the most exquisite kind, must, in some degree, form the ear of the inhabitants. ...

There was music every day, during dinner, and in the evening at the inn, where I lodged, which was the Golden Ox; but it was usually bad, particularly that of a band of wind instruments, which constantly attended the ordinary. This consisted of French horns, clarionets, oboes, and bassoons; all so miserably out of tune, that I wished them a hundred miles off.

In general I did not find that delicacy of ear among the German street musicians, which I had met with in people of the same rank and profession in Italy. The church organs being almost always out of tune here, may be occasioned by the parsimony or negligence of the clergy, bishop or superior of a church or convent; but the being, or stopping, in or out of tune, among street musicians, must depend on themselves, and on their organs being *acute* or *obtuse*. **"**

Dr Charles Burney's Continental Travels (1770–1772)
Compiled by Cedric Howard Glover
Pub. Blackie & Son, Glasgow, 192?

Outdoor entertainment

Hans Christian Andersen (1805–75), the Danish writer, recalls hearing the waltzes of Johann Strauss performed outdoors on a visit to Vienna.

" 'We are in Volcksgarten!' – Gentlemen and ladies stroll under the green trees in lively conversation; the waiters fly in all directions to procure ices. The tones of whole orchestra spread through the garden. In the midst of the musicians stands young man of dark complexion; his large brown eyes glance round about in restless manner; his head, arms, and whole body move; it is as if he were the heart in that great musical body, and, as we know, the blood flows through the heart, and here the blood is tones; these tones were born in him; he is the heart, and all Europe hears its musical beatings; its own pulse beats stronger when it hears them:– the man's name is – Strauss. **"**

Hans Christian Andersen, *A Poet's Bazaar*
Trans. Charles Beckwith, Pub. Richard Bentley, London, 184?

Mozart's lodgings

Wolfgang Amadeus Mozart (1756–91) moved to Vienna in 1781, and the following year he married Constanze Weber. The last nine years of his life saw an astonishing outpouring of masterpieces in every musical genre, but yet he was beset by constant financial hardships. The following extracts are from letters to his father on August 22, 1781, and then on May 3, 1783.

"I cannot let you know the address of my new lodging, as I have not yet got one. But I am bargaining about the prices of two, one of which I shall certainly take, as cannot stay here next month and so must move out. It appears that Herr von Auernhammer wrote and told you that I had actually found a lodging! I had one, is true, but what a habitation! Fit for rats and mice, but not for human beings. At noon I had to look for the stairs with a lantern. The room was a little closet and to get to it I had to pass through the kitchen. In the door there was a tiny window and although they promised me to put up a curtain inside, they asked me at the same time to draw it back as soon as I was dressed, for otherwise they would not be able to see anything either in the kitchen or in the adjoining rooms. The owner's wife herself called the house the rats' nest. ...**"**

"I simply cannot make up my mind to drive back into town so early. The weather far too lovely and it is far too delightful in the Prater today. We have taken our lunch out of doors and shall stay on until eight or nine in the evening. My whole

company consists of my little wife who is pregnant, and hers consists of her little husband, who is not pregnant, but fat and flourishing. ... I must ask you to wait patiently for a longer letter and the aria with variations – for, of course, I cannot finish them in the Prater; and for the sake of my dear little wife I cannot miss this fine weather. Exercise is good for her. So today I am only sending you a short letter to say that, thank God, we are both well and have received your last letter. Now farewell.**

THE LETTERS OF MOZART AND HIS FAMILY,
MACMILLAN PRESS, LONDON, 1985

THE DEATH OF MOZART

Mozart had been in poor health for some time and became bedridden about two weeks before his death on December 5, 1791. The following account of his last days was written by Sophie Haibel to her elder sister's husband Georg Nikolaus von Nissen.

**"I thought to myself, 'How I should love to know how Mozart is.' While I was thinking and gazing at the flame, it went out, as completely as if the lamp had never been burning. Not a spark remained on the big wick and yet there wasn't the slightest draught – that I can swear to. A horrible feeling came over me. I ran to our mother and told her all. She said: 'Well, take off your fine clothes and go into town and bring me back news of him at once. But be sure not to delay.' I hurried along as fast as I could. Alas, how frightened I was when my sister, who was almost despairing and yet trying to keep calm, came out to me, saying: 'Thank God that you have come, dear Sophie. Last night he was so ill that I thought he would not be alive this morning. Do stay with me today, for if he has another bad turn, he will pass away tonight. Go in to him for a little while and see how he is.' I tried to control myself and went to his bedside. He immediately called me to him and said: 'Ah, dear Sophie, how glad I am that you have come. You must stay here tonight and see me die.' I tried hard to be brave and to persuade him to the contrary. But to all my attempts he only replied: 'Why, I have already the taste of death on my tongue.' And, 'if you do not stay, who will support my dearest Constanze if you don't stay here?' 'Yes, yes, dear Mozart,' I assured him, 'but I must first go back to our mother and tell her that you would like me to stay with you today. Otherwise

she will think that some misfortune has befallen you.' 'Yes, do so,' said Mozart, 'bu
be sure and come back soon.' Good God, how distressed I felt! My poor siste
followed me to the door and begged me for Heaven's sake to go to the priests at S
Peter's, and implore one of them to come to Mozart – a chance call, as it were.
did so, but for a long time they refused to come and I had a great deal of trouble t
persuade one of those clerical brutes to go to him. Then I ran off to my mothe
who was anxiously awaiting me. It was already dark. Poor soul, how shocked she
was! ... I then ran back as fast as I could to my distracted siste
Süssmayr was at Mozart's bedside. The well-know
Requiem lay on the quilt and Mozart was explaining t
him how, in his opinion, he ought to finish it, when h
was gone. Further, he urged his wife to keep his death
secret until she should have informed Albrechtsberger
for the post should be his before God and the world
A long search was made for Dr Closset, who wa
found at the theatre, but who had to wait for th
end of the play. He came and ordered cold
poultices to be placed on Mozart's burning head
which, however, affected him to such an extent tha
he became unconscious and remained so until he died[2]
His last movement was an attempt to express with his mouth th
drum passages in the Requiem. That I can sti
hear.**"**

THE LETTERS OF MOZART AND HIS FAMILY
MACMILLAN PRESS, LONDON, 198

1 As Mozart intended, Albrechtsberger, the cou
organist, succeeded him as assistant to th
Kapellmeister at St Stephen's Cathedral, Leopol
Hofmann
2 Mozart died at 55 minutes past midnight o
December 5, 1791

SCHUBERT'S EVENING WALK
*On the evening of June 14, 1816, Franz
Schubert (1797–1828) described the
following walk in his diary. Währing and
Döbling were northwestern urban districts of
Vienna, easily reached from the Himmel-
fortgrund. The cemetery they passed was the
general one of Währing, just outside the Nussdorf
gate in the outer ring of fortifications bounding
the suburbs of Vienna.*

"I took an evening walk for once, as I had not don
for several months. There can be scarcely anythin
more agreeable than to enjoy the green country on a
evening after a hot summer's day, a pleasure for whic
the fields between Währing and Döbling seem to hav
been especially created. In the uncertain twilight and i
the company of my brother Karl, my heart warme
within me. 'How beautiful,' I thought and exclaime
standing still delightedly. A graveyard close by reminde
us of our dear mother. Thus, talking sadly an
intimately, we arrived at the point where the Döbling roa
divides. And, as from the heavenly home, I heard a familia
voice coming from a halting coach. I looked up – and it wa

Herr Weinmüller, just alighting and paying us his compliments in his cordial, honest voice. – In an instant our conversation turned to the outward cordiality of people's tone and language. How many attempt vainly to show their upright disposition by means of cordial honest language; how many would thus only expose themselves to derision. Such a thing may not be regarded as an acquisition, but only as a natural gift.**"**

SCHUBERT'S DIARY, QUOTED IN *SCHUBERT – A DOCUMENTARY BIOGRAPHY* BY OTTO ERIC DEUTSCH, PUB. J.M. DENT & SONS, LONDON, 1946

VIENNESE STYLE

THE RINGSTRASSE

Hermann Bahr (1863–1934) was a poet, essayist and art critic. Here he writes about the "artistic deceit" of the architecture of the Ringstrasse epoch.

"If you walk across the Ring, you have the impression of being in the midst of a real carnival. Everything masked, everything disguised ... Life has become too serious for that sort of thing. We want to look life in the face. This is what we mean when we talk of 'realist architecture', that is, that the building must not only serve its intended purpose, but must also express, not conceal, that purpose. ... To disguise it behind borrowed forms is both silly and ugly. Earlier, people used to require that a building should 'look like something'; we demand that it should 'be something'. We, the working people of today, should be ashamed to live in the style of the princes and patricians of yesterday. That we think of as a swindle. From the appearance of a house, we should be able to judge what is its purpose, who lives in it and how. We are not of the age of the Baroque, we don't live in the Renaissance, why should we act as if we did? Life has changed, costume has changed, our thoughts and feelings, our whole manner of living has changed, architecture must change too. ... These demands have now become audible, and will no longer be stifled.**"**

HERMANN BAHR, *SECESSION*, VIENNA, 1900

ADVICE ON THE WIENER WERKSTÄTTE

Charles Rennie Mackintosh (1868–1928), the Scottish architect and designer, wrote to Fritz Wärndorfer on March 17, 1903, two months before the foundation of the Wiener Werkstätte. Mackintosh traveled to Vienna on several occasions and was a great admirer of the city.

"If one wants to achieve an artistic success with your programme ... every object which you pass from your hand must carry an outspoken mark of individuality, beauty and most exact execution. From the outset your aim must be that every object which you produce is made for a certain purpose and place. Later ... you can emerge boldly into the full light of the world, attack the factory-trade on its own ground, and

Arthur

the greatest work that can be achieved in this century, you can achieve it: namely the production of objects of use in magnificent form and at such a price that they li within the buying range of the poorest. ... But till then years of hard, serious, honest work are still needed. ... First the 'artistic' (pardon the word) scoffers must be overcome; and those who are influenced by these scoffers must be taught... that the modern movement is not a silly hobby-horse of a few who wish to achieve fame comfortably through eccentricity, but that the modern movement is something living something good, the only possible art – for all and for the highest phase of our time. Yes – the plan which Hoffmann and Moser have designed is great and splendidly thought through, and if you have the means for it you are not taking any risk, and all I can say is: begin today! – If I were in Vienna, I would assist with a great strong shovel!**"**

E. SEKLER, *MACKINTOSH AND VIENNA*,
PUB. IN *ARCHITECTURAL REVIEW*, LONDON 1968.

THE FASHION IN DRESS

Martha Wilmot (1771–1873) was the wife of a chaplain at the British Embassy in Vienna. She wrote regularly to her friends in English society and particularly her sister Alicia.

"I must tell you that in expences we are disappointed – everything except luxuries is as dear as in England: dress, dearer, worse and a year behind us in fashion; *Tay* and *sugar* enormous. *However* there are glass konvaniences to be had in abundance, and fruit and flowers dirt cheap – parqué flours – Carpits if you chuse to give a daughters dowery for them, and if you do, the *Moths* eat them up to riddles in the summer. We happened luckily to bring a few knives with us which are invaluable, as is a small *tayput* – but the bedding!! No tongue can tell it, and as for a *double* bed, there is but one in Vienna … and that is Ld Stewart's, so English Turtle doves place two together to make believe tis one, and we have purchased *leather* sheets, exquisite things, one to serve as an under, the other as an upper blanket, for a blanket is not to be had for gold and precious stones. O had you seen Arnold cheapening said leather sheets! taking them on and off our bed, ballyragging in German! and finally beating the poor man down 15 florins on the pair! Such a thing as a bed curtain is not known, but the the turn out on the Prater of a Sunday Eve is Magnificent – 4, 6, 8 horses to *shell* like little carriages, footmen with streaming feathers. The Emperour and all his Court, young Napoleon (Wm saw a *child* in the Imperial Carriage), in fact from the Emperour to the Scavenger all turn out finer than butterflys. Not a *drab* of a Hussy that has not better broderie about her tail than *my best* and parterres of artificial flowers round her head. And à propos of dress, while I was in London I did my best to procure you a patinet *half* handkerchief and could not, such a thing was not to be had; well, in the Prater I saw *scores* on the trollops! How is this to be accounted for I beg to know? English second rate dress is so common here that every milk maid has our prints, our ginghams, our muslins, even our tabinets, but *stuffs* are rare (I have *not* one), ribbons are dear, and as for shawls, yr eyes are sickened of what look like Turkish ones, but what is in reality Cotton.**"**

MORE LETTERS FROM MARTHA WILMOT
EDITED BY THE MARCHIONESS OF LONDONDERRY
MACMILLAN PRESS, LONDON, 193

Schnitzler

CONVERSATION

Henry Reeve was a doctor who lived in Vienna in the winter of 1805–6 and wrote about his experiences in a journal. The work was published posthumously by his son.

"The Germans take very little for breakfast; a dish of coffee and a bit of bread suffices till dinner; many eat nothing at all. The usual hour of dinner is from one to three o'clock among all classes of people. They do not sit long at table; coffee is usually served in another room, and the company separate at six o'clock, when most people pay visits or go to the opera or to the theatre. The pleasures of social discussion and the gay fireside are quite unknown. The conversation is for the most part dull, languid, and uninteresting, often, in what is called *la bonne compagnie*, indecent and licentious. The married women are always expecting to be in love, and to have young men *faire la cour* to them; and the young misses are corrupted by what they hear, and are left to amuse themselves. With regard to literature, arts, and sciences, Vienna is far behind other towns even of Germany. Reading is in a manner forbidden by the Government not allowing the free circulation even of classical books; and many a man with a smattering of knowledge has a reputation of being a savant without being able to keep up a conversation for half-an-hour without betraying his gross ignorance. Literary men are not respected as at Paris, and it is one of the slowest ways to eminence to write a book."

HENRY REEVE, *JOURNAL OF A RESIDENCE IN VIENNA AND BERLIN*, LONGMANS, LONDON 1877

FREUD IN VIENNA

Sigmund Freud (1856–1939), the creator of psychoanalysis, practiced for many years in Vienna until Hitler's invasion of Austria drove him to London, where he died. The following piece is from a memoir written by his son Martin.

"My father began work at eight every morning and it was not uncommon for him to work through until perhaps three o'clock the following morning, with breaks for luncheon and dinner, the former extended to include a walk which nearly always took in the full circle of the Ringstrasse, although sometimes he shortened it by cutting across the inner city to collect, or deliver, proofs at his publishers. However, it must not be imagined that these excursions took the form of leisurely promenades designed to enjoy the beauty of the Ringstrasse and its flowering trees in springtime. My father marched at terrific speed. The Italian bersaglieri are celebrated for the speed of their marching; when, during my travels I saw these highly decorative soldiers tearing along, it occurred to me to think that each one of them marched like Sigmund Freud. Father might sometimes tell a favourite joke during our walks, one of a number which he had heard dozens of times without ever failing to be delighted. A certain part of Vienna, namely the Franzjosefskai, had, like all cities, its share of chimney-pots and other jutting-up adornments. My father often explained this phenomenon by telling us the story of the coffee party given by the devil's grandmother. It seems that this old lady for some reason or other was flying over Vienna with an enormous tray upon which she had put her very best coffee service, a large quantity of pots, jugs and cups and saucers of devilish design. Something happened, my father never explained just what, but I expect she entered an air pocket: at any rate the great tray turned over and the coffee service was distributed on to the roofs of Vienna, and each piece stuck. My father always enjoyed this joke as much as we did. …

I am not convinced that Sigmund Freud's often-expressed dislike of Vienna was either deep-seated or real. It is not difficult for a London man, or a New York man, both devoted to their respective home cities, to say: 'How I hate London: how I loathe New York.' They are speaking the truth of a day, of an hour or of a moment: not necessarily a fixed attitude. And my own feeling is that sometimes my father hated Vienna, and that sometimes he loved the old city, and that, in a general sense, he was devoted. He could have left Vienna at any time during the many secure years before the Hitler shadow began dimming the city's gay sky; but he never did, nor did he, so far as I know, ever seriously contemplate emigrating. And even at the end, when every consideration compelled him to leave, he left with great reluctance and only after strong persuasion.**"**

MARTIN FREUD, *GLORY REFLECTED*
ANGUS & ROBERTSON, LONDON, 195

FOOD AND DRINK

INTERNATIONAL INFLUENCES

Paul Hofmann wrote a very insightful guide to the Viennese, which was published in the US in 1988. The following piece examines the origins of some traditional Viennese dishes.

"Like the dialect, the cuisine of Vienna is the result of many influences from various directions. Take the schnitzel, considered the epitome of Danubia cooking. Actually, the Viennese way of breading and frying veal cutlets was copied from the Milanese when Lombardy was under Habsburg rule in the eighteenth and nineteenth centuries. The *scaloppina alla milanese* had been imported by the Spaniards, who were in control of the northern Italian city before the Austrian were, and the Spaniards had probably learned to fry meat in bread crumbs from the Byzantines at the eastern end of the Mediterranean. The strudel – thin doug

rolled and filled with apples or other fruits, curds, poppyseeds, or chopped cabbage – was probably brought from Hungary, as surely was goulash. Bohemia contributed dumplings and other farinaceous dishes to the Viennese tables; from Germany and Poland came a passion for sausages. Wieners are a Viennese staple but are always called frankfurters. Other popular sausage types are named after the cities of Cracow, Debrecen, and Paris. The sweet tooth of the Viennese, satisfied by their many kinds of torte and other rich desserts and by their indulgence in whipped cream, seems to be a very old characteristic of the city, one probably enhanced by its many contacts with the Turks. ... **"**

PAUL HOFMANN, *THE VIENNESE – SPLENDOR, TWILIGHT AND EXILE*, DOUBLEDAY, NEW YORK 1988

THE SCENTS OF THE CITY

William Sansom (1912–76), the English novelist and travel writer, describes here his sensual impressions of Vienna.

"Whiffs of incense, hot plaster, and Egyptian-smelling cigarettes seem to be the prevalent smells. Coffee, whipped cream, hockish white wine, paprika and, curiously, boiled beef (*Beinfleisch*) are the tastes. (The Schnitzel, as we know, hardly tastes of anything, unless it is a Kaiserschnitzel, larded with ham and Emmentaler cheese.)

FACKEL

Mix into these colours and smells the rumble of motor traffic and the grinding of trams, and the sound of the last piece of music, great or small that you heard in this most musical city of *Eroica* or *Schmaltz*; add the omnipresence of glittering gaswork-heavy baroque Prunk; place these impressions against miles and miles of pavement and caryatid-encrusted nineteenth century building, and sprinkle with the sense that although few people are rich there is a feeling somewhere of ease in most pockets – at least wine and beer and black coffee are cheap – and you will begin to feel some of the quality of this monstrously pleasant mirage. *Prunk* is a nice word, used for a show-room in a palace; 'pride' and 'hunk' combine in our ear to give a phonetically exact description of baroque.**"**

WILLIAM SANSOM, *BLUE SKIES, BROWN STUDIES*, 1960

COFFEE HOUSES

John Gunther (1901–70), a prolific and renowned travel writer, here describes the customs in Viennese coffee houses.

"Coffee houses, which continue to be the unalterable vital center of Viennese life, are everywhere. The visitor – or citizen – can sit for hour after hour over a single cup of coffee, which costs about 25 cents, while reading magazines and newspapers from all over the world, supplied free. Coffee exists in twenty or thirty different forms, from Mokka (jet black) to Weissen Ohne, which contains milk but is not topped by Schlagobers.

I had forgotten some piquant items in Viennese coffee-house lore and other customs, but they were quickly restored. In a café you normally get *two* glasses of water side by side – I don't know why – with your coffee; this drinking water is the best in Europe, coming from the Styrian hills ice-cold on even the hottest day. If you have a meal in a coffee house – or in a restaurant, for that matter – you must tell the headwaiter how many pieces of bread you have had when you are paying your bill, and these are charged for. Three different waiters must be tipped; 50 percent of the whole tip to the *Herr Ober*, who counts up the bill but does nothing else; 40 percent to the man who actually serves; 10 percent to the bus boy. This rule holds good even in the most humble cafés. Lightning mathematics is required.**"**

JOHN GUNTHER, *TWELVE CITIES*, HAMISH HAMILTON, LONDON, 1969

THE TURKS

Patrick Leigh Fermor (1915–), the English traveler, soldier and writer, journeyed on foot to Constantinople from the Hook of Holland in 1933 and passed through Vienna on the way. This part of his account relates the sole effect of Turkish influence on the city.

"I had never understood till now how near the Turks had got to taking Vienna. Of the first siege in Tudor times there were few mementoes in the museums. But the evidence of the second, more than a century later, and of the narrow escape of the city, was compellingly laid out. There were quivers and arrows and quarrels and bow-cases and tartar bows; scimitars, khanjars, yataghans, lances, bucklers, drums; helmets damascened and spiked and fitted with arrowy nasal-pieces; the turbans of janissaries, a pasha's tent, cannon and flags and horsetail banners with their bright brass crescents. Charles of Lorraine and John Sobiesky carocoled in their gilded frames and the breastplate of Rüdiger v. Starhemberg, the town's brave defender, gleamed with oiling and burnishing. (When John Sobiesky of Poland met the Emperor on

orseback in the fields after the city was saved, the two sovereigns conversed in Latin for want of a common tongue.) There, too, was the mace of Suleiman the Magnificent, and the skull of Kara Mustafa, the Grand Vizir strangled and decapitated at Belgrade by Suleiman's descendant for his failure to take Vienna; and beside it, the executioner's silken bowstring. The great drama had taken place in 1683, eighteen years after the Great Fire of London; but all the corroborative detail, the masses of old maps, the prints and the models of the city, turned it into a real and a recent event. ... It had been a close run thing. What if the Turks had taken Vienna, as they nearly did, and advanced westward? ... Martial spoils apart, the great contest has left little trace. It was the beginning of coffee-drinking in the West, or so the Viennese maintain. The earliest coffee houses, they insist, were kept by some of the Sultan's Greek and Serbian subjects who had sought sanctuary in Vienna. But the rolls which the Viennese dipped in the new drink were modelled on the half-moons of the Sultan's flag. The shape caught on all over the world. They mark the end of the age-old struggle between the hot-cross-bun and the croissant. **"**

PATRICK LEIGH FERMOR,
A TIME OF GIFTS,
JOHN MURRAY, LONDON, 1977

THE VIENNESE

INTERNATIONAL INFLUENCES
Washington Irving (1783–1859), the American journalist and essayist, wrote to his sister on November 10, 1822, about the array of nationalities to be met in Vienna.

"This is one of the most perplexing cities that I was ever in. It is extensive, irregular, crowded, dusty, dissipated, magnificent, and to me disagreeable. It has immense palaces, superb galleries of paintings, several theatres, public walks, and drives crowded with equipages. In short, everything bears the stamp of luxury and ostentation; for here is assembled and concentrated all the wealth, fashion, and nobility of the Austrian empire, and every one strives to eclipse his neighbour. The gentlemen all dress in the English fashion, and in walking the fashionable lounges you would imagine yourself surrounded by Bond Street dandies. The ladies dress in the Parisian mode, the equipages are in the English style though more gaudy; with all this, however, there is a mixture of foreign costumes, that gives a very motley look to the population in the streets. You meet here with Greeks, Turks, Polonaise, Jews, Sclavonians,

Croats, Hungarians, Tyroleans, all in
the dress of their several countries; and
you hear all kinds of languages spoken
around you . . . here the people think
only of sensual gratifications.**"**

WASHINGTON IRVING, LETTER TO HIS
SISTER, FROM *THE TRAVELLERS'
DICTIONARY OF QUOTATION*, ED. PETER
YAPP, ROUTLEDGE & KEGAN PAUL,
LONDON, 1983

STATELY AND COURTEOUS

*Richard Bassett's impression of the Viennese is that far from living up to
their reputation for gaiety, they are a cynical and lethargic people, with
the "past centuries of absolutist rule weighing down from high grey
façades".*

"The people of Vienna are completely different from western and Alpin
Austrians, with a different set of morals and attitudes from the rest of the countr
They regard their city as incomparable – as indeed it is, after a fashion. N
European capital has such a stately, imperial air – despite decades of Socialist rul
the double-headed eagle still broods overhead wherever you go – and no oth
European capital has such delightful surroundings. On a Sunday afternoo
wandering among the deserted cobbled streets around the Minorites Church, on
can almost hear Castlereagh's footsteps marking the way from the Pala
Dietrichstein, where he was lodged, to the Ballhausplatz during the Congress
Vienna. Close by, the chancery gates still seem firmly closed to the 1848 mob eag
for Metternich's blood, while across the grass the vast megalomaniac pile of th
New Hofburg, with its balcony overlooking the Heldenplatz, inevitably conjures u
that day in 1938 when Austrians stood roaring with delight at the only man ever t
have addressed them from this vantage point – Adolf Hitler. Through the Hofbur
in the Michaelerplatz, Adolf Loos flaunts his concept of streamlined architectur
free from 'the crime of ornament', in his bleak, classical Goldman and Salato
House. Through an arch on the right, the Palais Pallavicini still seems to resound t
Orson Welles' footsteps and the Harry Lime theme.

In all these places time seems to have stood still. Elsewhere, however, in the Café
Zartl in the Rasumofskystrasse on a late winter's evening, or in the Gmoa Keller o
the Heumarkt, smoky, shabby and run by two ancient Hungarian ladies whose wit,
manners and charm, like their rooms, have remained unchanged for decades, one
encounters a different Vienna. Beneath the appearance of gaiety among the
habitués there is evidence of much hard work; beneath the superficial politeness
there is much real courtesy; alongside the childishness, a great shrewdness and
knowledge of mankind; and amid scepticism and carelessness, a fabulous wealth o
talent.**"**

RICHARD BASSET
THE AUSTRIANS – STRANGE TALES FROM THE VIENNA WOOD
FABER & FABER, LONDON, 198

A FINAL WORD

*The British television presenter and writer Alan Whicker sums up his impressions
succinctly.*

"The nostalgic city with a streak of gentle hopefulness, where Freud discovere
sex. Baroque Vienna knows that an illusion which makes you happy is better than
reality which makes you sad.**"**

ALAN WHICKE
FROM *THE BEST OF EVERYTHING*, ED. WILLIAM DAVI
LONDON, 198

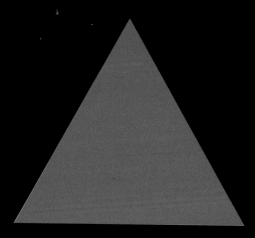

Itineraries in Vienna

▲ View of the 22nd District with the Prater on the right.

▼ The Danube Canal, alongside Morzinplatz...

▼ View of the 16th District (Ottakring).

...between the Salztorbrücke and Marienbrücke.

▲ The *Café Sperl*, on Gumpendorfer Strasse.

▼ The celebrated patisserie, *Demel*, on the Kohlmarkt.

▲ The *Café Central*, in the Ferstel Palace, on Herrengasse.

The *Café Schwarzenberg, on* Kärntner Ring. ▼ The *Café Griensteidl,* on Michaelerplatz

▲ The Lobau Park. ▼ The Tiergarten, a zoological garden in the Schönbrunn Park.

▼ The Augarten Palace and Gardens.

▲ The palace and the park of Schönbrunn, with the Naïad fountain in the center.

The Belvedere Gardens. ▼ View of Schönbrunn Park to the west of the parterres.

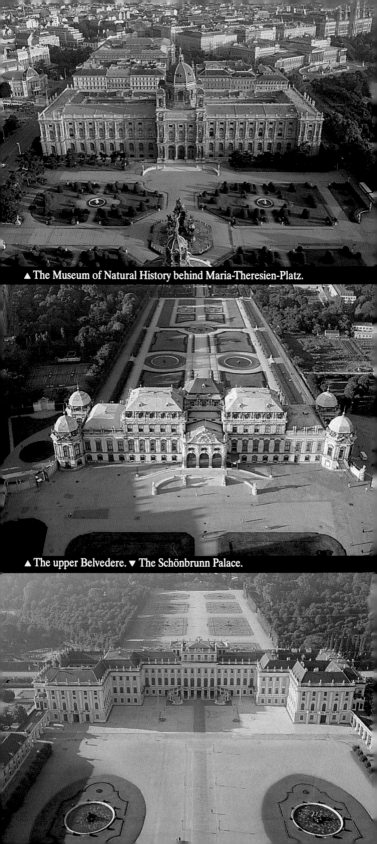

▲ The Museum of Natural History behind Maria-Theresien-Platz.

▲ The upper Belvedere. ▼ The Schönbrunn Palace.

The city center

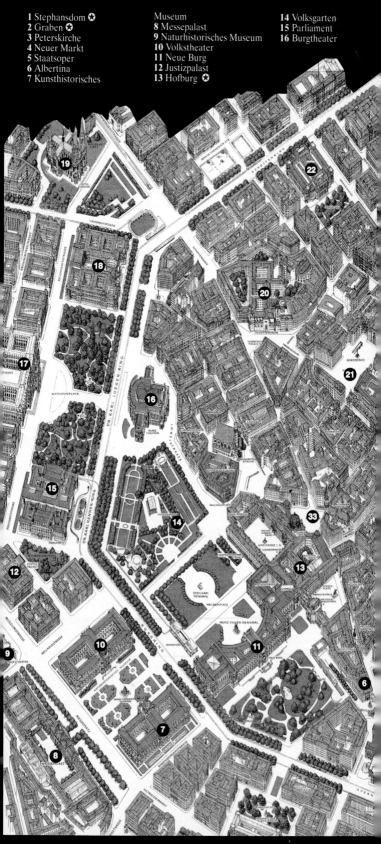

1 Stephansdom ✪
2 Graben ✪
3 Peterskirche
4 Neuer Markt
5 Staatsoper
6 Albertina
7 Kunsthistorisches
Museum
8 Messepalast
9 Naturhistorisches Museum
10 Volkstheater
11 Neue Burg
12 Justizpalast
13 Hofburg ✪
14 Volksgarten
15 Parlament
16 Burgtheater

7 Neues Rathaus
8 Universität
9 Votivkirche
0 Schottenstift

21 Am Hof
22 Börse
23 Stadtpark
24 Coburg Palace
25 Jesuitenkirche
26 Dominikanerkirche
27 Postsparkasse

28 Hoher Markt
29 Maria am Gestade
30 Altes Rathaus
31 (Ehemalige) Böhmische
     Hofkanzlei
32 Judenplatz
33 Michaelerplatz

STEPHANSDOM

St Stephen's Cathedral (Stephansdom) is at once the center of Vienna and its principal symbol. Its 390-foot spire is visible from all parts of the city and strikingly so from many miles away along the route of the old Budapest highway. The Viennese nickname for it is Stiffl, a diminutive of Stephan.

AN UNFINISHED MASTERPIECE. A 12th-century Romanesque basilica once stood on the site of the cathedral, built at the behest of the margraves of Babenberg ● 28 ● 302. After being ravaged by two fires, this basilica was completely rebuilt and consecrated in 1263 in the reign of Ottokar II of Bohemia. When the Habsburgs became Holy Roman Emperors in 1273 ● 29, Vienna – which already enjoyed the status of a free imperial city – aspired to become a bishopric. In anticipation of this, a worthy sanctuary was built, although Vienna did not get its bishop until the end of the 15th century. The first work on the cathedral was the construction of a Gothic choir, extending the old Romanesque basilica, between 1330 and 1339. The original church was demolished on the accession of Rudolph IV (1339–65), who was known as the founder because he financed the bulk of the new building. The only part that was preserved was the west façade (the Giant's Portal and the Pagans' Towers) which was framed by two Gothic chapels. The nave (1359) and the spire were built in the next century. Of the many architects and sculptors who took part in the construction of the cathedral, only those

> "The brown stone of this church puts forth wondrous refinements of feudal architecture."
>
> Gérard de Nerval

🏃 **Half a day**

◆ **A** C2-C3

COLORED TILES
Under restoration for several years following the 1945 fire, the high roof of St Stephen's is decorated with the Habsburg emblem: a two-headed eagle, bearing the imperial crown and a golden fleece.

A REMINDER OF THE 1451 CRUSADE
From this pulpit, overlooked by a statue of St Francis trampling on a Turk, the Italian Franciscan St John Capistrano (1386–1458), apostolic legate of Pope Nicolas V in Bavaria, Silesia, Poland and Austria, called for the Crusade.

involved in the final stages are remembered: Hans von Prachatitz completed the spire in 1433 and Hans Puchsbaum worked on the vaulting and the nave. The latter also attempted to add a second tower to the cathedral, but at the start of the 16th century the Viennese were concerned about a threatened Turkish invasion and were keener to invest in fortifications than in churches ▲ *198* . The north tower remained unfinished and was crowned with a Renaissance dome in 1578. In 1490, during the reign of Matthias Corvinus, King of Hungary ● *29*, the roof was covered with diamond patterns of polychrome tiles, and in 1511 the works were finally considered finished. St Stephen's was bombarded by the Turks in 1683 (a cannonball fired in that year may still be seen lodged in the wall above the sacristy) ● *34*, and again by the French in 1809 ● *31*. But neither of these sieges caused anything like the catastrophic damage of 1945 ● *42*.

THE RIESENTOR. On the west façade, the two 'PAGANS' TOWERS, (Heidentürme) which are the only vestiges of the old Romanesque basilica, and two GOTHIC CHAPELS with rose windows in a delicate tracery of stone, frame the main entrance. To enter the building you have to go through the Giant's Portal (Riesentor) on the north side, so called because the tibia of a mammoth dug up on this spot when the cathedral was under construction was thought at the time to be the shinbone of a giant drowned during the Flood. The tympanum over the portal and the columns on either side of it are covered with Romanesque sculptures representing Christ in glory, flanked by two angels and surrounded by innumerable saints and mythical creatures.

BISCHOFSTOR. If you walk round the cathedral's north side, you pass in front of the Bishop's Portal (Bischofstor), a Gothic feature which for many years was the entrance reserved for women. On the column is a statue of the *Virgin in a Mantle*.

Interior of
St Stephen's
Cathedral.

**THE MIRACULOUS
ICON**
The icon of the Virgin
of Potsch, in Hungary,
hangs beneath a
marble baldachin
(right). Real tears are
said to have poured
from its eyes in 1696,
during Prince
Eugène's campaign
● *35*, ▲ *147, 247*
against the Turks.
Leopold I acquired
the icon in 1697.

THE ADLERTURM. Continue along the line of the builder's
lodgings to the Eagle's Tower (Adlerturm), or North Tower,
which is unfinished. Since 1957, this tower has served as the
belltower for the celebrated Pummerin ● *43* on special
occasions; for example, its chimes at midnight are the signal
for the New Year's celebrations to begin. At the foot of the
tower is a warren of catacombs containing the bones of many
thousands of Viennese. Most of these were originally buried
in the cemetery surrounding the cathedral, before this was put
out of commission in the 18th century.
THE DUCAL CRYPT. At the center of the catacombs is the Ducal
Crypt, set up here during the reign of Rudolph IV; this
contains several bronze caskets and urns filled with viscera of
many of the Habsburgs ● *29* ▲ *143, 144–5, 176, 280*. A
baldachin, attributed to the master Puchsbaum, arcs over the
EAGLE PORCH (Adlertor) or Tower Porch. In the Middle Age
anybody who grasped the sanctuary ring sealed into one of
the columns, through this act, automatically came under

> "We possess the most majestic church nave on earth."
>
> Adolf Loos

hurch jurisdiction and could escape the fficers of the civil law. On the far east de of the cathedral stands a statue of hrist known colloquially as "Our Lord f the Toothache".

HE SPIRE ★. On the south side one can limb up 418 steps inside the spire to a latform, which offers a magnificent ew over the city. During the siege of 683 ● *34,* the Count of Starhemberg atched the Turkish forces from this ookout and sent up his rockets to summon the ing of Poland and he Duke of Lorraine.

INGERTOR. The Singer's Portal (Singertor), which was for enturies the men's entrance to the cathedral, has a 14th-entury tympanum decorated with sculptures that represent cenes from the life of St Paul. All around are Gothic statues f saints.

IEISTER PILGRAM'S PULPIT ∗. The interior of the cathedral, ith tall columns that support the transept's ogival vaulting, is lanned as a Latin cross with three naves of equal size. The hoir is lower than the main nave because it was built first, as n extension of the original Romanesque basilica. At first ght the Stephansdom appears to be a Gothic cathedral of reat splendor. Then one begins to notice 17th-century aroque additions, such as the altars backing on to the olumns of the nave or nestling in side chapels, and above all he high altar: all are loaded with statues and ornamentation n colored marble. The principal attraction, on the left of the entral nave, is a Gothic feature – the great pulpit sculpted in 500 by the master stone-carver Anton Pilgram.

HE EMPEROR'S TOMB. Other marvels of Gothic sculpture iay be seen all over the cathedral: the foot of the organ loft by Pilgram) on the lower left-hand side of the nave; the *Viener Neustädter Altar,* an altar screen from 1447 that shows ie Virgin between St Catherine and St Barba, in the left-and chapel of the choir; the tomb of Frederick III in the hapel to the right of the choir, designed by the late 15th-entury sculptor Nicolas of Leyden, among others; and finally ie fonts (1481) in the chapel of St Catherine at the foot of ie spire. A Gothic stone baldachin to the right of the ntrance shelters the *Virgin of Potsch* and a statue of the *Virgin, Patroness of Servant Girls.* This statue is said to have come to the

aid of a girl accused of stealing, by miraculously revealing the gem which her mistress had lost. Some of the medieval stained-glass windows were restored after World War Two and may now be seen in the collections of the choir (the remainder have been deposited in the Museum of Decorative Arts and the Vienna City Museum). They represent the Passion in a blaze of color dominated by red, yellow and green.

SELF-PORTRAITS
The man poking his head through the window of the pulpit

and the man at the foot of the organ (above) are both portraits of the Meister Pilgram, the sculptor, and carved by his own hand.

MEISTER PILGRAM'S PULPIT
In Vienna during the 16th century, the Gothic style was in its last flamboyant stage prior to the Renaissance; the sculptor decorated his pulpit with rosettes, perforated balustrades and ornaments in the form of stalactites, flames and foliage. The salamanders and toads pursuing one another along the hand rail symbolize good driving out evil.

The *Moor* marks the site of the former grocery store *Meinl* ● 72, ▲ 223 on St Stephen's Square. A bank of the same name has replaced the store (which has its shop-front on the Kohlmarkt). Nevertheless the statue has been left in place.

THE GRABEN IN ADVENT ✪
For a few weeks every year, the Graben takes on a festival atmosphere. During Advent (December 1–24), the late 19th- to early 20th-century façades of this elegant central thoroughfare become a kind of Advent calendar. A succession of twenty-four objects, which are different each year, are laid out all along the street.

STEPHANSPLATZ ★

In the Middle Ages the immediate vicinity of the cathedral was crammed with houses and street vendors, with a cemetery occupying what little space remained. At the close of the 18th century, after several epidemics of the plague, it was feared that the corpses buried so hastily there were a breeding ground for disease, so the cemetery was cleared and the bones transferred into the cathedral catacombs. The area was laid out as Stephansplatz and is now a pedestrian precinct.

VIRGILKAPELLE. The 13th-century Virgilkapelle was unearthed during the construction of the metro in the 1970's and 1980's. The remains of it are displayed behind a large plate-glass window inside the Stephansplatz metro station (in the 1st District).

ERZBISCHÖFLICHES PALACE. Directly on the square is the episcopal palace, housing the CATHEDRAL AND DIOCESAN MUSEUM (Dom- und Diozesanmuseum). The cathedral treasure is on display here (notably the reliquary of St Andrew, a reliquary cross dating from the 14th century, a Carolingian version of the Gospels, and an 18th-century monstrance), along with religious sculptures dating from the Middle Ages to the 19th century.

THE DIKES
The Graben, which today is a long, very elegant square, was originally no more than a deep dike (*Graben*) which was a part of the fortifications of the Roman camp of Vindobona. This small settlement extended into a rectangle enclosed by the Danube to the north, the Ottakring River to the northwest (now filled in), the Graben to the south, and another dike (which passed across the cathedral site) to the east. In the Middle Ages, Vienna spread beyond the limits of the original camp. In 1255 all the dikes were filled in, including the Graben, which became a fairground.

ST MARY MAGDALENE
This chapel on the south side of the
square was used for funeral
ceremonies; it was destroyed by fire in
1781. Its floor plan is commemorated
today with lines of red paving stones.

STOCK-IM-EISEN-PLATZ

This small square at the junction of Stephansplatz, the
Graben and the Kärntnerstrasse is in a way an antechamber
to the many pedestrian streets in this area. It owes its name to
the "post set in iron" into which apprentice locksmiths
traditionally drove a nail on their way through Vienna while
touring the area.

THE HAAS HAUS. When it opened in 1990, this shopping
center designed by Hans Hollein ● *94* caused a scandal
because of its total lack of harmony with the cathedral.
Nevertheless from the *Dom Café* inside it there is a superb
view of the cathedral and Stephansplatz from above.

THE GRABEN

The Graben and Stephansplatz together form a right angle,
with Stock-im-Eisen-Platz at its junction. Since the filling of
the dike (Graben), every form of trade has been pursued
here, especially prostitution: in the 18th century the "nymphs
of the Graben" were a notorious feature of Vienna. The
Habsburg court ▲ *144* organized major entertainments here,
since the Graben was one of the most attractive open
spaces in the inner city. Today, at the least sign of
sunshine, café tables ● *66* invade the square. The Graben
also boasts a string of luxury stores; all in all it is one of
Vienna's most elegant thoroughfares and a favorite haunt
of window-shoppers. Many of the Graben boutiques
are designed by famous architects – for example,
the *Knize* clothes shop (1913) is by Adolf Loos
● *86, 91*, ▲ *236, 287* and the
Schullin jewelry shop
(1982) is by Hans
Hollein.

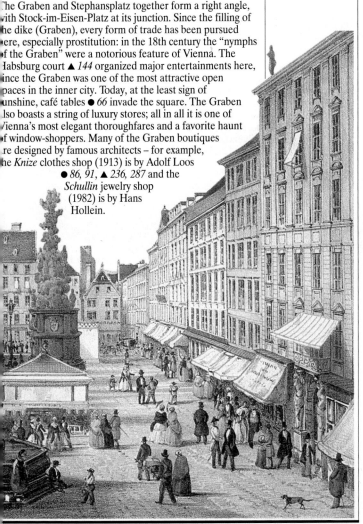

**MODERN DESIGN AND
OLD GOTHIC**
The Haas Haus
shopping center,
covered in plate glass,
never fails to make an
impact.

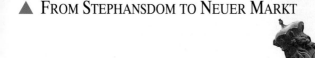

LEOPOLDSBRUNNEN AND JOSEPHS-BRUNNEN. The statue of Margrave Leopold (1096–1136, right) dominates the Fountain of St Leopold ● 46 , as does Joseph the fountain bearing his name. Both fountains have lions' masks (above) and stand beside the Graben.

PESTSÄULE. The Plague Column (Pestsäule, or Dreifältigkeitssäule) stands as a reminder of the epidemic that decimated the population of Europe during the 17th century. After London and Naples, the plague afflicted Vienna, claiming close to 100,000 victims. In gratitude to God for bringing an end to this disaster, Leopold I (1640–1705) decided to raise a monumental votive offering dedicated to the Holy Trinity. He commissioned J.B. Fischer von Erlach ● 74, 80, ▲ 147 in 1686; von Erlach had just returned from Rome, where he had been influenced by the Baroque sculptor Borromini, a rival of Bernini. The scrolls of sculpture winding upward around the column show the figure of the emperor on his knees before the Trinity; the ragged crone being thrust down to Hell by an angel symbolizes the plague. To one side of the column stands a statue of St Leopold, the patron saint of Lower Austria.

OTTO WAGNER – EARLY WORK. Most of the buildings along the Graben belong to the 1900 style; two of them, however, stand out as examples of Otto Wagner's early work ● 86, ▲ 228, 233, 237, 294. Between 1870 and 1880 Wagner was influenced by neo-Renaissance architecture, and at this time he tried his hand at the neo-classical GRABENHOF (nos. 14–15

and the ANKERHAUS (Anchor House, no. 10) on the corner of Spiegelgasse.

SPIEGELGASSE

Number 9 Spiegelgasse was the house of Franz von Schobert, where he lodged his friend Franz Schubert ● 50, ▲ 166, 227, 262. Schubert composed his *Unfinished Symphony* (No. 8) here in 1822, completing only two movements.

DOROTHEERGASSE

This street leading into the Graben is the preserve of Vienna's antique dealers; it is also the site of the DOROTHEUM, an auction house with several rooms, open daily. In the same street is the CAFÉ HAWELKA ★, formerly a well-known meeting-place for the intelligentsia ● 67, which is now jammed with students until 2am. This is where Vienna's artists come for their coffee at opening time every morning.

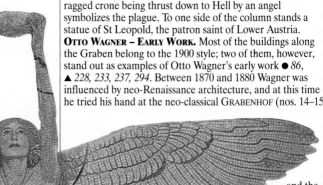

CAFÉ
LEOPOLD
HAWELKA

> "In the middle stands a monumental column that looks very much like a dice tumbler."
>
> Gérard de Nerval

TUCHLAUBEN

During the 1980's, when the house at no. 19 Tuchlauben (Drapers' Street) was being restored, a series of FRESCOES was discovered under

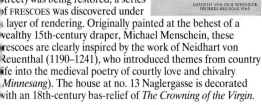

IN DIESEM HAUSE WOHNTE IM JAHRE 1840
CONRADIN KREUTZER
[1780 – 1849]
KOMPONIST UND KAPELLMEISTER
AM KÄRNTNERTOR- THEATER
GESTIFTET VON DR. H. SCHINDLER
FREIBURG/BREISGAU 1968

a layer of rendering. Originally painted at the behest of a wealthy 15th-century draper, Michael Menschein, these frescoes are clearly inspired by the work of Neidhart von Reuenthal (1190–1241), who introduced themes from country life into the medieval poetry of courtly love and chivalry (*Minnesang*). The house at no. 13 Naglergasse is decorated with an 18th-century bas-relief of *The Crowning of the Virgin*.

PETERSKIRCHE ★

On the cramped ST PETER'S SQUARE (Petersplatz), set back from the Graben, stands the church of the same name (Peterskirche) which, for lack of horizontal space, was constructed mainly skyward. The entrance is a fine Baroque porch by Andreas Altomonte. The oval dome is well lit by eight large windows, decorated with a fresco of the Assumption by Johann Michael Rottmayr ▲ *293*, and the altarpiece of the second chapel to the right is dedicated to St Francis de Sales. On the left of the choir, the Baroque pulpit designed by Matthias Steinl matches a Baroque ornamental altar by the sculptor Lorenzo Mattielli which is dedicated to St John Nepomuceno, confessor of the Queen of Bohemia, who was martyred in 1393 for refusing to betray his oath of confession to Wenceslas IV.

THE CHOIR. The choir with its trompe l'oeil dome was decorated by Antonio Galli-Bibiena. The high altar, by Santino Busti, has a screen by Martino Attomonte and a painting by Leopold Kupelwieser, *The Immaculate Conception*. Above, the Habsburg eagle ▲ *144* rises over one of two balconies. According to tradition, Empress Sissi ▲ *143, 144, 178* used to come incognito to one of these balconies late at night to pray.

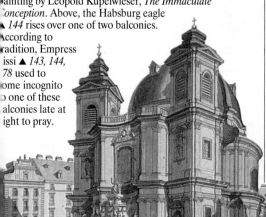

THE KREUTZER SONATA. In the Dorotheergasse there is a plaque to the violinist Rodolphe Kreutzer, to whom Beethoven dedicted his *Ninth Sonata For Piano and Violin*.

ENGEL-APOTHEKE A Jugendstil ● *86* fresco adorns the façade of the Angel Pharmacy on Bognergasse.

THE CHURCH OF ST PETER'S. It was built in the early 18th century by Gabriele Montani and Lukes von Hildebrandt ● *75, 81* on the site of the first church in Vienna (4th century) which was destroyed by fire.

139

THE ORDER OF ST JOHN OF MALTA
In 1530, Charles V ceded the island of Malta to the Knights of St John in perpetuity. The Saracens and Turks had driven the Knights successively from Jerusalem, Acre, Cyprus (12th–13th centuries) and Rhodes (1522).

HALLOWED RELICS.
The curious reliquaries on the altars on either side of the choir contain the skeletons of saints martyred at Rome – in particular that of St Benedict – covered in spangles and false precious stones. During the Counter Reformation, Baroque art ● *74, 82* was used as a weapon against heresy; the relics of saints, usually decorated and displayed as in this church, were also pressed into service for the cause.

KÄRNTNERSTRASSE ★

The pedestrian Kärntnerstrasse (Carinthia Street) in the center of the inner city is one of the two liveliest shopping streets in Vienna. The other is the Graben. People linger here throughout the day, to stare at the window displays and the street performers and sip coffee on the café terraces. The bustle continues at night, long after the smart shops, restaurants and terrace cafés have closed.

MALTESERKIRCHE. On the left going down Kärntnerstrasse from St Stephen's Cathedral toward the Ring stands the church of the Order of St John or the Knights of Malta (Malteserkirche), a Gothic building given a neo-classical façade during the 19th century. Founded in Jerusalem at the time of the Crusades, this order of hospitalers was originally intended to look after pilgrims during their sojourn in the Holy Land. In the 12th century, the Knights of St John became a military order whose purpose was to defend pilgrims, first against the Arabs, then against the Turks. Inside their Vienna Church is a monument to Jean de la Valette, the Grand Master who in 1565 defended Malta (the order's headquarters from 1530 until 1798) from the fleet of Suleyman the Magnificent. It is no accident that this great victory is commemorated in Vienna, seeing that in 1529 the forces of the selfsame sultan had laid siege to the capital of Austria ● *34*. The coats of arms of most of the families belonging to the order hang in the Malteserkirche. Just before the street joins the Ring ▲ *197* it is entered from the right by Philharmonikerstrasse, the street containing the State Opera ● *59* ▲ *223* and the *Sacher Hotel*.

THE FLEDERMAUS CABARET
Built during the Secession period ● 86, ▲ 232, this cabaret is named after the operetta *Die Fledermaus* (1874) by Strauss the Younger ● 56, a work popular with the Viennese.

THE "SACHER" HOTEL. The *Sacher* has been a Viennese institution since its founding in 1876 ● *66*, when its plush salons became the haunt of men of letters such as Arthur Schnitzler ▲ *141* ◆ *324;* since then it has been a favorite of the world's celebrities, royalty, diplomats and musicians. Many of the *Sacher*'s famous guests have sampled the celebrated *Sachertorte*, a recipe which was invented during the Congress f Vienna (1814–15) by an anonymous chef. Anna Sacher, the widow of the hotel's founder, was the first to serve this dish to er clients at the end of the 19th century. Among the latter vere the *Sacherbuben*, hard-up members of good Viennese amilies who came to the hotel not so much for the *Torte* as or the cash loans extended to them by Frau Sacher, who ventually became the city's principal moneylender.

NEUER MARKT ★

he Neuer Markt (New Market Square) is nked to

MARCO D'AVIANO
In a niche of the façade of the Capuchin Church is a statue of the Capuchin Marco D'Aviano, papal legate to the army of Charles of Lorraine. It was he who celebrated mass at the top of Mount Kahlenberg on the morning of the battle against the Turks.

Kärntnerstrasse boasts a casino, a series of bookshops, travel agents and souvenir shops (one of which sells *Sachertorte* ▲ *140*).

Kärntnerstrasse by Donnergasse. Its name is no longer ppropriate, since the flour market which was opened there in he 13th century has long ceased to exist. Nevertheless the Neuer Markt is one of the city's finest squares, today ongested with traffic.

DONNERBRUNNEN. In the middle of this square is Vienna's most graceful fountain, the Donnerbrunnen. It owes its name to the sculptor Georg Raphael Donner ▲ *170, 256, 304*, who designed it at the beginning of the 18th century; the statue of Providence on a plinth crowded with putti is its principal feature. Allegories representing each of the four tributaries of the Danube in Austria (the Traun, the Enns, the Ybbs and the March) used to stand at the fountain's corners. Maria Theresa thought the statues immodest, so they were removed. In the 19th century the Donner pieces, which had been cast in lead, were replaced by bronze copies. (The originals are now displayed in the Museum of Baroque Art ▲ *256* in the lower Belvedere.) A number of fine buildings stand around the square: at no. 18, the 18th-century Baroque façade of the former RAUCHMILLER PALACE can be seen, while nos. 10 and 11, festooned with floral reliefs, have an overhanging triangular

A SHAMELESS STATUE
To revenge himself on an erstwhile patron, Donner had one of his statues display its buttocks in front of his window!

141

THE TOMBS OF ELIZABETH-CHRISTINE AND CHARLES VI (detail) The tombs of both Maria Theresa and her father were sculpted by Balthasar Ferdinand Moll. Notice the crowned death's heads on the corners.

FRANZ-JOSEPH "The Emperor was an old man. He was the oldest emperor in the world. Around him, death had cut circle after circle and swathe after swathe. Already the field was entirely bare and only the Emperor still stood, like a forgotten stalk, waiting. For many years his clear, hard eyes had been trained on the vague distance. His pate was bald like a desert. His side-whiskers were as white as two snowy wings. The lines in his face were an impenetrable undergrowth in which the years nestled by the score."
Joseph Roth, *The Radetsky March*

projection). No. 2 was the lodging of Joseph Haydn ● *49,* ▲ *152, 162, 164* from 1795 to 1796, when he is supposed to have composed the quartet which was later to become the anthem of Imperial Austria.

AMERICAN BAR. On the north side of the Neuer Markt is the Kärntnerdurchgang, which overlooks the Kärntnerstrasse and the Seilergasse. This shopping street contains the *American Bar,* a jewel of modern architecture designed by Adolf Loos ● *86, 91,* ▲ *137, 174, 236, 287* in 1908 and a classified historical monument since 1959. Today it is a private club.

KAPUZINERKIRCHE. The Church of the Capuchins (Kapuzinerkirche), which fronts on to the Neuer Markt, is not much to look at, though the aesthetics of this 17th-century church do succeed in reflecting the outlook of the mendicant Capuchins, which was closely akin to that of the Franciscans. Indeed it was the rigorous austerity of the Kapuzinerkirche which led Emperor Matthias (1557–1619) and Empress Anne to select it as the Habsburg crypt. Members of the family have been buried here since 1633.

KAPUZINERGRUFT. About ten emperors, fifteen empresses and a hundred archdukes lie in the imperial vault (Kaisergruft) of the Capuchin crypt (Kapuzinergruft). Before each funeral, it was customary for the heart of the deceased to be taken out, placed in a casket and carried to the crypt of the Church of the Augustines, while the remaining viscera were moved to the crypt of St Stephen's Cathedral ▲ *132*. The official ceremonies only began after the body had been dressed in state robes, laid in a coffin and covered with flowers. The coffin would be displayed in the Assumption Chapel of the Palace so the public could pay its last respects (this was notably the case for the "Aiglon" ▲ *283*, son of Napoleon, and for Archduke Rudolph ♦ *323*). Then came the full state funeral at St Stephen's Cathedral, with the coffin finally coming to rest in the crypt of that cathedral, after the father superior had asked it the question: "Who art thou? Who asks to be admitted here?" The Great Chamberlain would reply, "I am His Majesty the Emperor of Austria, King of Hungary." "I know him not. Who asks to be admitted here?" "I am the Emperor Franz-Joseph, Apostolic King of Hungary, King of Bohemia, King of Jerusalem, Prince of Transylvania, Grand Duke of

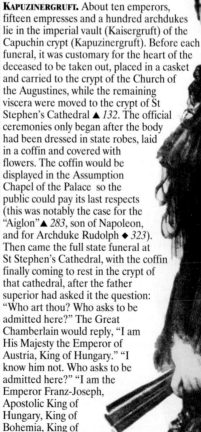

uscany and Cracow, Duke of Lorraine..." "I know him not. Who asks to be admitted here?" And at this point the Great Chamberlain knelt and answered humbly. "I am Franz-Joseph, a poor sinner, and I implore the Mercy of Our Lord God." "Then thou mayst enter."

MARIA-THERESIA-GRUFT. The imperial burial vault is made up of ten underground halls. In the first, which is the smallest, lie Emperor Matthias and the Empress Anne. Throughout these rooms, which are laid out in chronological order, there is a noteworthy contrast between the more lavish tombs and the simpler ones. The tomb of Maria Theresa (1717–80) and of her husband Francis of Lorraine (1708–65) ● *36*, designed by Balthasar Ferdinand Moll, is in the form of a huge state bed on which the two sovereigns are stretched out face-to-face. In addition to its generally Baroque style, this tomb is decorated with a series of bas-reliefs representing the coronation of the imperial couple. The tomb of Joseph II is in simple but direct contrast to that of his parents.

GUEST FROM OUTSIDE THE FAMILY. Although she was not of royal blood, Countess Fuchs-Mollardt was buried in the imperial vault because of her friendship with Maria Theresa, whose governess she had been. Marshal Radetsky nearly – but not quite – attained a similar honor at the request of Franz-Joseph, who greatly admired his achievements.

ABSENT HABSBURGS. All the Habsburgs ● *29,* ▲ *144-5, 176, 280* before Matthias were buried in places other than Vienna; most notably Charles V (1500–58) is interred at the Escorial in Spain. Among the other absentees are Marie-Antoinette, the wife of Louis XVI (who was buried on the spot in Paris after her execution), Napoleon's son, the "Aiglon" (the Germans transferred his ashes to the Invalides in Paris in 1940), the Archduke Ferdinand and his wife, and finally Charles I (who is buried at Funchal, Madeira).

The tombs of Joseph I, Ferdinand and Charles VI (top). An early 19th-century engraving (above).

THE HABSBURG PANTHEON
In the crypt are buried Marie-Louise, Empress of the French, her nephew Franz-Joseph and Empress Elizabeth ● *119,* ▲ *144, 178* (left), in mourning for her son Rudolph whose death mask is shown (above). Maximilian I of Mexico lies in the "new crypt". Like the tomb of Empress Sissi, this is permanently covered in flowers in the national colors of Hungary (green, white and red).

143

SALVATOR. The Archduke Salvator, nephew of Franz-Joseph, disappeared on his way to South America after breaking with his family and taking the name of Johann Orth in order to marry a girl from the Viennese bourgeoisie

Guillotined in 1793, Marie-Antoinette, the daughter of Maria Theresa, was the first member of the Austrian royal family to come to a tragic end. A century later, misfortune seemed to afflict the last of the Habsburgs and their relatives, confirming Franz-Joseph's bitter comment "I have been spared nothing". By the end of his reign, in 1916 during World War One, the Emperor was living as a virtual recluse in his apartments at the Hofburg and Schönbrunn. It is said that when a member of the Habsburgs was approaching his end a woman in white – the White Lady of the Habsburgs – appeared.

FRANZ-JOSEPH (1830–1916) AND ARCHDUKE OTTO (1912)
The 68-year reign of Franz-Joseph ● *41*, ▲ *142, 178* saw the change from absolute monarchy to a parliamentary system. His great-nephew Charles I (1887–1922), the last Emperor of Austria, succeeded him from 1916 to 1918. Then in 1919, Charles went into exile in Switzerland. After two attempts to return he was banished to Madeira, where he died of tuberculosis.

ELIZABETH (1837–98)
The Empress Elizabeth ▲ *142, 178*, who married Franz-Joseph in 1854, turned the court of Vienna into one of the most brilliant in Europe; but later she suffered from mental disorders after a series of bereavements. She traveled widely and, during a tour of Switzerland she was stabbed to death by Italian anarchist, Luigi Luchini.

MAXIMILIAN I (1832–67)
This archduke, the younger brother of Franz-Joseph, became Emperor of Mexico and was shot by partisans led by Benito Juárez in 1867. His wife Carlotta, daughter of Leopold I, King of the Belgians, subsequently went mad.

FRANZ-FERDINAND (1863–1914)
On June 28, 1914, the assassination of Archduke Franz-Ferdinand (the nephew of Franz-Joseph and heir to his throne since the death of Rudolf) and his wife Sophie in Sarajevo was the event that sparked off World War One.

FRANZ-FERDINAND'S TUNIC
The Army Museum ▲ *258* still displays the Archduke's bloodstained jacket (below) .

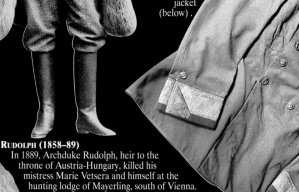

RUDOLPH (1858–89)
In 1889, Archduke Rudolph, heir to the throne of Austria-Hungary, killed his mistress Marie Vetsera and himself at the hunting lodge of Mayerling, south of Vienna. This episode has been a favorite topic for literature and the press ever since. The coffin of Marie Vetsera was later stolen from the Heiligenkreuz convent where she had been buried.

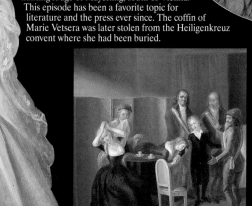

THE DAUPHIN'S PARTING FROM HIS FAMILY, JULY 3, 1793
Louis XVII, Duke of Normandy, the second son of Louis XVI and Marie-Antoinette, became Dauphin (heir to the French throne) on the death of his older brother in 1789. He was locked up in the Temple prison after the King's execution and died of scrofula on June 8, 1795.

🏃 Half a day
◆ A B3-B4-C3-D2-D3

"ANNAKIRCHE IN THE SNOW". A painting (right) by Hans Götzinger (1914).

"All of Austria, complete with the problems and contradictions which went unresolved until the collapse of 1918, is reflected in the work of Grillparzer, in his sensitivity and creative power."
Claudio Magris,
Le Mythe et l'Empire

THE BLUE CARP
The Blue Carp House (*Haus zum blauen Karpfen*, above) at no. 14 is one of the most singular buildings in Annagasse. The early 19th-century façade is decorated with frescoes and bas-reliefs, one of which represents a blue carp.

ANNAGASSE

LAVISH PALACES. Leading eastward from halfway along the Kärntnerstrasse, St Anne's Street (Annagasse) has a number of fine buildings. Most notable are the ESTERHÁZY PALACE ▲ *162* (no. 2) built in the 17th century and restored in the 18th; the KREMSMÜNSTERHOF (no. 4) with its elegant 17th-century façade; the Baroque HERZOGENBURGERHOF (no. 6); the DEYBELHOF, or Täuberlhof (no. 8), built in the 18th century to plans by Hildebrandt ● *75, 81,* ▲ *147, 247*; the 19th-century HAUS ZUM BLAUEN KARPFEN (Blue Carp House no. 14); and the ROMAN EMPEROR'S HOUSE (no. 18).

ANNAKIRCHE. The Annakirche ● *76,* a French parish church belonging to the congregation of lay brothers of St Francis of Sales, faces on to Annagasse. The building was constructed in the 15th century, and rebuilt in the Baroque style during the 18th century. The ceiling inside is decorated with a series of frescoes by Daniel Gran (1694–1757). Also look for the sculpted 15th-century group representing St Anne with the Virgin and Child, attributed to Veit Stoss (1448–1533), as well as the Baroque reliquary which is said to contain the hand of the saint.

THE PRINCE OF INTRIGUE. The bishop-turned-politician Charles-Maurice de Talleyrand-Périgord (1754–1838) dominated French foreign policy from 1797 to 1815. At Erfurt he betrayed Napoleon by persuading the Czar not to ally with him against Austria. He contributed to the Emperor's downfall by working for the restoration of the monarchy. At the Congress of Vienna (below) ● *38* he sought to curb the demands of the Allies, but the return of Napoleon in 1815 ruined his efforts.

OHANNESGASSE

RSULINENKIRCHE UND KLOSTER
ohannesgasse runs parallel to Annagasse; n it stands the church and convent of the Ursulines (Ursulinenkirche und Kloster), uilt in the 18th century by the Ursuline eaching order which was then established n about thirty countries. According to egend, their patroness, St Ursula, went to Cologne accompanied by eleven thousand irgins and was martyred there by the Huns who sacked the town because she ad refused to marry their king. In one ing of the church there is a small MUSEUM OF RELIGIOUS FOLK ART.
N JOHANNESGASSE. Opposite, at no. 15, ands the FOUNDATION FOR NOBLE LADIES (Savoyisches Damenstift). The IMPERIAL HOUSEHOLD RECORDS OFFICE Hofkammerarchiv) is at no. 16; stretching back in the irection of Annagasse, this building's two wings date from ne 18th and 19th centuries respectively. Franz Grillparzer as its director at one time. Near the Kärntnerstrasse is the UESTENBERG-KAUNITZ PALACE, built in the 18th century, hich was the residence of the brilliant French diplomat alleyrand.

IMMELPFORTGASSE

RINCE EUGÈNE'S WINTER PALACE ★. This palace dominates immelpfortgasse, a small street running parallel to ohannesgasse. The conqueror of the Turks ● *34* built himself everal palaces in Vienna (most notably the Belvedere ▲ *246*) hich he filled with works of art. The prince used the greatest chitects of his time, Johann Bernhard Fischer von Erlach d Johann Lukas von Hildebrandt, and did much to foster e rivalry between these two. For instance, Fischer von rlach worked on the Winter Palace from 1697 to 1698 and ildebrandt took over from 1702 to 1724. The former 74, 80, ▲ *138, 155, 164, 169, 275, 302* was responsible r the FORMAL STAIRCASE, which is remarkable for its las figures acting as caryatids, and the FOUNTAIN OF ERCULES on the landing. Hildebrandt gave fluidity to e façade with a system of fluted pilasters. Prince ugène died in this palace in 1736; since 1848 it has been ccupied by the Ministry of Finance.
E ERODÖDY-FÜRSTENBERG PALACE. Opposite Prince ugène's Winter Palace is the Baroque odödy-Fürstenberg Palace, whose early h-century façade has a magnificent portal namented with atlantes.

ENSTEINGASSE

'S DEATH. In 1847 a new building e dwelling at no. 8 asse where the debt- ● *40, 110* ▲ *150, 281* s return from

FRANZ GRILLPARZER
The son of a Viennese lawyer, Franz Grillparzer (1791–1872) is considered Austria's greatest playwright. His plays feature figures from classical antiquity such as Sappho, Medea and Leander, as well as Libuse, the founder of the city of Prague. A room at the Imperial Household Records Office is devoted to Grillparzer, who was its director from 1832 to 1856.

"I have reached the end before I could use my talent to the full. Life has been so beautiful, my career began under such happy auspices ... yet no-one can alter his own destiny. One must resign oneself to whatever shall be, for that is the will of Providence. So I am completing my song of mourning, which I must not leave unfinished behind me."
Mozart, September 1791

MOZART AND BEETHOVEN. The only meeting between the two geniuses took place in the house on Rauhensteingasse: at the time Beethoven ● 50 was seventeen and Mozart was thirty-one. Mozart singled out the younger man, telling his friends to "Watch that one; one day he will set the world talking about him".

FRANCISCAN CHURCH This was built between 1603 and 1611 in South German Renaissance style.

Prague in 1787. It was here that he composed many of his greatest masterpieces, notably *Don Giovanni, Cosi fan tutte, The Magic Flute* and the *Requiem*, which was unfinished at the time of his death. Mozart's star was on the rise until 1788, with the support of Joseph II himself; but after that date things grew increasingly difficult for him financially. Mozart was only thirty-five in November 1791 when he was forced to

take to his bed with a high fever; by the 28th his condition was desperate, and he died on the night of 4th to 5th December. On the following day the undertakers carried his coffin to the entrance of the cathedral catacombs for a final blessing ▲ *134*, and thence to St Mark's cemetery ▲ *262*.
BALLGASSE. A small alley, the Ballgasse, leads through a vaulted passage from midway along Rauhensteingasse to Franziskanerplatz.

FRANZISKANERPLATZ ★

THE MOSES FOUNTAIN. This pretty square has its own little church and fountain, as well as a number of fine old houses. The Fountain of Moses was designed by Johann Martin Fischer in 1798.

Detail of the Fountain of Moses.

FRANZISKANERKIRCHE. The Franciscan Church of St Jerome (Sankt Hieronymus, or Franziskanerkirche ● 74) belonged to the Order of St Francis and was the only place of worship in Vienna to receive a Renaissance façade at the beginning of the 17th century. The Baroque interior includes a fine high altar (1707) by Andrea Pozzo and an organ (1643) sculpted by J. Wöckerl.

KLEINES CAFÉ". Although it was built in the 1970's, the Art Deco *Kleines Café* (Little Café) on the square has nothing jarring in its décor. It was designed in retro style by the architect Hermann Czech.

SINGERSTRASSE

BAROQUE PALACES. North of Franziskanerplatz is Singerstrasse, a long thoroughfare which comes out at Stock-im-Eisen-Platz ▲ *137*. In this street are the ROTTAL PALACE (no. 17–19), built according to plans by Hildebrandt, which is now the PUBLIC DEBT BANK; and the NEPAUER-BREUNER PALACE (no. 16, below), likewise an 18th-century building, with a monumental doorway held up by figures of Atlas.

THE TEUTONIC ORDER IN VIENNA. The order of Teutonic Knights (Deutschorden) moved in the 14th century into a cluster of houses which included the Gothic Church of St Elizabeth. Originally an order of hospitalers, the Order's history dates back to the earliest crusades and it had its first base in the Holy Land at Acre. Later it became a military organization which fought against the Muslims. By the 13th century the Grand Master was no longer resident in the Holy Land but at Marienburg in Poland, from where he launched a crusade in central Europe. This campaign enabled the Order to colonize Prussia, Lithuania and Estonia, to such effect that by the 14th century they ruled over a sovereign state with about twenty provinces.

DEUTSCHORDEN
Sergei Eisenstein's film *Aleksandr Nevsky* (1938, below) presents the Teutonic Knights as fanatical soldier-monks.

SCHATZKAMMER DES DEUTSCHEN ORDENS. Several rooms within the Order's headquarters are used to display its treasures (Schatzkammer des Deutschen Ordens). These consist of coins, medals, and the rings and chains

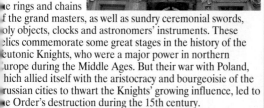

of the grand masters, as well as sundry ceremonial swords, holy objects, clocks and astronomers' instruments. These relics commemorate some great stages in the history of the Teutonic Knights, who were a major power in northern Europe during the Middle Ages. But their war with Poland, which allied itself with the aristocracy and bourgeoisie of the Prussian cities to thwart the Knights' growing influence, led to the Order's destruction during the 15th century.

DEUTSCHORDENSKIRCHE SANKT ELIZABETH. Built in the Gothic style during the 14th century and altered to some extent in the 18th century, the Church of Saint Elizabeth (Deutschordenskirche Sankt Elizabeth) possesses a fine 16th-century Dutch altarpiece. Mozart ● *48*, ▲ *147, 150, 262, 281*

In reality, the work of Germanization undertaken by the Teutonic Order eclipsed the influence of the Orthodox Russian religion. Ultimately, the states of northern Europe united against them. After a series of military disasters in the 15th century and the secularizations of the 16th century, the Order forfeited all its territories and fell back on its hospital vocation. In 1809 the Order was dissolved by Bonaparte, but was resurrected in Austria in 1840; since 1929 it has been limited to charitable functions.

Plaque on the Figarohaus.

HERMAN VON SALZA
In 1234 the Grand Master Hermann von Salza (1170–1239) launched a crusade against the Baltic Prussian peoples, who had remained pagan, with the blessing of Pope Gregory IX and the assent of Emperor Frederick II von Hohenstaufen. This crusade, one of the first "Marches Eastward" (*Drang nach Osten*), led to the establishment of a Christian state in northern Europe. The fact that Prussia was founded by a military order goes some way toward explaining the nation's traditional cult of discipline.

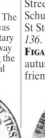

COATS OF ARMS
The interior of the Church of St Elizabeth is hung with the blazons of the knights of the Teutonic Order.

The Figarohaus.

lived in one of the Order's houses during one of his periods in Vienna, in the spring of 1781. Maria Theresa *36,* ▲ *158, 291* had just died and the Prince-Archbishop of Salzburg, Colloredo, had brought the Mozart family to Vienna for her funeral. At the same time Mozart's *Idomeneo*, written in Munich in January 1781, received acclaim in Vienna. A plaque commemorates the composer's brief residence here.

DOMGASSE

Blutgasse leads off Singerstrasse to the narrow Domgasse (Cathedral Street), which continues to Schulerstrasse in the vicinity of St Stephen's Square ▲ *132, 136.*

FIGAROHAUS ★. Mozart moved to no. 5 Domgasse in the autumn of 1784. There he composed chamber music with his friends including Haydn ● *48*, and at the end of 1785 he worked on one of his greatest operas, *The Marriage of Figaro*, with a libretto by Lorenzo da Ponte (1749–1838) who had already written the text for *Così fan tutte*. The *Marriage* was only a qualified success in Vienna, where it opened in May 1786, but it triumphed at Prague in the following year, when Mozart was given a hero's welcome on arriving conduct it. On his return to Vienna, however, Mozart found himself heavily in debt and was obliged to move from his fine house on Domgasse to much more modest lodgings on Rauhensteingasse ▲ *147*. Today there is a museum at no. 5 Domgasse (the only one of Mozart's various residences to have survived). The house is known as the Figarohaus, and has a collection of objects, paintings and musical scores that belonged to the composer.

HAUS "ZUM ROTEN KREUTZ". Vienna's first café opened in 1683 at no. 6 Domgasse ● *66*. Rebuilt in the 18th century, the building now bears the insignia of the Red Cross (Haus *zum roten Kreutz*).

FÜRSTENBERG PALACE. On the corner of Domgasse and Grünangergasse stands the 18th-century Fürstenberg Palace, with its magnificent façade and imposing sculpted staircase. The small streets in the vicinity of the cathedral are connected by a warren of underground passages, some of which contain shops and restaurants.

BÄCKERSTRASSE ★

After two shopping streets – Schulerstrasse (which owes its name either to a school for jurists established here in 1389, or to St Stephen's School, founded in 1237) and Wollzeile – one

FIGLMÜLLER

...aches Bäckerstrasse (Baker Street). Here there are several ...aces of interest, notably the courtyard of the ...CHWANENFELD HOUSE (no. 7). Opposite stands the 18th-...ntury SEILERN PALACE (no. 8), where Madame de Staël ...766–1817), author of the essay *On Germany* and a precursor ... Romanticism in France, stayed in 1808. Farther along is the ...LT WIEN café. Bäckerstrasse has several popular cafés, in ...rticular OSWALD & KALB, and the KIX, decorated with work ... contemporary artists.

...LTE UNIVERSITÄT. At its western end, Bäckerstrasse looks on ... LUGECKPLATZ, where there is a statue by Gutenberg and ...veral pleasant cafés and restaurants are sited, and to ...OTENTURMSTRASSE, a major shopping street. At its other end ...leads into DR-IGNAZ-SEIPEL-PLATZ, where the Alte ...niversität used to be. This building was reconstructed during ...e reign of Maria Theresa ● 36 by the French architect ...icolas Jadot de Ville-Issey (1753–5), who was brought here ...om Lunéville by Francis of Lorraine ▲ 280. Under ...rdinand (1847) ● 41 the building became the seat of the

ACADEMY OF SCIENCES (Akademie der Wissenschaften). **JESUITENKIRCHE.** In front of the academy stands the Jesuit Church (known as Jesuitenkirche or Universitätskirche) ● 77. Ferdinand II gave this order a monopoly on the teaching of philosophy and theology in the university, a task it fulfilled until Maria Theresa's reforms in

THE SCHWANENFELD HOUSE
The courtyard of this house, which is surrounded by galleries and arcades, is the only Renaissance construction of its type in Vienna. The rarity of Renaissance architecture is attributable to the Turkish threat: for several decades, any spare money was spent on ramparts. F. von Amerling, the 19th-century Habsburg portraitist, lived in this house, which now contains a collection of wrought ironwork; the best pieces may be seen in the courtyard.

1761 ▲ *291*.
Built in the 17th century by an anonymous architect, it looks rather dreary from the outside, but the Baroque interior is magnificent, devised in the early 18th century by the Italian Andrea Pozzo (1642–1709). Pozzo, a Jesuit lay brother, was a great painter who specialized in Baroque trompe l'oeil frescoes, with which he decorated the ceilings of many Italian churches (notably the one at San Ignatius, in Rome). While in Vienna, he worked on the Liechtenstein Palace, now the Museum of Modern Art, at n 9 Fürstengasse ▲ *292*, and on the ceiling of the Jesuit Churc where the trompe l'œil cupola is a major achievement. Don miss the magnificent PULPIT OF TRUTH, which is encrusted with mother-of-pearl and decorated with encrustation of Baroque sculpture.

POSTGASSE

THE ACADEMY OF SCIENCES
The old university building (the Academy of Sciences since 1847) has an imposing Baroque façade and a huge hall, in which a number of great composers (among them Beethoven ● *50* and Haydn ● *48*) played their own compositions.

DOMINIKANERKIRCHE UND KLOSTER.
Beyond the Jesuit Church is the Postgasse, site of the Dominican monastery and church (Dominikanerkirche und Kloster). This church, also known as the Rosary Basilica, is built on the foundations of several earlier sanctuaries, the first of which was constructed by the Dominicans in 1237. Destroyed by fi this was replaced by a Gothic church, which was in turn demolished during the siege of 1529 ● *34*. Today's Baroque church dates from the 17th century and is inspired by Roma

HAYDN AND "THE CREATION"
The oratorio *The Creation* was included in the last concert attended by Haydn. It was played in the old university's great hall on March 27, 1808, a year before the composer's death. Aged seventy-six and crippled, Haydn went to the event in a wheelchair and was greeted with drum rolls and a blare of trumpets by his many admirers and pupils, among them Princess Esterházy. Overwhelmed, he was obliged to leave the hall before the end of the concert: it was the old master's final public appearance. He died on May 31, 1809, a few days before the French army entered Vienna ● *32, 38*.

THE THREE RAVENS
The House of the Three Ravens (Haus zu den Drei Raben) is at no 21 Rotenturm-strasse.

SCHUMANN IN VIENNA
Robert Schumann (1810–56) stayed in Vienna on two occasions, in 1838 and 1846. Clara, his wife, had learned the piano there, and Robert was looking for a publisher for his review *Die neue Szeitschrift für Musik*. Vienna inspired the composer, even though he disapproved of the city's moral climate and felt that the Viennese did not understand his music.

...yles. The frescoes of the ceiling in the nave are by Matthias ...auchmiller. The CHAPEL OF ST THOMAS AQUINAS has an ...tarpiece dating from 1638.

...ANKT BARBARA KIRCHE. The small 17th-century Ukrainian ...urch of St Barbara has an interesting collection of old icons.

...CHÖNLATERNGASSE ★

...his street, which begins opposite the Dominican church, ...ves its name to the lantern on the front of the HOUSE OF THE ...EAUTIFUL LANTERN (Haus zur schönen Laterne) at no. 6 (this ...a copy; the original was long ago moved to a museum).
...EILIGENKREUZERHOF. At no. 5, a covered passage leads ...rough to a courtyard (Heiligenkreuzerhof) surrounded by buildings

...elonging to the monastery of Heiligenkreuz to the ...outhwest of Vienna. Constructed in the middle of the 17th ...entury and restored in the 18th, this complex includes the ...bot's residence, the monks' lodgings and the CHAPEL OF ...T BERNARD, whose Baroque interior is decorated with an ...tarpiece by Martino Altomonte (1657–1745).

BASILISKENHAUS. The Basiliskenhaus, at no. 7, is a 13th-century bakery; it is easily recognizable by a sandstone block which resembles the mythical basilisk.
ALTE SCHMIEDE. The composer Robert Schumann (1810–56) lived in the house next door, at no. 7a. On the same street are the museum of wrought iron (Alte Schmiede, no. 9) and the *WUNDER BAR* (1976). Schönlaterngasse leads back to SONNENFELSGASSE, a street full of cafés ● 66.

THE BASILISK
This mythical animal, believed to emerge from a serpent's egg hatched by a toad, could kill with a single glance. The basilisk poisoned a well with its breath and was slain by an intrepid baker, who held up a mirror to it.

FLEISCHMARKT ★

Via the Meat Market (Fleischmarkt), a street that was formerly the center of the butchers' district, one reaches the extreme north side of the inner city (Innerstadt). This is very much a night-time district, peopled by young Viennese and foreign tourists. Known as the "Bermuda Triangle", it lies between the Danube Canal, the

GRIECHENKIRCHE
The Greek Orthodox
Church has a domed
belltower. Details
include an angel
(above) and the
doorway (right).

**"DER LIEBER
AUGUSTIN"**
*"O, du lieber Augustin,
's Geld is hin,
's Mensch is hin,
O, du lieber Augustin,
alles is hin!"*
("Oh, my darling
Augustin, there's no
money, there are no
more people, Oh my
darling Augustin,
there's nothing
more!"). This song,
written in 1679 at the
height of the plague
epidemic, gave
courage to the sick
and to the survivors.
In the song, Augustin
gets drunk and falls
into a mass grave, but
he is so sodden with
alcohol that he is safe
from infection. The
melody was later
borrowed by Mozart
and Schönberg
(*Second Quartet*).

**THE BISHOP OF
SALZBURG.** Ruprecht,
the patron saint of
Bavaria (650–718),
was Bishop of Worms
in Germany before
coming to Salzburg
where he founded the
Abbey of St Peter.
Vienna's oldest
church is dedicated to
him.

Church of Our Lady and Franziskanerplatz. The more
fashionable restaurants here tend to be grouped around
Ruprechtskirche and the synagogue.

GRIECHENKIRCHE. The Greek Orthodox Church of St Georg
on the Fleischmarkt is of greater interest for its religious
ceremonies than for its architecture, which is an amalgam of
the 18th and 19th centuries. The orthodox services here are
very beautiful, with the priest in his miter and brocaded
chasuble, the clouds of incense, the deep-voiced choir,
and the icons glimmering in the candlelight.

"GREICHENBEISL". Formerly a haunt of such
luminaries as Mark Twain, Johannes Brahms ● *51*,
Johann Strauss ● *56* and Franz Grillparzer ▲ *147*,
the *Greek Tavern* (*Greichenbeisl*) next to the Greek
Orthodox Church is best known for the legendary
piper, hero and composer of the folk song
Der Lieber Augustin, who is commemorated
on its façade.

RUPRECHTSKIRCHE. Built on a former
defensive bastion, the Church of St
Rupert (Ruprechtskirche) ● *75* overlooks
Franz-Joseph Wharf ▲ *200, 229, 230*
and the Danube Canal ▲ *229*. It is
the oldest religious edifice in
Vienna, reputedly founded in 740, at which time the
site lay just to the north of the Roman camp of
Vindobona. A Romanesque church was later
constructed on the ruins of the original chapel in the

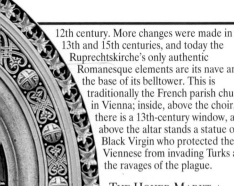

12th century. More changes were made in the 13th and 15th centuries, and today the Ruprechtskirche's only authentic Romanesque elements are its nave and the base of its belltower. This is traditionally the French parish church in Vienna; inside, above the choir, there is a 13th-century window, and above the altar stands a statue of the Black Virgin who protected the Viennese from invading Turks and the ravages of the plague.

THE HOHER MARKT ★

The Hoher Markt is Vienna's oldest marketplace and was originally the forum of the Roman camp of Vindobona. It is very probable that Marcus Aurelius died here of plague in 180 AD (facing no. 6 in nearby MARC AUREL STRASSE there is a statue of this emperor, who was a friend of Seneca and celebrated for his own philosophical writings). Roman remains have been excavated here (access is by way of no. 3); these consist of the ruins of two houses occupied by Roman officers belonging to the garrison of Vindobona in the first centuries AD. During the ascendancy of the Babenbergs, and later under the Habsburgs in the Middle Ages, the Hoher Markt was used for public executions (hangings) and for the markets after which it is named.

VERMÄHLUNGSBRUNNEN. The sinister tools of torture that used to stand here have today given way to much pleasanter monuments to look at. Leopold I (1640–1705) prayed that his son, the future Joseph I, would return safe and sound from the siege of Landau in 1702; when this prayer was granted, the emperor commissioned a first votive column of wood (Josephssäule), which was raised in the center of the square by J. B. Fischer von Ehrlach ● 74, 80, ▲ 138, 147, 164, 169, 302, in 1706. This was replaced in 1732 by the Betrothal Fountain (Vermählungsbrunnen), also known as Joseph's Column, in marble and bronze, which was created by Fischer von Erlach's son, Josef Emanuel ● 74, 80, ▲ 302, and sculpted by the Italian Antonio Corradini.

ANKERUHR ★. The anchor clock (Ankeruhr) by Franz von Matsch, which has long adorned the headquarters of the insurance company of the same name, somehow survived the bombardment of the square in 1945 ● 42. On the stroke of every hour, one of a number of different figurines appears: Marcus Aurelius, Charlemagne, Maria Theresa, Rudolph I,

A REMINDER OF THE GREAT SIEGE
This plaque retains three cannonballs fired into the city by its Turkish besiegers ● 34. There are similar grim mementos all over Vienna. A cannonball may still be seen embedded in the façade of St Stephen's Cathedral.

THE HOHER MARKT
The gallows remained in the Hoher Markt until the beginning of the 18th century, and the pillory until the 19th. The latter was used to punish bad bakers, who were locked in an iron cage and dunked three times in the Danube.

Detail of the synagogue's exterior.

He was only off by one year: the state of Israel came into being in 1948.

Walter von der Vogelweide and Prince Eugène are some of them. At noon, the whole cast troops forth. A scene from the film *The Third Man* ● 42, ▲ 192, 267 was set at the foot of the celebrated clock.

BEYOND THE HOHER MARKT

To the north of the square, one can make one's way back along Judengasse to Ruprechtskirche. Heading eastward, one reaches the huge Rotenturmstrasse which leads to St Stephen's Cathedral ▲ 132. To the west of the square, Tuchlaubengasse leads to the Graben ▲ 137.

SYNAGOGUE. The quiet synagogue in Seitenstettengasse obeyed to the letter the rules established by Joseph II in his Edict of Toleration (1781) that all non-Catholic denominations could practice freely, provided that they did not flaunt their differences. Outwardly similar to any other ordinary building, the great synagogue was able to survive the Fascist pogroms of the post-Anschluss years ● 42, during which the forty-odd other Jewish temples in Vienna were systematically burned to the ground.

THE JEWS IN VIENNA. The Jews were tolerated by the Habsburgs through to the end of the 19th century. At the beginning of Franz-Joseph's reign, new laws were passed to suppress all discrimination against them. Policies of economic liberalism after 1860, coupled with the growth of the empire, created a need for capital; moreover a number of official projects, including the grandiose new building projects on the Ring ▲ 197, required heavy financing. The crucial rôle played in this by the bourgeois Jewish families of Vienna led the emperor to ennoble some of them; but the stock exchange collapse of 1873 brought about a wave of anti-Semitism and certain politicians (notably the mayor of Vienna, Karl Lueger ● 87, ▲ 227, founder of the Social Democratic Party, and Georg von Schönerer, the Pan-Germanist and nationalist) used this sentiment as a vehicle to power. Ultimately, it was an Austrian who had lived in Vienna, Adolf Hitler, who committed the ultimate outrage. Of Vienna's two hundred thousand Jews, a third managed to emigrate and sixty-five thousand eventually perished in death camps.

"The Baroque, Imperial pomp of Vienna comes less
from the exaltation of power than from
awareness of its instability."

Guy Hocquenghem

**BAROQUE CARYATIDS
AND FIGURES OF
ATLAS**
"To be worthy of the
Ring, a building had
to display all the
caryatids and other
figures, all the urns,
and all the motifs and
small embellishments
imaginable, in the
decoration of its
façade. As to the
government
buildings, these
outclassed the private
ones in their sheer
opulence and in the
proliferation of their
styles."

George Clare,
*The Last Waltz in
Vienna*

⚑ Half a day
◆ A B1-B2-C1-C2

THE LAST ROMANTIC
As a Prussian high official, Joseph von Eichendorff (1788–1857) visited Vienna several times, where his literary talents were much admired. Known as "the last Romantic knight", he approached nature as a mystical theme.

For many years the *Sacher Hotel* ● 66, ▲ 140 and the *Café Demel* have been disputing the right to sell the *Original Sachertorte, Demel* maintaining that the chef who invented it left the *Sacher* to work for *Demel*. The Fellini window at *Demel* (below).

KOHLMARKT

Kohlmarkt is one of the most elegant streets in Vienna. *Kohl* means cabbage, and *Kohle*, coal, but since its recent restoration there is no sign of either cabbage or anthracite. There are only the façades of noble buildings and a line of shop windows, with the white-and-gold imperial palace (Hofburg) in the background.

"CAFÉ DEMEL" ★. At the Hofburg ▲ 173 end of Kohlmarkt is *Café Demel*, a tearoom and supplier of confectionery to the imperial court for more than two centuries. Founded in 1785 and taken over by Christoph Demel in 1857, this is one of Vienna's major gastronomic institutions ● 66. The waitresses wear black and white uniforms and address clients in the third person as they bring them delicious pastries on beautiful china.

BALLHAUSPLATZ

West of the Hofburg is the Ballhausplatz, dominated by the Federal Chancellery (Bundeskanzleramt).

BUNDESKANZLERAMT. The former imperial chancellery was built at the beginning of the 18th century under Charles VI, plans by Hildebrandt ● 75, 81, who was also constructing the two Belvedere palaces at that time ▲ 246, 256. Since its inception, the chancellery has been altered several times. What was once the nerve center of imperial Austria's diplomacy is now the headquarters of the Federal Chanceller and the Foreign Affairs Ministry. Under Maria Theresa, Chancellor Kaunitz ● 37, worked here to upset the Europear alliances and gain the friendship of France, Austria's traditional foe. This change enabled Maria Theresa ● 36 ▲ 291 to wage the Seven Years' War (1756–63) against Prussia and marry her daughter Marie-Antoinette to the future King of France, Louis XVI, in 1770. Kaunitz also served Joseph II and Leopold II. Participants in the Congress of Vienna ● 38 at the time of Prince Metternich met in the building. Finally, on Februar 25, 1934, four years before the Anschluss ● 44 whic united Austria and Germany, Chancellor Dollfuss was assassinated here.

HERRENGASSE

This street owes its name to the many fine houses lining it, all of which were built by members of the Lower Austrian aristocracy

THONET
WIEN.

Over forty million copies of Thonet's bistro chair have been sold worldwide. Michael Thonet (1796–1871), a native of the Rhineland, discovered a process for bending beechwood and created his first chair patterns in 1841. Thonet arrived in Vienna in 1842 and was immediately successful; his arrival coincided with the height of the Biedermeier period ● *62* when Viennese taste was for simple and comfortable furniture.

THE MURDER OF DOLLFUSS
Engelbert Dollfuss (1892–1934) became Chancellor of Austria

(erren) who wished to set themselves up in palaces close to e Hofburg. From St Michael's Square ▲ *174* to the Freyung, errengasse boasts every style of Austrian architecture from e Renaissance to our own time.

ε **WILCZEK AND MODENA PALACES.** The Wilczek Palace, at . 5, was built in the early 18th century to plans by Anton pel; between 1810 and 1812 it was the home of the German mantic poet Joseph von Eichendorff (1788–1857) and from 12 to 1813, that of the Austrian playwright Franz illparzer ▲ *147*, who was working at the imperial court rary at the time. The Modena Palace at no. 7 was rebuilt in 11 and is now the Interior Ministry.

EDERÖSTERREICHISCHES LANDESMUSEUM. Built at the end the 17th century, the MOLLARD-CLARY PALACE at no. 9 s been converted into the Lower ustria State Museum iederösterreichisches ndesmuseum). The collections the first and second floors are voted to prehistory, natural ience and the traditions of Lower stria. On the third floor, several oms have been transformed into a LLERY OF AUSTRIAN ART. Here are

displays of a number of fine altarpieces and Gothic wood carvings, some Baroque works by Maulbertsch, Altomonte and Rottmayr ▲ *139, 293*, and several paintings by Oskar Kokoschka ▲ *254*.

in 1932; National Socialists favoring Anschluss with Germany arranged his assassination.

THE FAÇADE OF THE FERSTEL PALACE
The Ferstel Palace was built in the mid-19th century by Heinrich von Ferstel (architect of the Votive Church) combining Romanesque and Renaissance elements.

VIENNA SEES RED
"...that morning Franz Tunda appeared on the crowded, sunny side of the Graben in the same clothes he had worn at the Moscow consulate, causing a sensation. He looked exactly like what a chemist (standing in the doorway of his odorous shop) described as a 'bolshevik'."
Joseph Roth,
The Endless Flight

LANDHAUS. The façade of no. 13, the Liechtenstein Palace (one of several of the same name in Vienna ▲ *161, 292*) is decorated with half a dozen pilasters; the building was formerly the seat of the Diet of Lower Austria. Today, it is t headquarters of the administration of Lower Austria and ha retained its title of Landhaus. Originally built in the 16th century with funds contributed by the nobility, it was entirel reconstructed between 1837 and 1848 by Aloïs Pichl. Conce were given here by Beethoven, Schubert and Liszt, and several important political events took place here: for example the riot preceding the 1848 revolution ● *40* began the courtyard, while the main hall was the scene of the proclamation of the Republic on October 21, 1918, followin the abdication of Charles I ● *33,* ▲ *144, 180*.

FERSTEL PALACE ★. This palace, with a labyrinthine interior staircases and corridors, was once the site of the Vienna Sto Exchange and the headquarters of the Bank of Austria. It h now been beautifully renovated and serves as a conference center, with one or two high-class shops.

"CAFÉ CENTRAL". You can reach the magnificent *Café Centr* ● *66* (left) through the corridors of the Ferstel Palace, or by way of the Herrengasse. The café has been a meeting place for Viennese intellectuals for more than 100 years. Stefan Zweig used to come he to meet his friends, among them the exiled revolutionary Lev Davidovitch Bronstein, otherwise known as Leon Trotsky.

PORCIA PALACE. Among Vienna's many Baroque an neo-classical palaces, the Porcia Palace at no. 23 stands out as a building from an earlier age. It was constructed around 1646.

PREMONITION
"Who will make the Russian revolution? Herr Bronstein at the *Café Central*, perhaps?", wrote a diplomat in the margin of a dispatch announcing the 1917 Soviet Revolution.

BANKGASSE

BAROQUE PALACES ★. Bankgasse, a narrow street running of Herrengasse, contains several fine Baroque palaces ● *80, 82* These include the BATTHYANY PALACE (no. 2) built at the close of the 17th century in the style of J. B. Fischer von Erlach ● *74, 80, 138, 147* and the joined TRAUTSON and

TRATTMANN-WINDISCHGRÄTZ PALACES (at nos. 4 and 6), redesigned by von Erlach's rival, Johann Lukas von Hildebrandt ● 75, 81, ▲ 147, 247. The latter palaces were formerly occupied by the chancellery of the Kingdom of Hungary, and now house the Hungarian Embassy.

STADTPALAIS LIECHTENSTEIN. Right at the end of the street, near the Volksgarten and the Burgtheater ▲ 204 stands one of the many residences which the princes of Liechtenstein (a small state which Charles VI created as a principality in 1719) built for themselves in Vienna: this one is a winter palace constructed between 1694 and 1706. Like the Liechtenstein summer palace ▲ 292 of the same date, it was built by Domenico Martinelli (1650–1718) and modeled on the Baroque palaces of Italy. The pilasters and statues of the majestic façade are particularly striking.

MINORITENPLATZ

MINORITENKIRCHE. In the center of Minoritenplatz stands the Church of the Minor Friars, the first order founded by St Francis of Assisi (1182–1226). The original monastery was destroyed at the beginning of the 20th century to make way for the ARCHIVE BUILDING at no. 1. Flanked by a small bellturret, the triangular façade has a broad entrance embellished by a handsome Gothic sculpture of *The Crucifixion*, by Franciscan friar, Jacques de Paris. At the rear of the church, several apses are clustered round the high octagonal tower (right), which is as slender as a chimneystack.

"THE LAST SUPPER". The principal curiosity of this church is a mosaic of twelve massive blocks which reproduces Leonardo da Vinci's *Last Supper* at Milan. This is the work of Giacomo Raffaelli; it was commissioned by Napoleon Bonaparte, who wished to take the original back to the Louvre, leaving this copy in Milan as a replacement. Bonaparte fell before this scheme could be carried out; and the mosaic was bought by the Austrian government, which

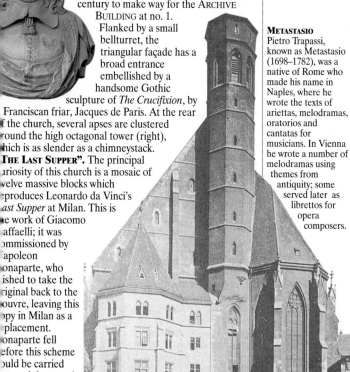

PORTAL OF THE MINORITENKIRCHE
This church was originally a chapel, built shortly after the death of St Francis. Later destroyed by fire, it was rebuilt in the Gothic style during the 14th century and altered several times in later years as a result of damage caused by the Turks ● 34. Every rebuilding was done in the spirit of the original Gothic style.

METASTASIO
Pietro Trapassi, known as Metastasio (1698–1782), was a native of Rome who made his name in Naples, where he wrote the texts of ariettas, melodramas, oratorios and cantatas for musicians. In Vienna he wrote a number of melodramas using themes from antiquity; some served later as librettos for opera composers.

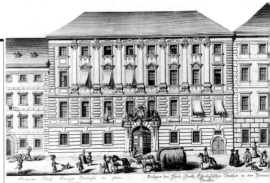

The Esterházy Palace.

NICHOLAS THE MAGNIFICENT (1765–1833)
The Hungarian prince Nicolas II Esterházy ● *49* (below) was made an imperial marshal in 1770. He was a lover of luxury and the arts, who preferred his country castle of Eisenstadt, a copy of Versailles, to Vienna.

had it transferred to the Minoritenkirche in the mid-19th century. Note also the tomb of the Italian poet Pietro Trapass (known as Metastasio, 1698–1782) and Rosselino's 18th-century bas-relief of the *Virgin*. The success of Metastasio's *Dido Abandoned* (1724) brought him to the attention of Charles VI, who invited him to his Viennese court. In 1750, the Italian met Joseph Haydn ● *49*, then living in the same building.

THE DIETRICHSTEIN AND STARHEMBERG PALACES. Also on Minoritenplatz are the 17th-century Dietrichstein Palace (no. 3) altered in the 18th century, and (no. 5) the 17th-century residence (also renovated) of Count Ernst Rüdiger Starhemberg, Vienna's defender in 1683 ▲ *31*.

WALLNERSTRASSE

Wallnerstrasse, which begins at the Kohlmarkt and enters Herrengasse near the Landhaus, can also boast some fine palaces; in particular those of the Esterházy clan.

THE ESTERHÁZY PALACE. The palace at no. 2 Wallnerstrasse was the second built by the Esterházy princes in Vienna, after that of Annagasse ▲ *142*. Imposing though they are, the two buildings cannot compare in magnificence with the castle built in the late 18th century at Lake Neusiedl ■ *24* by Prince Nicolas Esterházy. After distinguishing themselves in the war against the Turks, the Esterházys were raised to princely rank following the siege of Vienna ● *34*. Skillful diplomats and military leaders, the Esterházys lived in ostentatious luxury in times of peace.

JOSEPH HAYDN (1732–1809, right)
"Here I am now in my desert, abandoned like a poor orphan, almost without the company of human beings, full of precious memories of days past – alas, long past! And who knows when they will return?. ... Here at Estoras, nobody asks me 'Would you like some chocolate? With or without milk? Coffee, perhaps? Black coffee or café Liegois? What can I offer you, my dear Haydn? Would you care for an ice-cream? Vanilla or pineapple?' "
Letter from Joseph Haydn

HAYDN IN THE SERVICE OF THE ESTERHÁZYS. The Esterházys were great lovers and patrons of music, as well as of architecture. Musical performances were always an important feature at the lavish entertainments held at their palaces. They maintained a private orchestra, which was led by Joseph Haydn from 1762 to 1790, the year of his death. The great musician suffered agonies of boredom at the Esterházy country residence at Eisenstadt and longed for his employers to return to Vienna, where he could be reunited with his pupils, and his friends and admirers. Among his friends was Mozart ● *48, 110* ▲ *147, 281*, twenty-four years his junior; an among his pupils was the young Beethoven ● *51,* ▲ *262, 298.*

> "One day in the thirty-fourth year of my vagabond existence,
> I was sitting at the Café Central in Herrengasse in Vienna,
> in one of those gilded chairs in the English style."
>
> Peter Altenberg

THE CAPRARA-GEYMÜLLER PALACE. On the same side of the
street as the Esterházy Palace stands the 17th-century
Caprara-Geymüller Palace, altered in the 18th century, which
has a fine Baroque doorway framed by two figures of Atlas
● 82, ▲ 157. After the Treaty of Campo Formio (1797) which
ended Bonaparte's Italian campaign against the Austrians,
the Directoire government in France installed General
Bernadotte (1763–1844) in this palace as ambassador. (Jean
Bernadotte, a sergeant under Louis XVI, became an imperial
marshal under Napoleon and ended his life as King of
Sweden.) On his arrival in April 1798, the new ambassador
raised a Revolutionary tricolor flag on the building so
huge that it hung to the ground; the Viennese, who
were still smarting from Austria's defeats in Italy and
from the execution of Marie-Antoinette, immediately
tore it down, and Bernadotte left the city in disgrace.
The small street linking Wallnerstrasse to
Herrengasse is called Flag Street (Fahnengasse).

FREYUNG

This triangular-shaped square is one of the biggest in Vienna,
along with the Graben ▲ 137, Am Hof ▲ 166 and Hoher
Markt ▲ 155. Its name (*frei* means "free") evokes the right of
asylum which was accorded strangers and thieves – but not to
other criminals – who took refuge in the Scottish convent.

AUSTRIABRUNNEN. In the middle of the square is the Austria
Fountain (1846), made by the German Ludwig Schwanthaler.
Its various sculptures represent the principal rivers which
crossed the Austrian Empire: the Elbe, the Danube ● 20-1,
● 230, 271, the Vistula and the Po.

SCHOTTENKIRCHE. The buildings known respectively as the
Scottish Church and the Scottish Monastery (Schottenkirche
and Schottenstift) were actually founded by Irish Benedictine
monks at the beginning of the 12th century. This confusion
may be explained by the fact that the great Irish
missionary organization founded by
St Columba in the 6th century
originated on the island of
Iona off the northwest

**THE AUSTRIA
FOUNTAIN**
Goethe's
grand-daughter ▲ 222
is said to have posed
for the statue of
Austria (above). The
story has it that the
sculptor hid
contraband tobacco
in the fountain's
hollow figures but
arrived too late to
remove it: so that it is
there to this day!

The Freyung ● 96,
painted by R. Bernt
(1906).

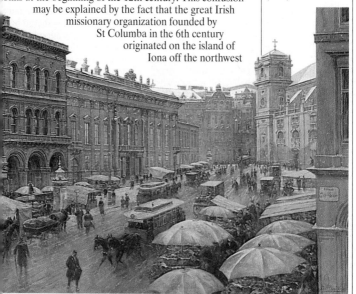

THE SCHOTTENSTIFT SCHOOL
"Whenever I meet a man with the slightly nasal, slightly snobbish accent of the old Schotten-gymnasium, I am rather attracted to him, in spite of myself."

Konrad Lorenz,
On Aggression

THE DEATH OF HAYDN
A mass was said on June 15, 1809, in memory of Haydn ● 49, ▲ 152, 162, who died on May 31 and was buried a few days later; Vienna, under siege by the French army, had just capitulated ● 38. This event overshadowed the death of the great composer in the eyes of the Viennese, but the French remembered that Haydn had been a corresponding member of the Institut Français and insisted that homage be accorded him. As an officer with the French army, Henri Beyle (the future Stendhal) took part in the Austrian campaign and attended this memorial service, which inspired him to write one of his first literary works, *Letter on Haydn*, in 1814.

coast of Scotland. From Iona a large number of missionaries spread out all over Europe, including these Benedictines, who stopped a while at Ratisbon in Germany before being summoned to Vienna by the Babenberg Duke Henry II Jasomirgott. The religious buildings of the Schottenkirche started off in Romanesque style and were then altered in the 14th, 15th and 17th centuries to the Gothic and Baroque styles. With its white and yellow rendering, the church we see today seems very sober for a Baroque building, with the exception of the onion-domed belltower soaring over the apse ● 76. Inside there are many handsome works of art, notably two 17th-century altarpieces by Tobias Pock and Joachim Sandrart, and a Baroque memorial by J. B. Fischer von Erlach ● 74, 80 to Count Rüdiger von Starhemberg, who defended Vienna against the Turks ● 31 ▲ 142. The statue of the Virgin in the church is venerated as miraculous by the Viennese and is the oldest Madonna in the city (c. 1250). In the crypt are the tombs of Duke Henry II Jasomirgott and his wife, the church's founders.

SCHOTTENSTIFT. The Scottish monastery is laid out around a large shady courtyard, the Schottenhof, which is shared by café terraces, restaurants, and a famous private school. The PICTURE GALLERY in this monastery possesses a number of masterpieces ranging from the 15th to the 19th centuries the star exhibit is a large GOTHIC ALTARPIECE painted by Tobias Pock and Joachim Sandrart at the end of the 15th century.

FRANZ LISZT'S HOUSE. The house in which the Hungarian musician Franz Liszt (1811–86) stayed when he visited Vienna for concerts and piano recitals also looks out onto the SCHOTTENHOF, which, like the Gothic-vaulted CAFÉ HAAG, is a real haven of peace.

THE DAUN-KINSKY PALACE. Johann Lukas von Hildebrandt ● 75, 81, who was to build the Belvedere ▲ 246, 256 shortly afterward, constructed one of his most beautiful buildings, the Daun-Kinsky Palace, on the Freyung in 1716. The façade is particularly refined, with a multitude of decorated pilasters and statues in addition to windows with carefully sculpted diments. The porch, which resembles a triumphal arch with its high columns and figures of atlantes ▲ *157, 163* leads through to an oval vestibule with a fine staircase and statues, and then to more courtyards.

THE HARRACH PALACE. On the corner of Freyung and the Herrengasse is the Ferstel Palace: next to it stands the Harrach Palace, which dates from the 17th century.

KUNST-FORUM. An extension of the Schottenkirche is the former monastery PRIORY built at the end of the 18th century; this is nicknamed the "commode" on account of its shape. Opposite stands the Kunst-Forum, a recently converted gallery which regularly stages exhibitions of contemporary art. Its décor is inspired by the Secession style ● *86, 88,* ▲ *232.*

HENRY II JASOMIRGOTT
Henry II inherited the Duchy of Bavaria and Austria from his brother Leopold IV von Babenberg in 1141. Frederick Barbarossa ● *28* made Austria a hereditary duchy in 1158, in exchange for Bavaria. Henry II became the first Duke of Austria in 1156, and founded the Scottish monastery in the same year.

RENNGASSE

THE BATTHYÁNY-SCHÖNBORN PALACE. In Renngasse, which begins between the "commode" and the Kunst-Forum, stands the handsome Batthyány-Schönborn Palace, converted by J. B. Fischer von Erlach ● *80,* ▲ *147, 247.* This mansion with its imposing sculpted façade used to the Vienna residence of the great Hungarian Batthyány mily, one of whose members, Charles-Joseph (1698–1772), rved as a general under Prince Eugène ● *35,* ▲ *147, 247* and bsequently commissioned this palace. Franz Schubert ● *50, 227* very rarely gave concerts, but one of them was at the rmer *Roman Emperor* Hotel across the street from the atthyány-Schönborn Palace. Schubert, who was only twenty-e at the time, played the *Complaint of the Shepherd,* spired by a text from Goethe.

OHENSTAUFENGASSE. This street, which crosses the enngasse, heads westward to the vicinity of the Stock xchange ▲ *201*, cutting across the Schottenring. The street ntains two remarkable buildings: the LANDERBANK, built in 82 by Otto Wagner ● *86, 88,* ▲ *228, 237, 240, 294* and the LAW FACULTY (Juridicum), an imposing construction dating from the 1970's.

THE FREYUNG
Fêtes and popular entertainments were held on the Freyung ● *96,* ▲ *163,* as well as the executions of traitors, who were drowned face down in a barrel of water.

MÖLKERBASTEI

MELKER HOF. The Melker Hof
the Vienna residence of the
Abbots of Melk, is on
Schottengasse. It was built in
the 15th century and altered i
the 18th, and includes a 16th-
century CHAPEL adorned with
frescoes by Johann Bergl
▲ *180, 278* and a painting by
Kremser Schmidt. It also has
Weinstube which serves wines
from Melk. Across the end o
Schottengasse runs the Ring
▲ *202*, with the Schottentor at the intersection.

PASQUALATIHAUS ★. Dominating the Ring is the
MÖLKERBASTEI, a remnant of the old ramparts ▲ *198* which
includes two or three outstanding buildings, especially the
Pasqualatihaus or Beethovenhaus, where Beethoven lived
● *51*, ▲ *298*. While he was here (between 1804 and 1815) the
composer wrote several masterpieces, among them the oper
Fidelio and the *Fourth* and *Fifth Symphonies*. A small museu
in this building displays scores, drawings and engravings fror
this period. Another major Viennese personality, Adalbert
Stifter resided in the building after Beethoven; examples of
his drawings and manuscripts are kept in a small separate
museum.

DREIMÄDERLHAUS. West of the Mölkerbastei, adjoining the
Pasqualitihaus in the little Schreyvogelgasse, stands the
handsome House of the Three Maidens (Dreimädlerhaus),
a Biedermeier ● *62* building in the early 19th-century
neo-Renaissance style. The windows of the façade are
embellished with garlands, as is the doorway with its twin
sculpted columns.

AM HOF

Am Hof is the largest square in central
Vienna. This "Royal Court" square earned
its name in the 12th century when
the Eastern Marches
(Ostmark) were transformed
into the Duchy of Austria by
Emperor Frederick
Barbarossa ● *28*. When the
first Duke, the Babenberg
Henry II Jasomirgott, moved
to Vienna ▲ *165* with his
court, he constructed a
palace on this square. Today
there is no trace of the
original Babenberg residence,
even though extensive
remains of the Roman camp
that once stood here have
been discovered in the
course of archaeological
excavations.

Mariensäule and Kirche Am Hof. In
the center of the square is the Virgin's
pillar (Mariensäule), sculpted with small
angels battling against the four scourges
of mankind: the plague (a basilisk),
heresy (a serpent), war (a lion) and
famine (a dragon). The Kirche
Am Hof, the great Church of
the Nine Choirs of Angels (zu
den neun Chören der Engel),
dominates the square. Built by
the Carmelites during the 14th
and 15th centuries in the
Gothic style, the church
today has a Baroque façade
heavily influenced by Rome.
It was altered in the 17th
century by the Italian
architect Carlo Antonio
Carlone ● 77 at the request
of the Jesuits who eventually took it
over from the Carmelites. Carlone
belonged to a family of Genoese sculptors and painters who
had worked on the decoration of several different churches in
Rome (including the Gesú). Joseph II appeared on the
balcony of this church to announce the end of the Holy
Roman Empire in 1806 ● 38, ▲ 176, 179; he thus became the
first hereditary Emperor of Austria, with the title of Joseph I.
Inside the church the best features are a magnificent organ
loft, some fine frescoes by Franz Anton Maulbertsch
(1724–96), J. J. Daringer's altarpiece at the high altar, and the
ceiling of the chapel of St Ignatius painted by the Italian
Jesuit Andrea Pozzo (1642–1709) ▲ 149, 152, 292, who also
decorated the Jesuit, or University Church.

Collalto Palace. To the north of the Am Hof square, on the
same side as the Kirche Am Hof and linked to it by a buttress,
stands the 17th–18th century Collalto Palace. Mozart held his
first concert here in 1762, at the age of six ● 48, ▲ 147, 281.

Bürgerliches Zeughaus ★. This thoroughly eccentric,
lavishly decorated fire station occupies the northwest corner
of the square. The firemen based here are quartered in
the old town arsenal (Bürgerliches Zeughaus), built
in the 16th century and converted to the Baroque
style ● 80, 82 by Anton Ospel at the
beginning of the 18th century. Apart from
the firemen's quarters and the fire-engine
garage, the barracks contain an interesting
FIREFIGHTING MUSEUM (Feuerwehr-
museum).

Roman remains. In the building next to the
fire station (no. 9) one can see remains of
the Roman camp of Vindobona, the original
city of Vienna ● 29.

Märkleinisches Haus. The original
Babenberg castle was sited at what is
now no. 7 Am Hof Square. After its
demolition, the Märkleinisches Haus
was built here to plans by Johann Lukas
von Hildebrandt ● 75, 81, ▲ 147, 247.

THE FIRE STATION
The Baroque-style
fire station with a
Greek pediment is
decorated with
sculptures by Lorenzo
Mattielli.

**MOZART AT THE
COLLALTO PALACE**
Leopold Mozart,
father of Wolfgang,
organized a
European tour to
"show the world a
miracle". The little
prodigy, Wolfgang
Amadeus, left his
native town of
Salzburg with his
sister Nannerl and his
father in 1762. After
passing through Ips,
Passau and Linz, the
Mozarts came to
Vienna, where they
gave a concert at the
Collalto Palace and
were received at
Schönbrunn ▲ 274.

JUDENPLATZ
A long time before World War Two, Vienna's Jewish community had been subjected to a series of brutal pogroms. The pogrom of 1421 removed all the buildings formerly occupied by Jews – their shops, schools, synagogue and the rabbi's house – from the Judenplatz (right). This occurred during the reign of Archduke Albert V the Illustrious, Holy Roman Emperor and the first Habsburg to assume the crown of Hungary.

Another example of this architect's particular style can be seen at no. 12.

SCHULHOF

The tiny Schulhof square behind the Kirche Am Hof is connected to Am Hof square by a covered passageway.
OBIZZI PALACE. This superb 17th-century mansion takes up the whole south side of the square. A CLOCK MUSEUM (Uhrenmuseum) and more recently a DOLL AND TOY MUSEUM (Puppen- und Spielzeug-Museum ◆ 332) have been

established here. In the former, the entire recent history of the clock is recounted through a display that covers several floors. Among other things, you can see the old cathedral clock, a 17th-century astronomical wall clock, small traveling clocks, painted and automatic timepieces, cuckoo clocks, wristwatches and precious fob watches, and several chiming clocks.
BEYOND THE SCHULHOF. Vienna's oldest restaurant, the GOLDEN DRAGON (*Haus zum Güldenen Drachen*), has been at no. 4 Steindlgasse since the 16th century. Steindlgasse leads on to Tuchlauben and Milchgasse, which in turn leads to Peterskirche ▲ 139. Kurrentgasse, a small street frequented by horse-drawn carriages and lined by 18th-century buildings, leads to the Judenplatz.

JUDENPLATZ

The Judenplatz is a small, narrow and particularly calm square that retains no traces of its days as the center of the Jewish ghetto.

> "He had a taste for Jewish stories and told them with wicked glee. The prefect didn't understand them, but still he said: 'Very good, Very good indeed!'"
>
> Joseph Roth

AUS ZUM GROSSEN JORDAN. To commemorate the
auto-da-fé that took place during the 1421 pogrom, a bas-
relief of the Baptism of Christ was carved on the House of the
Great Jordan (Haus zum grossen Jordan), a house built in the
14th century on the ghetto ruins. At no. 8 stands the HOUSE
OF THE TAILORS' GUILD, while no. 11 is one of the façades of
the former Chancellery of Bohemia, the entrance to which is
in Wipplingerstrasse.

JORDANGASSE

The tiny Jordangasse connects
Judenplatz with Wipplingerstrasse.
The great Baroque architect Johann
Bernhard Fischer von Erlach ● *74, 80,*
▲ *147, 155, 164, 169, 275, 302* died at
no. 5.

WIPPLINGERSTRASSE

EHEMALIGE BÖHMISCHE HOFKANZLEI★.
The former Chancellery of Bohemia
(Ehemalige Böhmische Hofkanzlei) at
no. 7 Wipplingerstrasse (built 1708–14)
was one of J.B. Fischer von Erlach's
major triumphs. After its enlargement
by Matthias Gerl in 1750, all that
remained of the original building was its
superb façade (1708) in a classical,
almost Palladian style interwoven with
French and Italian Baroque motifs.

ALTES RATHAUS. Facing the Bohemian Chancellery, the old
City Hall (Altes Rathaus) is yet another piece of magnificent
Baroque architecture. The original building here, which dated
from the Middle Ages, was given to the municipal authorities
by Frederick II the Handsome, Duke of
Austria (1286–1330), after it had been
confiscated from Otto Heims for his part in
the assassination plot against Albert I,
Duke Frederick's father. Reconstructed
at the beginning of the 18th century, the
Rathaus served as Vienna's City Hall
▲ *204* until 1883, when it was relocated
to a new building.

FREDERICK THE HANDSOME. Son of the
Habsburg Duke Albert I of Austria,
Frederick II the Handsome succeeded his
brother Rudolph II the Debonair in
1307. On the death of the Holy Roman
Emperor, Henry II of Luxembourg, in
1313, Frederick stood for election to his
throne, eventually resorting to arms to
defeat his rivals. He was finally defeated
at the battle of Mühldorf, where Ludwig IV
of Bavaria, who subsequently reigned as Emperor from 1314
to 1347, took him prisoner. After swearing on oath to cause
no more trouble, Frederick was reconciled with Ludwig, who
released him and even nominated him his deputy when he
went on a trip to Italy in 1326.

A house in
Kurrentgasse.

**TWO HOUSES
ASSOCIATED WITH
MOZART**
Mozart lived for a
time in nos. 3 and 4
Judenplatz: in the
former in 1783, a few
months after his
marriage to
Constanze Weber;
and in the latter from
1789 to 1790, the year
before his death ● *48,*
▲ *110, 147, 281.*

**THE BAPTISM OF
CHRIST**
(At no. 2 Judenplatz)
"By baptism in the
Jordan, the body is
washed clean of all
sin. Even secret
thoughts of sin
disappear. In 1421, a
thirst for vengeance
gripped the city, that
the Hebrew dogs
might expiate their
frightful crimes. Once
upon a time the world
was purified by the
flood: this time, the
evil was carried away
by fire."
    Inscription on the
    Haus zum grosse
    Jordan

THE BOHEMIAN CHANCELLERY
J. B. Fischer von Erlach installed dozens of ornamental features on the façade of this building (at top), including statues (figures of Atlas on either side of doors and windows) and ironwork (a wrought iron balcony is located above the doorway). All the statuary is by Lorenzo Mattielli ● 80.

THE OLD CITY HALL
The Altes Rathaus was built in 1699 by an unknown architect. The façade is in the style of J.B. Fischer von Erlach, with handsome doors framed by columns and allegorical figures of Justice and Bounty, by Johann Michael Fischer. These lead through to the courtyard (entrance at no. 8). A detail of the exterior is shown (right).

MUSEUM OF THE RESISTANCE. Several rooms inside the old City Hall are used as an archive center and record details of the Austrian resistance before and during World War Two. This museum sheds light on a number of little-known episodes in modern Austrian history. From 1934 onward, under the authoritarian rule of Engelbert Dollfuss and Kurt von Schuschnigg, numerous Austrians of every political and ethnic persuasion joined together to form a patriotic front, a kind of union against the German takeover of their country. was this union that forced Schuschnigg to organize the referendum on Austrian independence, which enraged Hitle and led him to unleash "Operation Otto", the military invasion of Austria and the proclamation of the Anschluss in March 1938 ● 42. During the war, the resistance went underground to organize acts of sabotage against the occupying Germans and guerrilla operations in the mountai of Styria, Carinthia, the Tyrol and Salzburg. With the help of Tito's Yugoslav partisans, they fought tenaciously against the divisions of the German "SS" and at the end of the war took possession of most of Austria's cities (with the exception of Vienna, which was occupied by the Soviet Army), thus thwarting the scorched-earth tactics of the SS. Nevertheless Austria paid a heavy price during the war: 3,000 resistance members were executed, 17,000 Austrians were taken hostag or killed in Gestapo prisons across Europe, and 140,000 others, particularly Jews, perished in concentration camps. I the total is taken to include all the soldiers who were killed fighting for the Wehrmacht and the large numbers of civilian killed by bombs, more than 600,000 Austrians lost their lives during World War Two.

ANDROMEDABRUNNEN ★. In the courtyard here stands a min masterpiece of Baroque sculpture: the Fountain of Andromeda (Andromedabrunnen) by Georg Raphael Donner ▲ 141, 304, which dates from 1741 (three years afte the Fountain of Providence on the Neuer Markt, also by

Donner ▲ 141). The Fountain of Andromeda represents Andromeda delivered by Perseus from the sea monster. A master of Baroque sculpture, Donner was trained in Italy before going to work in Strasbourg, Bratislava and Vienna. I addition to the Fountain of Andromeda and the Neuer Mar Fountain, he created several groups of statues which are nov on display at the Museum of Baroque Art ▲ 249 in the Low Belvedere.

TIEFER GRABEN

In Roman times, Vindobona was a small square of land surrounded on three sides by moats filled with water and on

THE FOUNTAIN OF ANDROMEDA
Framed by small angels perched on columns and with its own wrought iron balcony is a niche containing a sculpted group by Georg Raphael Donner (1693–1741). Andromeda was rescued by Perseus from the sea monster that was going to eat her. Cassiopeia, wife of Cepheus, King of Ethiopia, had proclaimed that she and Andromeda were more beautiful than the Nereids. Poseidon in fury created a monster that began to ravage the coasts. To make an example of Andromeda, he ordered that she should be tied to a rock in the monster's path. Once rescued, she married her savior.

THE ALSBACH
On the wall of a house on the Heidenschuss, a little square south of the Tiefer Graben, a plaque over the figure of a mounted Turk marks the place where the Alsbach was once forded.

MOZART AND BEETHOVEN
Mozart ● *48*, ▲ *147, 281* lived at no. 18 Tiefer Graben with his father Leopold during their third visit to Vienna. Then age seventeen, the composer had come from Salzburg to try for the position of music master of the court chapel. His candidacy failed, but Mozart used the time in Vienna to write six string quartets and a serenade. Beethoven ● *51*, ▲ *298* lived at nos. 8 and 10 at various times.

e fourth by the Danube. One of these moats was the
raben ▲ *137*, which connected with the Tiefer Graben (the
Deep Moat") through which flowed the Alsbach, a small
ibutary of the Danube. This river has been filled in since the
Middle Ages, and today the Tiefer Graben is a
broad thoroughfare which starts at the Freyung
and continues past the Church of Maria
am Gestade.

HOHER BRÜCKE. The metal Upper
Bridge (Hoher Brücke) across the
Tiefer Graben is a graceful
Jugendstil ● *86* work of art,
embellished with a number of
elegant floral garlands that
are in that style. Designed
by Joseph Hackhofer and
Karl Christl, the
bridge was completed
in 1903.

MARIA AM GESTADE ★.
The spire of the church of
Maria am Gestade, one
of Austria's loveliest
Gothic buildings, towers
over the Tiefer Graben.
Known as Our Lady of
the Steps (Maria

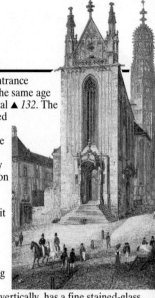

C.-M. HOFBAUER
A member of the congregation of the Holy Redeemer, the Bohemian Klemens Maria Hofbauer (1751–1820) instigated a Catholic renewal in Vienna at the beginning of the 19th century. His was a reaction against "Josephism", the politics of Joseph II, whose aim was to reduce the influence of the Pope and encourage religious toleration (notably of Jews and Protestants). His tomb is in the Church of Maria am Gestade.

THE PORTAL OF THE SALVATORKAPELLE
The two statues of knights in arms here are copies: the originals are kept in the Art History Museum ▲ 208.

Stiege) because of its entrance stairway, the church is the same age as St Stephen's Cathedral ▲ 132. The present building replaced a wooden Romanesque chapel which was a place of worship for the Danube boatmen: today the church's congregation is mostly Czech. Originally designed by Meister Michael Knab, it was restored on several different occasions, the belltower in particular being rebuilt after the damage sustained during the siege of 1683 ● 34.
The façade, which rises vertically, has a fine stained-glass window, a pediment and two slender sculpted pinnacles. The doorway is crowned by a stone baldachin and enlivened by a bas-relief representing John the Evangelist and John the Baptist. The interior of the church is surprisingly narrow, while the nave is set at an angle to the choir, because the builders were obliged to adapt themselves to the cramped urban conditions of the Middle Ages. The church, which is lit by 14th-century stained-glass windows, possesses several Gothic altarpieces (SAINT CLEMENT-MARIA CHAPEL), a fine organ case, and a Renaissance altar (ST JOHN'S CHAPEL). An anonymous painting of *The Annunciation* ★, dating from the 14th or 15th century, is alone worth the detour to Maria am Gestade.

SALVATORGASSE

This small street links Maria am Gestade with the Hoher Markt ▲ 155. The doorway of the SALVATORKAPELLE ● 74, at no. 5, built in 1530, is one of the very few examples of the Renaissance style in Vienna.

The Hofburg

THE DOME OF THE MICHAELERTO...
Baroque and neo-classical are the predominan...
architectural styles of the Imperial Palac...

The portal statues by
the early 18th-century
Baroque sculptor
Lorenzo Mattielli
● *80* represent the
Fall of the Angels.

THE HOFBURG ✪
The Hofburg is a
great labyrinth in
which countless
treasures are to be
found. A single visit
will hardly do it
justice. On the first
day, priority should
be given to the
imperial apartments,
then to the museums
and the churches.

**HERCULES AND THE
NEMEAN LION**
The Michaelertor is
embellished with
columns, balconies
and statues depicting
the labors of
Hercules. Like those
on the Michaeler-
kirche, the statues are
by Mattielli.

MICHAELERPLATZ

St Michael's Square (Michaelerplatz) stands at the
intersection of Vienna's two most elegant streets, Kohlmarkt
▲ *158* and Herrengasse ▲ *159*. The square leads to the
entrance of the Imperial Palace (the Hofburg). Roman
archeological remains excavated recently stand as evidence c
the earliest human occupation of this site, though they also
disfigure it to some degree.

MICHAELERKIRCHE. Acting as a foil to the Loos House, the
Church of St Michael (Michaelerkirche) has none of the
latter's stylistic unity. Initially a Romanesque building, it was
subsequently given a Gothic choir and belltower, a Baroque
portal and a stark neo-classical façade, with the only
ornament provided by pilasters. Inside the church, where the
imperial court once worshiped, there is a Baroque high altar
as well as vestiges of Romanesque frescoes and a Gothic
painting of Christ scourged (*Ecce Homo*, 1430). Also here is
the tomb of the Italian poet Metastasio ▲ *161*, who was a
friend of Haydn ● *49*, ▲ *152, 162, 164* and Mozart's librettist
● *48*, ▲ *147, 281*.

AN OSSUARY. The crypt of the church is somewhat macabre:
the whole area is strewn with bones and there are several
hundred coffins, several of which are open.

LOOSHAUS. No building in Vienna has provoked as mu...
controversy as the Looshaus, completed in
1911 at no. 3 Michaelerplatz. Franz-Joseph
thought it so ugly that he had the
curtains drawn in all the windows of
his palace looking out on to the
square! Nevertheless the simple,
functional style that Adolf Loos
(1870–1933) launched with this
building was destined to take the
world by storm. The building
clashes less than its critics would
claim with the rest of the
architecture on the square; using
fine materials such as green marble,
Loos constructed a colonnade which
matched those of the church and

> "The empire is built in the style of its houses –
> uninhabitable, but pretty."

Karl Kraus

t Michael's Gate. What is new about the building – apart from its deliberately austere outline – is the clear division of its functions. The ground floor and the mezzanine, which are in colored marble, were designed to contain shops and offices, while the four bare, white floors above were intended for apartments. As one becomes more familiar with the Looshaus, one gradually comes to appreciate the harmonious, muted tones of its façade. The use of veined marble in its lower portion gives it a discreet mobility to what would otherwise appear squat and foursquare.

"CAFÉ GRIENDSTEIDL". Reopened in 1992 at no. 2 Michaelerplatz after having closed in 1897, the *Café Griensteidl*, along with the *Central* ▲ *160* and the HERRENHOF, used to be a favored haunt of the great writers Arthur Schnitzler, Hugo von Hoffmannsthal, Herman Broch and Karl Kraus. To these "theaters of life", as Peter Altenberg ● *67* called them, came the musicians Hugo Wolf, Arnold Schönberg and Alban Berg ● *52*, the architect Loos, and even the revolutionary Leon Trotsky, all determined to remake the world. Most of the time, these were no more than "café revolutions". The new *Café Griensteidl* offers a discreet, genteel atmosphere, far from the smoky ambience of the time of Kraus's "joyous apocalypse".

MICHAELERTOR. The emperor and his family entered their private apartments, as well as the formal rooms of the palace, by way of the monumental Michaelertor ▲ *180*. The *dome* ▲ *174, 181* atop this gate forms a golden band above the entry porch. Beyond the door is a vestibule in the shape of a rotunda from which stairways lead to the imperial apartments and to the court collection of china and silver ▲ *186*.

THE HOFBURG

The buildings of the Imperial Palace (the Hofburg) seem to be laid out in no particular order. After the construction of the first palace by Rudolph I in the 13th century, his successors enlarged it without any coherent plan, tending at the same time to make alterations in the styles of their own times. Nevertheless, the architecture here is predominantly Baroque and neo-classical.

THE LOOSHAUS ● *86, 90*, ▲ *174, 236* "A building without eyebrows!" was the verdict of the Viennese on the Looshaus. Karl Kraus said of it, "That's not a house he has built for us, but a thought."

MICHAELERTOR
Built like a Roman triumphal arch, the Michaelertor was the main entrance to the Hofburg Palace in Habsburg times, guarded by soldiers who kept the public out. A superb wrought iron awning spreads over the porch. Inside are allegorical statues of the imperial mottoes: "Justice and Clemency" (Maria Theresa) ● *36*, "By Courage and Example" (Joseph II ● *36*), "By United Strength" (Franz-Joseph ● *41*).

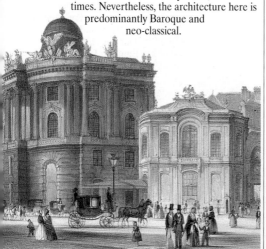

▲ THE HOFBURG

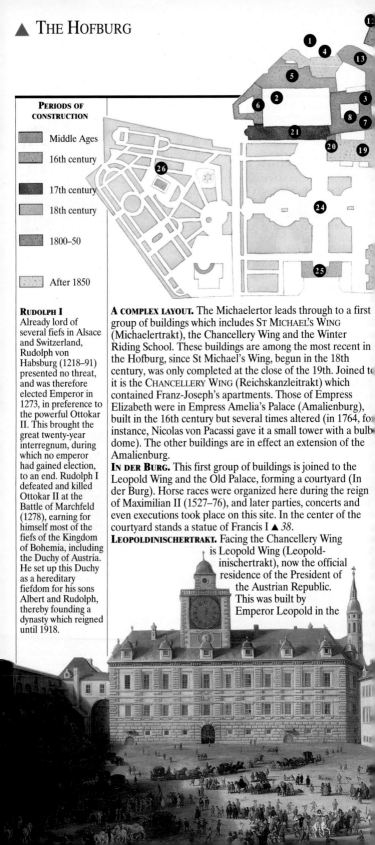

RUDOLPH I
Already lord of several fiefs in Alsace and Switzerland, Rudolph von Habsburg (1218–91) presented no threat, and was therefore elected Emperor in 1273, in preference to the powerful Ottokar II. This brought the great twenty-year interregnum, during which no emperor had gained election, to an end. Rudolph I defeated and killed Ottokar II at the Battle of Marchfeld (1278), earning for himself most of the fiefs of the Kingdom of Bohemia, including the Duchy of Austria. He set up this Duchy as a hereditary fiefdom for his sons Albert and Rudolph, thereby founding a dynasty which reigned until 1918.

A COMPLEX LAYOUT. The Michaelertor leads through to a first group of buildings which includes ST MICHAEL'S WING (Michaelertrakt), the Chancellery Wing and the Winter Riding School. These buildings are among the most recent in the Hofburg, since St Michael's Wing, begun in the 18th century, was only completed at the close of the 19th. Joined to it is the CHANCELLERY WING (Reichskanzleitrakt) which contained Franz-Joseph's apartments. Those of Empress Elizabeth were in Empress Amelia's Palace (Amalienburg), built in the 16th century but several times altered (in 1764, for instance, Nicolas von Pacassi gave it a small tower with a bulb dome). The other buildings are in effect an extension of the Amalienburg.

IN DER BURG. This first group of buildings is joined to the Leopold Wing and the Old Palace, forming a courtyard (In der Burg). Horse races were organized here during the reign of Maximilian II (1527–76), and later parties, concerts and even executions took place on this site. In the center of the courtyard stands a statue of Francis I ▲ 38.

LEOPOLDINISCHERTRAKT. Facing the Chancellery Wing is Leopold Wing (Leopold-inischertrakt), now the official residence of the President of the Austrian Republic. This was built by Emperor Leopold in the

Baroque style at the end of the 17th century. His granddaughter Maria Theresa lived here.

ALTE BURG. This palace, originally a stronghold, has been substantially altered. Several monarchs stayed there and, in the 19th century, the apartments were converted for the use of important guests, including Marshal Radetzky ▲ 143, 179. One passes from here through the SWISS COURTYARD (Schweizerhof) to the Palace Chapel of the Assumption (Burgkapelle) and treasury. The old palace is here extended by a group of buildings which includes the BALLROOM WING (Redoutensaaltrakt), the WINTER RIDING SCHOOL ▲ 190 (next the SUMMER RIDING SCHOOL) and the stables ▲ 188.

...WARD THE ALBERTINA. The STATE RECEPTION WING (Prunksaaltrakt), now the Austrian National Library, links the ballroom wing to the AUGUSTINIAN WING (Augustinertrakt), and forms the square of Josefsplatz. The latter wing is continued on one side by the hothouses, on the other by the Church of the Augustinians and the Albertina.

FESTSAALTRAKT. The Festsaaltrakt, which connects the Leopold Wing, the Old Palace and the New Palace, has been a convention center since ...58. It includes the reception hall (Festsaal) and the ...REMONIAL HALL (Zeremoniensaal), both former ...rone-rooms. The center also makes use of rooms ...the Leopold Wing (the Secret Council Room and ...e Marble Room), the Old Palace (the Knights' and ...lberdiers' Rooms, and the Radetzky ...artments) and the ballroom wing. Balls are ...en held here ● 58.

...UE BURG. Even more imposing than the rest of ...e Hofburg is the New Palace (Neue Burg), which ...ends right out to the Ring ● 84, ▲ 197. This ...o-Renaissance building (in the style of the Ring) ...uilt on a curve. There is a colonnade along the ...ond-floor gallery; the first-floor statuary tells of ...strian history, with likenesses of a Marcoman (a ...mber of the tribe that inhabited Austria in ...tiquity), a Roman legionnaire, a missionary ...obably Irish), a Slav, a Frankish noble, a ...agyar, a Crusader, a Lansquenet (a 16th-century ...rman foot-soldier), a Pole and a Tyrolean. The Neue Burg ...o houses the collections of the Ephesus Museum and the ...hnography Museum, along with certain departments of the ...strian National Library.

...IE IMPERIAL APARTMENTS

...e Leopold Wing (Leopoldinischertrakt) where Maria ...eresa lived is closed to the public, since it is the residence ...the President of the Republic. On the other hand, the

⏳ Half a day

◆ A C1-C2-D1-D2

THE BURNING OF THE REDOUTENSAAL
In November 1992, a fire swept through the Redoutensaal, the theater converted into a ballroom complex by Nicolas von Pacassi which was used for the imperial court's great entertainments and gala dinners. These rooms had served as a conference and congress center in more recent times; the Hunters' Ball and Redoutensaal Ball were both held here ● 58.

THE SCHWEIZERTOR
The Swiss gate leads from the main In der Burg courtyard to the

Swiss courtyard. It was built in 1522 as part of the façade of the Old Palace and survived Ferdinand I's (1503–64) alterations to the Hofburg during the Renaissance. The Habsburg eagle perches over it.

A ROYAL GYMNAST
The copper bath full of cold water into which Sissi ▲ 143, 144 plunged at 5 am each day, is perhaps less surprising than the toilet room with its wooden gymnastic fittings (below). Sissi ate very little, took frequent massages and practised gymnastics, walking and riding. This enabled her to retain a waistline

that was the envy of all throughout her life.

SISSI
"Tall and slender as she is, her movements are so noble and so natural that their grace is at once royal and animal. Beneath the mass of her chestnut hair, her little head might be that of a Greek goddess, were it not for the intense vitality which animates the perfection of her features, glitters in her shy, tender eyes, and in her magnetic glance with its nuances of sweetness and irony, audacity and modesty, dreaminess, gaiety and pity."

Comte de
Saint-Aulaire
(French Ambassador
to Vienna, 1882-91),
Franz-Joseph

apartments of Franz-Joseph I and Empress Elizabeth in the Chancellery wing (Reichskanzleitrakt), built in the 18th century by J. B. Fischer von Erlach ● 74, 80, ▲ 138, 147 and Johann Lukas von Hildebrandt ● 75, 81, ▲ 147 have been turned into a museum. This wing, overlooking the courtyard, was used as the offices of the Imperial Chancellery until 1806, when it was converted into apartments for Archduchess Maria Louisa. Her son the "Aiglon" ▲ 283 lived here, as well as at Schönbrunn, in his final years. Some of the rooms on the first floor were also occupied during the early years of Franz-Joseph's reign by his cousin Archduke Stephen, Palatine of Hungary. The Archduke lived here from 1848 to 1867: nowadays the apartments serve predominantly as reminders of the time of Franz-Joseph.

KAISERAPPARTEMENTS. These can be reached by way of the Michaelertor and the IMPERIAL STAIRCASE (Kaiserstiege), which leads from the rotunda to the first floor. This staircase looked on to the Halberdiers' Room (Trabantenstube). After the antechamber comes the suite of rooms said to be those of Archduke Stephen. The DINING ROOM (Speisezimmer) was where Franz-Joseph convened his general staff: the walls are covered with 16th-century Flemish tapestries illustrating the *Labors of Hercules*. After dinner, the officers would move into the CIRCLE ROOM (Cerclezimmer), hung with tapestries from Brussels of the life of the Roman Emperor Augustus, or else into the SMOKING ROOM (Rauchsalon), similarly decorated with tapestries and with a bust of Maximilian I. Immediately adjoining are the emperor's private apartments. In the HALBERDIERS' ROOM (Trabantenstube), the former bedroom of the "Aiglon", are a bust of Charles V and a scale model of the Old Hofburg. The AUDIENCE HALL

> "Like the Empress Sissi, her idol, the young girl used to jump with a mad briskness, spent hours in the stables and, like her model, had ridden the emperor's three hundred horses bareback."

> Paul Morand

Audienzsaal and Audienzzimmer) is lit by a huge Bohemian glass chandelier and decorated with frescoes of the life of Francis I ● 38 by Peter Krafft. In its corners are a bust of Francis I, and another of Franz-Joseph aged twenty-three. Franz-Joseph used to give audiences here twice a week. His aide-de-camp would summon petitioners one by one from the Audienszaal, and they would then be conducted to the Emperor's smaller audience chamber (Audienzzimmer) by his chamberlain, where Franz-Joseph awaited them. He stood behind a kind of lectern; the list of audiences appointed for January 3, 1910, still lies open on its top. On the walls of the chamber are portraits of Francis I, Ferdinand I and Franz-Joseph himself, aged forty-three. Franz-Joseph presided over his Council of Ministers in the COUNCIL CHAMBER (Konferenzzimmer). A portrait of him aged twenty hangs on the wall. The door at the back of the room gives on to the EMPEROR'S WARDROBE (Kaisergarderobe), which was the responsibility of his chamberlain, Ketterl. Franz-Joseph was always to be found wearing military uniform.

The EMPEROR'S BEDROOM (Schlafzimmer) is astonishing in its spartan simplicity. Above the small iron bedstead hang four portraits of his beloved wife Sissi, along with one of Archduchess Sophia, his mother, with Franz-Joseph himself aged two. On the side tables are busts of his parents. In the GRAND SALON (Grosser Salon, Kleiner Salon) are the famous portraits of Franz-Joseph and Sissi by Franz Xaver Winterhalter. The Small Salon (Kleiner Salon), which was used as a smoking room, contains an assortment of

souvenirs and a painting of Maximilian. Following on from the Emperor's apartments, those of the Empress occupy space in the AMALIENBURG, the Palace of Joseph I's widow, Empress Amelia (1678–1711), where Czar Alexander I resided during the Congress of Vienna ● 38. Like her husband, Sissi was content to sleep on an iron

From top to bottom: The dining room, the red salon (or Boucher Salon), the salon and bedroom of the Empress, and the Grand Salon.

179

bedstead, which was taken out each
morning to make more room in the
EMPRESS' SALON AND BEDROOM
(Wohn und Schlafenzimmer der
Kaiserin). In this beautiful room i
the Empress' small desk along with
her oratory, a Madonna ensconced
in a kind of Gothic niche. After the
bathroom (Badezimmer) and the
TOILET ROOM (Toilettenzimmer)
comes the red GRAND SALON (Grosser Salon), where the
imperial couple took breakfast together. Despite her
occasional breaches of protocol, Sissi never lost the
Emperor's love and respect; his apartments are full of
pictures of her. After her death, the Emperor forbade anyon
to enter the rooms where she had lived; they were later
partially reoccupied by Charles I. In the grand salon the mos
interesting objects are a statue of
Napoleon's elder sister Eliza, by Canova,
and two bisque statuettes of
Franz-Joseph aged fifty-seven and Sissi at
fifty. The red, white and gold SMALL
SALON (Kleiner Salon) is dedicated to the
memory of Sissi, with busts, a portrait
and a glass case containing objects that
belonged to her. Looking out over the
AMELIA COURTYARD (Amalienhof), the
BERGL SALON (Berglzimmer), which is
closed to the public, is decorated with exotic frescoes by
Johann Bergl ▲ 164, 278.

ALEXANDER I'S APARTMENTS. After the GRAND ANTECHAMBEF
(Grosser Vorzimmer), which contains a life-size statue of Sis
and portraits of the children of Maria Theresa ▲ 144
(including Marie-Antoinette), are the apartments of Czar
Alexander I. No trace remains of his having occupied these
richly decorated quarters, only a series of portraits of Charle
I, who used these apartments as an audience chamber and
work room. After the VESTIBULE (Eingangzimmer), with its
busts of Charles I and Zita, come the Rococo RECEPTION
SALON (Empfangsalon), with fine Gobelins tapestries on a
red background after cartoons by François Boucher. Thes
were a present from Marie-Antoinette to Joseph I on the
occasion of his visit to Paris in 1777. The STUDY
(Arbeitszimmer), covered in hangings made in
Brussels, is where Charles I signed his abdication.
The long royal table in the DINING ROOM
(Spiesezimmer), which was always set, could
seat up to ten diners. Etiquette required that
all knives and forks be set to the right of the
plates. The SMOKING ROOM is an extension of
the Czar's apartments; it is dedicated to Rudolp
and Franz-Ferdinand, the two archdukes who die
under tragic circumstances.

SCHATZKAMMER ★

The contents of the imperial treasury
(Schatzkammer) were assembled by Ferdinand I
(1503–64), then enriched by his successors, who

MICHAELERTOR
The Michaelertor
▲ 174, 175, 181 was
built in the 18th
century in the hollow
of the concave façade
of the North Wing
(Michaelertrakt). It is
a fine example of the
Baroque style, with
columns, balconies
and statues of the
labors of Hercules.
The façade is flanked
on either side by a
monumental
fountain, created by
Hellmer and Weyr at
the close of the 19th
century, which is an
allegory of the power
of the empire on land
and sea.

CHARLES I
The last
emperor of
Austria
abdicated in
1918 ▲ 144.

ROOFS OF THE
BURG
n left to right,
from top to
om: the

monument to Prince
Eugène which stands
in front of the
Heldenplatz wing
▲ 207, the

Michaelertor dome
▲ 174, 175, 180, a
detail of the Neue
Burg, the splendid
decoration on the

roof of the Austrian
National Library
▲ 192, and four
details of the
Michaelertor dome.

EMPEROR TWICE OVER
The 12th-century imperial orb of gold, silver and precious stones and the imperial crown (below). Joseph II's successor was crowned Holy Roman Emperor as Francis II (below); he donned

spread its various parts round the palace. It was not until the reign of Charles VI that the treasure was all brought together here.

INSIGNIA OF THE HOLY ROMAN EMPIRE. The crown of the Holy Roman Empire was the emblem of sovereignty over a major part of Europe for more than a thousand years. For a long time it was mistakenly known as the Crown of Charlemagne, though it was probably made in the 10th century for Otto II. Made of gold in the Byzantine and Carolingian style, it is topped by a cross, a hoop of gold and precious stones added during the 11th century for Conrad II. Other imperial insignia are the 12th-century golden Orb, the Gothic Scepter, the Imperial Cross (11th–13th centuries), the Carolingian gospel-book on which the emperor swore his oath, the Sword of Charlemagne (which is in fact an oriental saber), the Holy Lance and the Processional Cross. The first rooms also display the emblems of the Habsburgs as Kings of Bohemia and Hungary and Archdukes of Austria, including the crown, orb and scepter carved from a narwhal's tooth which was commissioned by Rudolph II from the goldsmiths of Prague. Mantles with long trains were used during formal imperial ceremonies; the purple one worn by Francis I at his coronation is embroidered with gold, with collar of ermine. Note also the magnificent robes embroidered by Maria Theresa herself for her grandchildren's christenings. Most of the principal gems of the Emperors, were carried into exile by the last Habsburgs; those that remain include the Columbian Emerald (1680 carats) the Golden Rose of the Pope given by Pius VII to Francis I's wife Carolina-Augusta, and a two-headed eagle made with an amethyst, an opal and a hyacinth. The cup passed at the Last Supper, in which Joseph of Arimathea caught the blood of Christ, was the subject of a great number of chivalric fables. For many centuries it was believed that the chalice (otherwise

the Crown of Charlemagne and carried the Orb. Then he became Francis I, first Emperor of Austria ● *38*.

known as the HOLY GRAIL) in the imperial treasury was indeed the true grail; this cup, fashioned from one of the largest agates in the world, in fact dates from the 4th century. Similarly, the narwhal tooth was thought to be the horn of a unicorn.

ROYAL HEIRLOOMS OF SICILY. Through numerous alliances and inheritances, the royal insignia of

seek the Golden Fleece and on his travels he overcame a race of giants, a terrible harvest of a crop of dragons' teeth sown in a field. Philip the Good, Duke of Burgundy, founded the Order of the Golden Fleece in 1429, Charles V gave it special kudos by recruiting its members from among Austria's higher nobility and men of state.

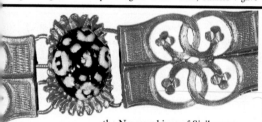

Shown here are the accoutrements of the members and heralds of the order: mantles of purple velvet, tabards embroidered with coats of arms, suits of armor, and jewelry, including the 18th-century Cross of the Oath and the goblet of Philip the Good.

the Norman kings of Sicily were handed down to the Hohenstaufens and subsequently to the Habsburgs. The finest piece is a red silk embroidered mantle that was worn by Roger II of Sicily on the day of his coronation.

THE GOLDEN FLEECE. A small gallery of portraits commemorates the principal members of the Valois-Burgundy family. Also displayed are various altar coverings and liturgical vestments. The Treasure of the Golden Fleece came from the dowry of Marie of Burgundy, daughter of Charles the Rash, who married Maximilian I.

MUSEUM OF RELIGIOUS ART. The ecclesiastical treasury contains a number of objects which were used at services attended by the court. St Stephen's purse – a reliquary which is said to have belonged to Charlemagne and to have contained the blood of the first Christian martyr – is thought to be the oldest item here. Other curiosities include a reliquary containing a nail from the True Cross, a casket containing fragments of wood from the same source, and a small

The 8th-century Holy Lance (Langobardish-Karolingisch, above); the Scepter of Austria (below).

temple-reliquary containing one of St Peter's teeth.

BURGKAPELLE

Next to the treasury is the Palace Chapel of the Assumption (Burgkapelle) which was built in the Gothic style by Frederick III in the 15th century (1415–93). The chapel was redecorated several times in subsequent years, but in the 19th century it was decided that it should be restored to its original form. The catafalque in which the coffins of deceased Habsburgs lay in state was traditionally placed in this chapel while members of the public were allowed to pay their last respects. Today the internationally renowned Vienna Boys' Choir ● *54*, ▲ *270* often put on performances here.

The Parthian Frieze

THE ARTEMISION
The Temple of
Artemis at Ephesus is
counted among the
Seven Wonders of the
World, as recorded by
a Byzantine sage.
Dedicated to Artemis
(Diana), it is said to
have been founded by
the Amazons and
according to the
Roman historian
Pliny was sacked
seven times. Croesus,
King of Lydia,
endowed the temple
with great splendor in
the 6th century BC;
destroyed by a
lunatic, Erostratus, in
365 BC, it was rebuilt
in exactly the same
form before being
demolished again by
the Goths in 263 AD.

EPHESOS-MUSEUM

Objects excavated in 1866 by Austrian archeologists at
Ephesus in Asia Minor are displayed in the Museum of
Ephesus in the New Hofburg. (Excavations are continuing
there today.) Ephesus became a major commercial port and
financial center of Asia Minor from the 8th century BC
onward, thanks to its trade with the Orient. It was also a
religious center for the cult of Artemis, to whom a great
temple, the Artemision, was erected in the 6th century BC.

Ephesus fell successively under the rule of
Croesus, the King of Lydia who was famous for
wealth; Cyrus, King of Persia; Alexander the
Great; Mithridates, King of Pontus; and the
Roman dictator Sylla. In 54 AD St Paul and
St John founded the first Christian communiti
at Ephesus, and the Virgin Mary died there.
Later Ephesus was visited by the Emperor
Hadrian (in whose honour a temple was built
before falling first into Byzantine and finally
into Turkish hands.

A MYSTICAL VISION. The German nun Anna
Katherina Emmerich (1774–1824) re-lived th
Passion of Christ on several occasions and was marke
with the stigmata. Her visions, recounting the life of
the Virgin and of Christ's Apostles, were transcribed
the German writer Clemens Brentano; forty years af
the death of the "Nun of Dülmen", her visions helpe
the archeologists working on the dig at Ephesus to
locate the house in which St Paul and St John are
thought to have lived.

FRAGMENTS OF THE TEMPLE OF ARTEMIS. Parts of th
Artemision, the Roman Theater, the Odeon, the
Temple of Hadrian, the stadium, the agora, the foru
the Library of Celsus and the road of Kouretes were

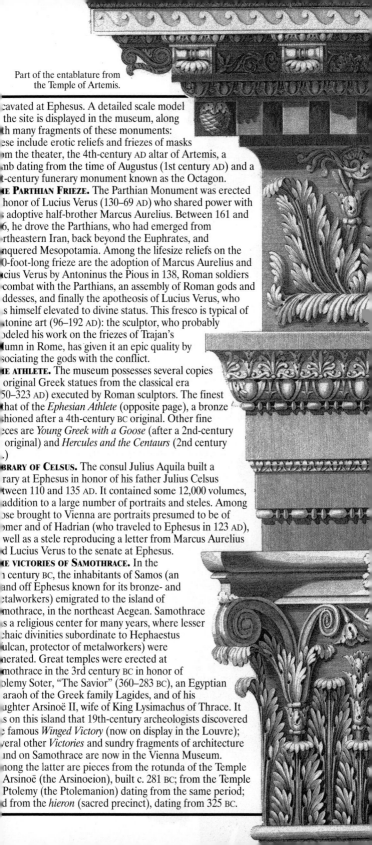

Part of the entablature from
the Temple of Artemis.

cavated at Ephesus. A detailed scale model
the site is displayed in the museum, along
th many fragments of these monuments:
ese include erotic reliefs and friezes of masks
m the theater, the 4th-century AD altar of Artemis, a
mb dating from the time of Augustus (1st century AD) and a
t-century funerary monument known as the Octagon.

IE PARTHIAN FRIEZE. The Parthian Monument was erected
honor of Lucius Verus (130–69 AD) who shared power with
adoptive half-brother Marcus Aurelius. Between 161 and
6, he drove the Parthians, who had emerged from
rtheastern Iran, back beyond the Euphrates, and
nquered Mesopotamia. Among the lifesize reliefs on the
0-foot-long frieze are the adoption of Marcus Aurelius and
ucius Verus by Antoninus the Pious in 138, Roman soldiers
combat with the Parthians, an assembly of Roman gods and
ddesses, and finally the apotheosis of Lucius Verus, who
s himself elevated to divine status. This fresco is typical of
tonine art (96–192 AD): the sculptor, who probably
odeled his work on the friezes of Trajan's
lumn in Rome, has given it an epic quality by
sociating the gods with the conflict.

IE ATHLETE. The museum possesses several copies
original Greek statues from the classical era
50–323 AD) executed by Roman sculptors. The finest
that of the *Ephesian Athlete* (opposite page), a bronze
shioned after a 4th-century BC original. Other fine
eces are *Young Greek with a Goose* (after a 2nd-century
original) and *Hercules and the Centaurs* (2nd century
.)

BRARY OF CELSUS. The consul Julius Aquila built a
rary at Ephesus in honor of his father Julius Celsus
tween 110 and 135 AD. It contained some 12,000 volumes,
addition to a large number of portraits and steles. Among
ose brought to Vienna are portraits presumed to be of
omer and of Hadrian (who traveled to Ephesus in 123 AD),
well as a stele reproducing a letter from Marcus Aurelius
d Lucius Verus to the senate at Ephesus.

IE VICTORIES OF SAMOTHRACE. In the
century BC, the inhabitants of Samos (an
and off Ephesus known for its bronze- and
etalworkers) emigrated to the island of
mothrace, in the northeast Aegean. Samothrace
s a religious center for many years, where lesser
chaic divinities subordinate to Hephaestus
ulcan, protector of metalworkers) were
nerated. Great temples were erected at
mothrace in the 3rd century BC in honor of
olemy Soter, "The Savior" (360–283 BC), an Egyptian
araoh of the Greek family Lagides, and of his
ughter Arsinoë II, wife of King Lysimachus of Thrace. It
s on this island that 19th-century archeologists discovered
e famous *Winged Victory* (now on display in the Louvre);
veral other *Victories* and sundry fragments of architecture
und on Samothrace are now in the Vienna Museum.
nong the latter are pieces from the rotunda of the Temple
Arsinoë (the Arsinoeion), built c. 281 BC; from the Temple
Ptolemy (the Ptolemanion) dating from the same period;
d from the *hieron* (sacred precinct), dating from 325 BC.

TWO PIECES OF SILVER TABLEWARE BELONGING TO MARIA THERESA
The court collection of china and silver in the Michaelertrakt includes sumptuous sets of tableware

from China, France (Sèvres), Germany (Saxe), Italy (Milan) and Austria (Augarten ▲ 269).

The breastplate and armor of Ferdinand I.

THE COLLECTIONS

The son of Ferdinand I and the brother of Maximilian II, Ferdinand of the Tyrol (1529–95) ▲ 210 like all the Renaissance princes, loved the arts. Using his own considerable fortune (along with that of his wife, the daughter of the banker Welser who had loaned money to Charles V to buy his election as Holy Roman Emperor in 1519), Ferdinand built up a collection of old weapons, musical instruments and ethnographic objects which were later passed on to the great museum of Vienna.

HOFTAFEL- UND SILBERKAMMER. Among the finest items in the court collection of china and silverware are the Milan Centerpiece, a gilded 100-foot-long bronze platter dating from the early 19th century, the English service given to Emperor Franz-Joseph by Queen Victoria, three Sèvres services given by Marie-Antoinette to her brother Joseph II when he visited Paris in 1777 (she also gave the tapestries now hanging in the red salon of the imperial apartments), and an extensive gilt silver service. This service, designed for a hundred and forty guests, was made by Guillaume Biennais (1764–1834), a Paris silversmith fashionable during the first French Empire. Most of Biennais' plates are modeled on the paintings of Louis David, the official portraitist of the Revolution and the Empire, who was a passionate student of Greek and Roman antiquity.

RÜSTUNGEN- UND WAFFENSAMMLUNG. The Hofburg's collection of arms and armor (Rüstungen-und Waffensammlung) is one of the largest in the world. It was started by Ernest I, Duke of Austria (1377–1424) in the 15th century, and enlarged by Archduke Ferdinand of the Tyrol (1529–95). Its oldest weapons date back to the Barbarian invasions of the 5th century AD, while the most splendid parts of the collection were fashioned during the Renaissance – notably the ceremonial armor of Charles V, and that of his son Philip II of Spain and of Francis of France, made in Milan during the 16th century. Note also Maximilian II's golden sword (1551), his rose-leaf ornamental accoutrements, and an extensive collection of Turkish weapons.

SAMMLUNG ALTER MUSIK-INSTRUMENTE ★. The finest pieces in the collection of old musical instruments (Sammlung alter Musik-Instrumente) come from the collections of Archduke Ferdinand of the Tyrol, which he assembled at Ambras. Others belonged to Archduke Ferdinand-Charles (1754–1806), son of Maria Theresa, who married Maria-Beatrice d'Este. The d'Este princes, a great North Italian family related to the Sforzas and the Borgias, had collected a large

umber of works of art in their various residences, in particular collectible musical instruments (some of these ere kept in the former property of the marquess of Obizzi, ear Padua).

MUSEUM FÜR VÖLKERKUNDE

he Museum of Ethnography (Museum für Völkerkunde) ossesses more than a hundred and fifty ousand objects from all over the world, ollected over the centuries either by the absburgs themselves or by ethnologists orking for the Austrian government.
ONTEZUMA'S DIADEM. The museum is articularly rich in objects from the Aztec mpire of ancient Mexico: it inherited both e collections sent by the conquistador ernán Cortés to Charles V after the king of Tenochtitlan in 1520, and also those of the ill-fated mperor of Mexico, Maximilian ▲ 145. It holds the feathered own of the Aztec Emperor Montezuma II (1466–1520) 207, who was killed in the revolt of the Aztecs against the rces of Cortés. Today, Mexico is calling for the return of this adem. Many other objects of Latin-American origin are ept here, especially pieces from Brazil. Francis I's daughter, e Archduchess Marie-Leopoldine, married Peter I of lcantara, Emperor of Brazil, in 1817. At that time Austria nt a team of scholars to Rio de Janeiro, among them the aturalist Johann Naterer (1787–1843) who provided the luseum of Ethnography with innumerable objects acquired om the Amazon Indians.
APTAIN COOK'S COLLECTIONS. The oceanic section of e museum was started off with the collections of Captain ook, purchased in London in 1806 by Francis I; Africa, ustralia and Asia, the destinations of many Austrian hnographic expeditions, are also well represented. l these elements complemented and enriched the ollections of Ferdinand of the Tyrol ▲ 210. Archduke

EUROPEAN CONCERT
The history of European music is retraced with a display of instruments. Note the clavicytherium, an ancestor of the harpsichord (17th-century), Maria Theresa's tortoise-shell violin (18th-century) and the trumpet of Ferdinand of the Tyrol (16th-century). A mandolin (Pandurina) and details of violas (above).

IN BLACK AND WHITE
Keyboard instruments which belonged to famous musicians are displayed. These include Haydn's harpsichord ● 49, ▲ 152, 162, 164, Mozart's pianoforte (*Hammerflügel*, above) ● 48, ▲ 162 the piano given by the Erhard Company to Beethoven ● 51, ▲ 298 in 1803, Liszt's organ-harmonium and the pianos of Schubert, Brahms ● 51, Schumann ▲ 153, Wolf and Mahler ● 52.

187

Captain James Cook (1728–79, above right) circumnavigated the world three times between 1768 and 1779.

Self-Portrait by Vincent Van Gogh (top); *Bather* by Pierre-Auguste Renoir (above).

An early 18th-century Indian warrior, from the Museum of Ethnology.

Franz-Ferdinand ▲ *145*, who traveled round the world in 1892–3, brought back with him no fewer than fourteen thousand Asian objects.

COLLECTION OF THE ART OF BENIN. One of the world's finest collections of the art of Benin, the kingdom that preceded today's Nigeria, is also displayed in the museum. Between the 18th and 19th centuries, a style of court art consisting of bas-reliefs and figurines evolved in Benin. These works were used to decorate the palaces of the *obas*, the powerful monarchs who reigned over the entire Gulf of Guinea. Most of the sculptures, which were cast using the lost wax method, represent the sovereign, the queen mother, warriors, servants or hunters. When the city of Benin was captured by the British Army in 1897, the *oba* went into exile and his property was sold at auction in London: Austria bought seventy-four bronzes.

SPANISCHE REITSCHULE ★

The Spanish Riding School ▲ *190* (Spanische Reitschule) occupies the STABLE BLOCK (Stallburg), at the far end of the Ballroom, and trains either in the winter or the summer school. It was originally based in quarters on Josefsplatz.

THE WINTERREITSCHULE. The winter manège (Winterreitschule) was built at the close of the 17th century, in the space once occupied by the apartments of Maximilian II; it was completed in 1729 and is the recognized Baroque masterpiece of its architect, Joseph Emanuel Fischer von Erlach ● *80*, ▲ *302*. The manège, which is painted white throughout, is surrounded by a double gallery and a high colonnade: a box crowned by a triangular pediment was included for the emperor's use, and stucco bas-reliefs of immaculate white add a further touch of refinement. The winter manège was opened in 1735 by Charles VI ● *36*, ▲ *192*, who had originally commissioned it; his monogram in relief and his portrait may be seen on the walls and in the emperor's box. Just as they do today, the riders would ride forth in impeccable order. Then they would go through the sequence of complex exercises which have since established the great renown of the Spanish Riding School.

THE SOMMERREITSCHULE.
In summer, the exhibitions of the Spanish Riding School are given at the summer manège (Sommerreitschule), which is in the courtyard adjoining the winter manège.

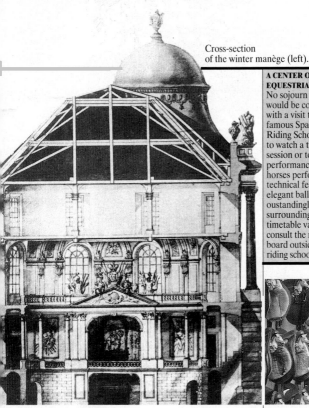

Cross-section of the winter manège (left).

A CENTER OF EQUESTRIAN ART ✪
No sojourn in Vienna would be complete with a visit to the famous Spanish Riding School, either to watch a training session or to attend a performance: see horses perform technical feats and elegant ballets in outstandingly fine surroundings. The timetable varies, so consult the notice-board outside the riding school.

LIPIZZANER MUSEUM. On the second floor of the stables is the Lipizzaner Museum, named after the white Lipizzan horses that are the pride of the Spanish Riding School. The original stud farm of these horses was at Lipizza, a hamlet in Slovenia; its founding was influenced by archduke Karl II who used the studs in the breeding of Spanish horses in the late 16th century. Their permanent home these days is on a stud farm in the Austrian province of Styria, where they were moved after the fall of the monarchy in 1920. The Lipizzaner Museum documents the history of the famous white horses from their origin to modern times. Paintings, engravings, drawings, photographs, horses' harnesses and video combine to give a fascinating and multifaceted overview of their history, breeding and training. One of highlights of the museum is a splendid view into the riding school. Two large glass windows offer visitors a look onto the boxes and provide a close-up of the horses' daily routine.

BALLS, CONCERTS AND CAROUSELS
The winter manège (below) was not just a theater for elaborate dressage. The Lipizzaners were also used for equestrian carousels and ballets, in which dancers and riders performed to the music of orchestras amid magnificent scenery. During the Congress of Vienna ● *38*, the aristocracy of Europe participated in balls organized in the manège, as well as attending concerts there.

JOSEFSPLATZ

This square is named after Joseph II (1741–90), whose equestrian statue by Franz Anton von Zauner (c. 1795–1807) may be seen in its center. The same architect, Nikolaus von Pacassi ▲ *192*, was employed to redesign all the surrounding façades between 1760 and 1770, and this is what gives the square its extraordinary unity. Before it was remodeled, it was used for tournaments and for training the horses of the Spanish Riding School.

189

SPANISH RIDING SCHOOL HORSEMAN
The riders are dressed
in brown dress coats
with gold buttons,
doeskin breeches and
two-cornered hats.

THE ART OF DRESSAGE
With the outbreak of the French Revolution in 1789, the great
stables of Versailles were abandoned and the Master of the Horse,
La Guérinière, left for Vienna, where he taught equestrian art at
the Spanish Riding School. Like the famed Cadre Noir at Saumur,
the Viennese school specializes in dressage – a highly skilled
discipline entirely different from show-jumping which became
popular in the 19th century. Many of the more advanced exercises
in dressage may be traced to the French tradition.

In 1562, Maximilian II's brother, Archduke Charles, who had inherited estates in the north of today's Slovenia, established several major studs at Lipizza, near Trieste, to which he brought Spanish thoroughbreds (hence the name of the school) for cross-breeding with Karst horses. The "Lipizzaner" strain was created at the end of the 16th century with these studs, which thereafter supplied horses to the Spanish Riding School and the Austrian Household Cavalry. When the Italians and subsequently the Yugoslavs annexed Trieste and Slovenia after World War One, Austria decided in 1920 to found its own Lipizzaner stud at Piber, near Graz, in Styria. Today the white horses of the Spanish Riding School are bred both at Lipizza (Lipice) and at Piber.

THE WINTER MANÈGE
The public is admitted several times a day to watch the demonstrations and schooling of riders in the winter manège
▲ *188* at the Hofburg.

THE "SILVER STALLIONS"
The Lipizzaners of the Spanish Riding School have been white ever since an imperial decree proclaimed that they should be so at the beginning of the 19th century. Before that time the Habsburgs were just as likely to select piebald, bay, spotted or chestnut horses. Empress Sissi was a keen collector of horses, but her preference, unlike her husband's, was not for "silver stallions", but for dark thoroughbreds.

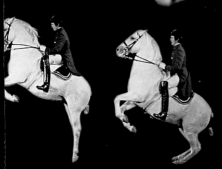

PACES
The riders have a huge repertoire of "paces", the advanced exercises which demonstrate the most elegant points of a horse. The paces are divided into low paces (pirouettes, pawing the ground, passage, changing leg on alternate steps of a canter, Spanish walk and trot) and high paces (curvets, cabrioles and croupades).

The ballroom, the Austrian National Library and the
Augustinian Church all look onto Josefsplatz, which adjoins
Augustinerstrasse.

PALLAVICINI PALACE. This palace at no. 5 has a remarkable
door framed by caryatids, the work of von Zauner in 1786
(like the later statue of Joseph II). This classical palace was
built in the same period by Ferdinand von Hohenburg on the
site of a former convent where Elizabeth of Austria, daughter
of Maximilian II and wife of Charles IX of France, died in
1592. Today it is used a convention center.

THE VIENNA WALTZ SCHOOL. Also facing the Hofburg, on the
corner of Bräunerstrasse, is the Ellmayer dancing school ● *58*

PALFFY PALACE. With its handsome Renaissance façade, the
Palffy Palace overlooking Josefsplatz was the
scene of Mozart's first performance of *The
Marriage of Figaro* ▲ *48* in 1785. This
palace stands on the site of the old
imperial chancellery; today it serves as
Austria House, scene of a wide variety
of cultural activities.

NATIONALBIBLIOTHEK

The imperial court's library, which
became the Austrian National Library
(Nationalbibliothek) in 1920, was scattered all
around the Hofburg before Charles VI commissioned
J. B. Fischer von Erlach ● *74, 80,* ▲ *138, 147, 302* and his son
Josef Emanuel to design a permanent building in 1722.

PRUNKSAAL ★. The result is the magnificent hall (Prunksaal)
in which the collections of the Habsburgs and Prince Eugène
● *35,* ▲ *147, 247* are stored (Joseph II purchased the prince's
books on his death in 1736). With marble, carved wainscoting,
a painted cupola covered in frescoes of the *Apotheosis of
Charles VI* by Daniel Gran, columns and statues, this room is
remarkably like a Baroque church interior, complete with
nave and oval transept. But the Prunksaal quickly became too
small to house the growing collections, and the library had to
expand into additional departments containing manuscripts,
maps and a Museum of Globes in the Augustinian wing;
papyri and musical scores, recordings and a film library in the
Albertina; periodicals, reading rooms, portraits, engravings
and more than eight hundred thousand photographs in the
Neue Hofburg.

THE GUTENBERG BIBLE. The sheer wealth of the library
makes it impossible to display all its treasures at one time, so
temporary exhibitions are organized all year round. In total,
the Austrian National Library possesses more than two and a
half million printed books, among them a Gutenberg Bible.

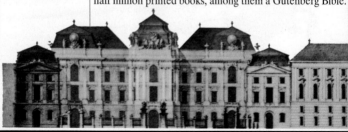

ie other great treasures include a Byzantine manuscript of 2 of a medical treatise by the Greek Dioscorides, who lived the 1st century AD; the 8th-century Gospel Books of Cuthbert and those of Johannes von Troppau (written by uke Albert III of Austria in 1368); a 12th-century tiphonal, or book of liturgical chants from St Peter's at lzburg; the Books of Hours of Charles the Rash and of aleazzo Sforza, Duke of Milan (both 15th century); and the leuerdank, a historical text written by Maximilian I 459–1519) printed in 1517.

LOBENMUSEUM. The museum of maps and globes ilobenmuseum) contains atlases by Willem Janszoon Blaeu *194*, and a globe made in 1541 for Charles V by the Flemish athematician and geographer ircator (1512–94). Four large obes made by the Venetian ographer Vincenzo

THE BLAEU ATLAS. In 1605, the Dutchman Willem Janszoon Blaeu (1571–1638) published a map of the world in Amsterdam, and followed it in 1619 with his famous atlases: *Theatrum Mundi* and *Theatrum Urbium et Monumentorum*.

Flat projections of t terrestrial globe in the *Atl* (opposite); a heliocentr armillary sphere (below

BLAEU AND VERMEER In Blaeu's time, the sea trade of the United Provinces was expanding into Northern Europe, Asia and Africa. All Europe was supplied by the

Coronelli (1650–1718) who worked at the court of Louis XIV are also displayed. Although it is a geographical map, the *Peutinger Table* is kept in the manuscript section; it is actually a superb 16th-century copy made by the German humanist Conrad Peutinger (1465–1547) of a 3rd- or 4th-century AD Roman map. Although the place names are somewhat misplaced, this map is ahead of its time in indicating reliefs, sites and mileages.

OTHER SECTIONS. The Austrian National Library also includes a restoration institute, the ESPERANTO MUSEUM and the theater archives that contain more than a million works, including photographs, maquettes and manuscrip of plays.

Low Countries. On his death, Blaeu's son Jan carried on his business. Vermeer of Delft ▲ *220*, a friend of the Blaeu family, often included maps in his paintings, for which he is said to have paid a fee.

AUGUSTINERKIRCHE UND KLOSTER

Integrated as they are into the Hofburg, the church and former monastery of the Augustinians (Augustinerkirche un Kloster) form a massive ensemble together with the Albertina and the hothouses (Palmenhaus). The Albertina, along with several sections of the Austrian National Library, occupies the monastery premises. The Gothic church is a favorite venue for aristocratic weddings, and the annual mass for Franz-Joseph is celebrated here on the anniversary of his death, November 21. Anton Bruckner

...2 frequently played on the old organ of the ...gustinerkirche, which originally came from the ...nolished Spanish Benedictine church ...hwarzspanier). It was here that he composed, ...played for the first time in public, his *Mass in F ...or* (1872). This musical tradition is kept up to ...day: a classical orchestra plays at mass every ...day in the Augustinerkirche.

E TOMB OF MARIA-CHRISTINA. Apart from the ...aculous statue at the church entrance, the most ...arkable features here are the handsome pulpit, ...high altar and, above all, the monumental tomb ...Maria-Christina of Saxony-Teschen (1742–98), ...ghter of Maria Theresa, who was the governor ...he Low Countries in 1778 (her husband Albert ...Saxony founded the gallery of drawings known as the ...ertina ▲ 196). This funerary monument is one of the ...sterpieces of the Italian sculptor Canova (1757–1822), who ...chiefly inspired by Greek and Roman sculpture and was

highly fashionable at the various European courts, including that of Napoleon, during the 19th century.

THE CRYPT OF THE HABSBURG HEARTS. A curiosity of the Augustinerkirche is the crypt (Habsburger Herzgruft) in which the hearts of the Habsburg family ● 29, ▲ 143, 144, 280 have been kept in silver urns ever since the reign of Matthias II in the early 17th century. Since that date, and following an unchanging ritual, the bodies of the imperial family have been literally dismantled after death: the hearts came to the Augustinerkirche, the viscera went to the crypt at St Stephen's Cathedral and what was left over was laid to rest in the crypt of the Capuchins ▲ 142.

ALBERTINAPLATZ

I. Stadt.
Augustiner-
Straße.

At the end of the AUGUSTINERSTRASSE, an old bastion of the Hofburg dominates Albertinaplatz. Above it stands the equestrian statue of Archduke Albert (1817–95) by Kaspar Zumbusch. Backing onto the bastion is the monumental, late 19th-century DANUBE FOUNTAIN (Donaubrunnen), the work of Mortiz von Löhr and Johann Meixner. The IMPERIAL GARDENS ▲ 207 and the GREENHOUSES are adjacent to the square.

WORKING IN THE FIELDS
A manuscript from the Abbey of St Peter, in Salzburg.

MERCATOR
In the 16th century, Gerhard Kremer Mercator (1512–94) achieved the first flat projection of the earth's surface, using principles that are still used by mapmakers today. For the time, his image of the world was astonishingly accurate.

PRINCELY NUPTIALS
The Augustinerkirche saw the weddings of Maria Theresa and Francis of Lorraine, in 1736, and of Elizabeth of Bavaria and Franz-Joseph in 1854. Also celebrated here were the proxy marriages of Marie-Antoinette and Maria Louisa of Habsburg-Lorraine with their absent husbands, Louis XVI, King of France, and Emperor Napoleon I – both of whom sent their wedding rings to represent them.

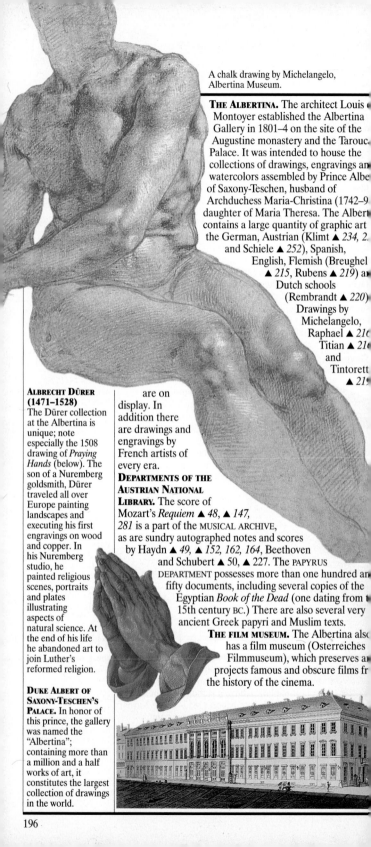

A chalk drawing by Michelangelo, Albertina Museum.

THE ALBERTINA. The architect Louis (Montoyer established the Albertina Gallery in 1801–4 on the site of the Augustine monastery and the Tarouc Palace. It was intended to house the collections of drawings, engravings an watercolors assembled by Prince Albe of Saxony-Teschen, husband of Archduchess Maria-Christina (1742–9 daughter of Maria Theresa. The Albert contains a large quantity of graphic art the German, Austrian (Klimt ▲ 234, 2. and Schiele ▲ 252), Spanish, English, Flemish (Breughel ▲ 215, Rubens ▲ 219) a Dutch schools (Rembrandt ▲ 220) Drawings by Michelangelo, Raphael ▲ 21(Titian ▲ 21(and Tintorett ▲ 21!

ALBRECHT DÜRER (1471–1528)
The Dürer collection at the Albertina is unique; note especially the 1508 drawing of *Praying Hands* (below). The son of a Nuremberg goldsmith, Dürer traveled all over Europe painting landscapes and executing his first engravings on wood and copper. In his Nuremberg studio, he painted religious scenes, portraits and plates illustrating aspects of natural science. At the end of his life he abandoned art to join Luther's reformed religion.

are on display. In addition there are drawings and engravings by French artists of every era.

DEPARTMENTS OF THE AUSTRIAN NATIONAL LIBRARY. The score of Mozart's *Requiem* ▲ 48, ▲ 147, 281 is a part of the MUSICAL ARCHIVE, as are sundry autographed notes and scores by Haydn ▲ 49, ▲ 152, 162, 164, Beethoven and Schubert ▲ 50, ▲ 227. The PAPYRUS DEPARTMENT possesses more than one hundred an fifty documents, including several copies of the Egyptian *Book of the Dead* (one dating from t 15th century BC.) There are also several very ancient Greek papyri and Muslim texts.

THE FILM MUSEUM. The Albertina also has a film museum (Osterreiches Filmmuseum), which preserves a projects famous and obscure films fr the history of the cinema.

DUKE ALBERT OF SAXONY-TESCHEN'S PALACE. In honor of this prince, the gallery was named the "Albertina"; containing more than a million and a half works of art, it constitutes the largest collection of drawings in the world.

196

as built in the second half of the 19th
to take the place of the original fortifica
ramparts, towers and bastions – which p
Vienna from the besieging Turks in 152
683. Military strategy evolved during th
nd 19th centuries, and armies preferre
ight in the open, where a decision coul
eached in a single day, rather than to e
rotracted sieges. Napoleon entered Vi

THE RING, AN IMPOSING BOULEVARD ✪

Two of the best – and certainly the least strenuous – ways of taking in all that this boulevard has to offer, including the monuments with which it is lined, is either to buy a tramway ticket and ride up and down to your heart's content (line 1 goes right round the Ring) or to settle comfortably in the seat of a hackney carriage.

THE RING BUILDING SITES

Along the Ring, new building sites sprang up everywhere. The State Opera was opened in 1869, followed by the Academy of Applied Arts, the Academy of Fine Arts, the Votive Church, the Parliament and the City Hall. Around ten public buildings and private palaces were constructed for the Viennese aristocracy and Austria's new captains of industry.

The greatest architects in Europe were summoned to Vienna; in conformity with Franz-Joseph's somewhat conservative taste, these architects invented no new styles, but sought inspiration in the past. The Ring gives the visitor a lesson in art history, from Greek antiquity to the Baroque period, by way of Romanesque, Gothic and Renaissance styles.

INAUGURATION PARADES AROUND THE RING
The Viennese were skeptical and even hostile to the Ring during early construction, but when the new promenade was finally opened in 1865 their delight knew no bounds. The imperial army paraded in full ceremonial uniform, and the people danced to Johann Strauss the Younger's *Demolition Polka*.

The Fruit Market on the Schanzel, by Aloïs Schorn.

The monument to the Hoch und Deutschmeister (formerly the Regiment of the City of Vienna) on Deutschmeisterplatz, stands in front of the Rossauerkaserne.

FRANZ-JOSEPHS-KAI ▲ 229, 30 The quays were heavily ombed in 1945 ● 42, and few of their original buildings remain.

ROSSAUERKASERNE The architecture of these large barracks, built in 1869, is similar to that of the Army Museum ▲ 258.

MONUMENT

DONAUKANAL

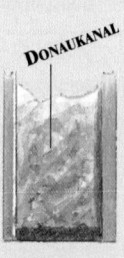

SCHOTTENRING

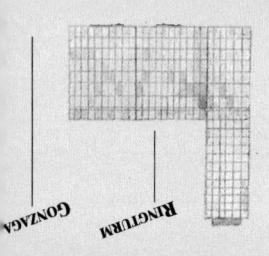
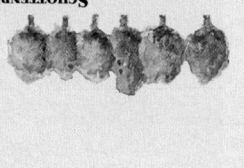

GONZAGA

RINGTURM

FRANZ-JOSEPHS-KAI

RINGTURM The Ring tower was completed in 1955.

Building on Franz-Josephs-Kai (right) and one on the corner of Franz-Josephs-Kai and Werdertorgasse (far right).

View of the Schanzel, near the Danube.

A A1-A2

The temporary Stock Exchange on the site of today's Börse was the scene of "Black Thursday", May 9, 1873. The stock market plunging on that day ended a period of prosperity, and its effects were felt even in the US.

No. 24
This fine building from the historicist epoch is now the site of the *Ring Cafeteria*.

BÖRSE
The Stock Exchange at no. 16 was designed by Theophil von Hansen (1871-7). It was partly burned down in 1956.

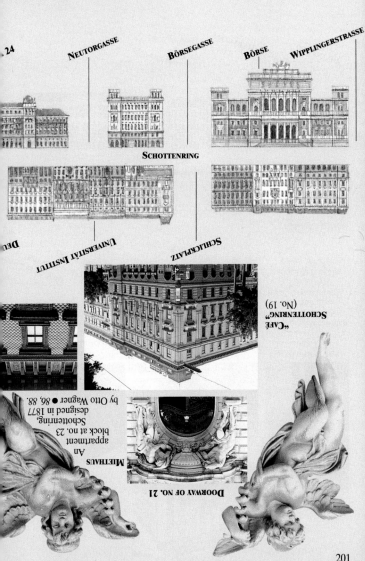

. 24

NEUTORGASSE

BÖRSEGASSE

BÖRSE

WIPPLINGERSTRASSE

SCHOTTENRING

DEU

UNIVERSITÄT INSTITUT

SCHLICKPLATZ

"CAFÉ SCHOTTENRING" (NO. 19)

MIETHAUS
An appartment block at no. 23 Schottenring, designed in 1877 by Otto Wagner ● 86, 88.

DOORWAY OF NO. 21

201

VOTIVKIRCHE
The neo-Gothic Votive Church was constructed by the architect Heinrich von Ferstel between 1856 and 1879.

"To have a play put on at the Burgtheater was the greatest dream of every Viennese writer."

Stefan Zwe[ig]

ZWEIG'S BIRTHPLACE
At no. 14 is the birthplace of the writer Stefan Zweig.

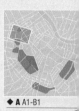

◆ A A1-B1

1.,Schotten[

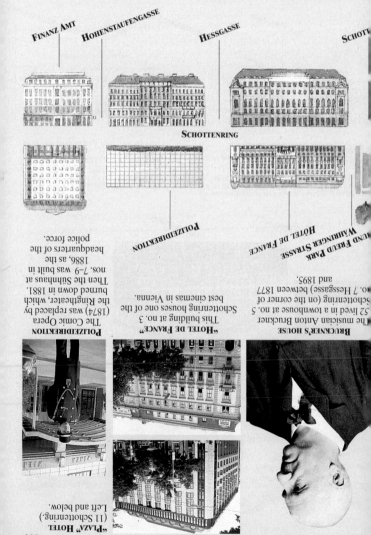

FINANZ AMT **HOHENSTAUFENGASSE** **HESSGASSE** SCHOTT[

SCHOTTENRING

POLIZEIDIREKTION
The Comic Opera (1874) was replaced by the Ringtheater, which burned down in 1881. Then the Sühnhaus at nos. 7–9 was built in 1886, as the headquarters of the police force.

"HOTEL DE FRANCE"
This building at no. 3 Schottenring houses one of the best cinemas in Vienna.

BRUCKNER'S HOUSE
The musician Anton Bruckner lived in a townhouse at no. 5 Schottenring (on the corner of no. 7 Hessgasse) between 1877 and 1895.

"PLAZA" HOTEL
(11 Schottenring.) Left and below.

202

PHRUSSI PALACE
...is palace at no. 14
...Karl Lueger Ring
...was designed by
Theophil von
...nsen, architect of
nearby Parliament
building (1873).

LIEBENBERG MEMORIAL
J. A. von Liebenberg
was mayor of Vienna
during the 1683 siege.
On the ruins of the
17th-century Melk
Bastion
(Mölkerbastei),
demolished in 1872,
stands the Pasqualati
house ▲ 166.

THE "CAFÉ LANDTMANN"
This establishment,
which has been managed
by several generations of
the Querfeld family, is a
favorite meeting place
for members of the
Parliament opposite, and
for people who have just
attended plays at the
nearby Burgtheater.

...SI PALACE   MÖLKERBASTEI   LIEBENBERG MEMORIAL   SCHREYVOGELGASSE   CAFÉ LANDTMANN   OPPOLZERGASSE

HOTTENRING   **DR KARL LUEGER RING**

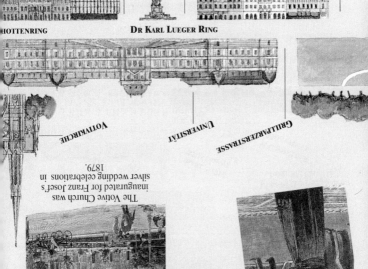

VOTIVKIRCHE   UNIVERSITÄT   GRILLPARZERSTRASSE

The Votive Church was
inaugurated for Franz Josef's
silver wedding celebrations in
1879.

**THE RINGTHEATER
FIRE**

The Votive Church
on Rooseveltplatz
commemorates the
assassination attempt
survived by Franz-
Joseph in 1853.

VOTIVKIRCHE ● 85

**INAUGURATION OF THE
NEW UNIVERSITY ON
OCTOBER 10, 1884.**

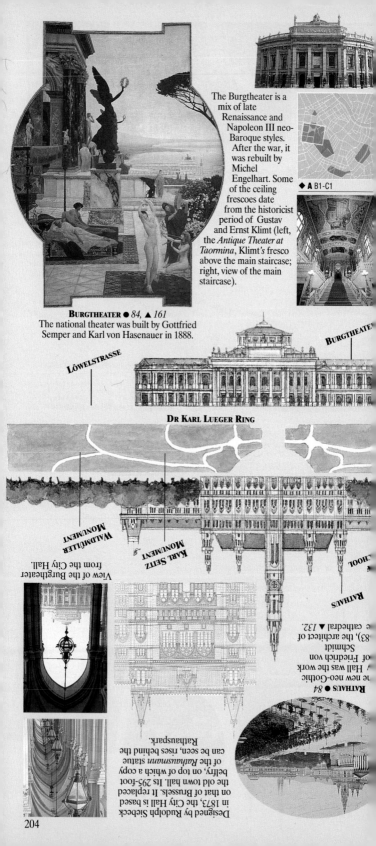

The Burgtheater is a mix of late Renaissance and Napoleon III neo-Baroque styles. After the war, it was rebuilt by Michel Engelhart. Some of the ceiling frescoes date from the historicist period of Gustav and Ernst Klimt (left, the *Antique Theater at Taormina*, Klimt's fresco above the main staircase; right, view of the main staircase).

◆ A B1-C1

BURGTHEATER ● *84,* ▲ *161*
The national theater was built by Gottfried Semper and Karl von Hasenauer in 1888.

LÖWELSTRASSE

BURGTHEATER

DR KARL LUEGER RING

WALDMÜLLER MONUMENT

KARL SEITZ MONUMENT

...SCHOOL

RATHAUS

View of the Burgtheater from the City Hall.

RATHAUS ● *84*
...e new neo-Gothic ...l Hall was the work of Friedrich von Schmidt ...83), the architect of ...e cathedral ▲ *132.*

Designed by Rudolph Siebeck in 1873, the City Hall is based on that of Brussels. It replaced the old town hall. Its 295-foot belfry, on top of which a copy of the *Rathausmann* statue can be seen, rises behind the Rathauspark.

204

VOLKSGARTEN

The Volksgarten is strewn with small buildings: the Temple of Theseus by Nobile (right, 1820), a miniature replica of the Theseion at Athens, with a statue by Müllner in front (1821); the monument to the Empress Elizabeth (1907); an octagonal café; and several pools (1866–80) with statues.

This garden, like the Burggarten, was laid out on the site of the fortifications destroyed by Napoleon in 1809. It was opened to the public as soon as it was completed in 1823.

EMPRESS ELISABETH MONUMENT

THESEUS TEMPLE

VOLKSGARTEN

DR KARL RENNER RING

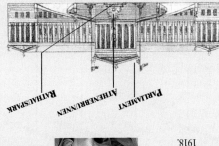

STRAUSS LANNER MONUMENT

RATHAUSPARK

ATHENEBRUNNEN

PARLIAMENT

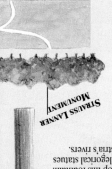

STRAUSS LANNER MONUMENT
The musicians Strauss and Lanner ● 56, rivals during their lifetimes, were reconciled by their sculptor in 1905.

FOUNTAIN OF ATHENE (1902) ● 85
Athene sits atop this fountain. At her feet, allegorical statues represent Austria's rivers.

RATHAUS

PARLIAMENT
The Parliament, built by Theophil von Hansen between 1874 and 1883, is inspired by Greek antiquity. The statues by the steps are of ancient historians. The Austrian Republic was proclaimed in front of the Parliament in 1918.

GRILLPARZER MEMORIAL Karl Kundmann, Karl von Hasenauer and Rudolf von Weyr collaborated on this monument, built in 1889.

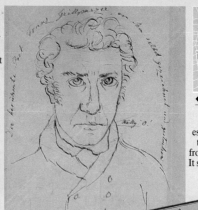

The bas-reliefs of the Grillparzer Memorial ● 60, 62, ▲ 147 reproduce some of the playwright's best-known scenes.

◆ A C1-D1

"CAFÉ MEIEREI
This open-air establishment adjo[...]
the university is c[...]
from April to Septe[...]
It serves several Vie[...]
specialties.

Café-Meierei Volksgarten

VOLKSGARTEN   **GRILLPARZER MONUMENT**

DR KARL RENNER RING

SCHMERLINGPLATZ **JUSTIZPALAST** **STADTSCHULERAT** **BELLARIASTRASSE** **NATURHISTORISCHES MUSEUM**

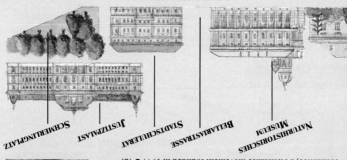

SCHMERLINGPLATZ
behind the Palace of Justice and the Volkstheater are the Auersperg Palace. The latter was the headquarters of the provisional national committee, a Resistance movement founded in 1944 ● 42.

JUSTIZPALAST
The Palace of Justice (1881), in the German Renaissance style, was burned down in 1927. From 1945 to 1955, it was the seat of the Allied High Command. Below, the main staircase.

HEADDRESS OF MONTEZUMA

This can be seen at the Museum of Ethnography ▲ 187 (Museum für Völkerkunde, Heldenplatz, 1) at the Neue Burg ▲ 177.

NEUE BURG

...e part of the Neue ...g (1881–1913) ...ch overlooks the ...g is known as the ...n building. It was ...ave been extended ...a triumphal arch ...r the Ring which ...ld have joined it ...he Art History ...seum. A similar ...lding was to have ...ed the Neue Burg, ...ted to the Natural ...tory Museum by ...other triumphal ...h: and the ...emble was to have ...med an imperial ...um.

...RGTOR

STRASSENBAHN HALTESTELLE

BURGTOR

Built by P. von Nobile (1824) to a design by L. Cagnola, the Burgtor was altered by R. Wondracek (1934), who turned it into a monument to the victims of World War One. A monument has now been added to it in memory of the Austrian Resistance.

HELDENPLATZ

The Burgtor leads to Heroes' Square, with its statues of Archduke Charles ● 38, ▲ 261 and Prince Eugène ● 35, ▲ 247, completed in 1860 and 1865, respectively.

NEUE BURG

BURGGARTEN

BURGRING

MARIA THERESI MONUMENT

MESSEPALAST

KUNSTHISTORISCHES MUSEUM

BABENBERG STRASSE

ESCHENBACHGASSE

MESSEPALAST. The exhibition hall occupies the former court stable block. It was started by J. B. Fischer von Erlach in 1719 and completed by his son Josef Emanuel in 1723. It was altered between 1850 and 1854.

MARIA THERESA MONUMENT

A work by the sculp... K. von Zumbusch (1830–1915). The riders are generals a... the statues of the central group are chancellors. The reliefs honor sixteen... individuals, among them Haydn and Mozart ● 48.

entrances on Maria-Theresienplatz are flanked by allegorical figures.

KUNSTHISTORISCHES MUSEUM ● 84, ▲ 208 AND NATURHISTORISCHES MUSEUM

The Museum of Art History and the Natural History Museum were built in the Italian Renaissance style by Karl von Hasenauer (interior decoration) and Gottfried Semper (façades) between 1872 and 1891. The main

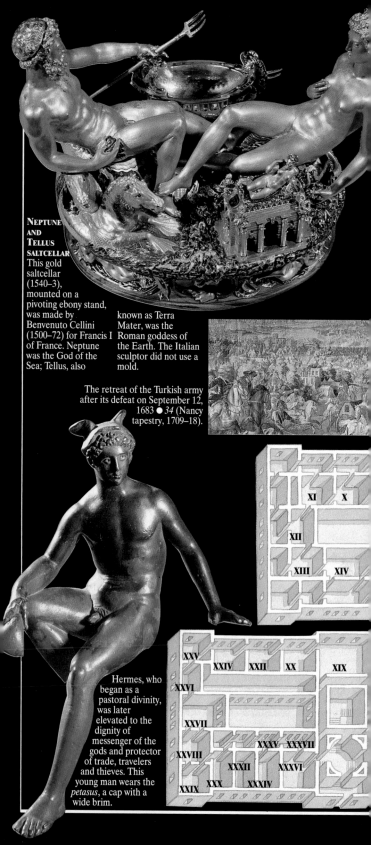

NEPTUNE AND TELLUS SALTCELLAR
This gold saltcellar (1540–3), mounted on a pivoting ebony stand, was made by Benvenuto Cellini (1500–72) for Francis I of France. Neptune was the God of the Sea; Tellus, also known as Terra Mater, was the Roman goddess of the Earth. The Italian sculptor did not use a mold.

The retreat of the Turkish army after its defeat on September 12, 1683 ● *34* (Nancy tapestry, 1709–18).

Hermes, who began as a pastoral divinity, was later elevated to the dignity of messenger of the gods and protector of trade, travelers and thieves. This young man wears the *petasus*, a cap with a wide brim.

XI X
XII
XIII XIV

XXV XXIV XXII XX XIX
XXVI
XXVII
XXVIII XXXV XXXVII
XXXII XXXVI
XXIX XXX XXXIV

HE GENIUS CELLINI
his goldsmith's
wel, made by the
ulptor for Francis I
France, is an
egory of the
niverse: an elephant carries the Earth while horses support Neptune. The four winds and the hours of the day also feature.

"BEZOAR"
This 16th-century Spanish bezoar stands on a tripod in the form of three lions, decorated with emeralds from the New World. The *bezoar*, a concretion formed by indigestible matter in the bodies of certain animals, was considered to be an excellent antidote for all sorts of poisons.

SECOND FLOOR
he coin collection (Münzkabinett) is kept on this floor.

I II III IV V
VI
VII
VIII
IX
III II I XIII XII XI X

I II III
IV
VII VI V

FIRST FLOOR
Devoted entirely to paintings, the first floor consists of two galleries (Gemäldegalerie): one of Italian and Spanish paintings; the other of Dutch, Flemish and German paintings.

TUTHMOSIS III
A black basalt bust of the 18th-Dynasty Pharaoh Tuthmosis (1504–1450 BC).

XIV XIII
XII
XI
VI VIa X
VII VIII IX

MEZZANINE
There are three different collections on the mezzanine floor: sculpture and decorative arts (Sammlung für Plastik und Kunstgewerbe), Greek, Etruscan and Roman antiquities (Antikensammlung) and Egyptian antiquities (Aegyptische Sammlung).

The Art History Museum of Vienna is one of the richest in Europe. The building was constructed to plans by Karl Hasenauer and Gottfried Semper (1870–91), and its collections ▲ *208* are divided into five departments, the painting section being the most extraordinary. Ferdinand I (1503–64) created a first "Cabinet Room of Arts and Wonders" at the Castle of Ambras near Innsbruck. His nephew Rudolph II assembled a large collection of paintings (notably by Brueghel) in his castle at Prague. His successor, Matthias, transferred the court of Prague to Vienna, bringing the collection with him. Leopold I inherited a number of Flemish and Italian pictures, and the Habsburgs' links with the Spanish branch of their family allowed the Austrian emperors to round off their collection very well.

Ferdinand of the Tyrol, son of Ferdinand I, himself a great collector, shown in a portrait by Francesco Terzio kept at Ambras; the Ambras collection is a part of the "Kunst". Below, *View of the Imperial Stables at the Hofburg*, by Franz Alt.

GIUSEPPE ARCIMBOLDO
The Emperors of Austria (Rudolph in particular) gave a warm welcome to this highly original Milanese painter. Arcimboldo (c. 1527–93) customarily painted faces in vegetable form. Thus in *Winter* (1573, opposite) he portrays Francis I of France as a tree trunk, using knots of wood and poisonous fungi to give him human features. The overall effect of phantasmagoria is very striking, but the details are perhaps more interesting still.

JAN VAN EYCK (C. 1390–1441)

The great master Jan van Eyck was treated like a prince all his life. He traveled all over Europe at a time when few people did so, visiting France, Spain and Portugal. Van Eyck far outstripped the fashions of his time; he freed his paintings from Gothic constraints and rediscovered the true simplicity of nature. Realism was the principal characteristic of his art. Though some of van Eyck's work was religious, he excelled at portraiture. His *Cardinal Nicolas Albergati* (1431) is one of his greatest works (right). This Polish cardinal is painted in an uncompromising manner but with no hint of caricature. The powerful physique and deeply-scored features indicate a strong personality; but the depth of understanding in the cardinal's eyes belie his physical appearance.

HANS HOLBEIN THE YOUNGER (1497–1543)

A century after van Eyck, Holbein the Younger raised German painting to its highest point. He settled in England in 1532, after the triumph of the Reformation, and reached the zenith of his career as official painter to the English court. He had the same objectivity and regard for detail as van Eyck, as is shown by his *Portrait of Jane Seymour* (right), and his faces have much the same gravity as those of the Dutchman. In a sense, in the painting of van Eyck and Holbein, Luther's philosophy canceled out the great discoveries of the Renaissance.

HIERONYMUS BOSCH (1450–1516)

The latent pessimism of the Reformation was exacerbated by Bosch, whose work is amply represented at Vienna. In his eyes Christ's *Bearing of the Cross* (right-hand page) becomes a masquerade of grimaces, gesticulations, ferocious faces, and shrieks. The painting in effect depicts a scene from hell. The peoples of northern Europe, despite the Renaissance, were allowing their demons to escape.

After the gaiety and convincing materialism of his *Village Wedding*, Pieter Brueghel the Elder (c. 1525–69) produced the heartbreaking landscape of *Hunters in Winter*. Elie Faure describes it as follows: "The violet and black winter is more painful, with its frozen ground crackling to the very tips of the tree-branches, than it is when snow has covered its naked carcass and muffled all its sounds – except for the voices of men who come forth; and are astonished to find themselves alone." More than half the known paintings of Brueghel the Elder are to be found in the Vienna Art History Museum.

215

GIORGIONE (1477–1510)

With Giorgione, Italian painting broke new ground. Not content with Giotto's literal transpositions or with Raphael's harmonious ones, Giorgione evolved a poetic, almost esoteric way of looking at the world. Every one of his paintings is an enigma. The *Three Philosophers* (right) has provoked much commentary: some critics believed the figures represented Pythagoras, Plato and Zoroaster, symbolizing the diversity of mankind. But this ingenious interpretation has recently been overturned by the results of an x-ray, which show the sages to be no more than a trio of astrologers. Strictly speaking, the works of Giorgione no longer have any particular meaning.

RAPHAEL (1483–1520)

"Raphael does not abandon himself to his theme", wrote Taine. "He remains sober and moderate; he studiously avoids going to extremes of movement or expression. He purifies types and arranges poses with great care. It is this taste for moderation and good measure, along with his spiritual delicacy, that carries him to the summit of his art." The *Madonna of the Meadows* (above), better known as the *Madonna of the Belvedere*, is a magnificent example of the classical style. The triangular composition, harmonious gestures and sweet expressions are entirely characteristic of the classical manner. The aim of symmetry in classicism is to establish contact with the spiritual world.

TITIAN (c. 1485–1576)

The approach of Titian, the "Doge of Color" and the painter of the *Madonna of the Cherries* (c. 1512–15, top right), is entirely different; beginning with a Raphael-style composition, he give color precedence over form. Palma the Younger said of his master Titian that he "roughed out his paintings by first brushing in blocks of color, which served as a bed or foundation for what he wished to express, and on these he could build afterward."

PETER PAUL RUBENS (1577–1640)
The *Nude of Hélène Fourment* (1638), sometimes called *Woman in a Fur Coat*, is a portrait of Ruben's second wife. The painter never tired of painting Hélène in all kinds of costumes, and in unabashedly sensual states of undress. Here (far left) she is seen half-naked under a fur-lined coat: laughing and blushing, she stares at her reflection in the mirror, while the painter himself seems confounded by such abundance of youth. The great design of Rubens, the heir of Titian, was not to express the harmony of reason like Raphael, nor the power of intelligence like Leonardo, but simply to express the infinite resources of life. He allowed himself to be carried away by life, dedicating his entire oeuvre to it. He was thus the precursor of Fragonard and Renoir.

TINTORETTO (1518–94)
The Biblical story of *Suzannah Bathing* (1560's, above) inspired several paintings by Tintoretto: another is in the Louvre. In the version in Vienna's Art History Museum, the painter seems to align himself with Veronese, and in doing so reaches the acme of his powers: the skillful handling of perspective, the extraordinary luminosity of the nude, the transparency of the veils, all combine to give this canvas a distinctly sensual flavor. Tintoretto did not stop at this material vision, however. Beyond its simple carnality, the work offers a moral lesson. The old men on the left, in a daring top-to-bottom perspective, seem plunged in the hell of unsatisfied desire, while Suzannah, gloriously haloed, represents innocence before the Fall.

VERMEER OF DELFT (1632–75)

The Artist in His Studio (right) is one of the museum's masterpieces, painted by Johannes Vermeer shortly before his death. From the point of view of its subject matter only, the picture seems banal; its powerful poetry lies in its rendering. "The letter is unimportant; so are the women. Likewise the world from which letters are brought. The world, in fact, has become a painting," wrote Malraux. The light, which comes from an invisible window, is unearthly; the painter (seen from behind) is mysterious; the girl dressed for a wedding is enigmatic. To crown all, an open map suggests fascinating voyages. The spectator feels himself to be in a theater; the heavy drapes held by a simple cord to the left will shortly fall like the curtain of a stage, and the play will be ended.

REMBRANDT VAN RIJN (1606–69)

The model for *The Portrait of Titus*, or *The Reader* (top right) was Rembrandt's fourth son from his union with Saskia. He was the only one of Rembrandt's children to survive into adulthood and this may explain the special tenderness with which the artist treats this young man. Only the hands and books are bathed in light; the face is not, and it is this that lends the portrait its strangeness.

In the paintings of Rembrandt, the light does not come from without, as it does in the work of Caravaggio, but from within. In this way he bares the souls of his subjects.

DIEGO VELAZQUEZ (1599–1660)
Velazquez' technique is entirely different: far from revealing his subjects' inner souls,

he treats them as the objects of pure poetry (above, portraits of the Infanta Margarita-Theresa, the Infanta Maria Theresa, and Don Felipe-Prosper). Margarita-Theresa, a little princess with an obstinate face, then aged eight, is transformed into a blue-and-gold gem by a few fluid brushstrokes.

BURGGARTEN

The garden of the Imperial Palace (1820), the former court promenade, was opened to the public in 1919. It has a number of fine statues, among them one of Mozart (below and

detail, far right, 1896), one of Francis of Lorraine (1781) and a monument to Franz-Joseph (1904).

GOETHE MONUMENT
The statue of Goethe (1900) by Edmund Hellmer stands in the middle of Goethestrasse.

◆ A D1-D2-D3

The palaces of the brewer A. Dreher (no. 4), the industrialist A. Ritter von Schoeller (no. 6) and the banker and art patron F. Schey (no. 8) line the north side of the Opernring.

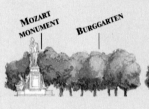

MOZART MONUMENT   BURGGARTEN   GOETHE MONUMENT   SCHEY PALACE   SCHOELLER PALACE   DREHER P

OPERNRING

FRANZ VON SUPPÉ'S HOUSE   ROBERT STOLZ PLATZ   HOTEL OPERNRING   SCHILLER MONUMENT   ER HAUS

THE SUPPÉ HOUSE
The operetta composer Franz von Suppé died at no. 23 Opernring.

SCHILLER MONUMENT
A statue of the poet F. von Schiller, by Schilling (1876), stands in front of the Fine Arts Academy.

OPERNRING AND OPERNRINGHOF
The houses at nos. 7 and 23 Opernring are typical of the first period of construction of the Ring (1861–3). The Opernringhof, a large modern building facing the Opera, is by Jonas Königswater (1956). It replaces the Heinrichhof, destroyed by bombs during World War Two ● 42.

AKADEMIE DER BILDENEN KÜNSTE
The Fine Arts Academy (1876), a neo-Renaissance building by Hansen, has a façade covered in antique statuary and, inside, a fresco of *The Fall of the Titans* by Anselm Feuerbach. There is also a gallery (Flemish, German, Spanish and Italian schools).

SECESSION ● 86.
The Secession Pavilion is set back somewhat from the Fine Arts Academy.

▲ 232.

STAATSOPER
Wrecked by bombing, the neo-Renaissance Opera by A. Siccard von Siccardsburg and E. van der Nüll (1869) was rebuilt by Erich Boltenstern in 1955.

The frescoes in the foyer by Moritz von Schwind illustrate (among other works) *Fidelio* (above) which was performed on the day of the reopening in 1955.

HOTEL SACHER (PHILHARMONIKER-STRASSE)
TOURIST OFFICE (KÄRNTNERSTRASSE)
WIENER PALACE (HOTEL BRISTOL)
TODESCO PALACE (MAHLERSTRASSE)

...ASSE **STAATSOPER**

OPERNRING

KÄRNTNER RING

OPERNRINGHOF

SIRK ECKE

MEINL ECKE

KÄRNTNERSTRASSE
The famous metro station designed by the architect Otto Wagner ● 86, 88 stands behind the Kunstlerhaus.

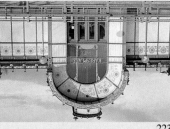

OPERNPASSAGE
The Opera Passage, an underground street at the intersection of the Ring and Kärntnerstrasse, contains a number of shops and the city tourist office.

"CAFÉ MUSEUM"
Designed by Loos in 1899 the café had chairs by the famous chair manufacturer Thonet ▲ 159.

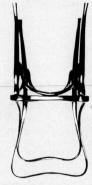

MEINL ECKE
The "Meinl Corner" is the headquarters of the coffee manufacturer Julius Meinl ● 72, ▲ 136.

223

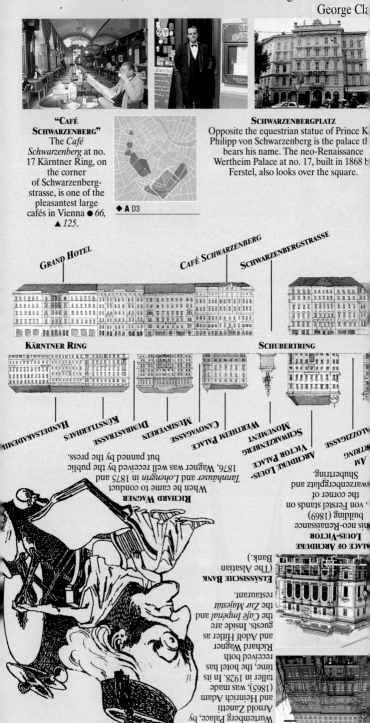

> "From the apartment at no. 3 Opernring, she could see, just on the other side of the Opernplatz, the celebrated Sirk Ecke, where Kärntnerstrasse met Ringstrasse"
>
> George Cla[...]

"CAFÉ SCHWARZENBERG"
The *Café Schwarzenberg* at no. 17 Kärntner Ring, on the corner of Schwarzenberg-strasse, is one of the pleasantest large cafés in Vienna ● *66*, ▲ *125*.

◆ **A** D3

SCHWARZENBERGPLATZ
Opposite the equestrian statue of Prince K[...] Philipp von Schwarzenberg is the palace th[...] bears his name. The neo-Renaissance Wertheim Palace at no. 17, built in 1868 b[...] Ferstel, also looks over the square.

GRAND HOTEL

CAFÉ SCHWARZENBERG

SCHWARZENBERGSTRASSE

KÄRNTNER RING

SCHUBERTRING

HANDELSAKADEMIE
KÜNSTLERHAUS
DUMBASTRASSE
MUSIKVEREIN
CANOVAGASSE
WERTHEIM PALACE
SCHWARZENBERG MONUMENT
ARCHDUKE LOUIS-VICTOR PALACE
AM
LOTZIGASSE
KARNTRING
MOZZIGASSE

RICHARD WAGNER
When he came to conduct *Tannhäuser* and *Lohengrin* in 1875 and 1876, Wagner was well received by the public but panned by the press.

LOUIS-VICTOR
[...]is neo-Renaissance building (1869) [...] von Ferstel stands on the corner of [S]warzenbergplatz and Shubertring.

PALACE OF ARCHDUKE LOUIS-VICTOR
AM MRTRING

ELSASSISCHE BANK (The Alsatian Bank.)

"HOTEL IMPERIAL"
The former Würtemberg Palace, by Arnold Zanetti and Heinrich Adam (1865), was made taller in 1928. In its time, the hotel has received both Richard Wagner and Adolf Hitler as guests. Inside are the *Café Imperial* and the *Zur Majestät* restaurant.

LEINTENBERGER PALACE

Built for the Austrian property owner and industrialist Baron Friedrich Leintenberger in 1871, this palace at no. 16 Parkring adjoins the Henckel Palace.

THE TRAMWAY

The red and white Viennese tramway is painted in the colors of the city.

SKENE AND KINSKY PALACES

The palace built in 1870 for the textile magnate and member of parliament Alfred Skene, and that of the

banker Eugen Kinsky occupy nos. 6 to 14.

A building on the corner of the Schubertring and Fichtegasse.

RINGSTRASSEN GALERIEN

The program for this portion of the ring is construction and restoration — hence the ensemble of hotels, shops and apartment buildings known as the Ringstrassen Galerien.

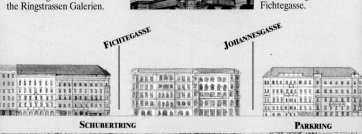

FICHTEGASSE · JOHANNESGASSE

SCHUBERTRING · PARKRING

CHRISTUSS · KONZERTHAUS · ADELIGES CASINO · BEETHOVEN PLATZ · Ö.A.M.T.C. · JOHANNESGASSE · KURSALON

WIENERFLUSSPORTAL

Vienna's favorite open-air spot in Stadtpark is known as the "Gate of the Vienna River'. An Art Nouveau ensemble ● 86 of kiosks, balustrades and stairways was built here in the early 1900's.

Ö.A.M.T.C.

The headquarters of the Austrian Automobile and Touring Club (Österreichischer Automobil Motor und Touringklub) is at no. 1 Schubertring.

"KURSALON"

This Renaissance-style tearoom may be entered via no. 33 Johannesgasse. Designed by Johann Graben (1865–7) it was a venue frequented by Eduard Strauss, brother of Johann Strauss Younger ● 57. Today, waltzes are still danced on the terrace in fine weather,

225

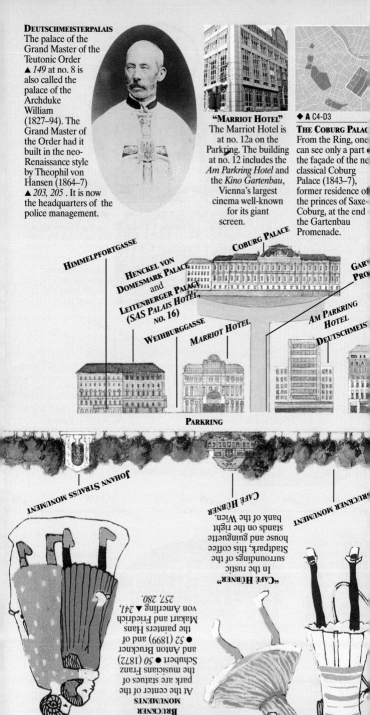

DEUTSCHMEISTERPALAIS
The palace of the Grand Master of the Teutonic Order ▲ 149 at no. 8 is also called the palace of the Archduke William (1827–94). The Grand Master of the Order had it built in the neo-Renaissance style by Theophil von Hansen (1864–7) ▲ 203, 205 . It is now the headquarters of the police management.

"MARRIOT HOTEL"
The Marriot Hotel is at no. 12a on the Parkring. The building at no. 12 includes the *Am Parkring Hotel* and the *Kino Gartenbau*, Vienna's largest cinema well-known for its giant screen.

◆ A C4-D3

THE COBURG PALACE
From the Ring, one can see only a part of the façade of the neo-classical Coburg Palace (1843–7), former residence of the princes of Saxe-Coburg, at the end of the Gartenbau Promenade.

HIMMELPFORTGASSE

HENCKEL VON DOMESMARK PALACE and LEITENBERGER PALACE (SAS PALAIS HOTEL, NO. 16)

COBURG PALACE

GAR PRO

WEIHBURGGASSE

MARRIOT HOTEL

AM PARKRING HOTEL

DEUTSCHMEIS

PARKRING

JOHANN STRAUSS MONUMENT

CAFÉ HÜBNER

BRUCKNER MONUMENT

"CAFÉ HÜBNER"
In the rustic surroundings of the Stadtpark, this coffee house and guinguette stands on the right bank of the Wien.

SCHUBERT AND BRUCKNER MONUMENTS
At the center of the park are statues of the musicians Franz Schubert ● 50 (1872) and Anton Bruckner ● 52 (1899) and of the painters Hans Makart and Friedrich von Amerling ▲ 241, 257, 280.

STADTPARK
The City Park ■ 16 was designed in 1862 by Rudolf Siebeck (who also laid out the garden of the city hall) after plans by Josef Selleny.

226

COLLOREDO PALACE

This private townhouse (no. 66) was lived in by the Colloredo family, whose most prominent member was the Prince-Archbishop of Salzburg who tyrannized Mozart.

DUMBA PALACE

This palace at no. 4 belonged to Nikolaus Dumba, an art patron of Greek extraction.

KARL LUEGER MONUMENT

The statue of the Mayor of Vienna (1897–1910) stands on the square named after him. Karl Lueger, who founded the Austrian Christian Socialist party, was a lawyer much loved by the common people because he installed modern public facilities managed by municipal companies in working-class areas. Above, a painting of Lueger by Wilhelm Gause.

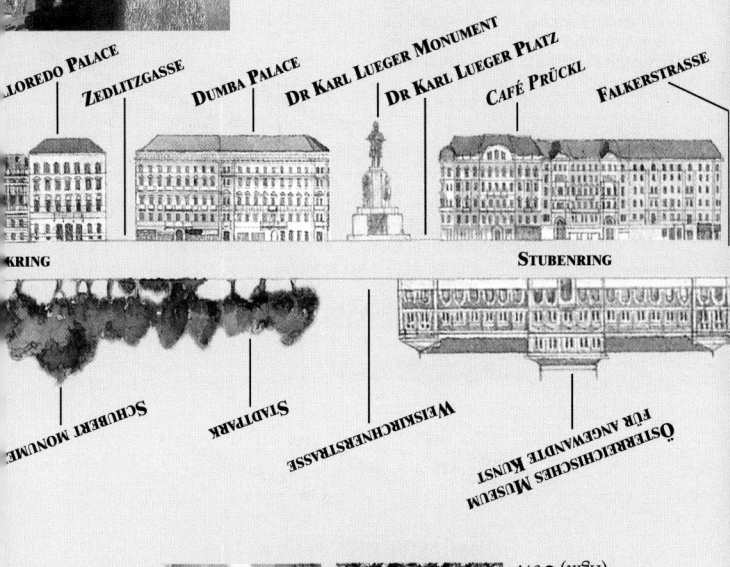

COLLOREDO PALACE — ZEDLITZGASSE — DUMBA PALACE — DR KARL LUEGER MONUMENT — DR KARL LUEGER PLATZ — CAFÉ PRÜCKL — FALKERSTRASSE

RING — STUBENRING

SCHUBERT MONUMENT — STADTPARK — WEISKIRCHNERSTRASSE — ÖSTERREICHISCHES MUSEUM FÜR ANGEWANDTE KUNST

FRANZ SCHUBERT

A painting by Gustav Klimt (1899) ▲ 20... representing 250 ... Schubert ● 50 at the piano (below), which was commissioned the Dumba Palace. This is a copy; the original was destroyed during World War Two.

JOHANN STRAUSS MONUMENT

In 1925, Edmund Hellmer installed a procession of marble naiads (far right) around the bronze statue of Strauss the younger (right) ● 57.

"COMBAT AT MINERBURG"

This tapestry dating from the first quarter of the 15th century is displayed at the Museum of Applied Arts (Österreichisches Museum für angewandte Kunst), at no. 5 Stubenring.

227

Aluminum air vent for the heating system at the Postsparkasse.

POSTSPARKASSE ● 88
The Post Office Savings Bank (1904–12) t[...] dominates Georg-Coch-Platz is the masterpiece of the Viennese Secession ▲ [...] architect Otto Wagner ● 86, ▲ 237, 240, 2[...] In front is the statue of the bank's founde[...] Georg Coch (1842–90).

◆ A C4-D4

THE CHAMBER OF COMMERCE
At nos. 8–10 Stubenring is a Jugendstil and neo-classical building by Baumann (1907) ● 86. It is now the Vienna Chamber of Commerce (Kammer der gewerblichen Wirtschaft für Wien).

"CAFÉ PRÜCKL"
This café, at no. 24, on the corner of Lueger Platz, is one of the most convivial establishments in Vienna.

POSTS[...]

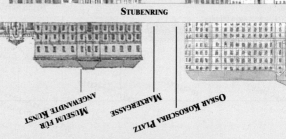

ROSENBURSENSTRASSE **KAMMER DER GEWERBLICHEN WIRTSCHAFT FÜR WIEN**

STUBENRING

MUSEUM FÜR ANGEWANDTE KUNST   **MARXERGASSE**   **OSKAR KOKOSCHKA PLATZ**

MUSEUM FÜR ANGEWANDTE KUNST
The Museum of Applied Arts and the academy next door, both built in the Italian Renaissance style (1871) by Heinrich von Ferstel ▲ 224, were enlarged by Ludwig Baumann in 1906-8. The museum contains collections of old furniture, ceramics, glassware, carpets and textiles. In front is the school is a statue of Oskar Kokoschka ▲ 254, by Alfred Hrlicka (1986).

HUNDERT-WASSERHAUS ● 94
In Löwengasse to the east of the Ring is the irregular, gaudy, golden-domed building designed by the painter Hundertwasser (1983-5).

FRANZ-JOSEPHS-KAI AND THE DANUBE CANAL ▲ 230

This quay runs along the Danube Canal and closes the circular Ring Boulevard to the northeast. Its broad avenue is dominated by Ruprechtskirche ● 75, ▲ 154 and lined with hotels and restaurant terraces. At the edge of Schwedenplatz is the landing stage for the river boats. A monument in Morzinplatz marks the site of the former Gestapo building, where many Viennese died.

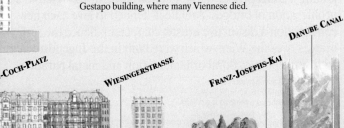

G-COCH-PLATZ   WIESINGERSTRASSE   FRANZ-JOSEPHS-KAI   DANUBE CANAL

UBENRING   JULIUS-RAAB-PLATZ

REGIERUNGSGEBÄU   REISCH-STRASSE   URANIASTRASSE   URANIA

The Urania build... contains observatory ar... large thea... concerts are s... staged h...

URANIA

This Jugendstil building ● 86 by Max Fabiani (1909–10) stands at no. 1 Uraniastrasse, beside the Danube Canal and Julius-Raab-Platz.

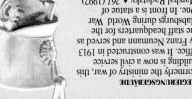

REGIERUNGSGEBÄUDE

Formerly the ministry of war, this building is now a civil service office. It was constructed in 1913 by Franz Neumann and served as the staff headquarters for the Habsburgs during World War One. In front is a statue of Marshal Radetzky ▲ 261 (1992).

The straightening of the Danube and the extension of the city (◀ joining Vienna proper to the Leopoldstadt, in 1850) led to a proliferation of bridges. Architects tended to give each new construction a distinctive artistic character – hence the series of bridges over the Wien, which were built in the Jugendstil manner with stone pilings, floral ornamentation and metal parapets.

SCHWEDENBRÜCKE
(Ferdinandsbrücke until 1920.)
The Ferdinandsbrücke (below) was Vienna's first solid bridge and opened on May 22, 1819. It replaced a pontoon and was built using the new technique of underwater construction.

FRANZENSBRÜCKE
(1803). Destroyed by the Viennese in 1809 while defending the city from the French, it was restored in 1899.

ASPERN BRÜCKE (reb and reopened in 1919 Aspernplatz (Julius Raab Platz since 197(dates from the early ? century. To its right is the "Kristallhof" (190 destroyed in 1945); th Urania was built in 1

SALZTORBRÜCKE
(Stephaniebrücke until 1920.)

SCHWEDENBRÜCKE, MARIENBRÜCKE AI SALZTORBRÜCKE. In the foreground is metro station by Otto Wagner ▲ *241*; on far side of the river, the old houses of Leopoldstadt ▲ 265.

From Secession to Musikvereinsgebäude

A poster (1898–9) by Joseph Maria Olbrich.

SECESSION ★

AN ART NOUVEAU MANIFESTO. The Secession Pavilion, built 1898, stands in the center of the major Friedrichstrasse intersection, to the south of the Opernring, beside the ACADEMY OF FINE ARTS ▲ 222. This large white cube toppe by a gilded dome was designed by Joseph Maria Olbrich ● a pupil of Otto Wagner ● 86, 88, ▲ 228, 237, 240 as a manifesto for the new movement launched by the Union o Young Artists. Its purpose was to stage the exhibitions of t Viennese avant-garde, which was at that time extolling the Jugendstil (Art Nouveau) ● 86. Built on the square plan, pavilion is not as stark as it might seem; floral friezes in b relief, Medusa masks and owls ornament the façade. As whole, the pavilion is a two-tone harmony of white and gold, all the more striking since its recent renovation.

THE SECESSIONIST MOVEMENT. The Secessionist movement was started in 1897 by a group of young painters, architects and decorators trained at the nearby Academy of Fine Arts, most of whom were pupils of the architect Otto Wagner; its leader was the painter Gustav Klimt ▲ 250. The movement was called "Secessionist" because these young artists began by "seceding" from the ARTISTS' ASSOCIATION (Künstlerhaus) ▲ 224, which they considered too "official" and mediocre, and from the esthe of historicism favored by Franz-Joseph ● 41, ▲ 142, 144, 17 which they considered thoroughly decadent. The composer Gustav Mahler ● 52, 301 was closely allied to the Secessionists. He entered their circle in 1902 following his marriage, in the Karlskirche ▲ 238, to Alma Schindler, the daughter of a painter who for a while had shared a studio w Hans Makart ● 103, and whose mother had remarried the Secessionist painter Carl Moll ● 104.

THE END OF HISTORICISM. During the second half of the 19 century, Franz-Joseph sanctioned the destruction of Vienna ramparts, which were replaced by the huge buildings along the Ring ● 84, ▲ 198 (the Votive Church, the new Universi the City Hall, the National Theater, the Parliament, and so on). All these buildings were designed in the Historicist styl with references and decorative motifs borrowed from Gree Gothic and Renaissance art. Toward the end of the century Viennese intellectuals began to call into question the value of liberal culture, and the architecture of the Ring became symbolic target of their attacks. Although Gustav Klimt an Otto Wagner had shone as historicists (the former was

SECESSION ✪ KÜNSTLERHAUS KARLSPLATZ KARLSKIRCHE MUSIKVEREINGEBÄUDE STEPHANSDOM ✪ HISTORISCHES MUSEUM DER STADT WIEN STADTPARK

IMMEUBLES JUGENDSTIL D'OTTO WAGNER

ponsible for the ceilings of the Burgtheater ● *204*, for
...mple), they joined up with the group which between 1897
... 1898 created the celebrated pavilion, whose bare,
...ometrical outlines caused as much of a furor as the bold
...tum inscribed on its pediment: "Der Zeit ihre Kunst, der
...nst ihre Freiheit" ("Every epoch has its art, and every art
... freedom"). A comment about Joseph Maria Olbrich by
...rk Varnedoe, taken from *Vienna 1900*, can be applied
...ually well to the entire Secessionist movement: "In his
...ction to the historicist stereotypes of the
...ngstrasse, Olbrich deliberately cast about for
...nething that would be indecipherable in
...ms of western convention, the symbolist
...stery of an 'enigmatic key to the registers of
...otion'."

...E GARDEN. Next to the sculpted bronze
...up representing the Roman general Mark
...tony seated in a chariot harnessed to lions (the
...rk of Arthur Strosser, 1854–1927), the garden is
...anged in terraces to accommodate the pavilion's
...FETERIA.

⧗ Half a day
◆ B A1-A2

THE SECESSIONISTS
Joseph Maria
Olbrich (left). In the
photo below: Anton
Stark, Gustav Klimt,
Koloman Moser,
Adolph Boehm,
Maximilian Lenz
(lying down), Ernst
Stoehr, Wilhelm List,
Emil Orlik, Maxi
Kurzweil, Leopold
Stolba (with
cigarette), Carl Moll
(lying down) and
Heinrich Vogeler.

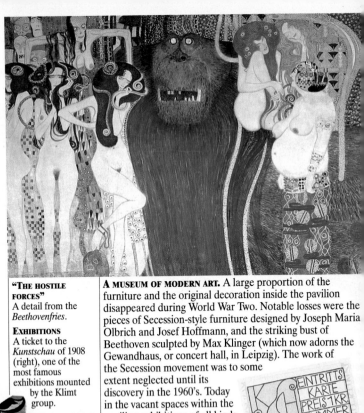

"THE HOSTILE FORCES"
A detail from the *Beethovenfries*.

EXHIBITIONS
A ticket to the *Kunstschau* of 1908 (right), one of the most famous exhibitions mounted by the Klimt group.

A piece of fabric printed with the "Secession" motif.

A MUSEUM OF MODERN ART. A large proportion of the furniture and the original decoration inside the pavilion disappeared during World War Two. Notable losses were the pieces of Secession-style furniture designed by Joseph Maria Olbrich and Josef Hoffmann, and the striking bust of Beethoven sculpted by Max Klinger (which now adorns the Gewandhaus, or concert hall, in Leipzig). The work of the Secession movement was to some extent neglected until its discovery in the 1960's. Today in the vacant spaces within the pavilion exhibitions of all kinds of contemporary art are regularly organized, and there is a bookshop which sells a wide range of exhibition catalogues, posters and postcards.

"BEETHOVENFRIES" ★ **.** There is a striking contrast between the Beethoven Frieze (Beethovenfries) and the frescoes of the Burgtheater ▲ *204* that Gustav Klimt had painted fifteen years earlier in 1888. In the interval, Klimt, the heir to historicism, invented a highly personal and radically innovative way of painting. For their fourteenth collective exhibition, which was scheduled for 1902, the Secessionist artists decided on the theme of the genius of Ludwig van Beethoven ● *50*, ▲ *298*. A gigantic sculpture by Max Klinger in honor of the master was displayed in the pavilion, representing him as an Olympian figure imposing order on the eagle of existence through the power of art. At the same time Gustav Klimt set about creating a monumental fresco for the building based on the composer, the Beethovenfries. The immense frieze is more than 110 feet long and extends across four walls of the pavilion; the work is executed in casein on a base of stucco encrusted with gemstones. It is considered today to be one of Klimt's masterpieces. The frieze was taken down after the 1902 exhibition, and belonged for many years to a private collector,

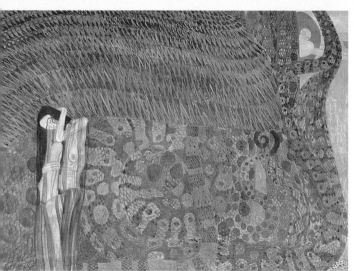

SECESSION

Posters by Koloman
Moser in 1902
(below) and Alfred
Roller in 1903 (below
left).

...fore being bought back by the Austrian
...vernment in the 1970's. After
...storation, it was replaced in its original
...sition in the renovated Secession
...vilion.

...MAZE OF SYMBOLS. On the left as you
...ter the room, the frieze begins with the
...eme of *Nostalgia for Past Happiness*,
...mbolized by flying figures. Then comes
...roup representing *The Pains of the
...ak*; the Weak (a kneeling couple) are
...n imploring the mercy of the Strong
...the person of a knight in armor). On
... small wall at the end of the room,
...imt painted *The Hostile Powers* (the
...nt Typheus and his daughters, the
...ree Gorgons) against whom the gods
...e shown to be striving in vain. Here
...o are allegories of sickness, madness,
...ath, sloth, luxury and intemperance,
...companied by the symbol of *Grief*, a
...ouching woman. On the long right-
...nd wall, the flying figures reappear, symbolizing happiness
...d the aspirations of humanity. *Poetry and Music* (the latter
...presented by a woman playing the lyre) and all the arts lead
...n to supreme happiness. The fresco is then interrupted by
...vindow embrasure, through which the statue of Beethoven
...n be seen. It continues on the far side of the window with a
group of women and a choir of angels
framing an embracing couple. These figures
are meant to illustrate the *Ode to Joy*, the
final movement of Beethoven's *Ninth
Symphony*. Gustav Mahler ● *52*, ▲ *301,* who
was a friend of Klimt's, is likely to have
advised him in his choice of themes. (In
addition to this frieze, the city of Vienna
possesses all the artist's preliminary
drawings, studies and sketches for it, which
are kept at the Albertina ▲ *196*.)

THE DECO ARTS
Josef Hoffmann
(1870–1956) and
Koloman Moser
(1868–1918) designed
furniture (opposite);
Otto Wagner often
created original
furniture for his
buildings; and the
other Secessionist
artists designed
jewelry, tableware,
silver and gold
objects, fabrics and
posters. They also
illustrated books,
along with their own
review, *Ver Sacrum.*

ADOLF LOOS (1870–1933)
The *Café Museum* ▲ *223*, an early building by Adolf Loos ● *86, 90*, ▲ *142, 174* was completed in 1899, one year after his break with the Secessionist movement.

FRIEDRICHSTRASSE

"CAFÉ MUSEUM". A few minutes walk from the Secession Pavilion at no. 6 Friedrichstrasse stands the *Café Museum*, built by Adolf Loos in 1889 (one year after the pavilion). Loos was a member of the Secession to start with, but decided to break with the movement in 1898 since he wante to develop a more functional and starker architectural aesthetic than that of his colleagues Joseph Maria Olbrich and Otto Wagner. Long before the public scandal caused by his Loos Haus on Michaelerplatz ▲ *174*, the *Café Museum* s perfectly represented the architect's new doctrine of severit and simplicity that Loos' contemporaries mischievously nicknamed it "The Nihilism Café". As such it became the principal meeting place for the writers, artists and musician of the Secessionist movement ● *67*. Today it is a student caf and has lost much of the purity of the original design; the furniture has been changed and posters have been put up, covering part of the walls, which were originally kept as bar as a monastery refectory. A pioneer of functional architecture whose

THE MARKETS
Wienzeile is best known for the FOOD MARKET (Naschmarkt), which is held all week long on its central reservation *(naschen* means "to nibble" or "eat with relish"). Many of the stalls are kept by Orientals, especially Chinese and Turks, selling exotic produce; Orientals also run the small restaurants which are scattered around the market. Every Saturday a FLEA MARKET is set up in the open air at the far end of the Naschmarkt.

"Wagner is to Viennese art what the emperor is to Austria-Hungary: the cement that holds together alliances which would be impossible without him."

Kirk Varnedoe

ment of glory was not to come until the 20th
tury, Loos built villas and shops and little else, all
is radical and distinctive style.

ENZEILE

enzeile (the banks of the Wien) is an avenue
ning southwest from Mariahilf in the 6th District
he way to the Schönbrunn Palace ▲ *274,* passing
Secession Pavilion on the way. It is a road with
eral broad curves following the lines of the
andering river Wien, part of which (from
chmarkt to the Stadtpark ▲ *226*) runs
erground. Perhaps the road really should be
ed Secession Avenue, since several of its buildings
vell as the Secession Pavilion are in the style of
movement.

LDINGS BY OTTO WAGNER. Two very fine
dential buildings on the avenue, nos. 38 and 40,
e designed by Otto Wagner ● *86, 88.* The façade
he spectacular MAJOLIKAHAUS is entirely covered
pattern of ceramic tiles representing a huge
ssoming tree with branches that spread all round
he building next door, occupying the corner, was also
t in 1898 (at the same time as the Secession Pavilion). It
a more refined décor, with a façade by Koloman Moser
ed medallions framing women's faces, golden palm fronds
golden climbing vines. The other buildings of special
rest here are the METRO STATIONS ▲ *240* designed by
o Wagner (Kettenbrückengasse, Pilgramgasse and
rgaretengürtel) and several further residential buildings in
Secession style.

AFÉ SPERL". The *Café Sperl* (1880), situated at
11 Gumpendorferstrasse, northwest of Wienzeile,
aains a favorite meeting-place for Viennese intellectuals
6.

JUGENDSTIL BUILDINGS
Buildings by Otto Wagner on the Linke Wienzeile (above), including the Medallion House, no. 38, and the Majolikahaus, no. 40.

MORNING COFFEE
"It was about seven in the morning when we arrived at the door of the *Café Magerl.* The first white rays of sunlight were visible, gilding the bread rolls, the poppyseed galettes and the salted baguette loaves. The first coffee, virginal, fresh-roasted and aromatic, wreathed us like a second morning. Joseph Branco sat beside me, dry, dark, southern, gay, wide awake and bursting with health. I was ashamed of my blond pallor and night-owl's fatigue."
Joseph Roth,
The Crypt of the Capuchins

KARLSKIRCHE

To the southeast of Karlsplatz, just before the great gardens, stands the church of St Charles Borromeo (Karlskirche). This is without doubt the most impressive Baroque building in Vienna. It was commissioned by J. B. Fischer von Erlach ● *74, 80,* ▲ *138, 147,* by Charles VI, who had made a vow to build a church dedicated to St Charles to mark his relief at the end of the plague epidemic in 1713. Fischer von Erlach directed the construction of Karlskirche from 1716 to 1723, and his son Josef Emanuel took over from 1723 to 1737 to complete the building. Facing the church is a work by the British sculptor Henry Moore, donated to the city of Vienna by the artist.

PLAGUE AND HERESY. Right from the time of Charles V and his son Philip II of Spain, the Habsburgs had taken the side the Popes against the Protestants. The Karlskirche is not merely a votive church; it is also intended to glorify the secular power of the Holy Roman Emperors and the Cathol faith they championed. The blend of Romanesque, Greek a Byzantine styles symbolizes these two aspects of the emperor's authority. Whether this blend succeeds is still a matter of some debate: some find it too disparate, others argue that the borrowings from ancient architecture, all of them perfectly integrated, are a tribute to the wide culture the church's architects.

GREEKS, ROMANS AND CHINESE. From the outside, Karlskirche is reminiscent of certain great Roman basilicas the Renaissance, notably St Peter's. More original is the framing of the dome by two columns which look like minare These are obviously inspired by the columns of Trajan and Marcus Aurelius in Rome ▲ *185.* From close up, the roofs o the two side pavilions seem to be borrowed from Chinese pagodas.

DUAL SYMBOLISM. The monuments and sculptures that cove the Karlskirche are loaded with symbolism. The Christian faith is glorified by sculpted angels (at the entrance), by the representation of virtues such as faith, hope and charity (ov the pediment and the side pavilions) and by the outsize statue of St Charles Borromeo (over the pediment). A further study of the church reveals other less obvious symbols of the power of the Habsburgs. The two columns, for exampl are a reference to the legendary Pillars of Hercules in Spain, which were included i the coat of arms of Charles V. Note also the eagles and imperial crowns carved the tops of these two columns, and th spiral bas-reliefs around them representing episodes from the li of St Charles Borromeo. Other decorative devices embody the two themes of steadfastness and courage – *Constantia et Fortitu* – the motto of Charles VI, wh

ST CHARLES BORROMEO
St Charles Borromeo, Archbishop of Milan (1538-84), took care of that city's plague victims in 1576, without a thought for his own health. He also played a leading role at the Council of Trent, which launched the Counter-Reformation, and prevented the rise of Protestantism in northern Italy. For these two reasons Emperor Charles VI chose him to be the patron saint of his new church.

As in all Baroque buildings, the décor is sumptuous; valuable materials are used, notably polychrome marble.

the patron of the church.

OVAL NAVE. Inside the church, one discovers that the dome [is n]ot round but oval, as is the nave below it. The natural light [com]ing from the windows around the dome blends softly with [the] muted artificial light rising from beneath. The fresco on [the] dome represents the apotheosis of St Charles [Bor]romeo: assisted by the Virgin, he implores [the] Holy Trinity to rid the world of the plague. [Sev]eral groups of angels and allegorical scenes, [arra]nged in a series of concentric circles, occupy [the] oval space. At its center is the turret of the [do]me, with the Dove of the Holy Spirit painted [at i]ts top. In the fresco, note on the left the angel [set]ting a torch to Luther's Bible. Johann [Mic]hael Rottmayr also painted the fresco above [the] organ loft, a celebration of music: *St Cecilia [an]d the Heavenly Choirs*.

THE ALTAR. The high altar represents St Charles Borromeo [asc]ending into heaven on a cloud surrounded by angels. Its [imp]act is overwhelming and theatrical, like that of all [Bar]oque works, and it was probably designed by Fischer von [Erl]ach. In addition, the church contains a number of [pai]ntings and altarpieces by other artists: *Jesus and the [Rom]an Centurion, The Healing of the [Par]alytic, St Elizabeth of Hungary* by [Dan]iel Gran, *The Resurrection [of th]e Son of the Widow of [Nai]m* by

THE DOME
The fresco by Johann Michael Rottmayr
▲ *139, 293* contains a range of old pinks and pale blues which harmonize with the other colors of the dome's interior.

The magnificent Karlskirche organ.

Karlsplatz (a postcard from the turn of the century).

239

Martino Altamonte and *The Assumption* by Sebastiano Ricci. The pulpit, choirstalls and confessionals are all high Baroque.

THE TREASURY. The best pieces here are the vestments of St Charles and a gold and silver reliquary bearing the imperial crown and the two-headed Habsburg eagle.

KARLSPLATZ

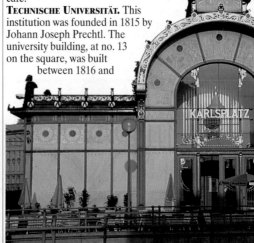

JOHANNES BRAHMS

A number of architects and urban designers have criticized the confused appearance of Karlsplatz, which has been altered several times with no particular log. The siting of the church at an angle in order to prolong Argentinierstrasse posed something of a problem; so did th Vienne River ▲ *225* running behind it. The church could no be moved, and yet it had somehow to be the dominant feature of the square. Many other difficulties also had to be faced, including the not inconsiderable one of diverting the river.

KARLSPLATZ STATION. Among the more recent buildings he are the splendid metro pavilions designed by Otto Wagner ● *86, 90,* ▲ *228, 237, 294.* Recently renovated, these compa structures of glass and metal were built at the end of the 19th century, when Otto Wagner was commissioned to des all Vienna's metro stations, galleries and bridges. Instead o settling for cold, functional architecture, Wagner determin to use all the Jugendstil resources and refinements he coul think of; and the resulting design was a riot of curves and gilded floral motifs which gives the stations a lavish appearance. Today, the two pavilions of Karlsplatz are hom to a small WAGNER MUSEUM and a minute café.

TECHNISCHE UNIVERSITÄT. This institution was founded in 1815 by Johann Joseph Prechtl. The university building, at no. 13 on the square, was built between 1816 and

KARLSPLATZ

18 in the neo-classical style, by Joseph Schemerl n Leytenbach. Its main façade of Ionic columns ces the Resselpark. Most of the statues in this park present Austrian inventors: Josef Ressel himself who signed propellors for ships, Siegfried Markus (the ternal combustion engine) and Joseph Madersperger (the wing machine). In the same company is a statue of the mposer Johannes Brahms by Rudolf Weyr.

ANDELSAKADEMIE. The neo-Gothic façade (1860–2) of the hool of commerce is decorated with statues of great inkers and discoverers including Adam Smith and hristopher Columbus. The sculptor of these was rdinand Fellner the Elder.

ISTORISCHES MUSEUM DER STADT WIEN. To the t of Karlskirche is Vienna's history museum Historisches Museum der Stadt Wien). Opened in 59, this institution contains a large collection of bjects and documents covering the history of the y from Neolithic times to the present. In the first oms are objects found during excavation of the oman camp of Vindobona and relics dating om the earliest Barbarian invasions. The iddle Ages are represented, among other ings, by a display of fragments of sculptures and ained glass from the Cathedral ▲ 132, along with weapons d armor from the era of the first Holy Roman Empire. ith the Renaissance came the Reformation, followed by the ounter-Reformation, followed by the first Turkish siege. A llection of sculptures, engravings, paintings and maquettes call Baroque Vienna during the time of the second siege 34 and the construction of the city's principal buildings. fter the 18th-century Age of Enlightenment comes the brief apoleonic interlude, followed by the Congress of Vienna 38. After this comes the Biedermeier epoque ● 62, ustrated by various paintings (Amerling ▲ 280, Fendi, hindler, Waldmüller, ● 100) and a recreation of the aywright Franz Grillparzer's ● 62, ▲ 147 apartment. The useum's final rooms are devoted to the Secession period 86, 88, with designs and plans by Otto Wagner, furniture by oloman Moser, paintings by Gustav Klimt ▲ 227, 250 and ally works by 20th-century artists including the xpressionists Egon Schiele ● 252 and Oskar Kokoscha ● 254 and sculptures by Fritz Wotruba ▲ 288.

AN ORANGE CUBE. For the time being, during the conversion of the imperial stables ▲ 189, 190 behind the Kunsthistorisches Museum ▲ 208 into a contemporary art gallery for the collections of the Museum of the 20th Century (Museum moderner Kunst in the Liechtenstein Palace ▲ 292), an ugly cube-shaped metal building has been installed almost directly opposite the Secession. Though temporary in nature, this hideous construction seems destined to remain in place for some years to come.

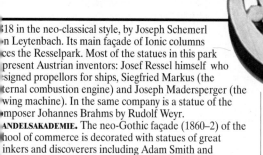

OTTO WAGNER AND THE METRO
Otto Wagner was appointed architectural adviser to the emperor in 1894, and commissioned by the Vienna municipality to design the city's public transport facilities. At that time Vienna was building one of the world's first underground train systems (after London, but before Paris). Becoming a member of the Secession movement in 1899, Otto Wagner designed about thirty stations, most of which looked like tiny palaces. Some of the prettiest are those at Karlsplatz, Schönbrunn (Hofpavilion) ▲ 286, and the Stadtpark ▲ 226.

A TEMPLE OF THE ARTS
The façade of the Künstlerhaus is adorned by statues of the great painters: Leonardo da Vinci, Michelangelo, Raphael ▲ 216, Titian ▲ 216, Dürer ▲ 196, and Velázquez ▲ 221

A poster by A. H. Schram in 1902, for the annual Künstlerhaus exhibition.

GOLDENE SAAL ● 54
Unlike most major concert halls, the one at the Musikvereinsgebäude is not inspired by the Italian model, with orchestra rows, boxes and balconies positioned around a kind of amphitheater. Instead, the huge gilded room is rectangular in form, and can hold up to two thousand people. In 1911, the auditorium, already embellished with large numbers of caryatids and muses (right), was improved by a coffered ceiling which altered its acoustics considerably.

BÖSENDORFERSTRASSE AND DUMBASTRASSE

KÜNSTLERHAUS. The Viennese Visual Artists' Cooperative was founded in 1861; it was in reaction to this humdrum institution that the adherents of Klimt ▲ 227, 250 started their Secession movement ▲ 222, 232 in 1897. The headquarters of the association (Künstlerhaus ▲ 224) was constructed between 1865 and 1868 by August Weber, in the style of the Italian Renaissance to plans by a consortium of architects. Today it serves as a theater and is also used by the history museum for exhibitions and conferences.

MUSIKVEREINSGEBÄUDE. The Friends of Music building (Musikvereinsgebäude) is on Dumbastrasse, in front of the Künstlerhaus. The music association was founded in 1812; its Renaissance-style headquarters, designed by Theophil von Hansen (1813–91), dates from 1867–9. Just as he did later when designing the Parliament ▲ 205, Hansen made free use of Greek elements of architecture. This building is now the home of the Vienna Philharmonic Orchestra ● 54, which the world's greatest conductors have directed for the last one hundred and fifty years. The concerts organized by the Friends of Music association are internationally famous; their "Goldene Saal", one of the finest auditoriums in Vienna, is the scene of the Strauss concert, held annually to celebrate the New Year, shown on television all over the world. This auditorium with exceptional acoustics is decorated with sixteen gilded caryatids facing one

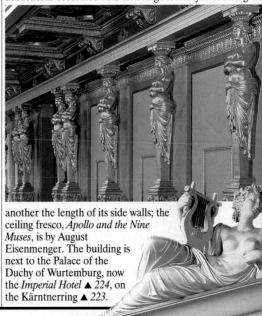

another the length of its side walls; the ceiling fresco, *Apollo and the Nine Muses*, is by August Eisenmenger. The building is next to the Palace of the Duchy of Wurtemburg, now the *Imperial Hotel* ▲ 224, on the Kärntnerring ▲ 223.

From Theresianum
to Zentralfriedhof

▲ THE THERESIANUM
TO THE ZENTRALFRIEDHOF

STEPHANSDOM ✪ SCHWARZENBERG PALACE ✪ UNTERES BELVEDERE ✪ OBERES BELVEDERE ✪ RIESENRAD ARSENAL

🚌 **Half a day**

◆ **B** A2-A3-B3-B4-C2-D4

THE THERESIANUM:
A SUMMER RESIDENCE
Leopold I ● *31, 35*
▲ *138, 275*, Joseph I
and Charles VI
▲ *142, 302* spent their
summers at the
Theresianum.

The façade of the
Theresianum,
decorated with
Francis II's coat of
arms.

South of the Ring
▲ *198* and karlskirche
▲ *238* are the neighborhoods
of WIEDEN (4th
District) and FAVORITEN
(10th District), both full of
handsome buildings which stand in
their own gardens.

THE THERESIANUM

FROM THE FAVORITA TO THE THERESIANUM. T.
Favorita was the Habsburgs' summer residenc
until it was destroyed by the Turks ● *34* in 1683. The newly
constructed Schönbrunn ▲ *274* then took over as the summ
palace. On the ruins of the old Favorita, the Italian architec
Ludovico Burnacini constructed the Theresianum (1687–90
a long, austere building fronting Favoritenstrasse. It was
named after Maria Theresa ● *36*, ▲ *260, 291*, who establishe
a college there to train young aristocrats for public-service
careers. Later it became the DIPLOMATIC SCHOOL
(Diplomatische Akademie). The headquarters
of Austrian Radio (Österreichische Rundfunk)
are now in the park of the Theresianum where
it fronts Argentinierstrasse.

"The Rudolfinerhaus is a private hospital in a city of socialized
dicine; its old stone walls are of the same Maria Theresa yellow as
he palace of Schönbrunn, or the Upper and Lower Belvederes."

J. Irving

WARZENBERGPLATZ

warzenbergplatz is named after Prince
warzenberg, the general who commanded the
d armies against the French at the Battle of
ozig in 1813, and whose statue – the
WARZENBERGDENKMAL – stands in the square.
SSEN DENKMAL. In the middle of the square (which
Russians rechristened "Stalinplatz") stands a
morial to the Liberation of Vienna by the Red Army
freiungsdenkmal der roten Armee), a replica of the ones
Budapest, Bucharest, Sofia, Warsaw and Riga. The
nnese call it the "Monument to the Unknown Looter". At
end of the Soviet occupation in 1955, Austria agreed to
ntain the memorial in good condition, but the promise
not kept. Today this last vestige of the Red Army in
nna has to be guarded round the clock by policemen, so
er are the city's memories of the Soviet interlude; but
bably the greatest injustice of the Russen Denkmal now is
it obscures part of the façade of the Schwarzenberg
ace.

THE SCHWARZENBERG PALACE. The palace, which looks
out on the square from behind the equestrian
statue of Prince Karl Philipp Schwarzenberg,
is now a luxury hotel (*Im Palais
Schwarzenberg*, no. 9). It was one of
the very first aristocratic
palaces to be built as a
summer residence
outside the city
walls. In
about

**DESTROYED
FRESCOES**
On either side of a
central building with
a colonnaded flight of
steps and a squat
tower are the two
wings, each decorated
with pilasters. The
lavish interior was
recently renovated,
but the frescoes by
Daniel Gran, which
were destroyed by
bombing during
World War Two ● *42*,
could not be saved.

ZENTRALFRIEDHOF

DR KARL
LUEGER KIRCHE

7,
nce
nsfeld-Fondi
mmissioned a first
lding from the great Baroque
hitect Johann Lukas von
debrandt ● *75, 81,* ▲ *147*; after this the
er's rival Johann Bernhard Fischer von
ach ● *74, 80,* ▲ *138* and his son Josef
anuel carried out alterations in about 1720
the Schwarzenberg princes.

NNWEG

EO-RENAISSANCE PALACE BY OTTO WAGNER. The broad
nnweg avenue begins at Schwarzenbergplatz, and
tinues toward the Lower Belvedere. Opposite the
warzenberg Palace is the splendid mansion that Otto
gner ● *86, 88* ▲ *228, 237, 240* built for himself in 1891. At
t time the architect had not yet joined the Secession
vement ▲ *232* and was drawing on the Italian Renaissance
inspiration. There is a noticeable difference between the
er and lower registers of the Wagner Palace (which was

The owner of the
Schwarzenberg
Palace, now a hotel, is
Prince Charles von
Schwarzenberg, from
Bohemia. In 1989 he
became general
secretary to the
President of the
Czech Republic in
Prague.

The Belvedere Palaces owe their name to the magnificent view from the Upper

Palace of Vienna and the Vienna woods ■ *18*.

later bought by the Hoyos family): on the first and second floors, the façade is very somber with projecting stonework while at the top of the building the windows are surrounded by garlands of flowers.

THE GARDENS. The GARDENS OF THE SCHWARZENBERG PALACE (Schwarzenberggarten) merge to the east with the magnificent Belvederegarten, the park surrounding the two BELVEDERE PALACES ★.
SALESIANERINENKIRCHE. The Baroque dome of the Church of the Salesian Convent (designed by Donato Felice d'Allio and built between 1717 and 1730) ▲ *303* precedes the far larger structure of the Belvedere.

GARDEKIRCHE. The Guards' Church (Gardekirche), which stands opposite the entrance to the Lower Belvedere on the far side of the Rennweg, originally belonged to the imperial hospital before becoming the Polish church. It was built by Nikolaus von Pacassi ▲ *192* in the Rococo style, shortly after the little theater at the Schönbrunn Palace ▲ *274*.

UNTERES BELVEDERE ★

The Rennweg runs past the old STABLES and thence to the entrance of the Lower Belvedere (Unteres Belvedere), former residence of Prince Eugène of Savoy.
HERCULES AND APOLLO. "He was short and ugly, with a snub nose, flaring nostrils and an upper lip so narrow that he could not close his mouth". The unprepossessing figure thus described by the Duchess of Orléans was none other than Prince Eugène, whom she met at Versailles. Perhaps it was somehow to compensate for his physical defects that the prince had himself represented as Apollo on the ceiling of his palace and devoted much of his time to the cultivation of beauty, amassing a fabulous collection of works of art. The two Belvedere Palaces, which almost outshine their contemporary, Schönbrunn ▲ *274*, were commissioned by Prince Eugène at a time when his military fame was at its height. He had succeeded in ejecting

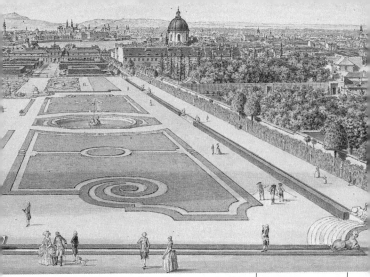

Turks from Hungary forever ● *34*, and now turned to his
[oth]er passion, as a patron of the arts. As a young general in
[168]3 he had bought himself a site for his future summer
[pal]ace. Twenty years later he was in a position to employ
[Joh]ann Lukas von Hildebrandt, one of the two
[gre]atest architects in Europe, to turn the project
[int]o reality. Hildebrandt's rival, J. B. Fischer
[vo]n Erlach ● *74, 80*, ▲ *138* was engrossed at
[the] time in the building of Schönbrunn; the
[tw]o architects had already collaborated on the
[pla]ns for Prince Eugène's winter palace ▲ *147*,
[be]gun in 1697–8. The Lower Belvedere was the
[fir]st of the two palaces to be completed; it stands on
[a si]te overlooking the Rennweg between the Schwarzenberg
[Pal]ace and the Salesian Convent. The Upper Belvedere was
[bu]ilt between 1721 and 1722 on a promontory dominating the
park and the Lower Belvedere.

CONQUEROR OF THE TURKS. Prince Eugène of
Savoy (1663–1736) was born in France; his
first ambition was a career in the church,
but he changed his mind and opted
instead to enter the army of Louis
XIV. When in 1683 the king
refused to give him command of a
regiment he went to Austria to
serve Emperor Leopold I against
the Turks. With his victory at Zenta
in 1697, Eugène enabled the empire
to recover Hungary and won fame
throughout Europe. As
commander-in-chief of the
Habsburg armies from 1697
(under Leopold I and
subsequently under his sons
Joseph I and Charles VI), Prince
Eugène won a series of victories
over the Ottoman Empire. In
1703 he was appointed
president of the Austrian
monarchy's war council;
he fought against the
armies of Louis XIV
during the War of the
Spanish Succession and

**THE FRENCH
GARDENS**
The gardens, which
ascend in terraces
from the Lower to
the Upper Belvedere,
were designed at the
beginning of the
18th century by
the French
landscape
architect
Dominique Girard.
They include wide
lawns, immense
parterres, several
pools and countless
statues including the
curious sphinxes near
the Upper Belvedere.
The enigmatic smile
of one of these
sphinxes is shown
opposite.

THE BELVEDERE ✪
The ensemble formed
by the two buildings of
the Belvedere is a
remarkable example
of late Baroque
architecture.
It also contains some
very fine museums: the
Museum of Medieval
Art and the Museum
of Baroque Art, in the
Lower Belvedere; and
the Gallery of 19th-
and 20th-Century
Austrian Art in the
Upper Belvedere.

247

Details of the architecture (top) and the gardens (above) of the Belvedere.

FAMOUS OCCUPANTS OF THE BELVEDERE
On Prince Eugène's death in 1736, the emperor bought his two palaces. For a few years, they were used for storing the art collections which are now displayed at the Art History Museum▲ 208. Anton Bruckner ● 52, ▲ 195, who was appointed organist to the court in 1868, lodged at the Belvedere and died there in 1896. At that time the Belvedere's most distinguished resident was Archduke Franz-Ferdinand, who lived here from 1894 until his assassination in 1914 ● 33, ▲ 145.

completed the eviction of the Turks from Hungarian territo between 1716 and 1717. Thanks to him, Austria embarked a long period of uninterrupted peace and prosperity, and during this time he himself constructed his winter palace ▲ 147 and the two palaces of the Belvedere. So vast was his influence on the conduct of Austrian affairs that he was nicknamed the "Backroom Emperor".

FRANZ-FERDINAND. After the suicide of his cousin Rudolph ▲ 145 at Mayerling ◆ 323, Archduke Franz-Ferdinand (1863–1914) became the heir to the throne. Bitter rivalry emerged between the aging Franz-Joseph ● 41, ▲ 142, 178 and the young archduke Franz-Ferdinand, who meddled constantly in affairs of state, rarely missing an opportunity criticize the policies of his uncle, whom he thought much to timid. On one occasion he wrote to the Pope to block the appointment of a bishop, and on another he sent a telegram to Austria's ambassadors countermanding official instructions. In effect he ran a kind of opposition governme which advocated more vigorous policies. Yet there was one point on which he was deeply vulnerable. Franz-Ferdinand had made a mésalliance which he was obliged to turn into a morganatic marriage, thus forfeiting for his heirs any claim the throne. When he was assassinated in 1914, the reaction Europe was one of relief that a future despot had been eliminated; but within months the continent was embroiled World War One.

TREATIES AND CONFERENCES. After their acquisition by the Austrian Republic, the two palaces were the scene of a

...mber of historic events. Hitler organized diplomatic
...nferences in them; and in 1955 the Belvedere Treaty, which
...ought to an end the Allied occupation of Austria ● 33, was
...gned in the Lower Belvedere by Antoine Pinay for France,
...hn Foster Dulles for the US, Molotov for the Soviet Union,
...arold Macmillan for Great Britain and Leopold Figl for
...ustria. The Austrian constitution was ratified there in the
...me year. Since the beginning of the century the Lower
...elvedere has housed the Museums of Austrian
...aroque and Medieval Art and the Upper
...elvedere has been the Gallery of 19th- and
...0th-Century Austrian Art.

...HE MAIN COURTYARD. A monumental gate
...ads through to the main courtyard of the
...lace. It is crowned by allegories of Strength
...d Wisdom, and by the Cross of Savoy, Prince
...ugène's coat of arms. From the courtyard one
...n see the orangery which houses the
...useum of Medieval Austrian Art
...useum mittelalterlicher
...sterreichischer Kunst ▲ 256) and the
...posing Baroque façade of the Lower
...elvedere. Designed by Hildebrandt at the
...ginning of the 18th century, the latter is a
...rmonious integration of seven buildings of varying lengths.
...e central building is ornamented with several pilasters,
...atues, and balustrades at attic level; it is flanked by two
...ngs, which sport small pavilions at each end. This first
...lace, Prince Eugène's summer residence (he also had a
...nter one ▲ 147 within the city walls) is a majestic edifice.

...ROCKMUSEUM. Inside, the Museum of Baroque Art ● 80-1
...s been organized in several different rooms, some of them
...ally splendid: the GALLERY OF MARBLES (Marmorgalerie);
...e mirror gallery, or GOLDEN ROOM (Goldenkabinett), with
...e gilded Rococo wainscoting; and the GALLERY OF
...OTESQUES (Groteskensaal), decorated with grotesque
...scoes by Jonas Drentwett, which include several grimacing
...sks by Franz Xavier Messerschmidt.

THE GROTESQUES
When the first frescoes were uncovered at Pompeii, they were buried by earth which had to be excavated. The motifs found in the "grottoes" were referred to as "grotesques".

GRIMACING FACES
The most startling items in the Museum of Baroque Art are Franz Xavier Messerschmidt's grimacing heads. He was a highly unconventional artist (1736–83), who was greatly appreciated at the Austrian court. To avenge himself on people who mocked his strange clothes and eccentric manners the sculptor sketched them as "heads of characters", but for the most part Messerschmidt's faces are based on his own.

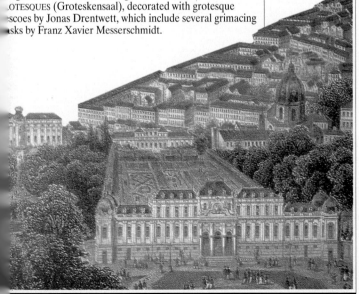

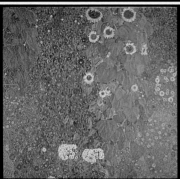

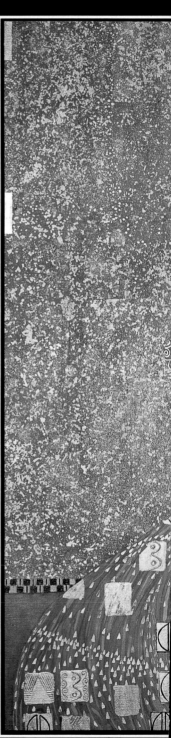

The year 1902, in which Gustav Klimt (1862–1918) unveiled his revolutionary *Beethovenfries* ▲ *234* at the Secession Exhibition ● *86,* ▲ *232,* was a turning point in his career. Both in his landscapes (above, *The Sunflower Garden*, 1905) and in his portraits of women (right, *Portrait of Adele Bloch-Bauer*, 1907), Klimt used a geometrical approach blending figures with their backgrounds in the same overall tones. Always stopping short of pure abstraction, he juggled with the ambiguities of form; in his paintings bodies, flowers and faces are liable to crop up at any moment in a cascade of color, as in

Bloch-Bauer, the decorative motifs suggest psychological conflicts. The mosaics of San Vitale at Ravenna, which Klimt visited in 1903, led him to this mannered primitivism, which became the trademark of early 20th-century Viennese decorative arts. This primitivism is seen in the vignettes by the illustrator Carl-Otto Czeschka (1878–1960) which influenced Fritz Lang's *Die Niebelungen,* and in the tunic worn by Klimt himself (below). This was designed by Emilie Flöge, who sold clothes inspired by the new aesthetic in her Vienna shop.

this astonishing portrait of a matriach of the Viennese Jewish community. Abstraction and symbolism characterize Klimt's paintings. In the *Portrait of Adele*

As recently as thirty years ago, Egon Schiele (1890–1918) was virtually forgotten in art history: today, he has taken his place alongside Modigliani and Van Gogh in the ranks of the great doomed artists, those who suffered materially and saw nothing in their lifetimes of the acclaim which was later to crown their work. His trial on a vice charge involving a beautiful young girl, the burning of an erotic drawing before the court, and his prison sentence are the best-known landmarks in Schiele's career. His short life was full of trauma, beginning with the death of his syphilitic father and ending with the artist's own death from the same epidemic which had already killed his wife Edith, pregnant at the time with their first child. Schiele, who was wont to represent himself as St Sebastian transfixed by the arrows of his critics, contributed considerably to his own legend. In the event, Egon Schiele was very young when he made contact with the collectors who were to enable him to achieve what is now rightly considered to be one of the great lifeworks of the 20th century. He was by nature anguished and oversensitive: "I must see something new, and explore it", he wrote. "I want to taste the dark waters, see the trees shiver to pieces, and come unawares upon life swarming in the hedges." This

voracious curiosity impelled him to seek in everything the vital shared pulse that breaks down the barrier between man and nature. His landscapes are much more than mere expressions of his mood; they are paintings of the fate of humankind (above, *The Trees*, 1917). He uses the naked human body, with mortified flesh, bleeding sex and jutting bones, as a means to investigate the nature of love and pain. In *The Family* (opposite, 1917) he can be recognized as the figure protecting his family with the gesture of an injured bird. However, Edith and the unborn child are not those represented in the picture, which was to be one of a series for a mausoleum.

"One need answer to no one for a work of art; but for a house one must answer to all the world. ... The work of art is revolutionary, the house is conservative."

Adolf Loos

Oskar Kokoschka (1886–1980) and Richard Gerstl (1883–1908) were both influenced by the works of Holder, Munch and Van Gogh, exhibited in Vienna between 1904 and 1906. Gerstl abandoned his ornamental arabesques to seek cruder harmonies through heavy brushwork and dislocated forms. There is no social message in this solitary artist's work, whose only interest was philosophy. Gerstl's only friends were musicians of the Vienna School ● 52, whose un-compromising aesthetic somehow legitimized his own. He was one of Arnold Schönberg's best friends, and indeed Schönberg's wife left him for Gerstl, who committed suicide shortly afterwards after destroying part of his work. His *Laughing Man* (above) is a self-portrait from 1907. Encouraged by his friend Adolf Loos ▲ 174, Kokoschka was also seduced by expressionism. He abandoned the stark graphics of his first years in Berlin and Vienna, in favor of an increasingly violent style. In his portraits from 1908 to 1915 the only thing that counts is the subject. His aim was to capture the essence of his models (opposite, *Portrait of Carl Moll* ● 104, 1914).

One of the gateways of the Upper Belvedere.

"Garp explained to her that the Upper Belvedere contained only the nineteenth- and twentieth-century paintings, but Jenny said that the nineteenth and twentieth centuries were enough for her.

3., Prinz Eugen-Straße

Garp explained that she could at least walk ... to the Lower Belvedere and see the Baroque collection, but Jenny shook her head; she had taken ... art history courses ... she'd had enough education, she said."
John Irving,
The World According to Garp

The museum also possesses the lead originals for sculptures by Georg Raphael Donner which adorn the Neuer Markt fountain ▲ *141*, as well as some Baroque paintings (many of them projects for frescoes) by Johann Michael Rottmayr ● *139, 159, 293* and Anton Franz Maulbertsch ▲ *167*.
MUSEUM MITTELALTERLICHER KUNST. The Museum of Medieval Art is housed in the former ORANGERY. It possesses some spectacular altarpieces, particularly from the 15th century.

OBERES BELVEDERE ★

Like the Lower Belvedere, the Upper Belvedere (Oberes Belvedere) is made up of seven different buildings skillfully united. The difference lies in its much greater elegance; the result is more Baroque, with an Oriental touch which lends it great charm.
A MASTERPIECE OF IRONWORK. The public entrance to the palace is by way of its south gate, which is flanked by two stone lions, or else by climbing up through the terraced gardens which open out in front of the Lower Belvedere. The gate is one of the great achievements of Baroque wrought iron.
A FAIRYTALE PALACE. The south façade of the Upper Belvedere is best viewed from the Landstrasser Gürtel. Its statues, Rococo decorations and elegant domed roofs are mirrored in an immense pool of water. During the 18th

...entury the Viennese began to take an interest in Orientalism
...nd inevitably they fell under the spell of the Upper
...elvedere Palace, which is more like something out of *The
...housand and One Nights* than the residence of a European
...rince. The illusion was all the more convincing when Prince
...ugène organized lavish masked balls and firework displays.
...rom many points of view this palace bears the imprint of the
...rient; the long roofs of the main buildings are similar to the
...remonial tents of the Turkish viziers who came to lay siege
... Vienna in 1683, while the pavilions on the wings have
...omes reminiscent of the mosques of Istanbul. Furthermore
...e façade's abundant decoration resembles a magnificent
...ece of Arab gold work.

HE VESTIBULE. The interior is just as sumptuous as the
...terior, with monumental Atlas figures ● *82,* ▲ *157*
...pporting the low vaults of the entrance vestibule.

**HE AUSTRIAN 19TH- AND 20TH-
...ENTURY GALLERY.** Since 1953, the
...pper Belvedere has been the home of
...e extraordinarily rich Gallery of 19th-
...d 20th-Century Austrian Art
...Österreichische Galerie des 19. und
.... Jahrhunderts). Here also is the
...orious Baroque MARBLE ROOM
...Grosser Marmorsaal), all in pink
...arble, with a fresco of the *Apotheosis
...Prince Eugène* by Carlo Carlone on
... ceiling. The Austrian Gallery
...ssesses nearly all the paintings of
...ustav Klimt ▲ *250* and Egon Schiele
... *252,* a large number of canvases by
...skar Kokoschka ▲ *254,* and works by
...rl Moll and the Norwegian painter Edvard Munch. From
...e 19th century, there is a highly representative collection of
...intings by Hans Makart ● *103,* Friedrich von Amerling
... *241, 280,* Ferdinand Georg Waldmüller ● *100* and Rudolf
...n Alt ● *103,* among others.

...CHWEIZERGARTEN

...USEUM DES 20. JAHRHUNDERTS. Vienna has two museums
...dicated to modern art: the Liechtenstein Palace ▲ *292* and
...e Museum of the 20th Century (Museum des 20. Jahr-
...nderts). Exhibitions
... contemporary art
... regularly
...ged in the
...ter.

View of Vienna from
the Upper Belvedere.

MARMORGALERIE
The Marble Room at
the Baroque Art
Museum is covered in
stucco ornaments and
decorated with a
magnificent ceiling
fresco by Martino
Altomonte
(1657–1745): *The
Triumph of Prince
Eugène, Conqueror of*

the Turks. This
Neapolitan painter
was also known as
Martin Hohenberg.
In 1684, he became
court painter to John
Sobieski, King of
Poland ● *34,* and
lived in Austria
from 1702 onward.

▲ THE THERESIANUM TO THE ZENTRALFRIEDHOF

In the Swiss garden (Schweizergarten) behind the pavilion is a park containing sculptures from all over the world.

MUSEUM OF THE 20TH CENTURY
The museum occupies a modern structure which was displayed at the 1958 Universal Exhibition in Brussels.

MUSEUM OF MILITARY HISTORY ★
After the 1848 Revolution ▲ 40, Franz-Joseph ▲ 144, 178 decided to build an arsenal and barracks near Vienna. The arsenal was designed in a Byzantine-Moorish style by Theophil von Hansen, architect of the Stock Exchange ▲ 201 and the Parliament ▲ 205.

HEERESGESCHICHTLICHES MUSEUM

ARSENAL. The imperial and royal artillery arsenal was built like a massive fortress between 1848 and 1856. It consists of no fewer than thirty-one buildings, one of which is the Museum of Military History (Heeresgeschichtliches Museum). All the collections accumulated by the Habsburgs since the 11th century were kept on these huge premises. Shortly after the opening of the museum in 1869 the collection of arms and armor was moved to the Hofburg ▲ 175; even so the museum's exhibits are more th sufficient to trace in detail the history of the imperial arme forces up to World War One.

MILITARY LEADERS. Taking the museum in more or less chronological order, begin on the first floor, which can be reached by way of the vaulted neo-Gothic vestibule. Backin onto each column here is the marble statue of one of the principal sovereigns or military commanders of the empir A staircase leads up to the second floor, which begins w THE HALL OF FAME. The frescoes in this room and in the ones adjoining it are all by Karl von Blaas (1815–94), whose particula brand of realism suited the taste of Franz-Joseph. The all depict battles, especiall the celebrated battle of Zenta (1697) against the Turks, and those of the campaigns against Napoleon ● 38.

THE THIRTY YEARS' WAR. The next rooms are devoted to the ⋯ th century, a time when the science of warfare was ⋯eloping apace all over Europe. The Thirty Years' War ⋯18–48) pitted the Catholic Habsburgs against the ⋯testant princes of Germany, and, together with the war ⋯inst the Turks, had a profound impact on military practice. ⋯e Low Countries under William of Orange, and Sweden ⋯er Gustavus Adolphus, began to use smaller, ⋯ter-trained, more mobile armies equipped with ⋯rwhelming firepower. The infantry (harquebusiers, musketeers and pikemen)

⋯yed a
⋯cial rôle,
⋯le the advent of brass and iron cannons
⋯ddenly made artillery much lighter and more
⋯ily maneuverable, turning it into an independent
⋯itary force. As to cavalry, the traditional cuirassier
⋯isions were bolstered by light dragoons. But while
⋯stavus Adolphus created a peasant army devoted to the
⋯se of Protestantism, the Habsburgs tended to hire
⋯rcenaries. The most famous of these was the
⋯ech Albrecht Valdstjin (1583–1634), known
⋯ Wallenstein in German, who placed his
⋯vate army at Ferdinand II's disposal.
⋯ other great mercenary figure was the
⋯nnese Octavio Piccolomini (1600–56)
⋯o fought the Swedes, notably at the
⋯ttle of Lutzen in 1632. In these first
⋯oms of the museum, there are
⋯merous objects, weapons and
⋯ntings that evoke this ruinous conflict
⋯ich was finally brought to an end by
⋯e Treaty of Westphalia in 1648.

⋯E WAR AGAINST THE TURKS.
⋯e empire was weakened by the
⋯irty Years' War and looked an easy
⋯get for the Turks, who had already
⋯nexed the Balkans. During the
⋯gn of Mehmet IV (1648–87)
⋯e Ottoman Empire launched
⋯ offensive which reached its
⋯max with the siege of
⋯nna in 1683 ● 34. The museum
⋯plays a number of trophies taken from⋯

The Reception Room (left), the Staircase (center) and the Chamber of Generals (right) in the Museum of Military History.

THE ASSASSINATION OF WALLENSTEIN
The German princes eventually dislodged Wallenstein, once Ferdinand II's paramount general. He negotiated with the enemy and was assassinated after he threatened to march on Prague.

PICCOLOMINI
Piccolomini played a major rôle in Wallenstein's assassination. During the Thirty Years' War he commanded the cavalry against the Swedes and the German Reformists at Nördlingen and defeated Richelieu's troops at Thionville (1640). Ferdinand III made him a prince of the empire in 1654.

"FIELD MARSHAL LAUDON ON HORSEBACK ON THE BATTLEFIELD OF KUNERSDORF"
This great general defeated Frederick II at Kunersdorf, on August 12, 1759. The painting is by Sigmund l'Allemand (1878).

MONTECUCCOLI
After the Thirty Years' War, Raimundo Montecuccoli (1609–80) fought the Turks as an Austrian marshal at Saint Gotthard (1664). He took part in the campaigns against the armies of Louis XIV from 1672. Montecuccoli wrote several books on military strategy.

the Turks, in addition to a *View of the Siege of Vienna*, showing the relief of the town by John Sobieski. Among other things, you can see the mortar that sparked the explosion of the powder magazine in Belgrade during the Turkish occupation of 1717, and the tent of the Grand Vizier Dahmat Ali, in which Prince Eugène dictated the news of his victory in a message to Charles VI. Prince Eugène also fought for Charles VI in the War of the Spanish Succession; this ended in 1715 to the advantage of Louis XIV, who put his grandson Philip V on the throne of Spain.
"MATER CASTRORUM" ● *36,* ▲ *158, 291.*
The reign of Maria Theresa (the "Mother of Encampments") was overshadowed by her rivalry with Frederick II of Prussia. From the day of her father's death, she fought Frederick for the right to the throne (the War of the Austrian Succession), later challenging the Prussian armies at Kolin (1757) during the Seven Years'

Turkish muskets from the 18th century (below left).

War (1756–63). At that time the imperial forces were commanded by Marshal von Daun (1705–66), one of the first soldiers to receive the Order of Maria Theresa. The museum has portraits and mementoes of other generals who served during the Seven Years' War, notably Lacy (1725–1801) and Laudon (1717–90).

STATUE OF THE ARCHDUKE CHARLES. The equestrian statue in the middle of the room assigned to Archduke Charles is a replica of the one in Heldenplatz ▲ 207. There are also portraits of the prince with his family and at the battle of Aspern ● 38. Francis II's brother, Archduke Charles von Habsburg (1771–1847), Duke of Teschen, led the imperial armies throughout the Revolutionary Wars. In 1792 he fought Dumouriez at Jemappes, at Amberg and at Wurzburg against Jourdan and Moreau (1796–7), and against Bonaparte during the Second Coalition's war with France (1799–1801). Appointed President of the Imperial War Council in 1801, he opposed an immediate declaration of war on Bonaparte. After Austerlitz (1805) he reorganized the Austrian army and fought Napoleon tenaciously at Eckmahl, Aspern-Essling and Wagram. After 1809, he retired to write books on military theory.

THE RADETZKY ROOM. During the 1848 revolution ● 38, the new chancellor Felix von Schwarzenberg (1800–52) and his father-in-law Windischgrätz put down the insurrections in Vienna ● 40 and Prague, while Marshal Radetzky (1766–1858) fought the nationalist movement in Italy. This room contains mementoes of the marshal and a painting of the battle of Novara (1849). There are also pictures of the defeats at Solferino (1859), against the French and the Piedmontese, and at Sadowa (1866), against the Prussians. After this period of waning influence in Europe, the Austro-Hungarian dual monarchy entered a period of peace which was only interrupted by the occupation of Bosnia-Herzegovina in 1878. Then in 1914 a Serbian nationalist assassinated Archduke Franz-Ferdinand at Sarajevo ▲ 145.

THE AUSTRIAN NAVY. In the rooms devoted to the navy, the most interesting items are the model of the frigate *Novara*, which sailed round the world between 1857 and 1859, and records of the expedition to the North Pole between 1872 and 1874, which resulted in the discovery of Franz-Josefs-land.

The colors of Prince Eugène of Savoy's Regiment of Dragoons, and a commemorative medal of Joseph II (above). A battalion banner of an imperial infantry regiment (below).

Austria was at war with France from 1792 on, not surprisingly, given that the guillotined Marie-Antoinette was Joseph II's sister. Under the Directoire regime in France (1795–9) Bonaparte led a brilliant campaign against Austria's forces in Italy; Austria then formed a coalition with the other monarchies of Europe, which Bonaparte defeated at Austerlitz (1805) and Wagram (1809) ● 32, before being himself defeated and sent into exile on Elba.

The Battle of Novara, March 23, 1849.

The bust of Brahms ● *51*
(below).

SANKT-MARXER-FRIEDHOF

THE MOZART CEMETERY. Southeast of the Museum of Mil
History is the tiny cemetery of St Mark, where Mozart
was buried on December 6, 1791. The snow and sle
prevented his friends and family from passing
through the city gates, so the hearse went
unaccompanied to the cemetery, which was the
the open countryside. The sexton threw Mozart's
into a common grave, and when the composer's wid
arrived later nobody was able to find
for her. The cemetery itself is in the
staunchest Biedermeier style ● *62*.

ZENTRALFRIEDHOF ★

At the end of the Rennweg, which is
extended by Simmeringer Hauptstra
is the central cemetery (Zentralfried
the largest graveyard in Austria (590
acres). Opened in 1874, it is said to
contain the remains of more than a
million people.

TOMBS OF THE FAMOUS. The
central avenue between the
gate and the church leads to
the crypt of the presidents
of the Austrian Republic
and other luminaries.
The best-known are
those of musicians,
though painters and
sculptors are also here,

notably Franz Alt ● *102*, Friedrich von
Amerling ▲ *241, 257, 280* and Makart.
In the Jewish sector are the tombs of
the writers Karl Kraus and
Arthur Schnitzler.

A FORGOTTEN IMPERIAL CASTLE. The
central cemetery continues on the
far side of Simmeringer Hauptstrasse.
Here are the CREMATORIUM, an extremely
handsome piece of architecture by
Clemens Holzmeister (1922) and the
remains of the castle of
Neugebäude. The latter was built
in the 16th century by
Maximilian II (1527–76), who
made it his summer residence (he
also acquired the old castle of
Katterburg ● *30* at the same time).
Following its conversion into a
powder magazine, Neugebäude
was stripped of whole sections of
its columns and decorations, which
were then used to build
Schönbrunn's Roman ruins and
the colonnade of the Gloriette
▲ *275, 284*.

The tombs of Joseph
Strauss, Johann
Strauss, Franz
Schubert and
Beethoven (above). A
memorial to Mozart
(below right).

**TOMBS OF THE
FAMOUS**
In the musicians'
precinct of the
central cemetery are
the tombs of Gluck,
Beethoven,
Schubert, Brahms,
Wolf and Schönberg,
the Strausses and
Lanner ● *48, 50, 52,
56, 58*. Haydn's
tomb is in the
Esterházy capital of
Eisenstadt ▲ *162*.
Mahler ▲ *232* is
buried in the
Grinzing cemetery,
while Bruckner's
tomb is in the crypt
of St Florian's
basilica.

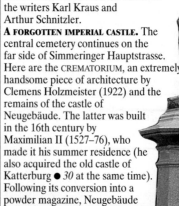

From the Prater
to the Danube

REISENRAD DONAUPARK DONAUTURM JUBILÄUMSKI VOLKS

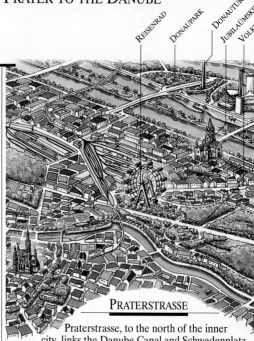

⌖ Half a day

◆ **A** A4–B4

A COMIC PLAYWRIGHT
An actor who became
a theater director in
Vienna, Johann
Nestroy (1801–62)
has remained popular
for his comedies of
manners ● *60*, which
are much cherished
by the Austrian
public. Nestroy's forte
was biting satire of
Viennese society
during the
Biedermeier era ● *62*,
which he lampooned
in dozens of farces,
comedies and
vaudevilles. His
best-known pieces are
*Der böse Geist
Lumpazivagabundus*
(1833), *Einen Jux will
er sich machen* (1842),
Der Unbeden Tende
(1846) and *Judith und
Holofernes* (1849).

THE STRAUSS HOUSE
Johann Strauss the
Younger ● *57* wrote
about two hundred
waltzes and was
known as the "Waltz
King". A critic wrote
of him in 1833, "One
might call Strauss the
Younger the very
incarnation of the
waltz".

PRATERSTRASSE

Praterstrasse, to the north of the inner
city, links the Danube Canal and Schwedenplatz
to the Praterstern intersection, which is near the park and t
fairground. The excursion boat *Johann Strauss*, moored at
FRANZ-JOSEFS-KAI ▲ *200, 229*, hosts exhibitions of Viennes
waltzes ● *56* nearly every night.
"THE BLUE DANUBE". Praterstrasse, which crosses
Leopoldstadt, has several interesting buildings, notably THE
GREEN HUNTER (no. 28) in which Joseph Lanner ● *56*, the
rival of the two Strausses, played his waltz music. Near
NESTROYPLATZ was the former site of the Carl Theater, whe
the celebrated writer Johann Nestroy (1801–62) was directo
between 1854 and 1860. Farther on, opposite the neo-
Byzantine CHURCH OF ST JOHN NEPOMUK (1846) i
the house of Johann Strauss the Younger (no. 54)
was in this building that Strauss composed his mo
famous waltz, *The Blue Danube*, in 1867. On the
same side of the road, at no. 70, the DOGES' PALA
(Dogenhof), a pastiche of a Venetian palazzo in a
Byzantine neo-Gothic style. This was probably bu
in the 19th century, at the same time as the area
known as the "Venice of Vienna" in the Prater, wh
people traveled along the canals in gondolas. This
site is now where the Ferris wheel ▲ *266* and the
merry-go-rounds of the fairground are located.
PRATERSTERN. Praterstrasse comes to an end at th
Praterstern crossroads, where the seven broad avenues that
cross Leopoldstadt converge. To the north of the crossroad:
stands the forbidding Vienna North railway station, while t
the east the famous Ferris wheel rises above the treetops of
the Prater Gardens. In the middle of the square is the
TEGETTHOFF MONUMENT, to the admiral who took part in t
sea battle of Heligoland against the Danes in 1864 and
decisively defeated the Italians at the battle of Lissa in 186
In 1867, Tegetthoff was assigned to bring the remains of
Maximilian ▲ *145* home from Mexico.
LEOPOLDSTADT. An extensive working class area at the
northern end of the inner city, Leopoldstadt (2nd District)

The *Johann-Strauss.*

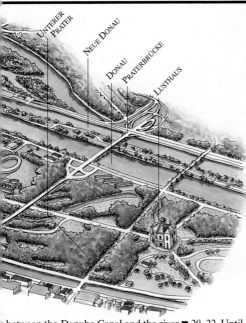

UNTERER PRATER

NEUE DONAU

DONAU

PRATERBRÜCKE

LUSTHAUS

...s between the Danube Canal and the river ■ *20, 22.* Until ...rld War Two, a number of Jewish shopkeepers and ...ftsmen lived and worked here. After the Anschluss ● *42* ... National Socialists deported the Jews of Leopoldstadt and ...troyed all their synagogues ▲ *156, 169.*

...E SCHÖNBERG HOUSE. The OBERE DONAUSTRASSE quay, ...ngside the Danube Canal, was the birthplace of Arnold ...önberg, father of dodecaphonics.

...E PRATER

...isit to the Prater has been a favorite excursion for the ...ennese ever since it was opened to the public in 1766 by ...eph II. As well as abundant green spaces in which to walk ...d jog, it also boasts a huge amusement park dominated by the Ferris wheel, numerous open-air cafés and restaurants (which tend to be very busy on weekends) and many sports facilities.

THE CONGRESS AT PLAY

During the Congress of Vienna ● *38,* kings and emperors with their suites of generals and diplomats converged from all over Europe on Vienna, where receptions and balls were held night and day. At the Prater, which for the duration became the most elegant promenade in Europe, a new dance – the waltz ● *56* – was all the rage.

ARNOLD SCHÖNBERG (1874–1951) ● *52*

Schönberg was influenced by Brahms ● *51,* Wagner and Mahler, as his *Transfigured Night* (1899) clearly shows; later his writing developed in the direction of atonality. Schönberg's *Treatise on Harmony* was published in 1911; his melodrama *Pierrot Lunaire* (1912), which employed the technique of speech-song (*Sprechgesang*), was a worldwide sensation. In 1933 Schönberg went into exile in the US, where he taught music.

PRATERSTRASSE

Joseph II was begged to open the Prater to the public, but replied that if he did so he would be "reduced to pacing the Crypt of the Capuchins, when I wish to be among my equals."

OUTLANDISH EXPLOITS

In 1898, Marie Kindl hung by her teeth from a cable hanging from one of the cabins on the Ferris wheel. In 1914 a Frenchwoman, Solange d'Atalide, rode a horse on the roof of one of its cabins. Between the wars, the Maningo Brothers did various acrobatics on the wheel for Pathé News; and in 1986 ecologists unfurled a banner at the top of it condemning nuclear power.

"VENICE IN VIENNA"

During the straightening of the Danube, small canals were dug and people used gondolas on them, hence the name of "Venice in Vienna".

FACTS AND FIGURES ABOUT THE WHEEL

The big wheel is held up by huge steel girders, and is 212 feet high; the diameter of the wheel is 200 feet. It includes 120 spokes made of steel cabling, weighs 474 tons, and spins at a rate of 2 feet 5 inches per second. Since World War Two it has had only 30 cabins, 15 of which bear an even number. For the wheel's 90th anniversary in 1987, cabin No. 30 was given special luxury fittings.

These swampy acres between the Danube Canal and the riv were turned into a game reserve in the 16th century by Maximilian II (1527–70), shortly after he had purchased the domain of Schönbrunn ▲ 274 for the same purpose. The Prater is nearly 3,200 acres in extent: its name probably derives from the Spanish word *prado* (plain). Many of the Habsburgs, notably Charles V, Ferdinand I and Charles VI spoke Spanish as fluently as German.

THE FUN FAIR. As soon as the Prater was opened to the public, icecream and coffee sellers as well as merry-go-round operators were granted the right to ply their trades there. By the end of 1766 there were more than a hundred structures – most of them tents – which sold wine, beer, coffee and pastries. In the following century the free-spending habits of the Prater crowds attracted more and more stall-keepers to the area. They tended to concentrate in the VOLKSPRATER (the People's Prater) or the WURSTELPRATER. This area is named after Wurstel, a tragicomic, resolutely unlucky character who symbolizes the Prater; a Viennese Don Quixote figure, he is persecuted by a crocodile but manages to win out after many struggles. The Wurstelprater was liked not only by ordinary Viennese for its merry-go-rounds and taverns but also by the upper classes for its dance hall-restaurants, where the "War of the Waltzes" between Strauss and Lanner ● *56* was waged.

ORSON WELLES IN "THE THIRD MAN" ● *42*, ▲ *192*
Reed's film, which took the Grand Prix at the Cannes Film
Festival in 1949, was hugely successful and contributed
significantly to the fame of the Prater's Ferris wheel. It was
here that he shot the confrontation between Holly Martins
(Joseph Cotten) and his friend Harry Lime (Orson Welles).

SENRAD. At the turn of the 19th and 20th centuries, when
canals of the "little Venice" area were being filled in,
ving only the Dogenhof on Praterstrasse, the Prater fun
was endowed with the Ferris wheel, or Riesenrad; this
ains its single greatest attraction. Walter Basset, a military
ineer working for Britain's Royal Navy, had the idea of
structing the wheel in imitation of those already in
stence at Paris, Blackpool, London and Chicago. Its
uguration in 1897 coincided with the Universal Exhibition
Brussels, which was opened a few weeks before Franz-
eph's jubilee ▲ *271*. The Ferris wheel narrowly escaped
truction in the first years of the 20th century, when its
ner's heirs put it up for sale as scrap metal. At the outbreak
World War One it was requisitioned as an observation post,
s escaping demolition. It was less fortunate in World War
● *42*, when it was blown to smithereens along with the
t of the Volksprater. Later it was rebuilt and modernized,
by May 1947 was back in operation, at the heart of a
ground in the throes of complete reconstruction.

GRAND HÔTEL VIENNE

LUSTHAUS

At the end of the main avenue is the Pleasure House (Lusthaus), now a café-restaurant. This former imperial hunting lodge was built by Isidorio Canevale ▲ 271 in 1784. For the first anniversary of the battle of Leipzig (1813) against Napoleon I, the Emperor of Austria and his allies organized a great banquet at the Lusthaus, while eighteen thousand of their troops picnicked in the surrounding park.

THE PLANETARIUM AND THE

PRATERMUSEUM. Next to the Ferris wheel is the Planetarium founded in 1927 by Zeiss, the manufacturer of optical instruments. It also contains a museum (the Pratermuseum which retraces the entire history of the Prater. A curious house in the form of a ball stands just beside the Planetarium this is known as the KUGELMUGEL. It is the home of a highly original character, Edwin Libburger, who proclaims it the "Smallest Republic in the World". Nearer the big wheel one can take the little train known as the LILLIPUTBAHN, which crosses part of the Prater from the fun fair to the STADIUM (Stadion).

MANNESMANN TOWER. Also between the main avenue (Hauptallee) of the Prater and the Ausstellungstrasse are the EXHIBITION GROUNDS (Messeländ with the 490-foot-tall Mannesmann Tower soaring overhead. The spring and autumn international

exhibitions are held here and in the Exhibition Palace (Messepalast) ▲ 207 each year.

SPORTING FACILITIES. Southeast of the exhibition grounds is a complex of sporting facilities, including a stadium, a swimming pool, a tennis court, a golf course and the Freudenau racecourse.

TABORSTRASSE

HAUPTALLEE

The main riding avenue (Hauptallee) crosses the Prater from end to end, from the Lower (Unterer) Prater to Freudenau. Running parallel to the Danube, this thoroughfare is now reserved for pedestrians. The aristocracy used to promenade here in carriages or on horseback.

Taborstrasse begins at the Danube Canal and Schwedenplatz and runs across Leopoldstadt.

BARMHERZIGE-BRÜDER-KIRCHE. On the right at the beginning of Taborstrasse is the monastery-hospice of the Brothers of Charity, with its huge church (Barmherzige-Brüder-Kirche) built in the 17th century. Before he became Music Master of the Esterházy Chapel ● 49, ▲ 162, Joseph Haydn ● 48 was intermittently employed as organist of this church between 1755 and 1758.

KARMELITERPLATZ. Taborstrasse

n passes through KARMELITERPLATZ, site of the 17th-tury Josefskirche, the former Carmelite Church, which ists a magnificent Baroque façade. On the same square is House of the Stag (Hirschenhaus), where the Strauss ily used to live ● 56.

GARTEN

A choir boy in the Augarten Palace.

the north of the inner city, the 130-acre Augarten Park ove) extends to the edges of Leopoldstadt (2nd District 64) and Brigittenau (20th District ▲ 296). The park was l out in the reign of Ferdinand II (1578–1637) and esigned in 1712 by the French gardener Jean Trehet, who s working on the gardens of the new Schönbrunn castle at time. Like the Prater, the Augarten was opened to the lic by Joseph II in 1775.

ZART AND BEETHOVEN. The park was formerly the site of Alte Favorita, Leopold I's (1640–1705) palace which was troyed during the siege of 1683 ● 34. An orangery was lt on the ruins, where musicians such as Mozart ● 48, 47, 281 and Beethoven ● 51 gave concerts before mbers of the imperial courts of Joseph II ● 36, 291, 292 l Francis I ● 38, ▲ 182.

RZELLANMANUFAKTUR AUGARTEN ★. This former orangery w serves as the Augarten china factory (Porzellan-nufaktur Augarten) ● 72, whose "beehive" monogram is lous all over the world. Founded in 1717 by a Dutchman, Paquier, the factory first operated from premises on zellangasse (Porcelain Street) in Vienna, before its move Augarten. Its products were particularly fashionable during Baroque era ● 80, 82 when it produced not only tableware also vases and trinkets which harmonized with the Rococo or of Viennese palaces. After a period of stiff competition m the factories of Meissen in Saxony and Sèvres in France, garten was given a new lease on life when Maria Theresa 6, ▲ 158, 280, 291 made it a state factory in 1744. At that e it was a training ground for decorators, whose ideas provided the factory with a constant source of renewal for its designs. The "Old Vienna" pattern, with its flowers and painted figures, became world-famous. After this Augarten began to draw inspiration from the French vogue for shepherds and shepherdesses, along with classical mythology and Rococo foliage and arabesques. At the close of the 18th

THE PORCELAIN FACTORY
In the 13th century Marco Polo brought the first pieces of porcelain back from China. Amsterdam merchants continued for many years to import Chinese porcelain for sale all over Europe; it was not until the end of the 17th century that Europeans discovered the secret of hard porcelain manufacture. At the beginning of the 18th century a number of factories were opened, notably that of Meissen in Saxony in 1710 and Augarten in 1717. At the close of the 18th century, Augarten was especially known for its mythological groups. Until 1744, each piece was stamped with a shield with blue stripes; after that date, Augarten ware bore the two-headed eagle of the Habsburgs ▲ 143, 144, 176, 280.

AUGARTEN CHOIRBOYS
● 54
This institution gives musical training and general instruction to a hundred and fifty children, who are divided into four choirs. The singers are boarded in the main palace; those whose voices have broken and who are no longer members of the choir lodge in the pavilion of Joseph II.

FLAKTURM
The mass of concrete which constitutes the anti-aircraft defense tower (Flakturm) is something of an eyesore in the Augarten. Six towers of this type were built in Vienna during World War Two and have since proved impossible to destroy. The city authorities have tried and failed to camouflage the Flakturms and are now transforming them into belvederes, exhibition rooms and (most recently) restaurants.

THE RAMPARTS AND THE SCHLAG BRÜCKE
To prevent the Danube from flooding, the Viennese embarked on a huge program to straighten its bed at the close of the 18th century. The branch of the river which ran directly below the ramparts became the Danube Canal, navigable for just over 10 miles.
As to the Danube proper, its bed was dredged straight for 12½ miles at the end of the 19th century, the banks being buttressed with stone and concrete. In 1975, the Neue Donau (New Danube) parallel branch was rearranged in the same fashion.

century, when all Europe was in raptures over the excavations at Herculaneum and Pompeii, Augarten tableware was covered in grotesques and antique figures inspired by Raphael. It also produced quantities of figurines, which were avidly collected all over Europe. The advent of Napoleon I and his period of residence at Schönbrunn ● 38 launched the Empire style, and later, after the Congress of Vienna, came the Biedermeier era ● 62. Biedermeier was particularly influential at Augarten; the factory hired a miniaturist painter, Daffinger, who launched what became known as the "idyll" pattern. The Viennese apartments of the time were filled with decorative porcelain whether plates made to be hung on walls or pipes, snuffboxes figurines, tea cups and teapots, all made not for use but for display in glass cabinets. With the fall of the Habsburg empire in 1918 ● 33, the factory experienced a period of difficulty, but before long it was back on its feet inventing new designs that reflected contemporary tastes.

THE AUGARTEN PALACES. Also in the Augarten is a Baroque Palace (AUGARTENPALAST) which was built at the end of the 17th century in the style of Fischer von Erlach ● 74, 80, ▲ 138, 147. Bought in 1780 by Joseph II, it was subsequently neglected by the emperor, who preferred the little pavilion (JOSEPHSSTÖCKL) nearby. This structure was built by the Italian architect Isidorio Canevale ▲ 268 in 1781. These palaces were used by Pope Pius VI in 1782 and by Emperor Charles I ● 33, ▲ 144, 180 during his

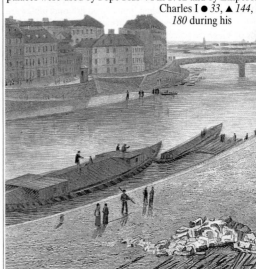

hood. Today the Vienna Boys' Choir (Wiener
gerknaben) ● *54* occupies the Augarten Palaces.
GITTAKAPELLE. The chapel of St Bridget, a Renaissance
lding that dates from between 1645 and 1681, stands
rounded by more recent structures in Adalbert-Stifter-
asse on the north side of the Augarten. Designed by
berto Lucchesi, it was probably a votive church,
structed during a period of concern over the threat of
dish invasion during the Thirty Years' War ▲ *259*.
XIKOPLATZ. It was in Mexikoplatz and the surrounding
rict between the NORTH STATION (Nordbahnhof) and the
ube that political refugees from eastern Europe found a
porary asylum before continuing their emigration to other
ntries.

E DANUBE

atrary to the normal perception, the Danube (Donau)
0, 22 does not flow past the walls of Vienna. Instead it
ns a broad inland delta here, with backwaters filled with
nds and islets.

REICHSBRÜCKE. The first part of the
huge imperial bridge (Reichsbrücke)
leads from Mexikoplatz across the
Danube. The river carries a wide
variety of boat traffic, including canal
boats, barges and bateaux-mouches
which head downstream to Budapest
in Hungary or else unload at the huge
river port of Vienna. This complex
includes a grain port at Albern, a
general cargo port at Freudenau,
the oil port of Lobau.
NAUINSEL. Next, the bridge spans the Danube island
nauinsel) 13 miles long, known as "Spaghetti Island,"
ween the Danube and the New Danube. Because
so long and thin it is known as
aghetti

**THE
JUBILÄUMSKIRCHE**
In 1898, the Viennese
decided to celebrate
Franz-Joseph's
fiftieth anniversary as
emperor ● *41*, ▲ *142,
144, 178* in proper
style. Banquets and
balls were given all
over town, and the
municipality began
constructing the
Jubilee Church
(Jubiläumskirche) on
Mexikoplatz. This
neo-Romanesque
building was not
completed until 1913,
by which time Franz-
Joseph had only three
more years to live.

DONAUTURM
The Danube Park is best known for the 820-foot Danube Tower (Donauturm), which has become its emblem. Two revolving restaurants in the building, one at 520 feet, the other at 560 feet, offer panoramic views of the entire Vienna region, the valley of the Danube, the Marchfeld plain and the hills of the Vienna Woods
■ 18,
● 68, 100.

Island". This strip of land boasts 26 miles of beaches and is mostly devoted to water sports (sailing, canoeing and swimming), as well as soccer, cycling and rollerskating. There are also fishing zones and an animal reserve, along with specially equipped areas in which handicapped people can practice various forms of exercise. The water sports are limited to the New Danube, which is closed to merchant shipping. Having crossed the Danube, the artificial Danube Island and the New Danube, the Reichsbrücke continues across the larger Danube Island and the Old Danube before connecting with the Donaustadt (22nd District) on the left bank of the river.

U.N. CITY. Built between 1973 and 1979, the United Nations complex consists of several parabolic tower blocks on the middle of the island between the Old and New Danubes. Opened in 1987, the AUSTRIA CENTER VIENNA which is next to the U.N. complex, contains fourteen auditoriums with capacities ranging from fifty to four thousand people. In addition to conferences and seminars, exhibitions, galas, plays and concerts are organized here; the center also has its own radio station, restaurants, banks, travel agencies and post office.

DONAUPARK. Laid out to the northwest of the U.N. complex to mark the occasion of the international flower show of 1964, the Donaupark is the second largest green area in Vienna after the Prater. A small train carries visitors around the gardens and the artificial lake, the IRISSEE, where there a THEATER that can seat four thousand spectators.

THE UNITED NATIONS BUILDINGS
The U.N. rents this complex from the Austrian government. It contains the headquarters of the Atomic Energy Agency and the United Nations Industrial Development Organization.

ALTE DONAU. To the southeast of the U.N. complex, the Danube Island is indented by the Kaiserwasser Bay; from here two channels lead through to the Old Danube (Alte Donau) and its islands (GROSS UND KLEIN GÄNSEHÄUFEL), favorite area for walkers. The Old Danube has remained in its original winding bed, but in effect it is a backwater, closed at both ends and lost in greenery – a perfect place for sailing, canoeing or picnicking.

From Schönbrunn to the Steinhof

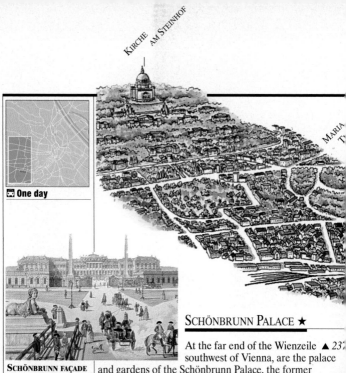

KIRCHE AM STEINHOF

MARIA T...

One day

SCHÖNBRUNN PALACE ★

At the far end of the Wienzeile ▲ *23?*
southwest of Vienna, are the palace
and gardens of the Schönbrunn Palace, the former
summer residence of the Habsburgs. The first building
here was the castle of Katterburg, which was
destroyed by the Turks in 1529 ● *34*; the
ruined site was bought in 1589 by
Maximilian II who wanted to set up
a hunting preserve in the vicinity,
with fishponds, a poultry farm
and a garden of rare plants.
The rebuilt castle of
Katterburg thus
became a hunting
lodge and a working
farm. It was enlarged by
Rudolph II, but once
again demolished in 1605 by
the Hungarian forces of Stefan
Bockai.

THE SPRING. Matthias II,
Rudolph II's brother, succeeded
him in 1612, and occasionally resided at
the castle after its reconstruction. One day, when he
was out hunting, he came on a beautiful spring in the woo□
(Schöner Brunnen) after which the site was eventually nar□
But the imperial family's obsession with "Schönbrunn" onl□
began in earnest with Eleonora Gonzaga, the wife of
Ferdinand II (1619–37). This Italian princess enlarged the
castle and laid out new gardens, residing there during the
summer months and organizing lavish entertainments.

SCHÖNBRUNN AND VERSAILLES. After the final victory over □
Turks in 1683 ● *34*, the Habsburg empire entered a period □
peace and prosperity. Leopold I and the princes attached ▮
the imperial court took advantage of this to build a numbe□
fine palaces in Vienna ● *80, 82*, ▲ *246*. Since Schönbrunn □
been destroyed in 1683, Leopold I determined to replace ▮
with an edifice worthy of the Habsburgs' newly recovered □
power. For this task he commissioned J. B. Fischer von Er□

SCHÖNBRUNN FAÇADE
Two obelisks crowned
with eagles frame the
entrance to the main
courtyard. These are
not two-headed
Habsburg eagles ● *29*,
▲ *143, 144, 195, 280*,
but Napoleonic ones,
placed here by
Bonaparte in the
course of his two visits
to Vienna ● *38*, after
Austerlitz (1805) and
Wagram (1809).
Bonaparte's father-in-
law, Francis I ▲ *182*,
retained the eagles,
even after the fall of
the French empire in
1815.

PURE SPRINGWATER
The water of the
"beautiful spring" was
exceptionally pure.
Franz-Joseph ● *41*,
▲ *178* offered it to his
guests at lunch and
dinner when he
entertained at the
palace.

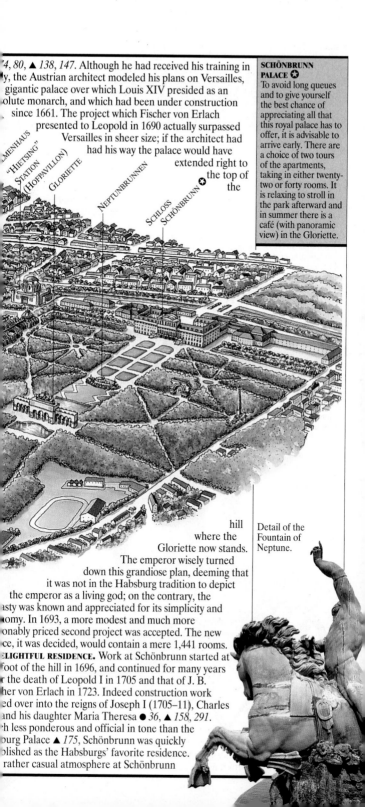

4, 80, ▲ *138, 147.* Although he had received his training in ...y, the Austrian architect modeled his plans on Versailles, ... gigantic palace over which Louis XIV presided as an ...olute monarch, and which had been under construction since 1661. The project which Fischer von Erlach presented to Leopold in 1690 actually surpassed Versailles in sheer size; if the architect had had his way the palace would have extended right to the top of the

...MENHAUS
"HIETSING" STATION (HOFPAVILLON)
GLORIETTE
NEPTUNBRUNNEN
SCHLOSS SCHÖNBRUNN ✪

SCHÖNBRUNN PALACE ✪
To avoid long queues and to give yourself the best chance of appreciating all that this royal palace has to offer, it is advisable to arrive early. There are a choice of two tours, taking in either twenty-two or forty rooms. It is relaxing to stroll in the park afterward and in summer there is a café (with panoramic view) in the Gloriette.

hill where the Gloriette now stands. The emperor wisely turned down this grandiose plan, deeming that it was not in the Habsburg tradition to depict the emperor as a living god; on the contrary, the ...asty was known and appreciated for its simplicity and ...omy. In 1693, a more modest and much more ...onably priced second project was accepted. The new ...ce, it was decided, would contain a mere 1,441 rooms.

Detail of the Fountain of Neptune.

...LIGHTFUL RESIDENCE. Work at Schönbrunn started at ...oot of the hill in 1696, and continued for many years ...r the death of Leopold I in 1705 and that of J. B. ...her von Erlach in 1723. Indeed construction work ...ed over into the reigns of Joseph I (1705–11), Charles ...and his daughter Maria Theresa ● *36,* ▲ *158, 291.* ...h less ponderous and official in tone than the ...burg Palace ▲ *175,* Schönbrunn was quickly ...blished as the Habsburgs' favorite residence. ...rather casual atmosphere at Schönbrunn

The courtyard of the castle.

was in marked contrast to the rigid etiquette of Versailles principally because the court did not lodge there. Maria Theresa wanted it to be a cosy domestic place where she could sit with her embroidery or her watercolors, in the company of her daughters. She had Schönbrunn redecora by Nikolaus von Pacassi ▲ 192 to make it more comfortab this was achieved by reducing the size of the private apartments to a more intimate scale, and by mitigating th somewhat pompous Baroque style of the building with touches of Rococo. In the 19th century, Schönbrunn was in the open countryside; today it is included in Hietzing (13th District ▲ 286).

EHRENHOF

The visitor enters the Schönbrunr Palace by way of the huge courtya (Ehrenhof; 66,000 feet) and the gateway (Haupttor).

NAPOLEON'S EAGLES. Two obelisks topped by Napoleonic eagles frame gateway. These were placed here by the French emperor during his two visits to Vienna, Austerlitz in 1805 and afte Wagram in 1809. In the courtyard are two fountains erect by Maria Theresa, which represent the principal rivers an kingdoms within the empire. This area has witnessed seve

takes the form of a gilded crown, with doors covered in paintings by artists of the school of Rubens ▲ 219. Pulled by eight horses, it was used for seven coronations, including that of Charles I in the middle of World War One. Archduke Rudolph's ▲ 145 berlin is shown at right.

significant historical events, notably the parade of Napoleon I's Grand Army, the arrival of the Russian, British and Austrian sovereigns for the Congress of Vienna ● 38, the takeover by Hitler's troops, and the meeting between Presidents Kennedy and Krushchev in

961. Schönbrunn served as the Soviet Army headquarters in
945, and that of the British Army from 1945 to 1948 ● 43.
MARIA THERESA YELLOW". The yellow paint which covers
e exterior of Schönbrunn later became standard for all
mperial buildings. It is thought that Schönbrunn's walls were
riginally pink, with gray pilasters. A new coat of paint
pplied to the palace recently seems less orange in tone than
s predecessors.

HE FAÇADE. The main body of the palace spreads along the
road esplanade. Its façade ▲ 284-5 is embellished with
lasters and covered with yellow ocher paint ("Maria
heresa Yellow"). Maria Theresa came out on the balcony
re to salute Count Kinsky, who had ridden from the
ttlefield to bring her news of the Austrian victory over the
ussians ● 36.

HE OUTBUILDINGS. In addition to the palace itself, the
ourtyard is hemmed in by a number of outbuildings, notably
e CARRIAGE MUSEUM (Wagenburg) in the former winter
anège. Sixty carriages of various kinds are exhibited here,
mong them the Berlin of Napoleon I, the phaeton of
iglon" and the barouche used by Sissi ▲ 119, 143, 144, 178
en she traveled incognito to Geneva in 1898. The red
arse displayed here was used for the funerals of archdukes,
d the black one for sovereigns. At Maria Theresa's request,
cassi ▲ 189, 192, 276 built the small Baroque SCHLOSS-
EATER in 1747. Mozart and Haydn both performed here
49. Today, the theater is used for the productions of the
enna Chamber Opera (Wiener Kammeroper) ● 54.

Sculptures in the park
▲ 284.

HE MAIN BUILDING

Schönbrunn's 1,441 rooms, only forty-two
the first floor are open to the public – the
mainder are rented out. These are entered
the courtyard as in the Hofburg ▲ 175.
ery room contains a large faience stove.

RGLRÄUME. The apartments and salons of
e first floor are preceded by the Bergl
lons (Berglräume) or "Indian Rooms",
ich are entirely decorated with exotic
scoes ▲ 180. The ceiling of the adjoining
CHAPEL (Schlosskapelle), constructed c. 1700, has a
fine fresco by Daniel Gran ▲ 146, 304.

THE GROSSE GALERIE. The Great Gallery
(Grosse Galerie) leads to the principal
STAIRCASE and the balcony overlooking the
esplanade. Some 140 feet in length, decorated
with white and gold paneling and crystal
chandeliers, the Grosse Galerie is still used
today for official banquets. In
1955, the closing reception
following the signature of the treaty
to end the Allied occupation of Vienna
was held here. In 1945, a bomb fell
straight through the ceiling fresco by
Gregorio Guglielmi ▲ 279 which
represents the territories of the empire
paying homage to Maria Theresa and Francis I,
but by an incredible stroke of luck failed to explode.

THE SMALL THEATER
Joseph II and his
sister Marie-
Antoinette (the
future Queen of
France) are shown
dancing in the ballet
The Triumph of Love
(1764) by Gluck ● 48.
The Habsburgs loved
and practiced all the
arts: especially dance,
music, theater and
painting. Mozart
conducted *The
Theater Director* at the
small theater; his *Don
Giovanni* was also
performed here.

Detail of a fresco in the Berglräume ▲ 277, by
Johann Bergl (1718–89).

KARUSSELLZIMMER AND LANTERNZIMMER. On either side of
the Grosse Galerie are the CAROUSEL ROOM (which owes its
name to a painting of the Spanish Riding School ▲ 190 by
Meytens ● 98; it also boasts a large portrait of Charles VI
● 36), and the LANTERN ROOM, which serve
as an antechamber.

KLEINE GALERIE. An extension of the Gross
Galerie overlooking the park, the Small
Gallery (Kleine Galerie) is also painte
white and gold, with a fresco by
Guglielmi ▲ 277, 279 (*The Union of the Hous
of Habsburg-Lorraine with the Holy Roman
Empire*). Decorated by Pacassi ▲ 189, 191,
276, the Kleine Galerie was formerly used for
children's parties and small banquets, and music
would sometimes be played here. On either side of the room
are the Chinese Cabinets, one round and one oval. The
former (Chinesischen Rundkabinett), which was Maria
Theresa's secret study, is linked via a bare staircase with the
floor above, where Chancellor von Kaunitz lodged.

THE ROSA SALONS. Originally the apartments of Joseph I,
these rooms are named after Joseph Rosa, who decorated
them with frescoes of Swiss and Italian landscapes
prefiguring Romantic art. The MAIN ROSA SALON contains a
fresco of the ruins of Habsburg, the
cradle of the imperial family.

THE RIGHT WING

**THE APARTMENTS OF FRANZ-JOSEPH AN
SISSI.** The imperial couple occupied
fifteen rooms in the right wing of the
palace. These are reached by a
monumental staircase above which is a
ceiling fresco by
Sebastiano Ricci
entitled *Allegory
the Princely Virtu*
(1702); in it an angel
symbolizing the "lov
of virtue" takes the
hand of the future
Joseph I and show
him the path he must follow.
first room, adjoining the
staircase, was used as a
GUARD ROOM; next is the
ANTECHAMBER
(Wartezimmer), with a
Biedermeier ● 62 billiard table, where
petitioners waited to be announced.
The AUDIENCE CHAMBER is also
known as the "Walnut Salon"
(Nusszimmer), because its wa
are covered in walnut
wainscoting whose brown ton
harmonize with the red dama
furniture. Among other thing
this salon contains busts of

> "We must have theatrical entertainments! Without them life in such a huge palace is impossible..."
>
> Maria Theresa

From top to bottom: The Mirror Gallery; the official Dining Room; Princess Sophia's salon; and the Garten Perronsaal Salon (19th-century engravings from the Museum of the City of Vienna ▲ *241*).

"I want to go to Schönbrunn!" said Herr von Trotta, and he drove to Schönbrunn. The persistent drizzle hid the palace and the Steinhof asylum alike. Herr von Trotta headed up the avenue, that same avenue which he had taken so long ago on his way to the secret audience, during the affair involving his son."

Joseph Roth,
The Radetsky March

A EUROPEAN PAINTER
The Baroque painter Gregorio Guglielmi (1714–73) was a truly European artist. Born in Rome, he worked at the studio of the great traveler Sebastiano Conca. From 1753 onward, Guglielmi followed the example of his master, first to Dresden, then to Vienna in 1755 before returning to Turin in 1765. He died at St Petersburg. During his time in Vienna he painted the ceilings of the great and small galleries, along with that of the Academy of Sciences ▲ *151*, at the request of Maria Theresa.

A FAMILY LIFE
Family life was vitally important to the Habsburgs and set firmly apart from their duties as monarchs. This was the case throughout the long reign of Maria Theresa, who with her husband and their sixteen children projected the image of a united family with simple tastes and pleasures including embroidery, painting and botany. Maria Theresa and her children at the Feast of St Nicolas (right); Joseph II at the bedside of his wife, newly delivered of yet another baby (opposite).

MARIA THERESA AND JOSEPH II
The personalities of Maria Theresa and her son Joseph II ● *36*, ▲ *291* left a deep imprint on Austria. The latter (below) ruled jointly with his mother (right) in mourning after the death of Francis I, from 1765 to 1780. (Both portraits are by Heinrich Friedrich Fueger, 1751–1818.)

FRANCIS I
Francis I of Lorraine, the husband of Maria Theresa, who became Francis I, Holy Roman Emperor, by election in 1745, must be distinguished from his grandson Francis II, who became Francis I, hereditary Emperor of Austria in 1806 ● *38*, ▲ *182*.

Franz-Joseph wearing the chain of the Order of the Golden Fleece ▲ *133, 183*, and of his father Archduke Franz-Karl. Next is Franz-Joseph's STUDY, which overlooks the courtyard; the walls and chairs are covered with brown ribbed fabric. This room and the one adjacent to it contain several portraits and statuettes of Franz-Joseph, Sissi and Archduke Rudolph ▲ *145*.

A BEDROOM. The ROOM IN WHICH FRANZ-JOSEPH DIED – a simple, comfortable chamber – is decorated in the same brown fabric. A painting on the wall depicts the deathbed scene on November 21, 1916. After visiting the two small cabinets, the visitor is led through to the DRESSING ROOM, which is hung with pink brocade. With its twin beds of dark wood and its prie-dieu, the BEDROOM shared by Franz-Jose and Sissi is as austere as a monk's cell. On the walls hang tw paintings of the *Madonna and Child*, one by Carlo Dolci, th other by Guido Reni.

EMPRESS ELIZABETH'S SALON. The walls of this room are covered in light gray brocade, and the furniture in flowered red silk. Several pastel portraits by Jean-Etienne Liotard of Maria Theresa's children decorate th room, which looks out onto the imperial privat garden. Note also the paintings by Hackert (*Th Grape Harvest, The Grain Harvest*).

Marie-Antoinette's salon, with its white and go paneling and chairs covered in red damask, is o of the largest rooms in the imperial apartments. is dominated by a huge portrait of Francis I in the costume of a Knight of the Order of the Golden Fleece ▲ *2* by Friedrich von Amerling (1803–87) ▲ *241*, the official cou painter.

THE CHILDREN'S BEDROOM. The chairs in this room, which also paneled in white and gold, are covered in pale blue damask. There are several portraits of Maria Theresa here, along with a wardrobe which was used as a desk by her daughter Marie-Antoinette; at one point this was removed Sissi and installed at her villa *Achilleion* on the Greek islanc of Corfu.

FRÜHSTÜCKZIMMER. The breakfast room, on the corner of the right wing of the palace, has a splendid view over the park. Its walls are studded with twenty-six medallions containing placemats embroidered by Maria Theresa and her daughters.

> **"The monarchy – our monarchy – is founded on piety, on the belief that God chose the Habsburgs to reign over so many Christian nations."**
>
> Joseph Roth

THE YELLOW SALON. This room takes its name from its chairs, which are covered in yellow damask. On the walls hang portraits of Maria Theresa's children by Liotard. The clock on the commode, made by the Parisian clockmaker Ridel, was a gift from Napoleon III to Franz-Joseph. Decorated in 1854, the BALCONY ROOM is the last of the apartments in the right wing. Once again the walls here are covered with white and red paneling and with portraits of Maria Theresa's children.

SPIEGELSAAL. The Yellow Salon communicates with the small MIRROR GALLERY, to which Maria Theresa's newly appointed ministers came to swear their oath of loyalty to the sovereign. Wolfgang Amadeus Mozart ● *48*, ▲ *147* gave one of his first recitals in this room.

The Porcelain Salon.

MOZART AT SCHÖNBRUNN
Mozart first came to Vienna in 1762, arriving from Salzburg with his father and his elder sister Nannerl. At the age of six, he gave his first concert in the small Mirror Gallery before a delighted Maria Theresa. When he slipped on the polished parquet, he was caught by the youthful Marie-Antoinette, and promptly declared that he wanted to marry her. And when he had finished playing he clambered onto the Empress' knees to give her a kiss, without the slightest regard for etiquette.

VIEUX-LACQUE-ZIMMER
In the 18th century, art from the Far East was fashionable in Europe; rooms were filled with Chinese prints, porcelain and exotic screens, which matched home-produced Rococo ornaments.

THE GLORIETTE
The view from Maria Theresa's bedroom, where Napoleon I later slept ● *38* when he was using Schönbrunn as his headquarters.

"Garp relaxed, when he wasn't writing, by going to the zoo; it was part of the great grounds and gardens surrounding the Schönbrunn Palace."
John Irving,
The World According to Garp

THE LEFT WING

ZEREMONIENSAAL. After the Carousel Room and the HORSE ROOM (stag-hunting scenes and portraits of horses along the walls), the tour continues into the left wing of the palace by way of the Hall of Ceremonies (Zeremoniensaal), also known as the Battle Room because of its gilded stucco ornaments interlacing banners and halberds. This spacious room was used for christenings, weddings and other ceremonies with the imperial family. On the walls are scenes of the wedding Joseph II by Martin von Meytens ● *98* and a full-length portrait of Maria Theresa ● *36*.

BLAUEN CHINESISCHEN SALON. The walls of the Blue Chine Salon, in which Charles I signed his abdication on November 11, 1918 ● *33*, are covered in wallpaper patterned with Chinese prints on a blue background. Lacquer wardrobes a Japanese porcelain vases complete this décor.

VIEUX-LAQUE-ZIMMER. Another room that shows a taste fo chinoiserie is the Old Lacquer Salon, in which the Rococo style may be seen at its best: here, framed by complex desig in gilt molding, are long lacquer panels representing Japan landscapes and flowers and birds engraved in fine gold. Th room also has a rich stucco ceiling and a superb marquetry floor.

MARIA THERESA'S BEDROOM. This chamber overlooking the park follows the Vieux-Laque-Zimmer; Napoleon I slept here, and his son the "Aiglon" was in this room when he breathed his last. The walls are lined with 18th-century Brussels tapestries showing scenes of military life.

THE PORCELAIN ROOM. This salon, Maria Theresa's former study, occupies the corner of the left wing. It looks out onto the CROWN PRINCE'S GARDEN (Kronprinzgarten), a private area cut off from the main park since the latter was opened the public in 1779. The Porcelain Room is decorated with wooden moldings painted blue in imitation of porcelain, in the shapes of flowers, fruit and Chinese parasols. On the w are two hundred and thirteen framed blue-wash drawings, done by Francis of Lorraine and his daughters. Fixed to the middle of the passe-partout mounting are four medallions bas-relief featuring portraits of Francis I, the archduchesse Elizabeth and Christina, and Duke Albert of Saxe-Teschen.

MILLIONENZIMMER. The Million Room, which was used for smaller audiences, is covered in rosewood paneling, into which are set two hundred and sixty Indian and Persian

Maria Theresa, Francis of Lorraine and their children.

niatures. These cost a million florins in the 18th century, nce the name of the room. If one looks at them closely, it comes clear that these miniatures were cut up and assembled to fit into their cartouches.

OBELINSALON. The tapestries in the Tapestry Salon obelinsalon) actually come from Brussels, rather than obelins. They show scenes from the lives of ntwerp fishermen; each of the six Rococo airs here is covered in a tapestry presenting two of the seasons. The tour ntinues through a small room which rves as a memorial to the "Aiglon". His rtrait as a child, his death mask, and (under ell glass), the stuffed corpse of the pet k which shared his itude, are all hibited here.

E RED SALON. is former reading om covered in scarlet mask is hung with several family portraits: seph II in coronation robes, his brother opold II, and Franz-Joseph I aged eighteen d again at sixty-four, wearing the insignia of e Golden Fleece ▲ 133, 183. The Red Salon mmunicates with a corner room which is corated with frescoes and tapestries of rose rlands, and looks out onto the courtyard.

E APARTMENTS OF FRANZ-JOSEPH'S RENTS. The living quarters of Sophia of varia and her husband Archduke Franz-Karl long to the left wing, overlooking the main urtyard. In the Archduchess' BEDROOM, the lls and bed are covered in red velvet (it took 0 pounds of silver just to embroider the dachin). Franz-Joseph was born in this room. ljoining are the STUDY and SALON of

THE "AIGLON" (1811–32). When Napoleon departed for St Helena, his son, the King of Rome, and his mother, Archduchess Maria Louisa, retired to Vienna. The boy was lodged at Schönbrunn by his grandfather Francis I, who made him Duke of Reichstadt to pre-empt a French title. Abandoned by his mother, who became Duchess of Parma, the

"Aiglon" died of consumption at the age of twenty-one, a much-loved member of the imperial family. He never saw his father again after Waterloo.

283

Archduke Franz-Karl. The salon and study contain a gallery of portraits that includes Maria Theresa, Francis of Lorraine and each of their sixteen children. The chandelier is made of Bohemian crystal.

SCHÖNBRUNN PARK

ANTIQUE STATUARY
The garden statues are by Johann Christian Meyer, who also sculpted the groups at the Fountain of Neptune ▲ 275 and the Fountain of the Naiads in the diagonal avenues.

While J. B. Fischer von Erlach was building the palace at the end of the 17th century, the gardens around it – which had been laid out first by Maximilian II and then by Eleonora Gonzaga – were reorganized, with geometrical paths and beds by Jean Trehet, c. 1691. Later, between 1750 and 1780, Joseph Hätzl and Adrian von Stockhoven made major changes, introducing a note of fantasy into the carefully aligned parterres and shrubberies.

From the foot of the palace, a broad, straight avenue opens up a perspective culminating at the FOUNTAIN OF NEPTUNE (Neptunbrunnen), by C. Bayer. **THE GLORIETTE AND THE LITTLE GLORIETTE.** This perspective is completed by the Gloriette, a monument perched at the top of the slope on the site of J. B. Fischer von Erlach's first, rejected project for Schönbrunn Palace. The Gloriette is a neo-classical triumphal arch built by Ferdinand von Hohenberg in 1775 to commemorate the Austrian victory at Kolin (1757) against the armies of Frederick II of Prussia (the sculpted trophies are by J. B. Hagenauer, and the décor and stuccoes by Benedikt Henrici). East of the hill stands the Little Gloriette, where Maria Theresa

ROMAN RUINS
The remains of Schloss Neugebäude were used to build these imitation ruins.

THE GLORIETTE
In front of and behind the Gloriette are two broad pools which supply the gardens and the zoo with water. There is a superb view of both Schönbrunn and Vienna from this site.

...netimes took her breakfast; it is now used as a ...blic tearoom.

...ROLEAN CHALETS. West of the hill are the GARDENS ...d chalets built at the request of Archduke John in 1800. ...MISCHE RUINE. At the foot of the slope are two ...numents built by Ferdinand von Hohenberg: the OBELISK, ...which are carved scenes from the history of the Habsburg ...nily ● 29, ▲ 143, 144, 195 and the Roman ruins (Römische ...ine). Around forty statues by Johann Christian Meyer ...presenting heroes of Greek mythology ...d Roman history are dotted here and ...re throughout the gardens.
...HÖNER BRUNNEN. Hidden in the ...ods on the left-hand side of the park ...oking out from the palace) is the ...ing after which Schönbrunn was ...ned. This spring, whose pure water ...s served at the imperial table, is ...used in an artificial grotto with a ...tue of the nymph Egeria holding an overflowing urn.

...TANISCHER GARTEN. Francis I ● 36, who was passionately ...erested in natural sciences, financed expeditions to remote ...untries with a view to enriching Schönbrunn's collection of ...e plants and animals. Even in Maximilian II's time, when ...16th-century Schloss Katterburg stood on this site, a ...mber of unusual plants and trees grew here, but it was ...ring the 18th-century reign of Francis that the Botanischer ...rten at Schönbrunn was seriously developed. During the ...ne period a menagerie was installed on the west side of the ...rk in 1752.
...ERGARTEN. The imperial family used to visit the octagonal ...vilion to observe their lions, tigers and leopards (this ...vilion is now a café-restaurant). The descendants of ...ncis I added a set of zoological gardens (Tiergarten) to the ...nagerie, one of the first of its kind in Europe, which today ...ome to around seven hundred and fifty animals.

...CHNISCHES MUSEUM
...R INDUSTRIE UND GEWERBE

...rth of Schönbrunn, on the other side of Vienna ▲ 225 and ...he extension of the AUER-WELSBACH PARK, is the ...hnical Museum of Industry and Craft. Part of the first

THE FAÇADE
This is arranged around two flights of steps that lead to the balcony of the second-floor piano nobile, and two wings extended by two large pavilions.

THE PALM HOUSE
The tropical greenhouse (Palmenhaus, 1883) made of glass and metal is a replica of the one at Kew Gardens in London.

▲ FROM SCHÖNBRUNN TO THE STEINHOF

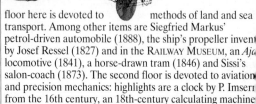

THE AUSTRIAN ICARUS
Between 1891 and 1896, Otto Lilienthal (1848–96) invented a series of gliders and took more than two thousand flights of between 100 and 200 yards. Finally he was killed trying out his latest flying machine, a biplane; he left behind him a treatise *Bird Flight as theBasis of the Flying Art*.

An airplane built by Wilhelm Kress, Siegfried Markus' first motorized automoobile, and Peter Mitterhofer's typewriter from 1864.

THE IMPERIAL METRO STATION
The Hietzing metro station (Hofpavillon), which serves Schönbrunn Palace, looks more like a temple than a railway station. It was built by Otto Wagner ● 86, 88, 90, ▲ 228, 240, 294 in 1898, and exclusively used at the time by members of the court. Its neo-Baroque building includes an octagonal hall topped by an elegant dome. Like all Wagner's constructions, it is decorated with great refinement.

floor here is devoted to methods of land and sea transport. Among other items are Siegfried Markus' petrol-driven automobile (1888), the ship's propeller inven by Josef Ressel (1827) and in the RAILWAY MUSEUM, an *Aja* locomotive (1841), a horse-drawn tram (1846) and Sissi's salon-coach (1873). The second floor is devoted to aviation and precision mechanics: highlights are a clock by P. Imsern from the 16th century, an 18th-century calculating machine Braun, a 19th-century typewriter by Mitterhofer, and 19th-century sewing machine by Madersberger. There are also exhibits from the textile, chemical and agricultural industries. On the third floor are various inventions from the history of the postal service (including the first postcard), and from musical instrument manufacture, computer science, photogra (notably Voigtländer's camera), and public works. Th is also a fascinating automaton made by Friedrich von Knaus (1760) which is capable of writing.

HIETZING

HIETZINGER FRIEDHOF. South of the TIROLER GARTEN Schönbrunn is the little cemetery of Hietzing (Hietzin Friedhof). A number of famous people are buried here, including the writer Franz Grillparzer ● 62, ▲ 147, 206, the painter Gustav Klimt ▲ 227, 250, the composer

WIENER STADTBAHN: HALTESTELLE HIETZING

> ## "To shake ourselves out of our complacency and comfort."
>
> Adolf Loos

an Berg ● *53* and Chancellor Engelbert Dollfuss ▲ *159*, . Room was also made here for the remains of n-Baptiste Hanet, known as Cléry, who together with nçois Hue was Louis XVI's valet while he was in prison in Temple until his execution in 1793. Cléry later published a ry of this historic period.

LA PRIMAVESI-SKYWA AND FÜRSTENHOF. Toward the of the 19th century a series of lavish dences were built in the vicinity of önbrunn by members of the elite among endstil ● *86*, ▲ *139* and Secession ● *86, 88, '32* architects. Thereafter Hietzing joined bling ▲ *294* and Währing ▲ *293* as one Vienna's aristocratic suburbs. To the west he Schönbrunn gardens on priettegasse stands the VILLA MAVESI-SKYWA, built by Josef ffman in 1915 ● *86, 90*, ▲ *142, 174*, le on Trauttmannsdoffgasse is the RSTENHOF building, which has a nderfully elegant façade in relief. It built by H. Dvorak in 1905.

Adolf Loos' Hornerhaus.

USES BY ADOLF LOOS. Nearby is the IEU HOUSE, on Larochegasse, which designed by Adolf Loos ▲ *142, 174* in 2, a year after his controversial building at no. 3 haelerplatz ▲ *174*, and in the same unadorned style. other building by Loos here, the HORNERHAUS (1913) on thartgasse, has a unique convex roof; further still to the t, the VILLA VOJCSIK ● *87* on Linzerstrasse was designed Otto Schönthal in 1901; this is a magnificent piece of endstil architecture, with a highly refined façade (note the doorway in particular).

VILLAS BY OTTO WAGNER. Nearly on Huttelberg-strasse

PAVILLON · DES · K ᴠɴᴅ K ALLERHOCHSTEN · HOFES

▲ FROM SCHÖNBRUNN TO THE STEINHOF

KIRCHE AM STEINHOF
● 87
St Leopold's Church is crowned by a broad dome covered in copper plaques, with a turret similar to those of Peterskirche ● 75, ▲ 139 and Karlskirche ● 74, ▲ 238.

The gilded bronze angels (above) atop the four columns are by Othmar Schimkowitz. The stained glass (right) is by Koloman Moser ▲ 235.

KIRCHE ZUR HEILIGSTEN DREIFALTIGKEIT ★
The Church of the Holy Trinity on St George's Hill on the edge of the Wienerwald ■ 18, ● 100 was designed in 1974–6 by Fritz Wotruba (1907–75).

are two villas by Otto Wagner ● 88, ▲ 228. The more celebrated of the pair is no. 28, situated on the slope o the hill, which has since been partly altered. The build can be reached by way of a double flight of steps which end at a classic portico framed by statues and frescoes.

KIRCHE AM STEINHOF ★

Just north of Schönbrunn, and west of the Ring, stands o of Otto Wagner's finest achievements: St Leopold's Churc (KIRCHE AM STEINHOF). This magnificent edifice was built in 1902, shortly before Wagner's Post Office Savings Bank ● 88, ▲ 228, and is a worthy neighbor to the imperial architecture all around it. The Kirche am Steinhof is part of the huge am Steinhof psychiatric hospital complex commissioned here in the early 1900's by the province of Lower Austria, which also includes a spacious garden for inmates and a number of pavilions. The complex was built on the side of a hill, the top of which is occupied by Otto Wagner's church, a Secession-style ● 86, 88, ▲ 232 building with a number of 18th-century Baroque features. Constructed in concrete, the Kirche am Steinhof is covered with a skin of thin marble, attached by studs that lend great elegance to its overall appearance. The main façade is flanked by twin belltowers, on the tops of which a statues of various saints by Richard Luksch. The PORTAL OF LEOPOLD, with four columns surmounted by ange is truly remarkable; on the inside the nave, transe choir and dome are, like the exterior, covered in plaques of white marble and flooded with light fr huge windows. Wagner did not stop with the building itself; he also designed its fittings (pews lamps) and its high altar and baldachin (the altar' decorations were executed by Othmar Schinkowi and its mosaics by Remigius Geyling).

From Josefstadt to Klosterneuburg

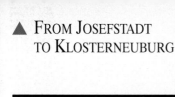

KAHLENBERGKIRCHE   GRINZING   LEOPOLDSKIRCHE   NU...

🚃 **Half a day**

◆ **D** B2 **E** D3

"When he drew his map of repressed Desire, meaning the unconscious, just as in earlier times … men had charted the lineaments of Sensitivity, Sigmund Freud brought into the world a sort of puppet resembling modern man – ambivalent, dreamy, neurotic. I repeat that the face of this creature … had more than anything the features of a Viennese."

Michel Guérin,
Le Deuil et la Mélancolie (in *Vienne*)

JOSEFSTADT

ALSERKIRCHE. The Church of the Holy Trinity (Alserkirche), an impressive Baroque edifice dating from the end of the 17th century, stands on Alserstrasse. Ludwig van Beethoven ● *51*, ▲ *298* was buried here on March 29, 1827. More than thirty thousand people accompanied the genius to a grave in the old Währing cemetery (the coffin was disinterred and moved to the Central Cemetery ▲ *262* in 1888). This church and the adjoining chapel

THE GENERAL HOSPITAL
Arthur Schnitzler began his career as a doctor at the General Hospital (above) in 1885. Sigmund Freud qualified as a doctor in 1881. He quickly abandoned his researches into physiology to study nervous diseases. This led him to invent the science of psychoanalysis.

SIGMUND FREUD AND HIS DAUGHTER ANNA (1913)

are plastered with ex-votos to St Anthony, patron saint of lost causes.
PIARISTENKIRCHE. The architect Johann Lukas von Hildebrandt's ● *75, 81* best-known buildings are his palaces. This is all the more reason to visit JODOK-FINK-PLATZ in the heart of Josefstadt (8th District) to see one of his other buildings, the Piarist Church of Mary the Faithful (Piaristenkirche Maria Treu). The Church belonged to the congregation of Piarists, whose calling was to educate poor children. The handsome Baroque façade topped with a fine pediment has

SCHANZPARK
KARL-MARX-HOF
NEUE DONAU
DANUBE
ALLGEMEINES
KRANKENHAUS

NARRENTURM
Isidor Canevale (1730–83), the architect of the
Lusthaus ▲ *268*, also built the Madmen's Tower
(the Narrenturm, below), the General Hospital and
the Josephinum ▲ *292*.

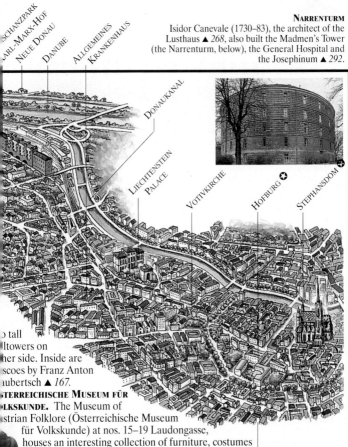

DONAUKANAL

LIECHTENSTEIN
PALACE

VOTIVKIRCHE

HOFBURG ✪

STEPHANSDOM

...o tall
...ltowers on
...her side. Inside are
...scoes by Franz Anton
...aubertsch ▲ *167*.

**...ÖSTERREICHISCHE MUSEUM FÜR
...OLKSKUNDE.** The Museum of
...ustrian Folklore (Österreichische Museum
für Volkskunde) at nos. 15–19 Laudongasse,
houses an interesting collection of furniture, costumes
● *64* , tools and cribs.

ALSERGRUND

The Alsergrund (9th District) was praised in the
novels of Heimito von Doderer (1896–1966),
one of Austria's greatest but least-celebrated
writers.

FREUD-HAUS. Sigmund Freud (1856–1939)
practiced psychoanalysis in a comfortable
house at no. 19 Berggasse, Alsergrund, between
1891 and 1938. In 1938 he fled from the Nazi
régime and installed himself in London. An office
identical to the one that he used has been
reconstructed here, with the same collection of
antique statuettes. Only the famous divan here
is a replica: the original is at the Freud Museum
in London.

ALLGEMEINES KRANKENHAUS. Like Maria
Theresa (1717–80), Joseph II (1740–90) ● *36*
helped create the basis for modern medicine in
Vienna by attracting respected specialists,
encouraging medical research and building
hospitals close to the city. In
1781 a military hospital was
founded so that surgeons and
doctors with practical
experience acquired on army

**FORETASTES OF
"JOSEPHISM"**
It is only partially true
to say that Joseph II
opened the Habsburg
monarchy to the ideas
of the Enlightenment
philosophers. In
reality, the era of
reform had already
begun during the
reign of his mother,
Maria Theresa
(1740–80). The men
who surrounded her
were full of the spirit
of the Enlightenment;
for example, the jurist
and philosopher
Joseph von
Sonnenfels
(1733–1817)
envisaged the
abolition of torture,
and Gerhard von
Swieten (1700–72),
the empress' personal
physician, presided
over the renovation
of the university and
inspired a general
reform of education.

291

The Josephinum.

THE TWO PALACES BY MARTINELLI

The Italian architect Domenico Martinelli built the two Liechtenstein Palaces virtually simultaneously: the

Summer Palace (above) between 1691 and 1704, and the Winter Palace between 1694 and 1706. Like Hildebrandt (1650–1718) Martinelli began in Rome as a pupil of Carlo Fontana. From there he traveled to Northern Europe, in particular to Prague and Vienna.

"ANATOMIA PLASTICA"

Joseph II had the idea for this collection of wax figures after visiting the anatomical museum in Bologna in 1769, and then seeing another collection of wax figurines in Florence. While in Florence he commissioned the artist who had done the figurines, Paolo Mascagni, to do a thousand like them for the Josephinum. The Viennese collection (*Anatomia Plastica*) is now world-famous and belongs to the medical history museum in the Josephinum.

campaigns could treat the sick of Vienna. They were also a to study medicine and surgery at the Military Academy, founded shortly afterward, which was known as the Josephinum. In 1784, the small military hospital was transferred to the premises of the present General Hospita (Allgemeines Krankenhaus); thereafter the hospital steadi added new facilities surrounded with courtyard-gardens, particularly the amazing MADMEN'S TOWER (Narrenturm), a style close to the Utopian architecture of Frenchmen Étienne-Louis Boullée and Claude-Nicolas Ledoux. Built on five floor this monster cylinder has more than one hundred and forty cells, in which those diagnosed as lunatics were incarcerated un 1866. Today it is the MUSEUM OF PATHOLOGY AND ANATOMY (Pathologisch-anatomisches Bundesmuseum), containing a startling collection of around 35,000 figurines and deformed limbs.

JOSEPHINUM ★. Like the General Hospital, the Josephinum (the former military academy of surgery and medicine) was founded by Joseph II. The emperor asked Carlo Canevale to model it on the Hôtel-Dieu hospital in Paris which he had seen during his official trip to France in 1777. The resulting structure, the Josephinum, is a conventional-looking building from the end of the Baroque age (1783–5), with an impressive library and above all a collection of wax figures for the study of anatomy. In addition to these flayed wax torsos, there are a number of mementoes of great Viennese physicians, notably some letters written by Sigmund Freud.

MUSEUM MODERNER KUNST. North of the Josephinum, in the heart of the Alsergrund, is the Liechtenstein Palace, which today houses the Museum of Modern Art (Museum moderner Kunst). This majestic Baroque palace ● *80, 82* set in its own gardens is one of the two residences built in Vienna by the princes of Liechtenstein at the close of the 17th century. Inside, the ceiling of the MAIN RECEPTION ROOM (Festsaal) is covered with frescoes by Andrea Pozzo ● *77,* ▲ *149, 152, 167* (*The Apotheosis of Hercules*). Other Baroque artists

ked on the palace's décor, notably Giovanni Giulani and
ann Michael Rottmayr ▲ *139, 159* on the sculptures, and
onio Belucci and Santino Bussi on the paintings. Most of
contemporary art movements (Jugendstil, Secession ● *86*,
ressionism, Cubism, Surrealism, Abstract Art, New
urative Art, Pop Art and so on) are represented in the
collections of the museum.
Temporary exhibitions are
also staged from time to time,
offering a glimpse of the current
international avant-garde.

SERVITENKIRCHE. Southeast of the Liechtenstein Palace
s the Servite Church (Servitenkirche), designed by Carlo
evale between 1651 and 1677. With an oval nave, this
ctuary is one of the first of its kind built in Vienna. The
rior is by Giovanni Battista Barberini.

ÄHRING

RUDELHOFSTEIGE (SCHUBERTPARK). The balustrades and
e lamps of the zigzag Strudelhof Steps (Strudelhofstiege),
ch have several different ramps and landings, make this
of the outstanding Jugendstil creations in Vienna. The
os link Liechtensteinstrasse to Währingerstrasse. As it
ceeds away from the Ring, Währingerstrasse cuts across
ssdorferstrasse, which continues as far as
ligenstadt and the Döblinger
rtelstrasse, which in turn
sses Oberdöbling and

**SCHUBERT'S
BIRTHPLACE**
Just west of the
Liechtenstein Palace,
in Nussdorferstrasse,
a small museum
devoted to Franz
Schubert (1797–1828)
● *50* has been set up
in the house of his
birth (Schuberts
Geburtshaus, no. 54),
at the sign of the *Red
Crayfish* (*Haus zum
roten Krebs*). Schubert
lived here during his
earliest childhood,
before moving to
another
house
nearby, at no.
3 Saulengasse.
He died aged
thirty-one in a house
on

Kettenbrückegasse,
not far from the
Naschmarkt ▲ *236*.

JOSEPH II
A bust of the
institution's
founder, Joseph
II, sits behind
one of the wax
figures at the
Josephinum.

Unterdöbling. This avenue runs parallel to the Danube Ca
■ *20, 22,* ▲ *271* and heads past THE UNIVERSITY COMPLEX
(Universitätszentrum).

WÄHRINGER FRIEDHOF. Before being transferred to the
Central Cemetery ▲ *262,* the body of Franz Schubert was
buried in the former Währing Cemetery (Währinger
Friedhof), which is now known as the Schubertpark, on
Währingerstrasse. Beethoven was also buried here and late
removed ▲ *290.*

JOHANNES-VON-NEPOMUK-KIRCHE. Still in the vicinity of th
General Hospital and the Liechtenstein Pala
is the pretty little church of St John of
Nepomuk on Währingergürtel, which was
built by Otto Wagner ● *86, 88,* ▲ *228, 23*
240 between 1895 and 1898.

VOLKSOPER. Nearby is the People's Opera
(Volksoper), constructed in 1898 to mark
Franz-Joseph's fiftieth jubilee. This impress
building really looks more like a circus th;
a theater. Ever since its opening it has
been a shrine for composers and lovers o
the operetta ● *60,* ▲ *299;* Mozart's *The
Magic Flute* ● *48,* ▲ *147, 281* is usually
performed here rather than in the State Op
on the Ring ▲ *223.*

GEYMÜLLER-SCHLÖSSEL. Northwest of the Währing, at
Pötzleinsdorf, stands the Geymüller-Schlössel manor hous
at no. 102 Pötzleinsdorfer Strasse, built in the 19th century
the banker J. H. Geymüller. The SOBECK COLLECTION of
clocks is exhibited here, with fine examples of wristwatches
fob watches, chimney clocks and grandfather clocks dating
from the 17th to the 19th centuries. The magnificent
Biedermeier décor ● *62* of this
house alone makes it worth the
visit.

DÖBLING

TÜRKENSCHANZ. Bridging Währing
(18th District) and Döbling (19th
District) is the Türkenschanz Park,
where part of Suleyman the
Magnificent's army was encamped
during the 1529 siege ● *34.* A 40-
acre park was created on this high
ground at the close of the 19th
century, and the area quickly
became a favorite resort of the
Viennese; it was very popular with

celebrated writer Arthur Schnitzler
'90.

LA GESSNER AND VILLA MOLLER. A
or residential area with many handsome
dings lies around the park and the
ERVATORY (Sternwarte). Buildings here
ude the Secession-style ● 86, ▲ 232 Villa
ssner (built in 1907 by Hubert and F.
ssner on Sternwartestrasse) and the Villa
ller on Starkfriedgasse (built by Adolf Loos
42, 174 in 1927–8) in the
sleinsdorf suburb.

RL-MARX-HOF. To the north of the
iversity complex is the remarkable
f-mile-long Karl-Marx-Hof municipal
sing project ● 92, which opens onto
ligenstädterstrasse. The red and ocher
tral part of this ensemble is particularly
king, with six tall towers crowned by
sts, and a series of statues and arcades
ng courtyards and gardens. Karl-
rx-Hof contains no fewer than
00 apartments and stands in the
ad green area between the hills of
bling and Heiligenstadt to the west,
the Heiligenstadt railway station to
east. It was one of the 398 workers'
jects – known as "red strongholds" –
ch were built around Vienna between
9 and 1934. This period was marked by
confrontation between Christian
ialists and Social Democrats in Austria; both of these
ups were also the sworn enemies of the Communist
tingent, Otto Bauer's Austro-Marxists, who were heavily
uenced by Marxist ideology. Administered by a Social
mocratic municipal council, Red Vienna was a veritable
te within a state. The municipal government tried to turn
nna into a showcase of the Socialist society of the future
t it wanted to promote, with a huge program of public

Posters for the
Social Democratic,
Christian Socialist
and Communist
parties from 1920,
1927 and 1919.

**FEAR OF JEWS
AND BOLSHEVIKS**
"No sooner did
our emperor's
eyes close for the
last time than we
shivered into a
hundred pieces. The
Balkans will be more
powerful than we.
Every nation will
organize its own
dirty little state and
the Jews
themselves will
proclaim a king in
Palestine. Vienna
already reeks of the
sweat of Democrats
and I can no longer
bear to be in
Ringstrasse. The
workers have red
flags and don't want
to work any more.
The priests are
already following the
people, the sermons
in the churches are
preached in Czech."
Joseph Roth,
The Radetsky March

The Socialist
municipality
promoted a campaign
for hygiene in the
schools during the
1920's.

"RED VIENNA"
Led by Karl Seitz (1869–1950, below), the mayor elected in 1923, "Red Vienna's" municipal team (H. Breitner, F. Siegel and A. Weber) laid special emphasis on public housing. Nearly all the housing built between 1923 and 1933 was within the framework of the *Höfe* complexes, projects designed for workers with collective facilities. Among the largest of

these were Sandleiten (1,587 units) in 1924, Rabenhof (1,109 units) in 1925, Karl-Seitz-Hof (1,173 units) in 1926, Karl-Marx-Hof (1,325 units) in 1927, George-

Washington-Hof (1,084 units) in 1927, Mithlingerhof (1,136 units) in 1929, and Engelsplatz (1,467 units) in 1930.

works and residential projects: between 1919 and 1934 over 64,000 new public housing units were built in the city. This housing was limited to a few districts on the north and south sides of Vienna because right up until 1918 the various class had been divided up quarter by quarter into aristocratic, bourgeois and working-class areas. Today more than five thousand people live in Karl-Marx-Hof, which is arranged around several large inner courtyards and garden areas, the latter taking up more than eighty percent of the space allotted.

KARL-MARX-HOF UNDER FIRE. During the civil war which broke out in Vienna in February 1934 ● *33* and only lasted a few days, Karl-Marx-Hof was the scene of a violent confrontation when it was taken over by a handful of rebels and was bombarded by the army acting on the orders of Chancellor Dollfuss. The buildings were partially destroyed and their defenders forced to surrender; subsequently an authoritarian government was installed which banned parti and unions and opened the way for the Anschluss ● *42*, wh was accomplished a few years later.

BRIGITTENAU

Between the Danube and the Danube Canal ● *20, 22,* ▲ *12 272* north of Leopoldstadt, lies Brigittenau (20th District), working-class area strewn with railway installations and mainline stations.

OTTO-HAAS-HOF. The city council of Red Vienna construct several workers' housing projects, comprising a total of 273 lodgings, on this site. The buildings were known collectively the Otto-Haus-Hof. The ensemble was built in 1924 by a te of architects that included Adolf Loos ● *86, 91,* ▲ *142, 174, 236.* Loos championed the idea of building small detached houses for the project, but without much

The façade of Karl-Marx-Hof (right).

FOR GREATER COMFORT
Built by the architect Karl Ehn between 1927 and 1930, the workers' housing project of Karl-Marx-Hof sought to give the working classes more comfortable lodgings. Hence this monster complex contains not only ten different kinds of apartments (with running water, city gas and electricity) but also various other social facilities: a swimming pool, laundries, children's playgrounds, a post office, a dispensary, a chemist, a library and shops.

cess; altogether, such houses (*Seidlungen*) made up only e percent of the new housing when it was completed. Huge rtment blocks were more in line with the prevailing ectivist dogmas.

NARSKYHOF. Another major project of 534 housing units is Winarskyhof, which includes a series of attractive rtyards in addition to creches, shops and swimming pools. e façade of Winarskyhof is lightened by Expressionist dings.

UMANNHOF ● *93*. The bust of Jakob Reumann, Vienna's t "red" mayor, stands in front of the public housing plex that bears his name. The Reumannhof was built ween 1924 and 1926 by Hubert Gessner, architect of the l-Marx-Hof.

GELSPLATZ. Adjoining the bridge over the Danube which ds to Floridsdorf is Engelsplatz. It is overlooked by a ssive residential complex of 1,467 apartments that were lt in the 1930's, toward the end of the Red Vienna eriment. Constructed around a series of rtyards, Engelsplatz is flanked by several numental-looking towers.

ORIDSDORF

s former village (now the 21st District) on left bank of the Danube is today a king-class area that is sandwiched ween the New Danube, the Old nube and a busy freeway junction. RL-SEITZ-HOF ● *92*. One of the gest projects (*Höfe*) to be structed in the Red Vienna rs, the Karl-Seitz-Hof (1,173 rtments) was built in 1926 by bert Gessner, one year before Karl-Marx-Hof and after the mannhof. The complex has a ctacular appearance because its arc- ped central block is crowned by a tower, which gives access to a e inner street. On the left-hand side he crescent is a clocktower. ices, creches, shops, laundries even a theater are features his remarkable dence.

> **"My musical works are the product of genius and wretchedness and those which give the public most pleasure are those which have given me the greatest pain."**
>
> Ludwig van Beeth⬚

Beethoven's Testament.

"As he gradually lost contact with the outside world, he focused more clearly on the one within him. As he grew more familiar with the management of his inner realm, he imposed, with ever greater awareness, his demands on the outer. He asked his protectors to cease paying him for his work, and instead to take care that he should never have to worry about the world, and thus be able to work for himself alone."
Richard Wagner, *Beethoven*

HEILIGENSTADT

This attractive village lying on the hillsides Kahlenburg and Leopoldsberg north of Vienna is less famous for its expanse of vineyards ■ *26*, ● *68* than for the time Lu⬚ van Beethoven ● *51* spent there at the en⬚ his life.

"I DON'T COMPOSE FOR THE GALLERY!" Li⬚ many other Romantics, Beethoven sought inspiration in the beauty and solitude of t⬚ Vienna woods ■ *18*, ● *100* or in bouts of seasonal work in the fields. During his visi⬚ Heiligenstadt in 1807–8, he composed his *Sixth Symphony*, known as the *Pastoral,* in which he attempted to translate the rhyth⬚ of the universe and the sensation of an all-pervading divinity into music.

"THE HEILIGENSTADT TESTAMENT". To music-lovers Heiligenstadt above all recalls Beethoven's first wretched period there in 1802. During his stay, the musician, who fo⬚ six years had done everything possible to conceal the fact t⬚ he was incurably deaf, finally admitted it in his *Heiligenstad⬚ Testament*, a document addressed to his brothers Kaspar a⬚ Johann. He also described his sense of desperation and wr⬚ that he was tempted to commit suicide: "These ordeals brought me to the brink of despair; I came close to killing myself. Art, and art alone, stayed my hand."

HEILIGENSTÄDTER-TESTAMENT-HAUS. The *Testament* was written in the modest house at no. 6 Probusgasse (above), was Beethoven's *Second Symphony*. Moreover, the *Third Symphony*, known as *Eroica,* was in all likelihood conceive⬚ while the composer was staying here. Pa⬚ the Testament-Haus has now been turn⬚ into a museum, where a collection of objects and engravings relating to Beethoven's time in the village is exhibite⬚

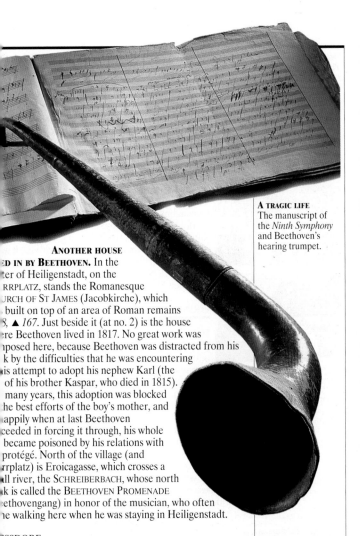

A TRAGIC LIFE
The manuscript of the *Ninth Symphony* and Beethoven's hearing trumpet.

ANOTHER HOUSE
⌐ED IN BY BEETHOVEN. In the
⌐er of Heiligenstadt, on the
⌐RRPLATZ, stands the Romanesque
⌐URCH OF ST JAMES (Jacobkirche), which
⌐ built on top of an area of Roman remains
⌐, ▲ 167. Just beside it (at no. 2) is the house
⌐re Beethoven lived in 1817. No great work was
⌐posed here, because Beethoven was distracted from his
⌐k by the difficulties that he was encountering
⌐is attempt to adopt his nephew Karl (the
⌐of his brother Kaspar, who died in 1815).
⌐ many years, this adoption was blocked
⌐he best efforts of the boy's mother, and
⌐appily when at last Beethoven
⌐ceeded in forcing it through, his whole
⌐became poisoned by his relations with
⌐protégé. North of the village (and
⌐rrplatz) is Eroicagasse, which crosses a
⌐ll river, the SCHREIBERBACH, whose north
⌐k is called the BEETHOVEN PROMENADE
⌐ethovengang) in honor of the musician, who often
⌐e walking here when he was staying in Heiligenstadt.

⌐SSDORF

⌐he hills to the north of Heiligenstadt is Nussdorf, which
⌐rlooks the Danube. Surrounded by vines ■ 26, Nussdorf is
⌐ous for its guingettes, or *Heurigen* ● 68.
⌐**E LEHAR-SCHIKANEDER-SCHLÖSSEL.** At no. 18
⌐ckhohergasse is Franz Lehár's castle (Lehár-Schikaneder-
⌐lössel) in which the celebrated operetta composer ● 60
⌐d until his death (there is a small MUSEUM here). A native
⌐Hungary, Lehár (1870–1948) continued in the great
⌐lition of operetta founded in the 19th century by Jacques
⌐enbach, a French composer of German extraction, and
⌐ann Strauss ● 56. Lehár had a number of triumphs,
⌐ably *The Merry Widow* (1905), *The Count of Luxembourg*
⌐08) and *The Land of Smiles* (1929). The Baroque building
⌐hich he lived belonged at one time to Emmanuel
⌐ikaneder, director of the Theater An der Wien ● 62.
⌐ikaneder commissioned *The Magic Flute* from Mozart
⌐8, ▲ 147, 281 and himself wrote the libretto for the opera.

"What could this ecstatic dreamer see, as he passed wide-eyed through the swarming streets of Vienna staring fixedly before him, inspired only by the world of harmonies, the one world that remained alive within him?"
Richard Wagner,
Beethoven

NEW WHITE WINE
The arrival of the *Heurigen* ■ *26*, ● *68* is welcomed with music in the guinguettes; it has made the reputation of Grinzing, a small village on the upper slopes of Döbling, north of Vienna

He resided at Nussdorf between 1802 to 1812 and during period met Beethoven, whom he encouraged to write ope
BEETHOVEN AGAIN. At no. 26 Kahlenbergerstrasse stands 18th-century house where Beethoven lived in 1824, the ye he finished his last, the *Ninth* (Choral) *Symphony*. Finally, the southeast side of Heiligenstadt, on Grinzingerstrasse a Michaelskirche, is no. 64, another 18th-century building th was occupied by Beethoven and the family of the poet Fra Grillparzer in 1808 ● *62*, ▲ *147, 206*. The Grillparzer fami finally was forced to decamp after a series of quarrels with composer.

NUSSDORFER WEHR. The entrance to the Danub Canal (Donaukanal) ▲ *230* is barred by a stupendous lock (Nussdorfer Wehr) which is overlooked by two bronze lions on tall pedestals Rudolph Weyr. This structure is a graceful combination of stone, glass and steel girders; it w designed by Otto Wagner ▲ *228, 237, 240* betwee 1884 and 1898, when he was a member of the Secession Movement ● *86, 88*, ▲ *232*.

GRINZING

(above). Other villages once famous for their wine, like Gumpendorf at Margareten (6th District), have become heavily populated residential areas. Karlskirche ▲ *238* and the Belvedere ▲ *246* were also surrounded by vines at one time.

HONORARY CITIZENS. Nowadays the guingettes (*Heurigen*) of Grinzing are increasingly being tur into tourist restaurants, and in summer the stree the village are often packed with people milling about whi looking for souvenirs. Even worse, speculators have taken advantage of Grinzing's fame to buy up a series of potenti building sites. An international campaign is now underway prevent such development which, if allowed to continue unchecked, would certainly lead to the destruction of the vineyards and of Grinzing's rustic character. In practice, th campaign works as a kind of club of "honorary citizens" of Grinzing. Every member of the club buys, for a nominal p a single vine which he or she is thereafter expected to prot Among these honorary vineyard owners are many stars an celebrities.

ɪNZINGER FRIEDHOF. Music-lovers will
h to make the pilgrimage to the Grinzing
netery (Grinzinger Friedhof) where
ʊsᴛᴀᴠ Mᴀʜʟᴇʀ (*Gruppe 6, Reihe 7*) ● *52,*
235 is buried.

ᴀʜʟᴇɴʙᴇʀɢ

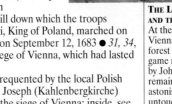

ᴏm Grinzing, two winding roads
ᴏblenzgasse and Höhenstrasse) lead up
ᴇ 1,588-foot Bald Mountain
ᴀhlenberg). This was the hill down which the troops
ᴍmanded by John Sobieski, King of Poland, marched on
ᴇir way to crush the Turks, on September 12, 1683 ● *31, 34,*
ᴅ thus ended the second siege of Vienna, which had lasted
ce July 14 that year.
ᴀʜʟᴇɴʙᴇʀɢᴋɪʀᴄʜᴇ. Much frequented by the local Polish
ᴍmunity, the Church of St Joseph (Kahlenbergkirche)
ᴍmemorates the lifting of the siege of Vienna; inside, see
ᴇ Sᴏʙɪᴇsᴋɪ Cʜᴀᴘᴇʟ and the replica of the *Black Virgin of*
ᴇstochowa.
ɪᴇ ᴠɪᴇᴡ ꜰʀᴏᴍ ᴛʜᴇ Kᴀʜʟᴇɴʙᴇʀɢ. The Kahlenberg offers a
ᴀgnificent view of Vienna and the Danube Valley ■ *20, 22,*
271. In 1809, during the French invasion of Austria, the
ᴇnnese climbed here to watch the maneuvers and battles
ᴋing place farther down the Danube at Essling-Aspern and
ᴀgram ● *38*.

ᴇᴏᴘᴏʟᴅsʙᴇʀɢ

ᴏhenstrasse connects the Kahlenberg to the 1,394-foot
ᴏunt Leopold (Leopoldsberg), which overlooks the
ᴀnube Valley from farther east. The view across the
ɢion from the top of the Leopoldsberg is remarkable.
ᴏᴏᴘᴏʟᴅsᴋɪʀᴄʜᴇ. Leopold I built a church here
ᴅicated to his namesake, St Leopold, in the 17th century.
ᴀis was destroyed during the second siege of Vienna by the
ʀks ● *31, 34,* then rebuilt in the Baroque style at the
ɢinning of the 18th century.

**THE LEOPOLDSBERG
AND THE KAHLENBERG**
At the gates of
Vienna, the huge
forest teeming with
game made famous
by Johann Strauss has
remained
astonishingly
untouched, despite
the bites taken out of
it by spreading
urbanization.

↖ Leopoldsberg

↖ Kahlenberg

"Contemplate the
landscape from the
top of the
Kahlenberg, and you
will understand what
I write and what I
am."
    Franz Grillparzer

THE LEOPOLDSBERG
This belvedere owes
its name to margrave
Leopold III von
Babenberg ● *28,*
▲ *138*, founder of the
abbey of
Klosterneuburg, who
was canonized in the
15th century. After its
destruction during
the 1529 siege, the
Babenberg castle at
the summit of the hill
was a ruin for many
years.

KLOSTERNEUBURG ★

The abbey of Klosterneuburg (Stift Klosterneuburg) was founded in the early 12th century by Margrave Leopold III Babenberg, whose fortress stood close by on the top of the Leopoldsberg. This was the capital of the Eastern March (Ostmark), the future Austria. In 1156, when Henry II

Jasomirgott of Babenberg was made Duke of Austria by the Holy Roman Emperor Frederick I Barbarossa (1122–90), he transferred his capital fr[o] Klosterneuburg to Vienna ● 28.

MARGRAVE AND SAINT. The extremely pious Margrave Leopold III refused to [be] drawn into the quarrels between the H[oly] Roman Emperors and the Popes (the dispute over investitures lasted betwee[n] 1059 and 1122), or into the rebellion of the German princes against the imperi[al] power. This policy allowed him to marr[y] Agnes, daughter of Emperor Henry II, [to] live in peace on his estates, and to dedicate his life to the Catholic religio[n.] He was canonized in the 15th century a[nd] is buried in the chapel.

AUGUSTINE ABBEY, AUSTRIAN ESCORIAL. The first abbey, which belonged to the Augustine Order, was built in the Romanesque style in imitation of the Cistercian abbeys that members of the Orders of Cluny and Citeaux had built across Europe. Several centuries later Charles VI hatched a series of projects designed to give new luster to Klosterneuburg, which had been damaged by fire in 1730. Taking as his model the Escorial Palace just outside

THE LEGEND OF THE LOST VEIL
Leopold III decided to build his abbey on the site where he had found a precious veil lost by his wife, Agnes of Franconia. A wooden panel (above) painted by Rueland Frueauf (1470–1547), from the altar of the abbey church.

Madrid (built between 1563 and 1584), Charles determined to construct a monastery-palace that would symbolize the grandeur both of the Austrian monarchy and of the Holy Roman Empire, as well as housing a majestic family burial vault close to the Habsburg capital of Vienna.

FROM FISCHER VON ERLACH TO D'ALLIO. Charles VI gave the project to Josef Emanuel Fischer von Erlach, son of Johann Bernhard ● 74, 80. Unfortunately the architect was involved in a plethora of other huge contracts at the time, notably the National Library ▲ 192, 196, the Winter Manège of the Spanish Riding School ▲ 188, 190 and the Chancellery Wing of the Hofburg ▲ 175, as well as the completion of Karlskirche ● 74, ▲ 240 and the Schönbrunn Palace ▲ 274. He therefore limited himself to a sketch for a grandiose project to build

LEOPOLD III (1070–1136)
Margrave Leopold III von Babenberg ▲ 138 is the patron saint of Lower Austria.

alace with four courtyards and nine domes. The Milanese
hitect Donato Felice d'Allio (1690–1780) was then called
o turn this into reality. Two difficulties immediately arose:
Habsburgs' chronic shortage of cash, and the death of
arles VI in 1740. As a result the works were limited to
ling a Baroque building to the original
manesque and Gothic abbey, with
y one courtyard and two copper
nes topped by the imperial crown and
archducal cap. Work was halted in
5, then resumed in the 19th century,
vhich time the architect Josef
rnhausel added a wing to the Baroque
lding to close off the courtyard.

E ABBEY CHURCH. From the esplanade
h its LANTERN COLUMN (Lichtsäule)
visitor passes into the Abbey Church
h its two belfries. Originally Romanesque, this Church was
ivily modified over the course of centuries, especially in the
h, when neo-Gothic additions were made. The
DIRSTALLS, the ORATORY OF THE IMPERIAL COURT, the
PIT and the ORGAN (on which Anton Bruckner ● 52, ▲
often played) are highlights of the interior.

E GOTHIC CLOISTER AND THE FREISINGERKAPELLE. Behind
Abbey Church is the Gothic cloister and the Freising
apel (Freisingerkapelle); the latter contains an effigy of
rthold von Wehingen, Bishop of Friesing in the 14th
tury.

OPOLDSKAPELLE. The Chapel of St Leopold
opoldskapelle) contains one of the greatest marvels of
dieval goldwork, the ALTARPIECE OF NIKOLAUS OF VERDUN
81). It shows scenes from the Bible, and is made up of
y-one plaques of gilded metal worked by the technique of
implevé enamel, whereby small sockets are drilled in the
tal and the liquid enamel is poured over and then fired. In
chapel is a silver reliquary containing the relics of St
opold Babenberg. The 14th- and 15th-century stained-glass
idows here are magnificent.

OPOLDSHOF. Dominated by an ancient fortified tower, the
irtyard of Leopold (Leopoldshof) is surrounded by Gothic
l Renaissance buildings. In its center is the 17th-century ST
OPOLD'S FOUNTAIN.

E MARBLE ROOM. Among the Baroque buildings
astructed under Charles VI are the imperial apartments

THE LANTERN COLUMN
This 15th-century memorial (below) stands in the middle of the esplanade.

St Leopold's Fountain (left).

THE ABBEY CHURCH
The Baroque interior contains fine frescoes from the late 17th and early 18th centuries, commissioned by Charles VI from such artists as Johann Michael Rottmayr ▲ 139, 160, 293, J. G. Schmidt and G. Fanti.

NIKOLAUS OF VERDUN
A pupil of the Flemish monk Godefroid de Claire, Nikolaus of Verdun perfected the art of champlevé enamel in the 12th century. This technique, inherited from Byzantine and Carolingian art, evolved in the workshops of Maastricht, Verdun and Liège along the River Meuse, and in Cologne, Coblenz and Aix-la-Chapelle along the Rhine.

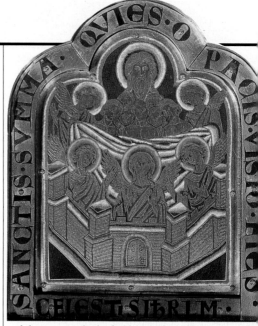

THE VERDUN ALTARPIECE
The altarpiece of Klosterneuburg (1181) is made up of illustrated enamel plaques from the Shrine of the Three Kings at Cologne Cathedral – one of the only pieces of medieval goldwork fashioned in solid gold – and from the Tournai reliquary (1205).

REMINDERS OF THE TURKS ● 34
As in Vienna itself, plaques here commemorate the presence of the Turkish armies, recalling a battle, or the site of a redoubt.

Franz Kafka, a native of Prague (1883–1924) was for part of his life a subject of the emperor of Austria. An obscure bureaucrat, Kafka spent his leisure time writing about a world of mental anguish that failed to interest the public until after his death.

and the museum, both of which overlook the courtyard (Kaiserhof). The upper floors are reached by a monumenta Baroque staircase (1723), never completed, which leads to MARBLE ROOM with its frescoes by Daniel Gran (*The Glory the House of Austria*, 1749). In the imperial apartments, not the TAPESTRY ROOM, which is decorated with 18th-century Brussels tapestries.

THE VIRGIN OF KLOSTERNEUBURG. The MUSEUM o the third floor contains several masterpieces, in particular a 14th-century marble Virgin of great sweetness and grace. The early 15th-century altarpiece of Albert II, the 15th-century Babenber family tree, the Italian Renaissance statues, and th *Mercury* by Georg Raphael Donner ▲ *170, 171,* wh sculpted the Neuer Markt Fountain ▲ *141,* are als well worth seeing.

TAUSENDEIMERFASS. Within the abbey precin are the GOTHIC CHAPEL OF ST SEBASTIAN, th CELLARHOUSE and the COOPER'S SHOP, containing the "thousand-bucket-barrel" (Tausendeimerfass) made in 1704. It can hold almost 15,000 US gallons of wine. On St Leopold's Day, November 15, an annual fête is held here, with barrel-rolling competitions; a reminder that the Klosterneuburg vineyard area is one of the largest in Austria.

KIERLING

THE DEATH OF KAFKA. The Kierling sanatorium was where Franz Kafka (1883–1924) died from tuberculosis. A small museum here contains mementoes of this great Bohemian writer.

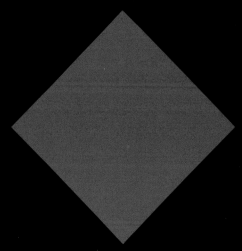

Practical information

Key

Ⅲ Air conditioning	♪ Live music
⚹ Children rates	P Parking
▬ Credit cards accepted	🏊 Swimming pool
▤ Credit cards not	☎ Telephone
accepted	▣ Television
♿ Facilities for the	↑ Terrace
disabled	☇ View
🍴 Garden	

ADDRESSES

→ IN THE UK

■ **Austrian Embassy and Consulate**
18 Belgrave Mews West
London SW1X 8HU
Tel. 020 7235 37 31
Fax 020 7344 02 92
embassy@austria.org.uk
www.bmaa.gv.at/emba
ssyluk/index.html.en

■ **Austrian National Tourist Office**
14 Cork Street
London W1X 1PF
Tel. 020 7629 04 61
www.austria–tourism.
at/index.htlm.en

■ **Austria on the Net (UK)**
www.austria-info.at
www.europeonline.c
om/aus/index–gb/htm
Visas and travel tips:
www.austria.org/
visa.htm

→ IN THE US

■ **Austrian Embassy**
3524 International Court
Washington, DC 20008
Tel. (202) 895 6700

■ **Austrian Consulate**
NEW YORK
Tel. 212 737 6400
austroko@interport.net
CHICAGO
Tel. 312 222 1515
LOS ANGELES
Tel. 310 444 9310
ausconsla@aol.com

■ **Austrian National Tourist Office**
NEW YORK
212 944 6880
LOS ANGELES
310 477 2038

■ **Austria on the Net (US)**
www.anto.at
www.austriaculture.net

BUDGET

→ CHEAP

■ **2 persons**
Hotel** £30–40/
$50–65 per day
per day.

→ FAMILY

■ **2 adults and 2 children**
Bed & breakfast £25/$40 per person per day (with a 30% reduction for children under 12).

→ COMFORTABLE

■ **2 persons**
Hotel***(*) central around £100/$160 per person per day.

CLIMATE

Moderately continental. Bright, but long and cold winters (Oct.–Apr., 22°F to 40°F). Short, sometimes wet, spring and fall. Moderate temperatures (60°F to 78°F) in summer.

FORMALITIES

Valid ID cards or passports for European Union members. US visitors need a valid passport. A visa is not required for stays (as a tourist) for up to three months. *A valid passport is required for excursions to the Czec Republic, Slovakia or Hungary.*

HEALTH

Form E111, issued by the Health Authorities of EU countries, entitles their members to emergency medical treatment in Austria. Non-EU members must take out personal medical insurance.

HOTEL RESERVATIONS

Essential during the high season (Apr.–Oct.). In low season (Nov.–Mar.), most hotels offer reductions.

■ **Tourist Office (Wien-Tourismus)**
Tel. 00 43 1
(211 14 444)
Fax (00 43 1)
211 14 445
rooms@info.wien.at
www.info.wien.at

MONEY

→ CURRENCY

The Austrian Schilling (ATS), subdivided into 100 Groschen.

→ EXCHANGE

£1 = 22.7 ATS
$1 = 15.1 ATS
1 Euro = 13.8 ats

→ CREDIT CARDS

Accepted by most hotels, restaurants and stores.

TELEPHONE

→ CALLING VIENNA FROM THE UK

Dial 00 + 43 1 + the number you wish to call.

→ CALLING VIENNA FROM THE US

Dial 011 + 43 1 + the number you wish to call.

TRAVEL

→ BY AIR

■ **From the UK**
There are regular flights from London and other UK cities direct to Vienna. A return flight from London can cost as little as £90, but generally costs £150–200 for economy class. Journey time 2¼ hrs.

■ **British Airways**
Tel. 0345 222111
www.british-airways.com

■ **Lauda Air**
Tel. 0800 767 737
www.laudaair.com

■ **Buzz**
Tel. 0870 240 7070
www.buzzaway.com

■ **From the US**
There are direct and one-stop flights from most major US cities to Vienna.
NEW YORK–VIENNA
From $750 return; journey time 8¾ hrs.
CHICAGO–VIENNA
From $780 return; journey time 9¼ hrs.
LOS ANGELES–VIENNA
About $940 return, with connections; journey time depends on connections, but generally about 14 hours.

■ **Lauda Air**
Tel. 1 800 588 8399
www.laudaair.com

■ **American Airlin**
1 800 433 7300
www.unitedairlin
com

■ **Delta**
1 800 223 5730
www.delta-air.co.

■ **United Airlines**
1 800 538 2929
www.unitedairlin
com

→ BY CAR

Take a car to Brus or Paris on the Shuttle through t Eurotunnel, then drive on to Vienn (Brussels–Vienna: 575 miles, Paris– Vienna: 782 miles.

■ **Eurotunnel**
Tel. (0990) 353 53
www.eurotunnel.c

Valid driving licer and the following documents:
■ International ca insurance, indicat the country of origin if it does n have the new European Union plate.
■ Austrian motorway tax dis sold at the border and at gas station Cost: 550 ATS (1 ye 70 ATS (10 days) 150 ATS (2 months

→ BY TRAIN

Take Eurostar fro London Waterloo Paris Gare du Nor then change for Gare de l'Est for a direct train to Vienna-Westbahnhof (tw trains daily).

■ **International ra enquiries (Londo**
Tel. 0990 848 848

■ **Eurostar**
Tel. 0990 186 186
www.eurostar.cor

■ **SNCF (Paris)**
Tel.08 36 35 35 35
www.sncf.fr

WHEN TO GO?

May–June and Sep.–Oct.: pleasa temperatures, no so many tourists. *Warning: Some museums are clos during the summe*

COMMODATION
LASSIFICATION
RATES
mping
camp sites
he vicinity
Vienna.
und 70 ATS
person per day,
an additional
o 80 ATS for the
h per day.
uesthouses/
sions per night
m 1 to 4 stars
* 3,000–4,000 ATS
2,000–3,000 ATS
,000–2,000 ATS
ss than 1,000 ATS
uests in private
hes per night
und 500 ATS
otels per night
m 1 to 5 stars
** over 4,000 ATS
* 3,000–4,000 ATS
2,000–3,000 ATS
,000–2,000 ATS
ss than 1,000 ATS
outh hostels per
ht
tengasse 7, VII

stiftgasse 85, VII
523 63 16

N-THE-SPOT
ERVATIONS
otel rooms
n private homes
RIST-INFORMATION
Albertinaplatz, I
513 88 92
216 84 82
n daily
–7pm
he airport
ival hall):
n daily
)am–9pm
VEL AGENTS
HE WESTBAHNHOF
opaplatz, XV
en Mon.–Fri.
–10pm
NA-AUHOF REST
A
stern Highway
)
en 8am–10pm
r.–Oct.),
m–6pm
v.–Mar.)

DRESSES
RITISH CONSULATE
restrasse 12, III
71613 5151
71613 5900
hancery@netway

→ US CONSULATE
Gartenbau-promenade 2/4, I
Tel. 31339/7532
Fax 512 58 35
www.usembassy–vienna.at

→ TOURIST INFORMATION
■ Jugend Info
Burgring/angle Babenberger Str.
Tel. 17 99
jugendinfo.wien@blackbox.at
Open Mon.–Sat. noon–7pm
Information for young people and students. Many advantages and reductions.
■ Tourist-information
Am Albertinaplatz, I
Tel. 513 88 92
Open daily

9am–7pm
At the airport (Arrival hall): open daily 8.30am–9pm
Desk indicated by an "i" for information.

ARRIVAL AND DEPARTURE
→ BY AIR
■ Airport
Wien–Schwechat (12 miles southeast of the city center)
Tel. 7007 0
FLIGHT INFORMATION
Tel. 7007 22 233
LOST PROPERTY
Tel. 7007 2193
AUSTRIAN AIRLINES
Tel. 7007 25 10
Open daily 6am–8pm
City center:
Kärntner Ring 18, I
Tel. 17 89
Open Mon.–Fri. 9am–5pm
BRITISH AIRWAYS
Schwechat airport:

Tel. 7007 2646/2939
Fax 7007 2637
City center:
Kärntner Ring 10, I
Tel. 506 60
Fax 5042 084
Open Mon.–Fri. 9am–5pm
LAUDA AIR
PO Box 51
Schwechat airport:
Tel. 711 10 2081 to 2084
Open Mon.–Fri 8.30am–5.30pm
City center:
Opernring 6
Tel. 514 770
Open Mon.–Fri. 9.30am–5.30pm
■ Airport–city link
BY BUS
(Vienna Airport Bus Service)
Tel. 5800-23 00
Between the airport and the City Air Terminal (Hilton Hotel, III), the Vienna International Center, the Südbahnhof and Westbahnhof.
Fixed fare: 70 ATS
BY EXPRESS TRAIN (S-Bahn, Line 7)
Between the airport and the Wien-Mitte station (Landstrasser Hauptstrasse, III)
Departure: every 30 mins.
Duration: 35 mins.
Fare: 38 ATS
BY TAXI
Taxi rank outside the airport arrival hall. Approx. 400 ATS from the airport to the city center.
BY SHARED TAXI
Outside the arrival gate. You share a taxi with other people. Fast and cheaper than taking a taxi on your own, circa 180 ATS.

→ BY CAR
■ Autoroutes
Autobahn
Indicated in white against a blue background. It is compulsory to have a current highway tax disk, which is sold at tobacconists' (Tabak-Trafik), gas stations, and at the border. Rented cars will already be issued with a tax disk.
Tariffs: 550 ATS (for 1 year)
70 ATS (10 days)
150 ATS (2 months)
■ Rescue service
ÖAMTC (TOURING CLUB)
Tel. 120
ARBÖ
Tel. 123

→ BY TRAIN
■ Westbahnhof (Western station)
Mariahilferstrasse 132, XV
Connections with the subway (U3 and U6) and various tramway lines.
INFORMATION
Tel. 1717 (24 hours a day)
RESERVATIONS
Tel. 1700 (daily 7am–10pm)

CELEBRATIONS AND PUBLIC HOLIDAYS
■ January 1 and 6
■ Easter Monday
■ May 1
■ Ascension
■ Pentecost Monday
■ Corpus Christi
■ August 15
■ October 26, National Day
■ November 1
■ December 8
■ December 25 and 26

CHILDREN
The most exciting places for children are:
■ The Prater and its Ferris wheel
■ The Schönbrunn Zoo (the oldest in the world, opened in 1752)

◆ STAYING IN VIENNA FROM A TO Z

Accommodation – addresses – arrival and departure – celebrations and public holidays – childre
cost of living – emergencies – food and drink – getting around – internet – language loss or the
mail – markets – money – newspapers – nightlife – opening times – parking – public transport –
shopping – taxis – telephone – time difference – tipping – tourist transport – tours and excursio

■ The Spanish Riding School
■ The Exotic Butterflies Conservatory (live butterflies), at the Burggarten
■ The Donauturm (820 feet high), located in the Donaupark (the highest point in the city with the best panoramic view) *See Places to Visit ◆ 328 for opening times.*

COST OF LIVING
■ Coffee: 35 ATS
■ Pint of beer: from 40 ATS
■ Bottle of wine: from 140 ATS
■ Standard meal: from 80 ATS
■ Admission to a museum: from 30 to 90 ATS
■ Admission to a theater: from 150 to 700 ATS
■ Admission to the Prater: 30 ATS
■ A single room: from 600 ATS

EMERGENCIES
■ Ambulances Tel. 144
■ Car rescue service Tel. 120 or 123
■ Drugstores Tel. 1550
■ Fire department Tel. 122
■ Hospital Tel. 144
■ Police Tel. 133 or Stephansplatz (Cathedral Square), U1 subway station Tel. 313 47 2023 Police station in the basement open 24 hours a day
■ Emergency doctors Tel. 141

FASCHING
See Nightlife (Balls) ◆ 310

FOOD AND DRINK
→ WHERE TO GO
■ Beisl
Bistrots serving cheap, traditional cuisine.

■ Heurigen
Open-air taverns with a convivial atmosphere. Heuriger means 'the seasonal new wine'. You can sit under arbors or at long white-wood tables and sample the wine while listening to *Schrammelmusik* (traditional tunes played on the violin, guitar, clarinet or accordeon). *Heurigen* are located on the northern and western hills above the city, some of

them on the winegrowers' farms. The entrance is usually marked by a pole with a bouquet or pine branches attached to it, which indicates that wine is served. Although *Heurigen* are not actual restaurants, they often serve cold buffets.
■ Kaffeehaus
The Viennese café – a place to relax for some, an office or a salon for others – is a true institution. It is without any doubt the best place to soak up the atmosphere of the city. Today there are about 400 traditional cafés, excluding cafés-restaurants, bars espresso and other coffee houses. You can spend the afternoon chatting with friends or reading the papers

(supplied by the café). Regular customers even receive their mail or invite their friends there. Simple food is usually served at lunchtime, and of course delicious Viennese pastries with a wide variety of coffees.
■ Keller
Bars where people go to drink wine or beer. Food is alo served.
■ Würstelstand
Small stalls on the sidewalks serving a choice of sausages with French fries.

→ WHAT TO HAVE
■ Durcheinander-Knödel
Balls made of bread, lard and flour.
■ Fritattensuppe
Broth with pieces of ceps (a type of mushroom).
■ Gebackene Champignons
Mushrooms in breadcrumbs.
■ Gulasch
Beef stew with paprika, from Hungary.
■ Knödel
Balls made of potatos, meat, liver, etc., to go with soups or meat dishes.
■ Leberknödelsuppe
Soup with balls made of liver.
■ Palatschinken
Pancakes with fresh cream, chocolate, jam or hazelnuts.
■ Sachertorte
Famous chocolate cake.
■ Strudel
Rolls made of puff pastry and filled

with apples, raisi and cinnamon (*Apfelstrudel*), or with cherries, strawberries, hazelnuts,dark-re plums, cranberrie or soft white che (*Topfenstrudel*).
■ Tafelspitz
Viennese boiled beef, served with horseradish.
■ Wiener Schnitz
Veal escalope in breadcrumbs.
■ Wiener Backhe
Fried boneless chicken in breadcrumbs.

GETTING AROU
→ BY BICYCLE
Vienna has exten cycle tracks, whic are well marked over town and o the outskirts.
RECOMMENDED READING:
Exploring Vienna Bicycle, available the City Tourist Office (Wien-Tourismus, Albertinaplatz).
■ Bicycle rental
RADVERLEIH CITY (Near Hundertwasserha Kegelgasse 43, III Tel. 713 93 95 Open Apr.–Oct. 9am–9pm

→ BY CAR
The rules for driv are no different t those prevailing elsewhere in Eur (priority to vehic approaching fron the right). *Tramways and travelers disembarking fro them always have priority.*
■ Alcohol levels
0.5 mg/l permitte
■ Speed limits
HIGHWAYS
80 mph (130 km/
ROADS
62 mph (100 km/
TOWN OR BUILT-UP AREAS
31 mph (50 km/h
■ Traffic jams
In the morning fi 7.30am until

0am, and in the
ening around
m. Avoid driving
the 1st District.
nleaded gas/98
prox. 13.90 ATS
iesel
prox. 10.80 ATS
ar rental
vers must be
er 21 and have
d a national
ving license for
least one year.
international
ving license
not necessary.
r rental
npanies can
found at the
port, at stations
d in the city
nter.
TES
0 ATS per day,
'00 ATS for a
ekend
;20 ATS for a
ek

EDESTRIANS
nnese
destrians are
diously respectful
traffic regulations
d will wait
ciently for the
ht to change
fore crossing
e street.
e also Public
nsport ◆ 311.

TERNET
afé Stein
hringer Strasse
X
. 319 724 1
ww.cafe-
in.co.at
en 8am–1am

NGUAGE
reign visitors who
a speak German
l have no
ficulty in
derstanding the
itten language.
wever the spoken
guage requires
it of practice:
ng vowels,
ked consonants
d the great
mber of local
pressions are
ficult for
trained ears.
e Useful Words
d Phrases ◆ 313

LOSS OR THEFT
→ DOCUMENTS
In the event of
loss or theft of
your ID or passport,
contact the nearest
police station (Tel.
133) as soon as
possible. This will
enable you to have
new documents
issued at your
consulate.
See Addresses
◆ 307

→ LOST PROPERTY
■ At the airport
In the Arrival hall
Tel. 7007 21 97
Open 9am–5pm
■ Fuudbüro
Wasagasse 22, IX
Tel. 313 44-9211
or 313 44-9217
Open Mon.–Fri.
8am–noon

**→ LOSS OR THEFT OF
BANKERS' CARDS**
Tel. 24 hours a day:
■ Diner's Club
501 355
■ EuroCard
and MasterCard
717 01 45 00
■ Visa
711 11 770

MAIL
■ Main post office
(*Hauptpost*)
Fleischmarkt 19, I
Open 24 hours
a day
■ Post offices
(*Postamt*)
Open Mon.–Fri.
8am–6pm; 24 hours
a day at railway
stations
■ Stamps
7 ATS for a postcard
and a letter under
20g to the UK.
Vending machines
can be found
outside the main
post offices.

Stamps are
also sold at
newsagents'.

MARKETS
→ ART AND ANTIQUES
■ Kunst und
Antikmarkt
On the banks of
the Danube
every weekend
from May to
September.

→ CHRISTMAS
Every year during
Advent:
■ Rathausplatz, I
(in front of
City Hall)
■ Freyung, I
■ Heiligen-
kreuzerhof, I
■ Schönbrunn, XIII
(in front of the
castle)
■ Spittelberg, VII

→ FLEAMARKETS
Wienzeile, VI
(near Ketten-
brückengasse
subway station)
Open Sat. 7am–2pm

**→ FRUIT, VEGETABLES
AND OTHER PRODUCE**
■ Naschmarkt
Linke Wienzeile, VI
Open Mon.–Fri.
7am–6pm,
Sat. 7am–noon
The largest market
in Vienna.
■ Rochusmarkt
Landstrasser
Hauptstrasse, III
Open Mon.–Fri.
7am–6pm,
Sat. 7am–noon

MONEY
→ BANKS
Open Mon.–Wed.
and Fri. 8am–
12.30pm and 1.30–
3pm, Thur. 8am–
12.30pm and
1.30–5.30pm

→ CURRENCY
■ Austrian Schilling
(ATS)
Subdivided into
100 Groschen
■ Coins
10 and 50 groschen,
1, 5, 10 and 20 ATS
■ Notes
20, 50 100, 500,
1,000 and 5,000 ATS

→ EXCHANGE
■ Auto-tellers
Outside many banks
in the city center,
with 24-hour access.
■ Bureaux de
change
AT THE AIRPORT
Open 6.30am–11pm
AT THE CITY AIR
TERMINAL (HILTON
HOTEL)
Open Mon.–Fri.
8.30am–1.30pm
and 2–6pm, Sat.–
Sun. 8.30am–1.30pm
AT STEPHANSPLATZ
(opposite the
cathedral) Open
daily 8am–6pm
AT THE WESTBAHNHOF
Open 7am–10pm

→ PAYMENTS
■ Credit cards
Accepted in most
hotels, restaurants
and stores.

→ TRAVELER'S CHECKS
Must be changed
into ATS in banks.

NEWSPAPERS
→ LOCAL NEWSPAPERS
■ Falter
Main source of
information on the
city's cultural life
(weekly, 25 ATS).
■ Wien Magazin
Monthly magazine
for visitors,
published in four
languages (28 ATS).
■ Der Standard,
Die Presse, Kurier
Vienna's main daily
newspapers (10 to
15 ATS).
■ Kronen Zeitung
Popular daily.

**→ FOREIGN
NEWSPAPERS**
Sold at newsagents'
in the city center, at
stations and at the
airport.

◆ STAYING IN VIENNA FROM A TO Z

Accommodation – addresses – arrival and departure – celebrations and public holidays – children
cost of living – emergencies – food and drink – getting around – internet – language loss or thef
mail – markets – money – newspapers – nightlife – opening times – parking – public transport –
shopping – taxis – telephone – time difference – tipping – tourist transport – tours and excursion

NIGHTLIFE

→ **BALLS (FASCHING)**
The season opens
on New Year's Eve
with the Emperor's
Ball in the salons
of the Hofburg. The
Opera Ball, which
takes place on the
Thursday before
Shrove Tuesday,
and the Vienna
Philharmonic Ball,
on the first Thursday
after Epiphany in
the salons of the
Musikverein, are
also among the
most prestigious
events. Many
receptions are
organized by
different trade
associations,
or arranged by
theme, during the
period ending on
Shrove Tuesday.
The Viennese
put on disguises
and form lively
processions in the
streets, parading
around the Ring
in carriages.
By invitation only.

→ **BARS AND
DISCOTHEQUES**
Viennese nightlife is
concentrated mostly
in two districts:
the now traditional
"Bermuda Triangle",
situated around
Ruprechtskirche,
and the more recent
Gürtel, on the
circular road
girdling Vienna.
More and more
people go to this
newly renovated
red district and
under the arcades
of Line U6 of the
aerial subway,
designed by
Otto Wagner at the
beginning of the
20th century.
See ◆ 322

→ **CONCERTS/THEATERS**
Concerts, plays
and opera usually
start at 7.30pm.
■ **Information**
Information
regarding shows
and events taking

place in Vienna can
be found at the
following Internet
site:
http://info.wien.at
For more details,
consult:
*inquiries@info.wien.
at*
■ **Reservations
and tickets**
ÖSTERREICHISCHER
BUNDESTHEATER-
VERBAND/BUNDES-
THÉATERKASSEN
For opera
and operetta,
Akadémietheater
and Burgtheater
Goethestr. 1

Hanuschgasse 1, I
Information:
(Tel. 514 44-2960)
Credit card
reservations
(Tel. 513 15 13)
WIEN-TICKET-PAVILLON
Kärntner Strasse,
(next to the opera
house).
Open daily
10am–7pm.
Reduced tickets
for same-day
performances.
No supplement
payable and no
reservation
necessary. Tuesdays:
2 tickets for the
price of 1.
*Ask your hotel
receptionist about
the best way to
get tickets.*

Also useful:
*www.wienerphilam
oniker.at*
www.konzerthaus.at

→ **NEW YEAR'S
DAY CONCERT**
All the applications
received on the
first day of the
previous year
(for example,
apply on Tuesday,
January 2, 2001
for the concert
taking place on
January 1st, 2002)
are placed in a
lottery and drawn
by lots.

■ **Wiener
Philharmoniker**
Bösendorfer
Strasse 12, I

OPENING TIMES
■ **Banks**
Open Mon.–Wed.
and Fri. 8am–
12.30pm,1.30–3pm;
Thur. 8am–12.30pm,
1–5.30pm
■ **Stores**
Open Mon.–Fri.
9am–6pm,
Sat. 9am–1pm
(until 5pm on the
first Sat. of the
month)
*Stores located in
the main shopping
streets are open
until 5pm every Sat.*
■ **Grocery stores**
Open Mon.–Fri.

7.30am–7.30pm;
Sat. 7.30am–5pm
■ **Museums**
*See Places to Visit
◆ 328*
■ **Restaurants**
LUNCH
Between noon
and 2pm.
DINNER
From 6pm.
Restaurants will
not usually take
orders after 10pm
However, the bars
and restaurants
situated between
Schwedenplatz an
the Wollzeile stay
open until about
1am.

ORIENTATION
Vienna is divided
into 23 districts
(*Bezirke*), spiraling
outward from the
1st District (*Innere
Stadt*) to the histo
center girdled by
the Ring. When
writing an address
in Vienna, districts
are indicated by th
second and third
digits in the posta
code, for example
1st District (I)
= 1010
15th District (XV)
= 1150
20th District (XX)
= 1200

PARKING
Controlled betwee
7am and 7pm
(except Sun.) in
1st to 9th districts
and permitted for
a maximum perio
of 2 hours.

→ **PARKING COUPON**
Are compulsory
and can be
purchased from
tobacconists
(Tabak-Trafik).
They have to be
filled in and clear
displayed behind
your windshield.
■ 6 ATS for 30 mins
■ 12 ATS for 60 mi
■ 18 ATS for 90 mi

→ **PARKING PLACES**
Indicated by blue
lines painted on
the road

ARKING LOTS
ere are numerous
king lots in the
center, but these
generally quite
all and all too
en filled to
acity. However,
nna is a relatively
all city and has an
ellent public
nsport system,
t is perfectly
ssible to have an
oyable day out
hout needing a

BLIC
ANSPORT
nna has an
ellent and
eap public
nsport system.

NFORMATION
7909 105

USES
routes cover
th the center and
periphery,
ssing the tram
tes.
perating times
ween 5am
midnight.
ht bus ("N") on
and Sat. from
30–4am between
main Ring
ersections and
outer districts
ats).
nformation
rlsplatz,
phansplatz,
terstern and
ladelphiabrücke
way stations.

BAHN
HNELLBAHN)
ress train linking
city center to
periphery, and
icated by a white
in the shape of
ash of lightning.
perating times
ween 4am and
dnight.

UBWAY
BAHN)
subway symbol
white "U"
inst a blue
kground. Five
es: U1, U2, U3, U4
d U6.

■ Operating times
Between 4am and
midnight.

→ TRAMWAY
(STRASSENBAHN)
Vienna's fastest
means of transport,
with a network
running around
the Ring in both
directions and
branching off it.
The tram lines
bear numbers 1 to
71 and letters B to
O. Lines 1 and 2
and part of lines J
and D do the
whole circuit of
the Ring.

■ Operating times
Between 4am and
midnight.

→ TICKETS
One ticket gives
access to all
destinations and
means of transport
for an unbroken
journey.
■ Single ticket
22 ATS (9,50 ATS
for children
between 6 and 15)
■ Book of 4 tickets
76 ATS
**■ Cards and
passes**
Valid for journeys
on the subway,
buses and tramways
everywhere in the
city.

24-HOUR CARD
60 ATS
72-HOUR CARD
150 ATS
PERSONAL WEEKLY
CARD
(Wochenkarte)
Valid Mon.–Sun.
155 ATS
■ Children
Children under the
age of 6 travel free
all year round.
■ Young people
Free transport for
children under 15
on Sundays, public
and the Vienna
Academy school
holidays (for dates,
call: Tel. 790 91 05).

→ WIENKARTE
May be used in
the subway,
as well as on
tramways and buses
for 72 hours.
It also entitles the
holder to reductions
to 150 museums,
monuments,
theaters, concerts,
shops, restaurants,
cafés and Heurigen
and on the shuttle
linking the airport
to the city center.
This card can be
purchased from
the Tourist office,
in some hotels
or by telephoning
from abroad and
paying by credit
card

(Tel. + 43 1 798
44 00 28).
Cost: 210 ATS

→ SALES OUTLETS
Apart from the
ticket offices of
subway stations,
tickets and cards can
be purchase from:
■ Tabak-Trafic
Bus, subway
tickets and parking
coupons.
■ Vending machines
On buses and
tramways (have the
right change ready).
*Bus and tramway
drivers do not sell
tickets.*

SHOPPING
Typical items
to buy while you
are in Vienna:
■ Lodens
■ Augarten
porcelain
■ Petit-point
embroidery
■ Art-nouveau
fabrics
■ Painted wooden
toys
■ Antiques (old
books, paintings,
coins, medals)
■ Apricot, apple,
pear or plum
brandies (*Schnäpse*)
■ Mozart Kugeln:
chocolates filled
with marzipan and
nougat

→ MAIN SHOPPING
STREETS
**■ Kärntnerstrasse-
Graben-Kohlmarkt**
Trendy and
expensive
pedestrian zone.
■ Mariahilferstrasse
The longest and
most popular
shopping street in
Vienna. You will
find all the main
department stores
there, as well as
small boutiques.

→ SALES TAXES
VAT is 20%.

TAXIS
→ RANKS
There are taxi
ranks near stations,
outside major

◆ STAYING IN VIENNA FROM A TO Z

Accommodation – addresses – arrival and departure – celebrations and public holidays – childre
cost of living – emergencies – food and drink – getting around – internet – language loss or the
mail – markets – money – newspapers – nightlife – opening times – parking – public transport –
shopping – taxis – telephone – time difference – tipping – tourist transport – tours and excursior

hotels, at the
Am Hof, Hofburg,
Stephansplatz and
the Opera
■ **Radio-Taxis:**
Tel. 31 300, 40 100,
60 160 or 81 400

→ TARIFFS
Basic: 30 ATS
Between 8pm and
6am, on Sundays
and public hols:
40 ATS

TELEPHONE
**→ PUBLIC
TELEPHONES**
These are quite
scarce in Vienna.
They operate
with a telephone
card (50 or 100 ATS),
sold at tobacconists'
(Tabak-Trafic).

**→ TO CALL THE
UK AND THE US
FROM VIENNA**
■ **UK**
Dial 00 44 followed
by the number you
wish to call,
omitting the
inital 0.
■ **US**
Dial 00 1 followed
by the number you
wish to call.
■ **Reduced rates**
Cheaper before
8am and after
6pm and on
public hols.
*Hotels charge much
higher rates if you
make calls from
your room.*
■ **Mobiles**
*Additional charges
may be incurred
when calls are made
from mobile
phones, depending
on the agreement
between the
operators.*

**→ TO CALL WITHIN
VIENNA**
Dial the number
you wish to call,
omitting the
prefix 1.

**→ TO CALL FROM
VIENNA TO ANOTHER
REGION IN AUSTRIA**
Dial the prefix
(0 + one number),
followed by the
number you wish
to call.

TIME DIFFERENCE
Austria is on
Central European
Time, which is one
hour ahead of
Greenwich Mean
Time (GMT).
When it is noon in
Vienna it is 11am in
London and 6am in
New York.

TIPPING
**→ CAFÉS AND
RESTAURANTS**
A 10–15% tip is
usually included
in the bill, but it is
customary to leave
an additional tip
(around 10% of
the bill).

→ SHOWS
Around 10% of the
price of the ticket.

→ TAXIS
Round up the fare
by 5 to 10 ATS.

TOURIST
TRANSPORT
→ BY 1920S TRAMWAY
Two-hour circuit
around the city's
main monuments as
far as Schönbrunn in
a 1929 tramway.
■ **Departure**
From Karlsplatz
(in front of Otto
Wagner's Pavilion)

■ **Operating dates
and times**
May 4–Oct. 6
Sat. 11.30am and
1.30pm, Sun.
and public hols.
9.30am, 11.30am
and 1.30pm.
■ **Cost**
150 ATS
(50 ATS for children).
Tickets for sale at
the Public Transport
Information Office,
Karlsplatz
Tel. 7909-44026

**→ HORSE-DRAWN
CARRIAGES**
The hackney
carriage is a
charming way for a
small group of
between 4 and 6
people to explore
Vienna during
the spring and
summer.
■ **Carriage ranks**
Are located at
Stephansplatz,
Am Graben, Am Hof
and at the Hofburg.
■ **Fees**
400 (for 20 mins)
to 800 ats (for 40
mins) per carriage.

TOURS
AND EXCURSIONS
**→ BUS TOURS WITH
RUNNING
COMMENTARY**
■ **Vienna
Sightseeing Tours**
Stelzhammergasse
4/11, III
Tel. 712 46 83-0
Tour of the city
(3½ hrs), including a
visit to Schönbrunn

(390 ATS, children
160 ATS).
■ **Cityrama
Sightseeing**
Börsegasse 1, I
Tel. 534 130
Tour of the city
(3 hrs, 390 ATS,
children 160 ATS)
■ **Alternative
Stadtrundfahrten
City Tours**
Kolingasse 6, IX
Tel. 317 33 84
"Dreams and
Reality" tour (3 h
focuses on the
1870–1930 period
(Jugendstil and
Red Vienna).
Tue. and Thur. 1p
Sat. 10am by
appointment
(280 ATS).

**→ CRUISES ON
THE DANUBE**
■ **DDSG**
DDSG Blue Danub
Friedrichstrasse 7,
Tel. 588 800
Cruises and
excursions on the
river in and aroun
Vienna. (Some wi
dinner and
dancing).
Departure
from the
Schwedenplatz
landing stage.

→ EXCURSIONS
■ **Niederösterreic
information**
Walfischgasse 6, I
Tel. 513 80 22
Open Mon.–Fri.
9am–6pm
Information
on Vienna's
surrounding
area (Lower
Austria).
■ **Österreich
Urlaubsinformati**
Margaretenstrass
1, IV
Tel. 587 200-0
Open Mon.–Fri.
10am–5pm
(Thur. 6pm)
Information on al
Austria.

CITY

irk: district
isse: street
se: small street
ang: beginning
le: end
: courtyard
g: ring, circular
d around the city
ter
tel: belt or
ular road
ten: garden
haus: town hall
us: house
tz: square
sgänger:
estrians
sgängerzone:
estrian area
iis, Palast: palace
seum: museum
the: church
ster: monastery
Bahn: subway
assenbahn:
mway
: train
inhof: station
leitung: deviation
sicht!: warning!
rzparkzone:
rt stay parking
e (such as for
pping someone

el: island
: embankment
er: bank
cke: bridge
: lake
d: forest
tobahn: highway

BUSINESSES/
TRADES

en: open
chlossen: closed
feehaus: café
kerei: baker's
nditorei: patisserie
uriger: open-air café
thaus: inn
sl: restaurant
ak-
fik: tobacconist's
velier: jeweler
ik: bank
chselstube: bureau
change
kt: market
ifhäus:
artment store
kstelle: gas station
nsprecher:
phone
efmarken: stamps
nkenhaus:
pital
otheke:
gstore

GOING OUT

Right: rechts
Left: links
Guide: Fremdenführer
Monument:
Sehenswürdigkeit
Visit: Besichtigung
Tickets: Karten
Concert: Konzert
Open-air concerts:
Gartenkonzert
Religious music:
Kirchenmusik
Chamber music:
Kammermusik
Movie theater: Kino
Theater: Theater
Play: Theaterstück
Go to the
theater: das Theater
besuchen

FOOD

Eat: essen
Drink: trinken
Cold: kalt
Hot: heiss
Salt: Salz
Sugar: Zucker
Breakfast: Frühstück
Lunch: Mittagessen
Tea time: Jause
Dinner: Abendessen
Pork: Schweinefleisch
Beef: Rindfleisch
Stewed beef: Tafelspitz
Veal: Kalbfleisch
Fish: Fisch
Sausage: Wurst
Potatoes: Kartoffeln
Rice: Reis
Bread: Brot
Small bread: Semmel
Cake: Kuchen
Strudel: Strudel
New wine:
Heuriger
White wine: Weisswein
Red wine: Rotwein
Beer: Bier
Fruit juice: Fruchtsaft
Mineral water:
Mineralwasser
Coffee: Kaffee
Waiter: Herr Ober
Menu: Speisekarte
The bill, please:
Zahlen, bitte!

CAFÉS

Brauner: dark coffee
with a little milk
Doppelschlag: more
whipped cream than
coffee
Einspänner: traditional
Viennese coffee,
served in a glass with
whipped cream
(Schlagobers, or
Schlag)

Eiskaffee: vanilla ice
cream with black
coffee and whipped
cream topping, served
with wafers.
Fiaker: with rum
Franziskaner: coffee
with milk, cream and
chocolate chips
Grosser Schwarzer:
large black coffee
Kapuziner: Viennese
cappucino
Kleiner Schwarzer:
small black coffee
Mazagran: cold coffee
with ice cubes and a
dash of rum, served
with a straw
Melange mit Schlag:
large cup of coffee
with milk and whipped
cream
Schale Gold: light
coffee
Teeschale licht: a large
cup of tea with a lot of
milk
Türkischer: Turkish
coffee
Verkehrt: very milky
coffee

MONEY

Credit card:
Kreditkarte
Traveler's checks:
Reisescheck
Car rental:
Autovermietung
Buy: kaufen
Hire/Rent: mieten
Cheap: billig
Expensive: teuer

ACCOMMODATION

Guesthouse, small
hotel: eine Pension
Hotel: ein Hotel
Single bedroom:
Einzelzimmer
Twin bedroom:
Doppelzimmer
What's the price per
night?:
Was kostet
eine Übernachtung?
Youth hostels:
Jugendherberge

GREETINGS

Mrs: Frau
Miss: Fräulein
Mr: Herr
Hello: Grüss
Gott!: (typical Austrian
expression)
Good day: Guten Tag!
(in the morning) or
Good morning:
Guten Morgen!

Good evening:
Guten Abend!
Goodbye: Auf
Wiedersehen!
Hi!: Servus!
(among friends in
Vienna)
Goodbye!: Baba!
(other familiar
Viennese expression)
Thanks: Danke schön
Please: Bitte!
I beg your pardon:
Verzeihung!
I don't understand:
Ich verstehe nicht
Do you speak
English?: Sprechen
Sie Englisch?
Yes: ja
No: nein
I would like…:
Ich möchte…

DAYS

Monday: Montag
Tuesday: Dienstag
Wednesday: Mittwoch
Thursday: Donnerstag
Friday: Freitag
Saturday: Samstag
Sunday: Sonntag
Week: Woche
Weekend:
Wochenende
Public holiday:
Feiertag, Festtag

MONTHS

January: Januar
February: Februar
March: März
April: April
May: Mai
June: Juni
July: Juli
August: August
September:
September
October: Oktober
November: November
December:
Dezember

NUMBERS

1: eins
2: zwei
3: drei
4: vier
5: fünf
6: sechs
7: sieben
8: acht
9: neun
10: zehn
20: zwanzig
21: einundzwanzig
30: dreissig
50: fünfzig
100: hundert
1,000: tausend

◆ HOTELS

Addresses are listed by district and in alphabetical order.
◆ refers to the maps at the end of this guide.
A list of symbols can be found on page 305.

A list of symbols can be found on page 305.

INSIDE THE RING
1ST DISTRICT

Ambassador
◆ **A** C2
Kärntner Strasse
22
Tel. 514 66
Fax 513 29 99
reservations@
ambassador.at
105 rooms
21 suites
*Situated halfway
between the
Opera and
St Stephen's
Cathedral, this
hotel has been
offering top-
quality service for
over a century.
Refined, friendly
setting and spacious
rooms.*
▦▤▱P▨▭▥▥

Ana Grand Hotel
◆ **A** D2-D3
Kärntner Ring 9
Tel. 515 80 0
Fax 515 13 13
reservation@
anagrand.com
www.anagrand.com
205 rooms
30 suites
*Opened in 1994, this
is one of the most
luxurious hotels in
Vienna. Quiet
rooms. Direct
access to the
Ringstrassen-
galerien commercial
center.*
▦▱▭▤▥▥

**Appartment-
Pension
Riemergasse**
◆ **A** C3
Riemergasse 8
Tel. 512 722 00
Fax 513 77 78
20 apartments
*Apartments for rent
in a Jugendstil
building (from a 80-
square-foot studio
to a 295-square-foot
apartment).
All are quiet and
functional, with
their own
kitchenette.
The establishment
offers the same
service as those
provided
by hotels.*
▱▱▤▥▥

✪ Austria
◆ **A** B3
Fleischmarkt 20
Tel. 513 23
Fax 515 23 506
hotelaus@eunet.at
www.ping.at/
members/hotelaus
42 rooms
4 apartments
*In a side street near
the Donaukanal,
this is a haven of
peace and quiet.
Surroundings are
typically late
19th–early 20th
century Viennese.
Decent size
bedrooms, hearty
buffet breakfast.
Recommended.*
▱▤▭▥▥

AMBASSADOR

ANA GRAND HOTEL

Capricorno
◆ **A** B3-B4
Schwedenplatz
3–4
Tel. 533 310 40
Fax 533 767 14
capricorno@schick-
hotels.com
www.schick-
hotels.com
*Standard, rather
dull, 1950
architecture, but
the rooms are
large and pleasant.
One of them
was used by
Carol Reed to
shoot one of the
scenes from
The Third Man.*
▱▱▭▤▥▥

Domizil
◆ **A** C3
Schulerstrasse 14
Tel. 513 31 99 0
Fax 512 34 84
domizil@gmx.net
40 rooms
*Tranquil family
guesthouse with
an ideal location
near Stephansplatz.*
▱▤▭▥▥

Graben Hotel
◆ **A** C2
Dorotheergasse 3
Tel. 512 153 10
Fax 512 153 120
graben@kremsleh
ner.hotels.or.at
www.kremslehner.
hotels.or.at/graben
*At the turn of the
20th century this
hotel was the
meeting place of
such literary figures
as Peter Altenberg,
Franz Kafka and
Max Brod. The
Jugendstil style of
furnishings in most
of the rooms is a
reminder of that
period.*
▱▤▭▥▥

Hotel Amadeus
◆ **A** B2-B3
Wildpretmarkt 5
Tel. 533 87 38
Fax 533 87 38 38
30 rooms
*The Amadeus still
boasts its original*

Biedermeier
furniture. Cliente
of artists, student
and business peop
▱▤▭▥▥

**Hotel Am
Schubertring**
◆ **A** D3
Schubertring 11
Tel. 717 02 0
Fax 713 99 66
aschu@atnet.at
39 rooms
3 suites
*Small, delightful
modern hotel
opened in 1984 an
located in a build
dating from the e
of the 19th centu
between the
Schwarzenbergpla
and the Stadtpark
Quiet, comfortabl
rooms with pretty
Biedermeier or
Jugendstil furnitu*
▱▤▭▥

**Hotel Am
Stephansplatz**
◆ **A** C2-C3
Stephansplatz 9
Tel. 534 05 0
Fax 534 05 711
hotel@stephanspl.
co.at
*Centrally located
hotel offering
parking facilities,
invaluable in this
area. Pleasant roo
with an exception
view of St Stephe
Cathedral.*
▱P▤▭▥

✪ Hotel Bristol
◆ **A** D2
Kärntner Ring 1
Tel. 515 16 0
Fax 515 16 550
131 rooms
11 suites
Hotel-Bristol@
sheraton.com
www.luxurycollecti
com/Bristol
*One of Vienna's
finest hotels.
Founded in 1892
and recently
extended and
renovated, it
combines all the
modern comforts
with an old-
fashioned décor,
with works of art
and fine period*

ELS
< 1,000 ATS
1,000–2,000 ATS
2,000–3,000 ATS
> 3,000 ATS

✪ The editor's choice

niture. The rooms
the front of the
ilding look out
to the Opera,
ile those at the
ck look out on
hlerstrasse.
e entire floor is
erved for
siness with
nference rooms
d offices.
🛆 🗆 🖾 🖻

tel Europa
A C2
rntner Strasse 18
515 94 0
513 81 38
ropa.wien@
stria-trend.at
vw.austria-
nd.at
the comforts you
uld expect from a
ently renovated
tel. Functional
d modern.
🗆 🖾 🖻 Ⅲ

tel Royal
A C2-C3
gerstrasse 3
515 68 0
513 96 98
al@kremslehner.
tels.or.at
vw.kremslehner.
tels.or.at/royal
rooms
partments
50s hotel with a
rrace looking out
er Vienna and the
autiful tiled roof
St Stephen's
thedral. Its
staurant, Firenze
oteca, has the
est cellars in
stria, with the
st wines from
ly.
🗆 🖾 🖻

tel Sacher
A D2
lharmoniker
asse 4
514 56 0
514 568 10
tel@sacher.com
vw.sacher.com
3 rooms, 27 suites
e best-known
d most luxurious
tel in Vienna. It
that atmosphere
t is so unique
the city.
🗆 🖾 🖻 Ⅲ

Hotel Wandl
◆ A C2
Petersplatz 9
Tel. 534 55 0
Fax 534 55 77
reservation@hotel-
wandl.com
www.nethotels.com/
wandl
138 rooms
*Family hotel tucked
away at the back of
Peterskirche, a few
steps away from the
Graben, Michaeler
Platz and the
majestic entrance
of the Hofburg.*
🛆 🗆 🖾 🖻

✪ Imperial
◆ A D2-D3
Kärntner Ring 16
Tel. 501 10 333/423
Fax 501 10 410
Hotel-Imperial@
sheraton.com
www.luxurycollection.
com/Imperial
*Located in a former
prince's palace, the
Imperial first
opened in 1873.
A butler welcomes
each visitor and
remains at their
disposal 24 hours a
day throughout
their stay. The
furniture of the
huge rooms is as
sumptuous as the
architectural setting.
Charlie Chaplin
considered the
rooms at the
Imperial the most
beautiful he had
ever seen.*
🖩 🅿 🗆 🖾 🖻 Ⅲ

✪ Kärntnerhof
◆ A B3
Grashofgasse 4
Tel. 512 19 23
Fax 513 222 833
kaerntnerhof@
netway.at
*Very old
establishment
hidden away in a
small, quiet street
near the cathedral.
Excellent welcome.
Book in advance.*
🗆 🖾 🖻

Kaiserin Elisabeth
◆ A C2-C3
Weihburggasse 3
Tel. 515 26 0

Fax 515 267
kaiserin@ins.at
*Typical Viennese
atmosphere, warm
welcome and
impeccable service
in this hotel named
after the popular
empress of Austria.*
🛆 🗆 🖾 🖻

König von Ungarn
◆ A C3
Schulerstrasse 10
Tel. 515 84 0
Fax 515 84 8
www.tiscover.com/
koenig.ungarn
33 rooms
*Very close to the
cathedral and to
the house where
Mozart composed
his Marriage of
Figaro. The quiet,
comfortable rooms
have all been
recently renovated.
Excellent restaurant
on the first floor, as
well as a bar on the
hotel patio.*
🛆 🗆 🖾 🖻

Mailberger Hof
◆ A D2-D3
Annagasse 7
Tel. 512 06 41
Fax 512 06 41 10
40 rooms
6 apartments
*Tranquil 1970s hotel
situated in a listed
Baroque building.
Good location
in a small, quiet
street near Kärntner
Strasse, in the heart
of the pedestrian
zone.*
🛆 🅿 🗆 🖻

Marc Aurel
◆ A B3
Marc-Aurel-Strasse 8
Tel. 533 36 40
Fax 533 00 78
18 rooms
*Small, modern hotel
near a very lively
(day and night!)
district known as
the "Bermuda
Triangle".*
🗆 🗆 🅿 🖾 🖻 🛆

Pension am
Operneck
◆ A D2
Kärntner Str 47
Tel. 512 93 10

Fax 512 93 10 20
7 rooms
*Opposite the
Opera.*
🗆 🗆 🖾 🖻 🛆

Pension Aviano
◆ A D2
Marco-D'Aviano-
Gasse 1
Tel. 512 83 30
Fax 512 83 306
aviano@pertschy.
com
www.pertschy.com
17 rooms
*This guesthouse
occupies the top
floor of a building
dating from the end
of the 19th century.
Some rooms are
equipped with a
mini kitchen. Very
reasonable prices.
Book in advance*
🗆 🗆 🖾 🖻

Pension City
◆ A C2-C3
Bauermarkt 10
Tel. 533 95 21
Fax 535 52 16
19 rooms
*Ideal location in a
quiet street near the
cathedral. Warm
welcome and very
reasonable prices.
The rooms, which
have been recently
renovated, happily
combine 19th-
century and modern
furniture. The bust
and commemorative
plaque at the
entrance pay
homage to the
Austrian playwright
and poet Franz
Grillparzer, who was
born in the same
building in 1791.*
🗆 🗆 🖾 🖻

Pension Christina
◆ A B3
Hafnersteig 7
Tel. 533 29 61
Fax 533 29 61 11
christina@pertschy.
com
www.pertschy.com
33 rooms
*Close to the
Ruprechtskirche, in
a quiet street in the
oldest part of
Vienna.*
🗆 🗆 🖾 🖻

◆ HOTELS

Addresses are listed by district and in alphabetical order.
◆ refers to the maps at the end of this guide.
A list of symbols can be found on page 305.

Pension Nossek
◆ **A** C2
Graben 17
Tel. 533 704 10
Fax 535 36 46
26 rooms
Friendly welcome, pleasant setting and reasonable prices at this centrally-located hotel.
🔲🔲🔲🔲

Pension Pertschy
Im Palais Cavriani
◆ **A** C2
Habsburgergasse 5
Tel. 534 49 0
Fax 534 49 49
www.pertschy.com
47 rooms
Pleasant welcome and spacious rooms. The ocher-colored courtyard gives a Mediterranean touch to this quiet Viennese hotel. As with the three other Pertschy pensions, a very good address for a moderately priced hotel in central Vienna. Book in advance.
🔲🔲🔲🔲🔲

Post
◆ **A** B3
Fleischmarkt 24
Tel. 515 83 0
Fax 515 83 808
107 rooms
Very central hotel in a small street in the old part of Vienna. Spacious, high ceilinged rooms. This hotel has a lot of charm and its price certainly makes it even more agreeable.
🔲🔲🔲🔲🔲🔲

Radisson SAS
Palais Hotel
◆ **A** D3
Parkring 16
Tel. 515 17 0
Fax 512 22 16
246 rooms
52 suites
sales@viezh.rdsas.com
Luxury hotel situated in two elegant buildings (Henckel von Donnersmarck and Leitenberg

palaces), dating from the end of the 19th century. It has all the comforts you can expect from a 5-star hotel, including a sauna, solarium, fitness rooms, etc. View over the Statdpark, beyond the Ring. Good fish restaurant, Le Siècle.
🔲🔲🔲🔲🔲

Römischer
Kaiser
◆ **A** D2-D3
Annagasse 16
Tel. 512 775 1
Fax 512 775 113
24 rooms
Well-kept hotel with elegant, comfortable rooms. Run by the same family since 1904.
🔲🔲🔲🔲🔲

HOTEL IM PALAIS SCHWARZENBERG

ALTSTADT

Zur Wiener
Staatsoper
◆ **A** D2-D3
Krugerstrasse 11
Tel. 513 127 4
Fax 513 127 415
office@zurwiener
staatsoper.at
www.zurwiener
staatsoper.at
This family hotel is just a few steps away from the Opera house. Delightful rooms, all individually decorated.
🔲🔲🔲🔲

Academia
◆ **D** C2-C3
Pfeilgasse 3a, VIII
Tel. 401 76
Fax 401 76 20
acahot@academia-
hotels.co.at
300 rooms
This students' hall of residence becomes a cheap, basic hotel during the months of July and August when its usual residents are away.
🔲🔲🔲🔲🔲🔲

Admiral
◆ **D** D4
Karl-Schweighofer-
Gasse 7, VII
Tel. 521 41 0
Fax 521 41 76
64 rooms
Modest hotel

located near Mariahilferstrasse, one of the main shopping avenues in Vienna.
🔲🔲🔲🔲🔲🔲

Altstadt
◆ **D** D3
Kirchengasse 41, VII
Tel. 526 33 99
Fax 523 49 01
alt.vie@magnet.at
25 rooms
6 suites
The corridors and reception rooms of this 18th-century

residence boast many works of ar All the rooms are spacious and comfortable, with different décor. Y can choose betwe the "noble" floor with its pastel co and stuccoed ceilings, and a ro with a sloping ceiling under the roof.
🔲🔲🔲🔲

Biedermeier
Im Sünnhof
◆ **A** C4
Landstrasser
Hauptstrasse 28,
Tel. 716 71 0
Fax 716 71 503
hotel.vienna@dor
rogner.com
203 rooms
9 suites
Intimate, comfortable and unpretentious ho in the pure Biedermeier tradition. Ideally located near the terminal of the airport shuttle and good public transport connections.
🔲🔲🔲🔲🔲

Carlton Opera
◆ **B** B1
Schikanedergasse
IV
Tel. 587 53 02
Fax 581 25 11
Situated in a small, quiet stree the Carlton is especially popula with artists.
🔲🔲🔲🔲🔲🔲🔲

Hotel im Palais
Schwarzenberg
◆ **B** B3
Schwarzenberg-
platz 9, III
Tel. 798 45 15
Fax 798 47 14
palais@schwarzer
rg.via.at
www.relaischatea
frlschwarzenberg
44 rooms
8 suites
Former residence of an aristocratic family converted into a hotel in 19

ELS
< 1,000 ATS
1,000–2,000 ATS
2,000–3,000 ATS
> 3,000 ATS

❂ The editor's choice

re is a suite of
ons with a décor
trompe-l'œil
scoes, splendid
ms with period
niture, and a
taurant with a
race looking over
agnificent park
ich almost joins
h the Belvedere
k. One of the
st elegant
ablishments
Vienna.
🔲🔲🔲Ⅲ❂

tel-Pension
neider
◆ A1
reidemarkt
/I
, 588 38 0
: 588 38 212
rooms
s charming,
mate hotel is a
orite with opera
gers. Friendly
lcome and ideal
ation, with a
w over the
ession Pavilion
the Naschmarkt.
u can choose
tween a room
an apartment
th with a fully
uipped kitchen),
her of which
be rented on a
nthly basis.
🔲🔲🔲

tel Savoy
◆ A3
dengasse 12, VII
, 523 46 46
: 523 46 40
rooms
re you will find
ne of the
ervescence of the
ger hotels. The
voy has a discreet,
nost meditative,
mosphere. The
ff at reception
l give you all the
ormation and
ggestions you
ed to make the
st of your stay
Vienna.
🔲🔲🔲

ton Vienna
◆ C4
Stadtpark, III
. 717 00 0
: 713 06 91

business.center
@vienna-hilton.
telecom.at
www.telecom.at/
viennahilton
600 rooms
50 suites
Hotel situated near
the terminal of the
shuttle bus
operating between
Vienna's airport and
the city center. One
entire floor is
reserved for
business. All the
rooms facing north
have a fine view
over the Stadtpark
and the historic
center.
🔲🔲🔲🔲Ⅲ

HILTON VIENNA

K+K HOTEL MARIA THERESIA

K+K Hotel
Maria Theresia
◆ D D4
Kirchberggasse
6–8, VII
Tel. 521 23
Fax 521 23 70
www.kkhotels.com
123 rooms
Restful atmosphere
in the heart of the
charming
Spittelberg
neighborhood,
an area that
used to be popular
with artists.
All the rooms
have modern
conveniences and
air conditioning,
some have terraces.
🔲🔲🔲🔲Ⅲ

Mozart
Theobaldgasse 15
Tel. and fax
587 85 05
14 rooms
Unpretentious
hotel near the lively
Mariahilferstrasse.
🔲🔲

Pension Hargita
◆ C B2-B3
Andreasgasse 1
Tel. 526 19 28
Fax 526 04 92
10 rooms
Friendly guesthouse
whose interior
decoration is
reminiscent of
Hungary, the
owner's native
country. Only
10 minutes
away from the
Westbahnhof
(Western station),
at the far end
of Mariahilfer
Strasse, where
you will find
all the most famous
fashion labels.
🔲🔲

Pension Kraml
◆ C B2-B3
Bräuergasse, VI
Tel. 587 85 88
Fax 586 75 73
14 rooms
Small, well-
kept guesthouse
situated in the
vicinity of the

Westbahnhof
(Western station),
just a few minutes
away from the
stores on
Mariahilfer Strasse
and a small flea
market open every
Saturday morning.
Excellent value for
money.
🔲🔲

Pension Residenz
◆ D B4
Ebendorferstrasse
10, I
Tel. 406 47 86 0
Fax 406 47 86 50
vienna@pension-
residenz.co.at
15 rooms
Small family
hotel in a quiet
neighborhood
behind the
University, and
close to the
center.
🔲🔲🔲🔲

Rathaus
Lange Gasse
13, VIII
Tel. 406 01 23
Fax 408 42 72
43 rooms
Located in the
former middle-class
district which has
managed to retain
its special charm.
🔲🔲🔲🔲🔲

Roter Hahn
Tourotel
Landstrasser
Hauptstrasse 40, I
Tel. 713 25 68 0
Fax 713 25 68 190
46 rooms
Traditional
establishment
founded 300
years ago and
located in a busy
high street.
🔲🔲🔲🔲🔲

Vera
◆ D A3
Alser Strasse 18, IX
Tel. 402 77 11
Fax 402 77 11 26
26 rooms
Unpretentious
family hotel, ideal
for small budgets.
Can be noisy
though.
🔲🔲🔲🔲🔲

◆ RESTAURANTS

Addresses are listed by district and in alphabetical order.
◆ refers to the maps at the end of this guide.
A list of symbols can be found on page 305.

RESTAURANTS
■ < 200 ATS
■ 200–300 ATS
■ 300–400 ATS
⊞ > 400 ATS

INSIDE THE RING
1ST DISTRICT

Barbaro's
◆ A C2-C3
Kärntner Strasse 19
(in the Steffl
commercial
center)
Tel. 513 171 225
Open noon–4pm
and 6pm–1am
Italian and multi-
ethnic cuisine
*A panoramic
elevator operates up
and down the front
of the building.
The view from
this restaurant
is magnificent,
encompassing St
Stephen's Cathedral
and the rooftops of
Vienna. Sober and
elegant atmosphere,
and foreign-inspired
(mostly Asian and
Italian) cuisine.*
⊞ ■ � ※

Bei Max
◆ A B1
Landhausgasse 2/
Herrengasse
Tel. 533 73 59
Open Mon.–Fri.
11am–10pm
Cuisine from
Carinthia
*The perfect place to
try Käsnudeln or
Kletzennudeln,
typical pastry balls
filled with cheese or
fruit. Max also
serves traditional
Austrian dishes.
Draft beer from
Carinthia, good
wines and strong
brandies (Schnäpse).*
■

۞ Do & Co
◆ A C2
Stephansplatz 12
Tel. 353 969
Open noon–3pm
and 6pm–midnight
*Do & Co occupies
the top floor of the
crystal palace
designed by Hans
Hollein opposite
the cathedral.
The international
menu includes
American,
Mediterranean and
Japanese dishes.*
⊞ ■ � ᔕ ↟

Drei Husaren
◆ A C2-C3
Weihburggasse 4
Tel. 512 10 92
Open noon–3pm
and 6pm–1am
Viennese gourmet
cuisine
*The oldest of
all luxurious
restaurants in the
Austrian capital.
Aristocratic charm,
and traditional
cuisine that includes
a trolley of
legendary hors-
d'œuvres, as well as
unforgettable fish
dishes and desserts.*
⊞ ■ � ♫

È Tricaffè
◆ A B2
Am Hof 2/
Bognergasse 4
Tel. 533 84 90
Open Mon.–Sat.
8am–midnight
Snack bar
11.30am–2.30pm
and 6–11pm
Italian cuisine
*Friendly, relaxed
atmosphere and a
décor in the best
of Italian taste.
Good sandwiches,
excellent hors-
d'œuvres, meat
and fish dishes
full of flavor.*
■ ■ &

Fadinger
◆ A B2
Wipplingerstrasse 29
Tel. 533 434 1
Open Mon.–Fri.
11am–3pm
and 5.30–10pm
Viennese cuisine
*Small, unpretentious
restaurant serving
food prepared by
one of the most
inventive chefs in
Vienna, Josef
Fadinger.*
■

۞ Hansen
◆ A A2
Wipplingerstrasse
34
Tel. 532 05 42
Open Mon.–Fri.
9am–8pm,
Sat. 9am–5pm
Creative cuisine
*Light, unusual and
inventive cuisine
served in a
luxuriantly green
décor of plants.
Traditional Viennese
dishes are mixed
with Mediterranean
and Asian flavors
which suit the most
figure-conscious of
gourmets: every
item on the menu
comes in half
portions. Note: the
restaurant closes at
the same time as the
Garden Center in
which it is located.
You can also buy
groceries like oil,
vinegar, preserves
and pasta.*
■ ■ ※

۞ Korso
◆ A D2
Mahlerstrasse 2
Tel. 515 165 46
Open Mon.–Fri
noon–2pm
and 7–11pm
Traditional Viennese
cuisine
*Reinhard Gerer's
restaurant is a
favorite with both
local and foreign
gourmets. This chef,
one of the most
creative in Austria,
combines the purest
Viennese culinary
tradition (Tafelspitz
– stew) with
international classics
in a splendid late-
19th-century décor.
Fine cellar and
impeccable service.*
⊞ ■ ⓜ

Lustig Essen
◆ A B2-B3
Salvatorgasse 6/
Marc-Aurel-Strasse
Tel. 533 30 37
Open 11.30am–
midnight
Creative cuisine
*Ideal for those
who need a quick
snack but can't make
up their minds where
to go. Lustig Essen
serves small helpings
which enable one to
sample a whole array
of hors-d'œuvre,
main dishes and
desserts.*
■ ■

Neu Wien
◆ A C3
Bäckerstrasse 5
Tel. 513 06 66
Open 6pm–1am
Mediterranean
cuisine
*Fine vaulted dinin
room decorated
with modern
paintings
by Christian Ludw
Attersee – a regul
client here. Popul
with the local
intelligentsia, this
restaurant offers
light Mediterrane
cuisine. Good cho
of wines. The bar
next door is popu
with Viennese nig
owls.*
■ ■

Oswald & Kalb
◆ A C3
Bäckerstrasse 14
Tel. 512 137 1
Open 6pm–2am
Cuisine from Vien
and Styria
*Typical Beisl. Artis
and intellectuals
enjoy coming her
for a salad (with
dressing of pump
oil produced in
Styria) or for a le
of lamb served w
a glass of fine ros
wine.*
■ ■

Palmenhaus
◆ A D2
Im Burggarten
Tel. 533 10 33
Fax 533 10 33 10
Open 10am–2am
Mediterranean
cuisine
*The perfect place
for breakfast in a
leafy garden on a
fine summer
morning, or for a
lunch break befo
or after visiting th
city's museums. Th
Palmenhaus has j
been renovated a
offers light and
inventive dishes i
refined décor.*
■ ■ ┿ ※

۞ Plachutta
◆ A C4
Wollzeile 38
Tel. 512 15 77

318

512 15 77 20
en 11.30am–
Opm and 6–10pm
ditional Viennese
sine
modern setting
ed with period
niture, the
chutta family
ves traditional
nnese dishes
ed on beef.
ips or Tafelspitz
w) are given
ority, but fish is
on the menu.
various
parations
delicate
d creative,
the desserts
eringues with
ntilly cream,
barb strudel,
nolina cake
h raspberry
ce) are the
cialties of the
se. The winelist
Judes fine
nnese whites.
◻↑

Salzamt
B3
orechtsplatz 1
533 53 32
en 5pm–1am,
5pm–2am
nnese and
diterranean
sine
uated in the heart
Vienna's oldest
trict, known
ay as the
ermuda Triangle",
Salzamt is
oular with artists,
hitects
I the Viennese
hion world.
ellent Austrian
sine, mixed with
diterranean
vors. Sober and
gant setting,
asant terrace and
y drinkable
nes.
↑≋

**Schwarzes
meel**
B2
gnergasse
533 89 67
en Mon.–Fri.
Oam–8pm,
8.30am–3pm
re), noon–3pm

(restaurant)
Appetizers and
Viennese cuisine
*This establishment
houses a*
Delikatessen *store
which sells excellent
dried meats,
cold dishes and
sandwiches to eat
in or take out, as
well as a bar and a
restaurant that
offers traditional
dishes in
a Jugendstil décor.
Fabulous treasures
in the cellars!*
◼ ✿ ◻

**AROUND THE RING
1ST–9TH DISTRICTS**

Academie
Untere Viaduktgasse
45, III
Landstrasse subway
station (U3)
Tel. 713 82 56
Open Mon.–Fri.
noon–2.30pm
and 7–10.30pm
Creative gourmet
cuisine
*Meinrad
Neunkirchen is an
absolute master
at extracting the
delicious essences
of herbs and flowers
and mixing their
subtle flavors and
scents to give his
unusual dishes a
unique flavor.
Don't miss the
fried sardines with
bitter-sweet
gherkins and
dandelion.*
⊞ ◻

Al Cappello
◆ **D** D2
Hermanngasse 30,
VII
Tel. 524 68 88
Open Mon.–Sat.
5–11pm
Italian cuisine
*A fine mix of
flavors from
the Italian region
of Friuli at the
furthest points
of Italy, Austria and
Slovenia, with its
mountain food
mixed with
specialites from
Venezia. Irresistible
antipasti (hors-*

◆ RESTAURANTS

Addresses are listed by district and in alphabetical order.
◆ refers to the maps at the end of this guide.
A list of symbols can be found on page 305.

RESTAURANTS
◼ < 200 ATS
◼ 200–300 ATS
◼ 300–400 ATS
⊞ > 400 ATS

d'œuvres), soups and stews. Delicious meats grilled on a wood fire on Tuesdays and Wednesdays.
◼ ◻

Bodega Española
◆ **B** C3
Belvederegasse 10, IV
Tel. 504 55 00
Open Tue.–Sat.
6pm–midnight
Spanish cuisine
Tapas to please all tastes and the famous "pata negra" ham, as well as traditional meat and fish dishes, and crema catalana for dessert. The wines and spirits, also from Spain, are of top quality.
◼

Demi Tass
◆ **B** B3
Prinz-Eugen-Strasse 28, IV
Tel. 504 31 19
Open Mon.–Sat.
11am–2pm and 6–11pm
Indian and French cuisine
This restaurant has achieved an incredible mix of culinary traditions. Here French and Indian cuisines are harmoniously combined, presenting the classic dishes of the former with the delicious spicy specialties of the latter.
⊞ ◻ ◻

Dubrovnik
◆ **A** D4
Am Heumarkt 5, III
Tel. 713 27 55
Open Mon.–Fri.
11am–3pm and 5.30pm–midnight, all day Sun. and public hols.
Cuisine from the Balkans
Traditional cuisine and an atmosphere that is fascinating and melancholy:

every evening, while aromatic entrees and delicious fish or grilled meats dishes are being prepared, a pianist plays nostalgic melodies from times gone by.
◼ ◻

Green Cottage
◆ **C** B4
Kettenbrückengasse 3, V
Tel. 586 65 81
Open Mon.–Sat.
6–11.30pm
Chinese cuisine
Tradition and creativity meet here in dishes that are served in a modern and luxurious setting. Specialties include duck in spicy sauce, medallions of venison on tea leaves and rice balls with ginger.
◼ ◻

Grünauer
◆ **D** D2
Hermanngasse 32, VII
Tel. 526 40 80
Open Tue.–Fri.
11.30am–2.30pm, Sat.–Mon.
6–10.30pm
Austrian cuisine
Long-established restaurant with paneled walls and Spartan furnishings. Austrian culinary classics are brought up-to-date and adapted for modern tastes. Excellent selection of wines and brandies (Schnäpse). Reservations recommended.
◼

Gusshaus
◆ **B** B2
Gusshausstrasse 23, IV
Tel. 504 47 50
Fax 504 94 64
Open Mon.–Fri.
11am–2.30pm and 6–11pm, Sat. 6–10pm
Creative cuisine
This Beisl is full of surprises. Viennese and Mediterranean

specialties can be savored in a pleasant and welcoming atmosphere, complemented perfectly by wines, draft beers and brandies.
◼ ◻ ◻

Piccini Piccolo Gourmet
◆ **B** A1
Linke Wienzeile 4, VI
Tel. 587 52 54
Open Mon.–Fri.
10am–7pm, Sat. 9am–2pm
The most famous Italian restaurant in Vienna. The menu includes delicious antipasti (hors-d'œuvres), pasta, fish soup, and in the fall, dishes made with truffles.
◼

Prinz Ferdinand
◆ **D** B2
Bennoplatz 2, VIII
Tel. 402 94 17
Open Tue.–Sun.
11am–2.45pm and 6–10.45pm
Viennese cuisine
This picture-postcard of a Beisl is located in a remarkable Biedermeier building which boasts a pleasant shady garden in the summer. Excellent menu and good selection of wines and brandies.
◼ ◻ ◻

Schwarzer Adler
◆ **C** C3-C4
Schönbrunner Strasse 40, V
Tel. 544 11 09
Open Tue.–Sat.
11am–2.30pm and 6–11pm
Viennese cuisine
Typical Viennese gourmet dishes are prepared with consummate skill in this restaurant which also serves some Mediterranean specialties such

as raviolis filled with ceps and cheeses. There is a fine selection of Austrian and Italian wines as well as beers, and a wide range of delicious gâteaux. Family atmosphe...
◼ ◻ ◻

Stein's Diner
◆ **A** A1
Kolingasse 1, IV
Tel. 310 95 15
Open Mon.–Sat.
7pm–1am
Modern cuisine
A restaurant with modern, minimal design occupies t... cellar of the café the same name. T... sophisticated me... offers traditional Viennese dishes as well as some Mediterranean specialties recrea... with a more Asia... flavor.
◼ ◻

✪ Steirereck
Rasumofskygasse III
Rochusgasse subv... station (U3)
Tel. 713 31 68
Open Mon.–Fri.
noon–3pm and 7–11pm
Austrian gourmet cuisine
This luxurious restaurant serves specialties from Styria – where the owner was born. You can savor such dishes as Gabelfrühstück, a generous breakfa... consisting of Viennese specialt... at lunchtime together with the Mittagsmenu, an... in the evening, after the show, y... can let yourself b... tempted by the Restelessen. Try t... oysters with ging... the beef Styrian-style, the assortm... of cakes or the semolina omelet (Griesschmarrn).
⊞ ◻ ◻

✪ The editor's choice

**en drei
hteln**
B4
rgasse 9, V
587 83 65
n Mon–Sat.
pm
ine from
emia
cal dishes from
emia such as
utfleckerln
ta with
bage) and
fenhaluska
cchis with
white cheese),
t balls made
ork, and fried
erts such as
anzen and
vidltascherln.
arkable
ice of wines
beers from
emia.

**bener
e und
er Stock**
D4
ggasse 13, VII
523 62 54
n Tue.–Fri.
n–2.30pm
6–11.30pm,
6–11.30pm
restaurant is
ted on the
floor of a tiny
ermeier
ding, in the
Spittelberg
a, and serves
ginative, refined
nese cuisine.
on the first
r.
🔲

**Goldenen
el**
01
arettgasse 6, IX
405 83 63

Open Thur.–Mon.
9am–3pm and
6–11pm
Viennese cuisine
Authentic Beisl
*offering Viennese
cuisine together
with quality beers
and excellent
Austrian wines.
Special dining room
for non smokers and
entertainment area
for children.*
🔲🔲

OUTSIDE THE RING
10TH–23RD DISTRICTS

Kierlinger
Kahlenbergerstrasse
20, XIX
Tel. 370 22 64

Open Mon.–Sat.
3.30pm–midnight,
Sun. 3–11pm
*This inn belongs to
the Kierlinger
family, famous
for the grapes
produced in their*

*Rheinriesling and
Weissburgunder
vineyards. You can
have a drink at the
counter, in one of
the dining rooms
or in the garden
under the linden
and chestnut trees.
A buffet includes
hot and cold meat
dishes, and the
specialty of the
house: the* Liptauer
*(herb and fromage
frais cheescake).*
🔲🔲

**Mayer
Am Pfarrplatz**
Pfarrplatz 2, XIX
Tel. 370 12 87

Open 4pm–
midnight; Sun.
and public hols
11am–midnight
*Beethoven stayed
here in 1817. Today
this house is a
famous inn where*

*one can sample
remarkable wines
such as Nussberger,
Alsegger Riesling
and Traminer.
Mayer, the engineer
who runs it with his
family, is a pioneer
of high-quality
Viennese wine
growing. His label
"Vienna classic"
has brought fame to
Viennese wines.*
🔲🔲🔲

Sirbu
Kahlenbergerstrasse
210, XIX
Tel. 320 59 28
Open beg. Apr.–
mid Oct., Mon.–Sat.
3pm–midnight
*Situated on
Nussberg Heights,
this inn offers a
splendid panoramic
view of Kahlenberg,
Leopoldsberg
and the Danube.
Amongs wines,
all excellent, the
Nussdorfer Riesling
stands out in
particular. A buffet
offers robust dishes,
some of which are
prepared with
organic ingredients.*
🔲🔲🔲🔲

Zimmermann
Armbrustergasse 5,
XIX
Tel. 370 22
Open 5pm–midnight
Closed Sun. and
public hols.
*Spacious inn
where wines and
bubblies from the
Klosterneuburg
reserve can be
sampled, together
with quality dishes.*
🔲🔲🔲

◆ CAFÉS, BARS, NIGHTCLUBS AND CONCERT HALLS

INSIDE THE RING
1ST DISTRICT
→ CAFÉS AND BISTROS

Café Bräunerhof
◆ A C2
Stallburggasse 2
Tel. 512 38 93
Open. Mon–Fri.
7.30am–8.30pm,
Sat. 7.30am–
6pm, Sun. and
public hols.
10am–6pm
*Thomas Bernhard
was a regular
customer of this
typical Viennese
café. On Saturdays,
Sundays and
public holidays,
a charming trio
(including a
pianist) plays
Austrian music
from 3 until 6pm.*

Café Central
◆ A B2-C2
Herrengasse 14
Tel. 533 37 63 26
Open 8am–8pm
(summer),
8am–10pm (winter)
Closed Sun. and
public hols.
*Situated in Ferstel
palace, this is
one of the
most distinguished
and cosmopolitan
cafés in the
Austrian capital.
However, despite its
sumptuous décor
and superb choice
of pâtisseries,
this café seems to
be more popular
with tourists than
with the Viennese.
Live music from
4 until 7pm.*

Café Griensteidl
◆ A C2
Michaelerplatz 2
Tel. 535 26 92
Open 8am–
midnight
*One of the oldest
cafés in Vienna, and
the meeting place
of many Austrian
intellectuals and
artists, such as
Hofmannsthal,
Schnitzler, Kraus,
Wolf and
Schönberg.
Entirely renovated.*

Café Hawelka
◆ A C2
Dorotheergasse 6
Tel. 512 82 30
Open Tue.–Sat.
8am–2pm,
Sun. and public h
10am–2am
Closed Mon.
*Don't miss the
delicious Buchtel
(small cakes filled
with prune
preserve) prepare
by Frau Hawelka*

Haas & Haas
◆ A C3
Stephansplatz 4
Tel. 513 191 60
Fax 513 191 612
Open Mon.–Fri.
9am–8pm,
Sat. 9am–6pm
Sandwiches
and patisseries
*Delicious cakes
and light appetiz
served with coffe
In summer you ca
sit on the terrace
the shade of the
cathedral or in th
charming mediev
courtyard of the
Deutschordenha*

Kecks Feine Kost
◆ A B1
Herrengasse 15
Tel. 533 63 67
Open Mon.–Fri.
9am–6.30pm
Appetizers, snack
*Excellent place to
sample inventive
Austrian snacks:
salads, flans and
mouth-watering
cakes, as well as
good-quality
Weisswürste on
Wednesdays.*

Trzesniewski
◆ A C2
Dorotheergasse
Tel. 512 32 91
Open Mon.–Fri.
8.30am–7.30pm,
Sat. 9am–5pm
Bread with a vari
of toppings
*Half-Polish, half-
Viennese institut
serving only
Aufstrichbrot –
sliced bread with
various toppings
(delicious chicke
liver paté, speck,*

*lobster,
ers with a bit of
, etc.). Beers or
kling wines to
rith your bread.*

-Vis
3
zeile 5
eria)
12 93 50
n Mon.–Fri.
30pm
*tiny, crowded
e is among the
Beisl in Vienna.
llent appetizers
erved, made
ham,
adella, cheese
olives, as well as
ious white
s served by the
. Sober setting.*

**RS AND
OTHEQUES
land**
33
z-Josephs-
29
533 25 75
erts start at
nd 9pm
ission fees
vary
entic jazz
with live
s'n'boogie, folk,
g, traditional
modern jazz
erts. Food is
lable before,
g or after the
ert.

Krah
33
ensteig 8
533 81 93
n Mon. am,
and public hols.
n–1pm
ission free
y tavern
ted in the
muda Triangle"
. A wide range
eers is on offer
, as well as a
concert and
ch or lunch
y Sunday
veen 11am
3pm.

Isco
33
asse 9
535 99 95
n Fri.–Sat.

11am–6am
*Discotheque
located near the
area known as the
"Bermuda Triangle".
An absolute must
for techno
enthusiasts.*

Santo Spirito
◆ A C3
Kumpfgasse 7
Tel. 512 99 98
Open Mon.–Fri.
11am–2am,
Sat. 11am–3am,
Sun. 10am–2am
*Bar for classical
music lovers, with
an emphasis on
Baroque music.
Dinner available.*

→ **CONCERT HALLS,
THEATERS AND OTHER
VENUES**
Burgtheater
◆ A B1-C1
Dr.-Karl-Lueger-
Ring 2
Tel. (1) 514 44 29 59
Fax (1) 514 44 41 47
Season: Sep.–June
Reservations by
telephone minimum
4 weeks before the
performance:
Mon.–Fri 10am–6pm,
Sat.–Sun. and public
hols. 10am–noon.
*The program has
consisted mostly
of German classics
since the opening of
the theater in 1888
with Esther by Franz
Grillparzer.*

**Spanish Riding
School**
◆ A C2
Hofburg
Reservations
by fax 535 01 86
Times may vary
(check the Spanische
Reitschule, Wiener
Sängerknaben
board at the Spanish
Riding School).
*Three main types
of shows: galas,
equestrian displays
with music and
dressage.*

Kammerspiele
◆ A B3
Rotenturmstrasse 20
Tel. (1) 427 003 00
Small avant-garde

*theater, where
Schnizler's Merry-
Go-Round caused
a scandal at the
beginning of the
20th century.*

Vienna Boys' Choir
◆ A C2 B A2
Concerts at the
Musikverein
and sung mass
(Jan.–June and
Sep.–Dec. 9.15am)
at the Burgkapelle
Reservations by fax
for the sung mass:
533 99 27 75.
Free standing
(no reservations
required).

Staatsoper
◆ A D2
Opernring 2
Tel. 514 44 29 59
or 514 44 29 60
Season: Sep.–June
Reservations by tel.
Mon.–Fri. 8am–6pm,
Sat.–Sun. and public
hols. 9am–noon
(1st Sat. of the
month 9am–5pm) or
Internet
www.culturall.com
*With over 40 operas
and some 300
performances every
season, the Vienna
opera house is the
largest repertory
theater in the
world. Seats are
hard to come by,
but if you are lucky,
you may be able to
get a seat in the
stalls or one of
the 800 standing
places, sold one
hour before the
performance (the
ticket office is in the
main foyer).*

**Wiener
Kammeroper**
◆ A B3
Fleischmarkt 24
Tel. 513 60 72
Light opera

AROUND THE RING
IST–9TH DISTRICTS
→ **CAFÉS AND BISTROS**
Café Im Kunsthaus
Weissgerberlände
14, III
Landstrasse or
Rochusgasse subway

station (U3)
Tel. 712 04 97
*Fine café, with a
pleasant green
setting and located
very near the
Hundertwasserhaus.
Perfect for relaxing
while having a
drink.*

Café Sperl
◆ C A4
Gumpendorfer
Strasse 11, VI
Tel. 586 41 58
Open Mon.–Sat.
7am–11pm,
Sun. and public hols.
3–11pm.
Closed Sun and
public hols.
July–Aug.
*Tranquil old
Viennese café where
time seems to have
stood still. Billiard
tables for amateurs.*

Plutzer Bräu
◆ D D4
Schrankgasse 2, VII
Tel. 526 12 15
Open 11.30am–2am
*Large tavern
situated in the heart
of the Spittelberg
district. House beer
and delicious bread
snacks. Warm
atmosphere.*

→ **BARS AND
DISCOTHEQUES**
Blue Box
◆ B B2
Richtergasse 8, VII
Tel. 523 26 82
Open Tue.–Sun.
10am–2am,
Mon. 6pm–2am
Admission free
*Friends love to meet
in this club whose
convivial
atmosphere is
enhanced by the
DJ's choice of soft,
discreet music.*

B 72
◆ D A2
Hernalser Gürtel,
U-Bahnbögen 72/73,
VIII
Tel. 409 21 28
Open 8pm–4am
Admission free
until 10pm
*Situated under the
red brick arcades*

◆ CAFÉS, BARS, NIGHTCLUBS AND CONCERT HALLS

of the overhead subway, this club has a dance floor and a different DJ every night. Theme evenings.

Chelsea
◆ D B1
Lerchenfelder Gürtel, U-Bahnbögen 29/31, VIII
Tel. 407 93 09
Open 8am–4am
Underground institution founded in 1986 and playing mostly pop music. Different DJ every night. The Chelsea produces a music fanzine four times a year. Cider, whisky and Irish beer flow rather more freely when English or Austrian football matches are on, shown live on the club's television screens.

Flex
◆ A A2
Donaukanal/Augartenbrücke, I
Tel. 533 75 25
Admission: 100 ATS
One of the temples of electronic music in Vienna, set up in a former warehouse on the banks of the Donaukanal. Theme evenings with performances by groups representing different musical styles.

Meierei Im Stadtpark
◆ A D4
Am Heumarkt 2a, III
Tel. 714 61 59
Open Fri.–Sat. 10pm–4am
Old-fashioned building in the middle of the municipal park dating from the end of the 19th century. Two different dance floors with jungle and house music. In summer a third DJ plays records in this Biergarten.

Miles Smiles
◆ D B3
Langegasse 51, VIII
Tel. 405 95 17
Open Sun.–Thur. 8pm–2am, Fri.–Sat. 8pm–4am
You can enjoy a drink or a snack in this convivial establishment while listening to 1950s contemporary jazz. Two or three concerts take place every month.

Rhiz
◆ D B1
Lerchenfelder Gürtel, U-Bahnbögen 29/31, VIII
Tel. 409 25 05
Open 6pm–4am
Admission: 100 ATS
New electronic venue where different musicians appear practically every night (at 8pm). A DJ takes over when the atmosphere has become sufficiently heated.

Schultz
◆ C A2A 3
Siebensterngasse 31, VII
Tel. 522 91 20
One of the most popular cocktail bars in Vienna for pre-dinner drinks. Warm atmosphere in spite of the rather cold décor. Impressive range of drinks.

Stein
◆ A A1
Währinger Strasse 6, IX
Tel. 319 724 1
www.cafe-stein.co.at
Open 8am–1am
Vienna's first cybercafé. Good-quality, trendy but rather loud music. The terrace in the afternoon is best for those who want to chat quietly over a drink.

Tunnel
◆ D B2
Florianigasse 39, VIII
Tel. 405 34 65
Open 9am–2am
Performances start at 9pm
With its reasonable admission fees the Tunnel is a favorite with students. There is a special room for live jazz performances. Occasional incursions into different styles of music such as blues, rock and bossa nova. Free admission for "Jazz Live" every Sunday from 8pm.

Titanic
◆ C A4
Theobaldgasse 11, VI
Tel. 587 47 58
Open Thur.–Sat. from 9.30pm
Free admission
Two dance floors in the basement, one mostly for hip-hop, the other for 1980's revival.

→ CONCERT HALLS AND THEATERS
Musikverein
◆ B A2
Bösendorferstr. 12, VI
Tel. 505 81 90
Season: Sep.–June. Reservations by tel. Mon.–Fri. 9am–6pm, Sat. 9am–5pm
The season is divided into the Brahmssaal (chamber music) and the Grosser Saal (symphonic concerts). It is in this sumptuous hall that the famous New Year concert given by the Vienna Philharmonic Orchestra takes place.

Raimund Theater
◆ C C1
Wallgasse 18, VI
Ticket office open 10am–7pm

Closed Jul.–Aug.
Reservations by tel. 588 85
One of the temples of musicals. Grease, Lady and the Tramp, The Kiss of Spider Woman and The of the Vampires (produced by Roman Polanski 1997 with music Jim Steinman) h all been perform here.

Theater an der Wien
◆ B A1
Linke Wienzeile VI
Tel. 588 30 33
Performances Mon.–Sat. 7.30p Sun. 6pm
Closed Wed.
Beethoven's Fid (1805) and Joha Strauss's Die Fliedermaus (18 had their first performance in this hall. Today the Theater an Wien also puts popular musical and operas duri such festivals as the Wiener Festwochen (May–June) and the Klangboger (Jul.–Aug.).

Theater in der Josefstadt
Josefstädter Stra 24–26, VIII
Tel. 427 00 300
Reservations by tel. minimum 14 days before the performance
One of the oldest recitative theaters in Vienna (1788). The great direct Max Rheinhardt the theater's manager from 1 to 1933 before emigrating to th United States. Works by Schniz and Hofmannst are performed here with great panache and fervor.

324

CAFÉS, BARS, NIGHTCLUBS ◆
AND CONCERT HALLS

...nna's English ...eater
...efsgasse
... VIII
... 40212 60
...ason:
... Sep.– mid Jul.
...formances
...n.–Sat. 7.30pm
...unded in 1963
...a summer
...eater for English-
...aking visitors, it
...n developed a
...gular program.
...ace Kelly,
...anne Moreau,
...n Fontaine,
...thony Queen,
...torio Gassman
...d Jean-Louis
...rrault are among
...e great actors
...o have
...rformed here.
...art from
...5 or 6 yearly
...glish-language
...oductions, it also
...ts on regular
...rks in French
...d Italian.

...kstheater
...❿ D4
...ustiftgasse 1, VII
... 524 72 63
...ason: Sep.–June
...is theater was
...ilt between 1887
...d 1889 as an
...ernative to the
...ry official
...rgtheater,
...anks to the
...tiative of a
...nnese association
...at wished to
...ke popular
...ssics and
...ntemporary
...rks available
...a larger audience.

...ener
...nzerthaus
...❽ A3
...thringerstrasse
... III
... 712 12 11
...servations by tel.
...n.–Fri.
...m–6.30pm,
...t.–Sun. and public
...ls. 10am–1pm
...d 4–6.30pm
...ket@konzerthaus.

...ww.konzerthaus.at
...e second finest
...nnese concert

hall with an
international
reputation.
The program is
often more diverse
and audacious
than that of the
Musikverein. The
contemporary
music festival
"Wien Modern"
takes place here
every year in
the fall.

Wiener Volksoper
◆ E C2
Währinger Strasse
78, IX
Tel. 514 44 29 59
or 514 44 29 60
Season: Sep.–June
Reservations
by tel. Mon.–Fri.
8am–6pm, Sat.–Sun.
and public hols.
9am–noon.
*The temple of
Viennese operetta.
The repertory
includes* Hänsel and
Gretel, *as well as
works by Franz
Lehár and Johann
Strauss.*

OUTISDE THE RING
10TH–23RD
DISTRICTS

→BARS
AND DISCOTHEQUES
Reigen
Hadikgasse 62, XIV
Tel. 894 00 94
Open 6pm–4am
Evening starts at
9pm
*An evening to be
combined with a
visit to the
Schönbrunn Castle.
Jazz concerts almost
every night,
with emphasis on
Latin-American
rhythms. Salsa
every Saturday
night.*

U4
◆ C D1
Schönbrunner
Strasse 222, VII
Tel. 815 83 07
Open 10pm–5am
Admission:
60–100 ATS
*A Viennese classic.
Two halls and
various types of
music.*

◆ SHOPPING

INSIDE THE RING
1ST DISTRICT

→ ANTIQUES
Antiquitäten D&S
◆ A C2
Dorotheergasse 13
Tel. 512 58 85
Open Mon.–Fri.
10am–6pm,
Sat. 10am–1pm
Closed Sat. in
summer
*Magnificent clocks
and Biedermeier
mantelpieces, as
well as fine
furniture dating
from the 18th and
19th centuries.*

→ BOOKS AND
RECORDS
Arcadia
◆ A D2
Kärtner Str. 40
(under the arcades
of the opera house)
Tel. 513 95 68
Open Mon.-Sat.
9.30am–6.30pm,
Sun. 10am–6.30pm
*Huge choice of
opera records. A
music lover's
paradise.*

Prachtner
◆ A D2
Kärntner Strasse 30
Tel. 512 85 490
*One of the largest
bookstores in town,
with a large
selection of works
on Vienna.*

→ DEPARTMENT
STORES
Steffl
◆ A C2-C3
Kärntner Strasse 19
Tel. 514 310
Open Mon.–Fri.
9.30am–7pm,
Sat. 9am–5pm
*Steffl has developed
a new shopping
concept: clients
describe what they
are looking for by
telephone and the
store assistants
select suitable items.
An appointment is
then made for the
presentation of
the various items
selected. A special
room is used for
this purpose with
no extra charge.*

Beauty products and
accessories can be
found on the first
floor; top fashion
labels for both men
and women are
located on the
2nd, 3rd, 4th and
5th floors, while
books, music
and multimedia
items are in
the "Amadeus"
section on the 6th
and 7th floors.
You can relax in
the restaurant or
American bar on
the 9th floor, which
offers a fine view
of St Stephen's
Cathedral and across
the Vienna roof
tops.

→ FASHION
Braun & Co
◆ A C2
Graben 8
Tel. 512 550 50
Open Mon.–Fri.
10am–6pm,
Sat. 9.30am–5pm
*Extremely elegant
store, whose curved
windows resemble
caskets for the fine
clothes on display.
Sophisticated décor
of beautiful wood
paneling and period
furniture, used for
the presentation
of the most famous
names and labels in
prêt-à-porter.*

Helmut Lang
◆ A C2
Seilergasse 6
Tel. 513 25 88
Open Mon.–Fri.
9.30am–6pm,
Sat. 10am–5pm
*The Viennese
designer is one
of the most*

famous names in
international prêt-à-
porter. Renowned
for his choice of
original materials,
such as vinyl and
rubber. Beautiful
store with the
barest of décors.

Oberwalder & Co
◆ A D2
Kärntner Strasse 39
Tel. (1) 512 28 41
Open Mon.–Fri.
9am–7pm,
Sat. 9am–5pm
*Famous for its hats,
notably the classic
loden model to
which small
decorations, such as
feathers or animal
hairs, can be added.*

KUNST UND ANTIQUITÄTEN MARKT AM DONAUKANAL

Palmers
◆ A C2
Graben 14
Tel. 532 40 58
Open Mon.–Fri.
9am–6pm,
Sat. 9am–5pm
*Famous name in
Austrian lingerie,
whose numerous
stores are easily
spotted thanks to
their green-and-
gold shop sign.*

Tostmann & Co
◆ A B1
Schottengasse
3a
Tel. 533 53 31
Open Mon.–Fri.
10am–6.30pm,
Sat. 9.30am–5pm
*Here you will find
the finest Dirndl
(traditional female
costumes). The
store also sells
clothes for men
and children, and
has a suit hiring
service.*

UUM Beschorner
◆ A B1
Schottengasse 2
Tel. 533 14 28
Open Mon.–Fri.
10am–6pm,
Sat. 10am–5pm
*Established in 185
this is the oldest
glove store in
Vienna, easily
recognizable by it
shop sign. Gloves
come in many sty.
with traditional o
modern design,
and are made of
different materia.
Fine selection of
scarves as well.*

Wolford
◆ A C2-C3
Kärntner Strasse 2
Tel. 512 87 31
Open Mon.–Fri.
9am–6pm,
Sat. 9am–5pm
*Well-known bran
of hosiery. Wolfo.
stockings, panty
hoses and bodies
are expensive
but of undeniable
quality.*

→ FOOD
Meinl am Graben
◆ A C2
Graben 19
Tel. 532 33 34
Open Mon.–Fri.
8.30am–7pm,
Sat. 8am–5pm
*The best grocery
and delicatessen
store in Vienna. T
Austrian specialtie
and exotic produc
sold here can be
sampled in the
restaurant of the
same name next
door (open 11am–
midnight).*

**Vinothek Sankt-
Stephan**
◆ A C3
Stephansplatz 6
Tel. 512 68 58
Open Mon.–Fri.
9.30am–6.30pm,
Sat. 9.30am–1pm
*Welcoming store
with an excellent
selection of Austr
wines, as well as
vintages from oth
countries. Possibil
of wine tasting.*

**TERIOR
RATION
Köchert**
C2
er Markt 15
512 58 28
n Mon.–Fri.
–6pm,
9am–5pm
ner jewelers
he Austrian
erial house. A
nond tiara with
tars was created
e for the empress
abeth. It was
eated in 1998
ommemorate
centenary of
death.

arten Wien
D2
k-im-Eisen-
z 3
512 14 94
n Mon.–Fri.
am–6pm,
9.30am–5pm
he porcelain
nufactured by
house of
arten is hand-
le in the finest
trian tradition.
roductions of
roughbreds from
Spanish Riding
ol are also
here.

unden
C2
ntner Durchgang
512 58 24
n Mon.–Fri.
–6pm,
9.30am–5pm
largest pottery
nufacturers in
tral Europe
be found in
unden, a small
n in Upper
tria. All the
es are hand-
ated with floral
reen-stripe
terns, and there
more than
0 different
dels of coffee
, vases, jars,
d bowls, etc.

ze & Kater
B1-B2
is Ferstel,
rengasse 14/
ung 2
535 43 72

Open Mon.–Fri.
10am–6pm,
Sat. 10am–5pm
*Katze & Kater
sell the largest
collection of cat
figurines in Europe
(over 2,500 pieces).
Made of ceramic,
wood, bronze, glass
or metal, most are
hand-crafted and
reasonably priced.*

Lobmeyr
◆ A D2
Kärntner Strasse 26
Tel. 512 05 08
Open Mon.–Fri.
9am–6pm,
Sat. 10am–5pm
*Huge choice of
wine glasses and
carafes – there are
25 different models
of champagne
flutes. The store also
houses a small
glass museum.*

Rasper & Söhne
◆ A C2
Graben 15
Tel. (1) 534 33
Open Mon.–Fri.
9.30am–6pm,
Sat. 10am–5pm
*This store represents
Riedel, the Austrian
glassmakers
known to all wine
connoisseurs. Claus
Riedel was the first
to adapt the glasses'
shapes to suit the
specific qualities of
the different wines.
Today the "Wine
waiter" collection
comes in 30
different styles.*

Theyer & Hardtmuth
◆ A C2-C3
Kärntner Strasse 9
Tel. 512 36 78
Open Mon.–Fri.
9.30am–6pm,
Sat. 10am–5pm
*This store sells
crystal miniatures
(small animals,
musical instruments,
multi-faceted fruit),
as well as jewelry
(brooches,
pendants) and key
holders bearing the
famous Austrian
name of Swarovski,
whom it represents.*

**→ PATISSERIES,
CONFECTIONERS
Altmann & Kühne**
Graben 30
Tel. 533 09 27
Open Mon.–Fri.
9am–6.30pm,
Sat. 10am–5pm
*Located in a
fine Secession
building, these
confectioners still
use traditional
recipes. Handcrafted
sweets such as the
miniature Liliput,
presented in pretty
boxes with unusual
shapes (chests of
drawers, treasure
chests, books, etc.),
demand the type
of craftsmanship
that this house is
famous for.*

Demel
◆ A C2
Kohlmarkt 14
Herrengasse
Tel. 5351 717 39
Open daily
10am–7pm
*The temple of
cakemaking in
Vienna. The velvet
interior decoration
and impeccable
service are equal
to the reputation
of this fine
establishment.
Sweets are
presented in
luxurious boxes
that were created
by Demel for
the Wiener
Werkstätte at
the beginning
of the 20th century.*

Oberlaa-Stadthaus
◆ A C2
Neuer Markt 16
Tel. 513 29 36
Open 8am–10pm
*Light cakes, sweet-
smelling petits
fours to savor with
coffee, as well
as sophisticated
sandwiches,
salads and other
snacks. The
Faschingskrapfen
(doughnuts sold
during the Carnaval)
made in this store
are reputed to be
the best in Vienna.*

*Don't leave
the Austrian
capital without
taking with you a
specialty from this
store – the
wrapping is as
delightful as the
contents!*

Sacher
◆ A D2
Kärntner Strasse 38
Tel. 514 568 52
Open Mon.-Sat.
9am–6pm
*Delicious cakes
and, of course, the
world-renowned
Sachertorte,
invented by
Franz Sache
in 1840.*

**AROUND THE RING
1ST–9TH
DISTRICTS**

**→ANTIQUES,
FLEAMARKETS
Flohmarkt
Am Naschmarkt**
Naschmarkt, VI
Tel. 546 344 30
Open Sat. (except
public hols.)
6am–6pm
*This fleamarket,
in the continuation
of the Naschmarkt
(the great food
market), is the
largest and most
famous in Vienna.
Professional antique
dealers as well as
second-hand stall
holders and
individuals gather
here every Saturday
to sell all kinds of
objects. It is best to
come early in the
morning.*

**Kunst und
Antiquitäten Markt
Am Donaukanal**
Donaukanal, XX
Tel. 531 144 31
Open May–Sep.
Sat. noon–8pm,
Sun. 8am–8pm
*Small second-
hand goods
and crafts stalls
set up on the banks
of the Danube,
on the old town
side between the
Augarten and
Aspern ridges.*

◆ PLACES TO VISIT

Places to visit are listed alphabetically.
The ▲ symbol refers to the Itineraries section, while the ◆ refers to the maps.

VIENNA

ACADEMY OF SCIENCES *Akademie der Wissenschaften* *Alte Universität*	*Not open to the public.*	◆ ▲
ALBERTINA Im Akademiehof/Makartgasse 3 Tel. 581 306 021	*Open Tue.–Sun. 10am–5pm.*	◆ ▲
ANCHOR CLOCK *Ankeruhr* Hoher Markt 10/11	*Chimes and figurine procession daily at noon.*	◆ ▲
ARCHIVES OF THE AUSTRIAN RESISTANCE *Dokumentationsarchiv des* *Österreichischen Widerstandes* Altes Rathaus Wipplingerstrasse 8 Tel. 534 36 01 779	*Open Mon., Wed.–Thur. 9am–5pm.*	◆ ▲
ART HISTORY MUSEUM *Kunsthistorisches Museum* Maria-Theresien-Platz Burgring 5 Tel. 525 240	*Open Tue.–Sun. 10am–6pm,* *late-night opening Thur. 10am–9pm.*	◆ ▲
AUGARTEN PARK AND CHINA FACTORY *Augarten* Obere Augartenstrasse 1 Tel. 211 24 11	*Guided tours Mon.–Fri. 9.30am.* *Closed public hols.*	▲
AUSTRIAN 19TH- AND 20TH-CENTURY GALLERY *Österreichische Galerie* *des 19. und 20. Jahrhunderts* Prinz-Eugen-Strasse 27 Oberes Belvedere (Upper Belvedere) Tel. 795 570	*Open Tue.–Sun. 10am–5pm.*	◆ ▲
BATTHYANY-SCHÖNBORN PALACE Renngasse	*Not open to the public.*	◆
BUILDINGS BY OTTO WAGNER Wienzeile	*Not open to the public.*	▲
BURGTHEATER Dr. Karl Lueger Ring 2 Tel. 514 44 2218	*Guided tour by appointment.*	◆ ▲
CAPRARA-GEYMÜLLER PALACE Wallnerstrasse	*Not open to the public.*	◆ ♪
CARRIAGE MUSEUM *Wagenburg* Schloss Schönbrunn Tel. 877 32 44	*Open Nov.–Mar 10am–4pm and* *Apr.–Oct. 9am–6pm.* *Closed Mon.*	◆ ◆ ▲
CATHEDRAL AND DIOCESAN MUSEUM *Dom- und Diözesanmuseum* Stephansplatz 6 Tel. 515 52 35 60	*Open Tue.–Sat. 10am–5pm.*	◆
CENTRAL CEMETARY *Zentralfriedhof* Simmeringer Haupstrasse 234 Tel. 760 410	*Open Mar.–Apr. and Sep.–Oct. 7am–6pm;* *May–Aug. 7am–7pm; Nov.–Feb. 8am–5pm.*	▲
CEREMONIAL ROOM OF THE NATIONAL LIBRARY *Prunksaal der* *Nationalbibliothek* Josefsplatz 1 Tel. 534 10 397	*Open May 7–Oct. 26 Mon.–Wed., Fri.–Sat.* *10am–4pm, Thur. 10am–7pm,* *Sun. and public hols. 10am–2pm;* *Oct. 27–May 6 Mon.–Sat. 10am–2pm.*	◆
CHAPEL OF ST BIRGIT *Brigittakapelle*	*Open daily 9am–5pm.*	◆
CHAPEL OF ST VIRGIL *Virgilkapelle* Stephansplatz Tel. 513 58 42	*Open 9am–12.15pm and 1–4.30pm.* *Closed Mon.*	◆ ◆

URCH AND CONVENT **THE URSULINES** *rsulinenkirche und Kloster* *hannesgasse*	Open for services: Sun. mass at 10am.	◆ A D3 ▲ 147
URCH AND MONASTERY **THE DOMINICANS** *ominikanerkirche und Kloster* *stgasse*	Open daily 7am–7pm (9pm Sun. and public hols.).	◆ A B4 ▲ 152
URCH OF ST ANNE *nnakirche* *nnagasse*	Open daily 6.30am–6.30pm.	◆ A D3 ▲ 146
URCH OF ST BARBARA *nkt Barbara Kirche* *stgasse*	Guided tour by appointment (Tel. 512 21 33).	◆ A B-C4 ▲ 153
URCH OF ST CHARLES **RROMEO** *rlskirche* *rlsplatz*	Open daily 9am–6pm.	◆ B A2 ▲ 238
URCH OF ST ELIZABETH *eutschordenskirche* *nkt Elizabeth* *ngerstrasse*	Open daily 6.30am–7pm.	◆ A C3 ▲ 149
URCH OF ST JEROME *anziskanerkirche* *anziskanerplatz*	Open daily 6.30am–5.30pm.	◆ A C3 ▲ 149
URCH OF ST LEOPOLD *rche am Steinhof* *aumgartner Höhe 1*	Open Mon.–Fri. 8am–3pm. Guided tour Sat. at 3pm.	◆ A B2 ▲ 288
URCH OF ST MARY'S **N THE BANK** *aria am Gestade* *assauerplatz*	Open for services: Sat. 6.30pm, Sun. and public hols. 7.30am, 9.30am, 11am, 7pm.	◆ A B2 ▲ 172
URCH OF ST MICHAEL *ichaelerkirche* *ichaelerplatz*	Open daily 11am–5pm.	◆ A C2 ▲ 174
URCH OF ST PETER *terskirche* *etersplatz*	Open Mon.–Sat. 10.30am–6pm, Sun. and public hols. 9am–6pm.	◆ A C2 ▲ 139
URCH OF ST RUPERT *uprechtskirche* *uprechtsplatz*	Open Mon.–Fri. 10am–1pm and 4–6pm.	◆ A B3 ▲ 154
URCH OF THE BROTHERS **CHARITY** *armherzige-Brüder-Kirche* *borstrasse*	Open daily 7am–7pm.	◆ A A4 ▲ 268
URCH OF THE HOLY TRINITY *serkirche* *serstrasse*	Open daily 7am–7pm.	◆ D A3 ▲ 290
URCH OF THE HOLY TRINITY *rche zur* *eiligsten Dreifaltigkeit* *eorgsgasse/Rysergasse Mauer*	Open Sat. 2–8pm, Sun. and public hols. 9am–5pm, Thur.–Fri. 2–4pm. Guided tour by appointment (Tel. 88 85 003).	◆ C D1 ▲ 288
URCH OF THE MINOR FRIARS *inoritenkirche* *inoritenplatz*	Open daily 7am–7pm.	◆ A C1 ▲ 161
Y HALL *athaus* *iedrich-Schmidt-Platz* *l. 525 50*	Group visits Mon., Wed., Fri. 1pm. Apply in writing at least one month in advance.	◆ D B4 ▲ 204
OCK MUSEUM *hrenmuseum der Stadt* *ien* *lais Obizzi, Schulhof 2* *l. 533 22 65*	Open daily 9am–4.30pm. Closed Mon.	◆ A B2 ▲ 168
LLALTO PALACE *m Hof*	Not open to the public.	◆ A B2 ▲ 167
LLECTION OF ARMS AND **MOR** *stungen und* *affensammlung* *eue Burg, Heldenplatz*	Open 10am–6pm. Closed Tue.	◆ A D1-2 ▲ 186

CRYPT OF THE CAPUCHINS *Kapuzinergruft* Neuer Markt Tel. 512 68 53 12	Open daily 9.30am–3.30pm.	◆ A ▲ 1
CRYPT OF THE HASBURG HEARTS *Herzgruft der Habsburger* Augustinerkirche Augustinerstrasse 3 Tel. 533 70 99	Visit by appointment Mon.–Sat. 10am–5pm.	◆ A ▲ 1
DAUN-KINSKY PALACE Freyung	Not open to the public.	◆ A ▲ 1
DIETRICHSTEIN PALACE Minoritenplatz	Not open to the public.	◆ A ▲ 1
DOLL AND TOY MUSEUM *Puppen- und Spielzeugmuseum* Palais Obizzi, Schulhof 2 Tel. 535 686-0	Open Tue.–Sun. 10am–6pm.	◆ A ▲ 1
EPHESOS-MUSEUM Neue Burg 1 Heldenplatz Tel. 525 476	Open 10am–6pm. Closed Tue.	◆ A ▲ 1
ERDORY-FÜRSTEMBERG PALACE Himmelpfortgasse	Not open to the public.	◆ A C ▲ 1
ESTERHAZY PALACE Wallnerstrasse	Free admission to the courtyard.	◆ A ▲ 1
EXOTIC BUTTERFLIES **CONSERVATORY** *Schmetterlinghaus* Burggarten Tel. 533 85 70	Open daily Apr.–Oct. 10am–5pm, Nov.–Mar. 10am–4pm.	◆ A B
FEDERAL CHANCELLERY *Bundeskanzleramt*	Not open to the public.	◆ A ▲ 1
FERSTEL PALACE Herrengasse	Free admission to the internal staircase and corridors.	◆ A ▲ 1
FIGARO'S HOUSE *Figarohaus* Domgasse 5 Tel. 513 62 94	Open Tue.–Sun. 9am–6pm.	◆ A ▲ 1
FINE ARTS ACADEMY *Akademie der bildenden Künste* Schillerplatz 3 Tel. 588 16 225 or 228	Open Tue.–Sun. 10am–4pm.	◆ A C ▲ 2
FIREFIGHTING MUSEUM *Feuerwehrmuseum* Am Hof 7 Tel. 531 99	Open Sun. and public hols. 9am–noon.	◆ A ▲ 1
FORMER CHANCELLERY OF **BOHEMIA** *Ehemalige Böhmische* *Hofkanzlei*	Not open to the public.	◆ A ▲ 1
FORMER CITY HALL *Altes Rathaus*	See Archives of the Austrian Resistance.	◆ A ▲ 1
FRIENDS OF MUSIC BUILDING *Musikvereinsgebäude* Dumbastrasse	Only open for concerts.	◆ B ▲ 2
FÜRSTEMBERG PALACE Domgasse	Not open to the public.	◆ A ▲ 1
"GANZ OHR" THEATER *Klangtheater "Ganz Ohr"* Austrian Radio House Argentinierstr. 30a Tel. 505 22 22	Open daily 9am–7pm.	◆ B C3
GREEK ORTHODOX CHURCH *Griechenkirche* Fleischmarkt 13	Open for services: Sun. mass 11am. Guided tour by appointment Mon.–Fri. 9am–4pm (Tel. 533 29 65).	◆ A ▲ 1
HARRACH PALACE Hunting Museum and weapon and armor collection *Jagd-und Waffenmuseum* Freyung 3 Tel. 523 17 53	Open daily 10am–6pm.	◆ A ▲ 1

YDN MUSEUM aydngasse 19 l. 596 13 07	*Open Tue.–Sun. 9am–12.15pm and 1–4.30pm.*	◆ C B2
ILIGENKREUZ MONASTERY ND ST BERNARD'S CHAPEL eiligenkreuzerhof hönlaterngasse 5	*Visit of the chapel by appointment (Tel. 513 18 91).*	◆ A B4 ▲ 153
RBERT-VON-KARAJAN-CENTRUM rntnerring 4 l. 506 00 100	*Open Tue., Thur.–Fri. 2–6pm, Wed. 2–8pm, Sat. noon–4pm. Works by the famous conductor and temporary exhibitions.*	◆ A D2-3
RMES VILLA rmesvilla inzer Tiergarten trance on Hermesstrasse l. 804 13 24	*Open Apr.–Sep. 10am–6pm, Oct.–Mar. 9am–4.30pm. Closed Mon.*	
ETZING SUBWAY STATION adtbahn Hofpavillon hönbrunner Schloßstraße l. 877 15 71	*Open Tue.–Sun. 1.30–4.30pm.*	▲ 286
OUSE OF JOHANN STRAUSS hann-Strauss-Gedenkstätte aterstrasse 54 l. 214 01 21	*Open Tue.–Sun. 9am–12.15pm and 1–4.30pm.*	◆ A B4 ▲ 264
OUSE OF THE GREAT JORDAN aus zum grossen Jordan denplatz	*Not open to the public.*	◆ A B2 ▲ 169
OUSE OF THE HEILIGENSTADT STAMENT (BEETHOVEN'S) eiligenstädter-Testament-Haus obusgasse 6 l. 37 54 08	*Open Tue.–Sun. 9am–12.15pm and 1–4.30pm.*	▲ 298
OUSE OF THE THREE MAIDENS reimäderlhaus hreyvogelgasse	*Not open to the public.*	◆ A B1 ▲ 166
NDERTWASSER'S HOUSE ndertwasserhaus orner of Kögelgasse d Löwengasse	*Not open to the public.*	▲ 228
PERIAL FURNITURE COLLECTION iserliches Hofmobiliendepot ndreasgasse 7 l. 524 33 570	*Open daily 9am–5pm. Restored imperial furniture, from Biedermeier to Jugenstil.*	◆ A C2
PERIAL TREASURY hatzkammer ofburg, Schweizerhof l. 533 79 31	*Open 10am–6pm. Closed Tue.*	◆ A C1 ▲ 180
SUIT CHURCH suitenkirche ckerstrasse	*Open daily 7am–8pm.*	◆ A C3 ▲ 151
WISH MUSEUM THE CITY OF VIENNA disches Museum r Stadt Wien lais Eskeles orotheergasse 11 l. 535 04 31	*Open 10am–6pm, late-night opening Thur. 10am–9pm. Closed Sat.*	◆ A C2
AISER'S APARTMENTS LVER AND CHINA COLLECTIONS aiserappartements ofsilber und Tafelkammer ichaelerplatz l. 533 75 70	*Open daily 9am–5pm.*	◆ A C2 ▲ 178
NST-FORUM eyung 8 l. 532 06 44	*Open daily 10am–6pm, late-night opening Wed. 10am–9pm.*	◆ A B2 ▲ 165
NSTHALLE arlsplatz	*Open daily 10am–6pm, late-night opening Thur. 10am–10pm.*	◆ B A2
CHTENSTEIN PALACE ndhaus errengasse	*Not open to the public.*	◆ E C3 ▲ 160

LOOSHAUS Michaelerplatz	*Not open to the public.*
LOWER AUSTRIA STATE MUSEUM *Niederösterreichisches* *Landesmuseum* Herrengasse 9 Tel. 531 10-3505	*Open Tue.–Fri. 9am–5pm, Sat. noon–5pm,* *Sun. 9.30am–1pm.*
MÄRKLEIN HOUSE *Märkleinisches Haus* Am Hof	*Not open to the public.*
MUSEUM OF APPLIED ARTS *Österreichisches Museum* *für Angewandte Kunst* Stubenring 5 Tel. 711 36-0	*Open 10am–6pm,* *late-night opening Thur. 10am–9pm.* *Closed Mon.*
MUSEUM OF AUSTRIAN **FOLKLORE** *Österreichisches Museum* *für Volkskunde* Laudongasse 15–19 Tel. 406 89 05	*Open Tue.–Fri. 9am–5pm,* *Sat. 9am–noon and Sun. 9am–1pm.*
MUSEUM OF BAROQUE ART *Österreichisches Barockmuseum* Rennweg 6a Unteres Belvedere (Lower Belvedere) Tel. 795 57 134	*Open Tue.–Sun. 10am–5pm.*
MUSEUM OF ETHNOGRAPHY *Museum für Völkerkunde* Neue Burg, Heldenplatz Tel. 534 300	*Open 10am–4pm.* *Closed Tue.*
MUSEUM OF MAPS AND GLOBES *Globenmuseum* Nationalbibliothek Josefsplatz 1, 3rd floor Tel. 534 10 297	*Open Mon.–Wed. and Fri. 11am–noon,* *Thur. 2–3pm. Closed Sat.–Sun.*
MUSEUM OF MEDIEVAL ART *Museum mittelalterlicher* *österreichischer Kunst* Rennweg 6a Unteres Belvedere (Lower Belvedere) Tel. 795 57 134	*Open Tue.–Sun. 10am–5pm.*
MUSEUM OF MILITARY HISTORY *Heeresgeschichtliches Museum* Arsenalstrasse Bat.18 Tel. 795 61 0	*Open 10am–5pm.* *Closed Fri.*
MUSEUM OF MODERN ART *Museum Moderner Kunst* *Fondation Ludwig* Liechtenstein Palace Fürstengasse 1 Tel. 317 69 00	*Due to reopen on Dec. 1, 2001.*
MUSEUM OF MOVING PICTURES *Filmmuseum* Albertina Augustinerstrasse 1 Tel. 533 70 54-0	*Showing of films Oct.–May, Mon.–Sat. 6pm and* *8pm.*
MUSEUM OF PATHOLOGY **AND ANATOMY** *Pathologisch-anatomisches* *Bundesmuseum* Altes Allgemeines Krankenhaus Narrentum Alser Strasse 4, Spitalgasse 2 Tel. 406 86 72	*Open Wed. 3–8pm, Thur. 8–11am,* *1st Sat. of the month 10am–1pm.* *Closed public hols.*
MUSEUM OF SURGERY **AND MEDECINE** *Josephinum* Währingerstrasse 25/1 Tel. 427 76 34 01	*Open 9am–3pm.* *Closed Sat.–Sun. and public hols.*

JSEUM OF TEDDY BEARS *iener Teddybärenmuseum* *rahtgasse 3* l. 533 47 55	Open Mon.–Sat. 10am–6pm and Sun. 2–6pm.	◆ A B2
USEUM OF THE HISTORY VIENNA *storisches Museum* *er Stadt Wien* *arlsplatz* l. 505 87 47 - 84 021	Open Tue.–Sun. 9am–6pm.	◆ B A2 ▲ 241
ATURAL HISTORY MUSEUM *aturhistorisches Museum* *aria-Theresien-Platz* *urgring 7 (2nd floor)* l. 521 77-0	Open 9am–6.30pm, late-night opening Wed. 9am–9pm. Closed Tue.	◆ A D1 ▲ 207
D MUSICAL INSTRUMENTS OLLECTION *mmlung Alter* *usikinstrumente* *eue Burg, Heldenplatz* l. 525 24 471	Open 10am–6pm. Closed Tue.	◆ A D1-2 ▲ 186
LACE CHAPEL *urgkapelle* *ofburg Schweizerhof* l. 533 99 2771	Guided tours: mid Sep.–end June Mon.–Thur. 11am–3pm, Fri. 11am–1pm. Mass: Jan.–June and Sep.–Dec. Sun. 9.15am, with the Vienna Boys Choir (reservations compulsory: fax 533 9927 75)	◆ A C2 ▲ 183
LLAVICINI PALACE *rmanent "Dali" exhibition* *sefsplatz 5* l. 512 25 49	Open daily 10am–6pm.	◆ A C2 ▲ 192
ARLIAMENT *arlament or Reichsrat* *r.-Karl-Renner-Ring 3* l. 401 10 2211	Guided tours Mon.–Fri. (except when in session) at 11am and 3pm. In July–Aug. additional visits at 9am, 10am, 11am, 1pm, 2pm and 3pm.	◆ A BC1 ▲ 205
SQUALATI HOUSE *eethovenhaus-Pasqualatihaus* *ölker Bastei 8* l. 535 89 05	Open Tue.–Sun. 9am–12.15pm and 1–4.30pm.	◆ A B1 ▲ 166
ARIST CHURCH *aristenkirche* *dok-Fink-Platz*	Open daily 7am–6pm.	◆ D B3 ▲ 290
ANETARIUM *ater, Hauptallee* l. 729 54 94	Guided tours Sun. 3pm, 5pm and by appointment. Closed Aug. 12–Sep. 13.	◆ A A4 ▲ 268
ORCIA PALACE *errengasse*	Not open to the public.	◆ E C3 ▲ 160
ATER MUSEUM *atermuseum* *ater Hauptallee* l. 726 76 83	Open Tue.–Fri. 9am–12.15pm and 1–4.30pm, Sat.–Sun. and public hols. 2–6.30pm.	◆ A A4 ▲ 268
IVATE MUSEUM OF IE PAINTER ERNST FUCHS *nst Fuchs Privatmuseum* *lla Otto Wagner 1* *üttelbergstrasse 26* l. 914 85 75 14	Open Tue.–Fri. 10am–4pm.	
SIDENCE OF THE ABBOTS MELK CHAPEL *elker Hof*	Not open to the public.	◆ A B1 ▲ 166
OMAN REMAINS *ömische Baureste am Hof* *m Hof 9* l. 505 87 47-84 016	Open Sat.–Sun. and public hols. 11am–1pm.	◆ A B2 ▲ 167
OMAN REMAINS *omische Ruinen* *nter dem Hohen Markt* *oher Markt 3* l. 535 56 06	Open Tue.–Sun. 9am–12.15pm and 1–4.30pm.	◆ A B3 ▲ 155
MARK CEMETERY *nkt-Marxer-Friedhof* *berstrasse 6–8*	Open June–Aug. 7am–7pm, Sep.–May 7am–6pm.	◆ B B4 ▲ 262

◆ PLACES TO VISIT

ST STEPHEN'S CATHEDRAL *Stephansdom* Stephansplatz Tel. 515 52 536	CATHEDRAL: *guided tour Mon.–Sat. 10.30am, 3pm; Sun. and public hols. 3pm, and Sat. at 7pm in July–Aug.* CATACOMBS: *guided tours Mon.–Sat. 10am, 11am, 11.30am, 2pm, 2.30pm, 3.30pm, 4pm, 4.30pm; Sun. and public hols. 2pm, 2.30pm, 3.30pm, 4pm, 4.30pm.* SOUTH TOWER: *open daily 9am–5.30pm.* NORTH TOWER (PUMMERIN): *elevator: Apr.–Sep. 9am–6pm; Oct.–Mar. 8am–5pm.* HIGH MASS: *Sun. and public hols. at 10am.*
SCHÖNBRUNN PALACE AND PARK *Schloss Schönbrunn* Schönbrunner-Schloss-Strasse Tel. 811 13 238	*Open Apr.–Oct. daily 8.30am–5pm; Nov.–Mar. daily 8.30am–4.30pm.*
SCHUBERT MUSEUM (BIRTHPLACE) *Schubert-Museum* Nussdorfertrasse 54 Tel. 317 36 01	*Open Tue.–Sun. 9am–12.15pm and 1–4.30pm.*
SCHUBERT'S HOUSE *Schuberts Sterbezimmer* Kettenbrückengasse 6 Tel. 581 6730	*Open Tue.–Sun. 1.30–4.30pm.*
SCOTTISH CHURCH *Schottenkirche* Freyung	*Open daily 6am–8pm.*
SCOTTISH MONASTERY *Schottenstift* Pinakothek, Freyung 6 Tel. 534 98 600	*Open Thur.–Sat. 10am–5pm, Sun. noon–5pm.*
SECESSION PAVILION *Secession* Friedrichstrasse 12 Tel. 587 53 07	*Open Tue.–Fri. 10am–6pm, Sat.–Sun. and public hols. 10am–4pm. Closed Mon.*
SERVITE CHURCH *Servitenkirche* Alsergrund	*Open daily 9am–6pm.*
SIGMUND FREUD MUSEUM *Sigmund-Freud-Museum* Berggasse 19 Tel. 319 15 96	*Open daily July–Sep. 9am–6pm, Oct.–June 9am–4pm.*
SPANISH RIDING SCHOOL *Spanische Reitschule* Hofburg Fax 535 01 86	*Times of shows may vary. Check the* Spanische Reitschule Wiener Sängerknaben *board updated by the Spanish Riding School.*
SPANISH RIDING SCHOOL'S MUSEUM *Lipizzanermuseum* Stallburg/Hofburg Reitschulgasse 2 Tel. 526 41 84 30	*Open daily 9am–6pm. Guided tours daily at 11am and by prior arrangement.*
STARHEMBERG PALACE Minoritenplatz	*Not open to the public.*
SUBWAY PAVILIONS *Station Karlsplatz*	*Open Apr.–Oct. Tue.–Sun. 1.30–4.30pm.*
SYNAGOGUE Seitenstettengasse 4 Tel. 531 04 15	*Guided tour by appointment.*
TEUTONIC KNIGHTS' TREASURY *Schatzkammer des Deutschen Ordens* Singerstrasse 7 Tel. 512 10 65	*Open Nov.–Apr. Mon. and Thur. 10am–noon, Wed. and Fri. 3–5pm, Sat. 10am–noon and 3–5pm; May–Oct. Mon., Thur.–Sun. 10am–noon, Wed., Fri.–Sat. 3–5pm.*
THEATER MUSEUM (COLLECTION OF SKETCHES, PHOTOGRAPHS, THEATER SETS AND COSTUMES) *Theatermuseum* Lobkowitzplatz 2 Tel. 512 88 000	*Open Tue.–Sun. 10am–5pm, late-night opening Wed. 10am–9pm.*
VIENNA STATE OPERA *Staatsoper* Opernring 2 Tel. 514 44-2613	*Guided tour by appointment.*

TIVE CHURCH *tivkirche* *oseveltplatz*	*Open daily 7am–8pm.*	◆ **D** A4 ▲ *202*
NTER PALACE OF PRINCE EUGENE *interpalais des Prinz Eugen* *mmelpfortgasse*	*Not open to the public.*	◆ **A** C3 ▲ *147*
NTER PALACE OF THE **NCES OF LIECHTENSTEIN** *adtpalais Liechtenstein* *nkgasse*	*Not open to the public.*	◆ **A** C1 ▲ *161*
O *rgarten Schönbrunn* *nönbrunner Schlosspark* *trance Hietzinger Tor* . 877 92 940	*Open Nov.–Jan. daily 9am–4.30pm;* *Feb. and Oct. 9am–5pm; Mar. 9am–5.30pm;* *Apr. 9am–6pm, May–Sep. 9am–6.30pm.*	◆ **C** D1 ▲ *285*

RINZING

INZING CEMETARY *inzinger Friedhof* den Langen Lüssen 33	*Open Nov.–Feb. 8am–5pm, Mar.–Apr. 7am–6pm,* *May–Aug. 7am–7pm, Sep.–Oct. 7am–6pm*	▲ *301*

HLENBERG

URCH OF ST JOSEPH *hlenbergkirche*	*Open daily 9am–6pm.*	▲ *301*

JSSDORF

ANZ LEHÁR'S CASTLE *hár-Schikander-Schlössl* *ackhohergasse 18* . 318 54 16	*Visits by appointment.*	▲ *299*

◆ BIBLIOGRAPHY

ESSENTIAL READING

◆ CRANKSHAW (E.): *Vienna, the Image of a Culture in Decline*, London and New York, 1938
◆ GRIEBEN GUIDEBOOKS, NO 199: *Vienna and Its Environs*, Vienna, many editions
◆ LEHMAN (J.) and BASSET (R.): *Vienna, a Traveller's Companion*, London, 1988
◆ MICHELIN (PUB): *Austria*, English edition
◆ MEHLING (F .N.): *Austria, Phaidon Cultural Guides*, London, 1985
◆ RICKETT (R.): *A Brief Survey of Austrian History*, London, 1973

GENERAL BOOKS AND GUIDES

◆ BAREA (I.): *Vienna, Legend and Reality*, London, 1992
◆ CERMAK (A.): *Vienna - A Book of Photographs*, London, 1963
◆ COOK (T.) (PUB): *Traveller's Guide to Venice*, London, 1993
◆ FUERSTEIN (G.): *Vienna Past and Present*, Vienna, 1976
◆ HOOTZ (R.): *Wien*, Munich and Berlin, 1968
◆ MAHAN (J.A.): *Vienna Yesterday and Today*, Vienna, 1928
◆ MCGUIGAN (D.): *Vienna Today, a Complete Guide*, New York, 1955
◆ NEUWIRTH (W.), KÖLBEL (A.) AND AUBÖCK (M.) : *Die Wiener Porzellan Manufaktur Augarten*, Vienna, 1992
◆ ROBERTSON (I.): *Austria, Blue Guides*, London, 1992
◆ SCHMIED (W.) : *Der Zeicher Alfred Kubin*, éditions Residenz, Salzbourg, 1967
◆ VESTNER (H.): *Vienna, Insight Cityguides*, London 1989
◆ WERKNER (P.): *Austrian Expressionism*, éditions Palo Alto, California, 1993
◆ WILLIAMSON (A.): *The Lure of Vienna*, London, 1926

ART AND ARCHITECTURE

◆ ACADEMY EDITIONS (pub): *Gustav Klimt*, London, 1976
◆ AURENHAMMER (H.): *Fischer von Erlach*, London, 1973
◆ BORSI (F.) and GODOLI (E.): *Vienna 1900, Architecture and Design*, London, 1986
◆ BRANDSTATTER (C):

Vienna, éditions Molden, Vienna, 1981
◆ BULTMAN (B): *Oskar Kokoschka*, New York, 1961
◆ BUXBAUM (G.): *Mode aus Wien*, éditions Residenz, Salzburg, 1986
◆ COMINI (A.): *Edon Schiele*, London, 1974
◆ GRIESSMAIER (V.): *Austria, Her Landscape and Her Art*, Vienna, 1950
◆ HANSEN (T.): *Wiener Werkstatte*, éditions Brandstatter, Vienna, 1984
◆ HAUSNER (E.): *Wien*, éditions Jugend und Volk, Vienna-Munich, 1975
◆ HOFFMANN (E.): *Kokoschka, Life and Work*, London, 1947
◆ HURLIMANN (M.): *Vienna*, London, 1970
◆ KALLIER (J.): *Viennese Design and the Wiener Werkstatte*, London, 1986
◆ KOMAREK (R.): *Wien*, Éditions Kremayer and Scheriau, Vienna, 1990
◆ KRUCKENHAUSER (S.): *Heritage of Beauty*, Innsbruck, 1965
◆ MANG (K. and E.): *Viennese Architecture, 1860-1930 in Drawings*, New York, 1979
◆ MANG (K.): *Thonet Bugholzmobel*, éditions Brandstatter, Vienna, 1982
◆ MARTINEK (T.): *Kaffeehauser in Wien*, éditions Falter, Vienna
◆ MUNZ (L.) and KUNSTLER (G.): *Adolf Loos, Pioneer of Modern Architecture*, London, 1966
◆ POWELL (N.): *The Sacred Spring, the Arts in Vienna, 1898-1918*, London, 1974
◆ PRINTARIC (V.H.): *Vienna 1900, the Architecture of Otto Wagner*, London, 1989
◆ VERGO (R.): *Art in Vienna, 1898-1918: Klimt, Kokoschka, Schiele and Their Contemporaries*, London, 1975
◆ *Vienna in the Age of Schubert, the Biedermeier Interior*, exhibition catalogue, London, 1979
◆ WEBER (H.): *Wien*, editions Brandstatter, Vienna-Munich, 1984
◆ WEISSENBERGER (R.): *Vienna in the Biedermeier Era, 1815-1848*, New York, 1986
◆ WEISSENBERGER (R.): *Vienna Secession*, London, 1977
◆ WILSON (S.): *Egon Schiele*, Oxford, 1980
◆ WINGLER (H.M.):

Oskar Kokoschka, the Work of the Painter, London, 1962

HISTORY

◆ BAGGER (E.): *Francis Joseph*, New York, 1927
◆ CRANKSHAW (E.): *Maria Theresa*, London, 1989
◆ CRANKSHAW (E.): *The Fall of the House of Hapsburg*, London, 1963
◆ HASLIP (J.): *The Emperor and the Actress*, London, 1982
◆ JOHNSTON (W.H.): *Vienna, the Golden Age, 1815-1914*, New York, 1981
◆ LEVETUS (A.S.): *Imperial Vienna*, London and New York, 1905
◆ LEHNE (I.) and JOHNSON (L.): *Vienna, the Past in the Present*, Vienna, 1985
◆ LONYAY (C.): *Rudolf, the Tragedy of Mayerling*, London, 1950
◆ MUSULIN (S.): *Vienna in the Age of Metternich*, London, 1975
◆ REDLICH (O.): *Emperor Francis Joseph of Austria*, London, 1929
◆ RUMBOLD (SIR H.): *The Austrian Court in the Nineteenth Century*, London, 1909
◆ SPEIL (H.): *Vienna's Golden Autumn, 1866-1938*, London, 1987
◆ TAYLOR (A.J.P.): *The Hapsburg Monarchy*, Harmondsworth, 1976
◆ TSCHUPPIK (K.): *The Reign of the Emperor Franz Joseph*, 1930

HISTORY OF IDEAS

◆ BARTLEY (W. W.): *Wittgenstein*, London, 1974
◆ BROME (V.): *Freud*, London, 1984
◆ CLARK (R. W.): *Freud*, London, 1980
◆ FRANCIS (M.) (ED.): *The Viennese Enlightenment*, London, 1985
◆ GAL (H.): *The Golden Age of Vienna*, New York, 1948
◆ GRIFFIN (R.A.): *High Baroque Culture and Theatre in Vienna*, New York, 1972
◆ GRIMSTAD (K.): *Masks of the Prophet: the Theatrical World of Karl Kraus*, Toronto and London, 1982
◆ JANIK (A.) and TOULMIN (S.): *Wittgenstein's Vienna*, London, 1973
◆ JONES (E.): *The Life and Times of Sigmund Freud*, London, 1962

◆ MCGUINESS (B.) (ed.) *Wittgenstein and His Times*, Oxford, 1982
◆ PEARS (D.): *Wittgenstein*, London 1971
◆ RHEES (R.) (ed.): *Ludwig Wittgenstein*, Oxford, 1981
◆ SZASZ (T.): *Karl Kraus and the Soul Doctor*, London, 1977
◆ TIMMS (E.): *Karl Kraus Apocalyptic Satirist: Culture and Catastrophe in Habsburg Vienna*, New Haven and London, 1986
◆ WIJDEVELD (P.): *Ludwig Wittgenstein Architect*, London, 1994
◆ YATES (W.E.) and MCKENZIE (J.R.P.): *Viennese Popular Theatre*, Exeter, 1985
◆ ZWEIG (S.): *The World of Yesterday* London 1943

LITERATURE

◆ BRIGHT (R.): *Travel from Vienna in the Year 1814*, Edinburgh and London, 1818
◆ CASANOVA (G.): *History of My Life*, Eng trans. London, 1970 (especially Volume 1)
◆ DODERER (H. VON): *The Waterfalls of Slu* London, 1966
◆ GREENE (G.): *The Third Man*, London, 1950
◆ KRAUS (K.): *In The Great Times*, Manchester, 1984
◆ KRAUS (K.): *Half-Truths and One-and-half Truths,* Manches 1986
◆ MUSIL (R.): *The Man without Qualities*, London, 1953
◆ SCHNITZLER (A.): *Vienna 1900, Games with Love and Death* London, 1985
◆ SCHNITZLER (A.):*My Youth in Vienna*, London, 1971
◆ TROLLOPE (F.): *Vienn and the Austrians*, London, 1838
◆ WORTLEY-MONTAGU (LADY M.): *Letters* (many editions)

MUSIC

◆ ABRAHAM (G.) (ed.): *Schubert, A Symposium*, London 1947
◆ANDERSON (E.) (ed. and trans.): *The Letter of Beethoven*, London 1961
◆ BORY (R.): *Ludwig Beethoven, His Life a His Work in Pictures,* New York, 1960
◆ BRION (M.): *Daily Li in the Vienna of Moz and Schubert,* Lond

...1
ROWN (M.J.E.):
...ubert, a Critical
...graphy, London
...8

◆ JURNEY (C.): Musical
...rs in Europe, 1772
... Scholes, London,
...9

...ARNER (M.): Alban
...g, London, 1975
...OOPER (M.):
...ethoven, the Last
...cade, 1817-1827,
...don, 1970

A PONTE (L.):
...moirs, New York,
...9 (reprinted)
...NDLER (F.): Vienna,
...uide to its Music
...d Musicians,
...tland, Oregon,
...9

...LOWER (N.): Franz
...ubert, the Man and
... Circle, London,
...8

...RAF (M.): Legend of
...usical City, New
...k, 1945

...AMBURGER (M.) (ed.
...trans.): Beethoven:
...ers, Journals and
...versations, London,
...6

...ANSLICK (E.):
...nna's Golden Years
...Music, 1850-1900,
...don, 1951

...UGHES (R.) (ed.): A
...zart Pilgrimage,
...ng the Travel Diaries
...incent and Mary
...velle, London, 1955

...ELLY (M.):
...miniscences,
...don, 1826

...ANDON (H.C.R.):
...zart and Vienna,
...don, 1991

...ANDON (H.C.R.):
...zart, the Golden
...rs, London, 1989

...ANDON (H.C.R.):
...1, Mozart's Last
...r, London and New
...k, 1988

...ANDON (H.C.R.):
...ays in the Viennese
...ssical Style, London,
...0

...ITTAG (E.): The
...nna Philharmonic,
...nna, 1954

...OLDENHAUER (H.):
...on von Webern,
...ronicles of His Life
...d Works, London,
... New York, 1978

...OZART (W.A.):
...ers (many editions)

...EWLIN (D.): Bruckner,
...hler, Schoenberg,
...w York, 1947

...AYNE (A.):
...hoenberg, London,
...8

...EDLICH (H.): Alban
...rg, the Man and His
...sic, London, 1951

...EICH (W.): Alban
...rg, London, 1965

...ICKETT (R.): Music
...d Musicians in
...nna, London, 1973

...ELLESZ (E.): Arnold
Schoenberg, London,
1925

◆ WIESMAN (S.) (ed.):
Gustav Mahler in
Vienna, New York, 1976

◆ WILDGANS (F.): Anton
Webern, London, 1966

MISCELLANEOUS

◆ BRAUNEIS and
ROSENER: Die
Umgebumgen Wiens,
editions P. Zsolnay,
Vienna, 1978

◆ COLLECTIF: Wien
Wirklich, editions
Gesellschaftskritik,
Vienna, 1992

◆ GRUNAUER (G.), KISLER
(A.) and FRIEDMAN
(D.F.): Viennese
Cuisine, the New
Approach, London,
1989

◆ SINHUBER (B.F.): Das
Grosse Buch vom
Wiener Heuriger,
editions Orac Pietsch,
Vienna, 1980

ACKNOWLEDGEMENTS

**The Architectural
Review**: Excerpt from
Mackintosh and Vienna,
article by E. Seckler
published in the
Architectural Review,
London, in 1967.
Reprinted by
permission of the
Architectural Review,
London.

Faber & Faber:
Excerpt from Nightwood
by Djuna Barnes,
published by Faber &
Faber in 1958.
Reprinted by
permission of Faber &
Faber Ltd, London.

**J.M. Dent & Sons
Ltd**: Diary entry of
Franz Schubert on
June 14, 1816, from
Schubert – A
Documentary
Biography by Otto Eric
Deutsch, translated by
Eric Blom (J. M. Dent &
Sons, London 1946).
Reprinted by
permission of J. M. Dent
& Sons Ltd.

**Northern Illinois
University Press**:
Excerpt from The Travel
Diary of Peter Tolstoi,
translated by Max J.
Okenfuss, copyright ©
1987 by Northern
Illinois University
Press. Reprinted by
permission of Northern
Illinois University
Press.

**Penguin Books
USA, Inc**: Excerpt
from March 20, 1891,
letter of Anton Chekhov
from The Letters of
Anton Chekhov, by
Anton Chekhov,
translated by Avrahm
Yarmolinsky, translation
copyright © 1973 by
Avrahm Yarmolinsky,
copyright © 1947, 1968
by the Viking Press.
Reprinted by
permission of Viking
Penguin, a division of
Penguin Books USA,
Inc.

**Penguin Books
USA, Inc. and John
Murray (Publishers)
Ltd**: Excerpt from
A Time of Gifts by
Patrick Leigh Fermor.
Copyright © 1977 by
Patrick Leigh Fermor.
Rights outside the
U.S. administered by
John Murray
(Publishers) Ltd,
London. Reprinted by
permission of Viking
Penguin, a division of
Penguin Books USA,
Inc., and John Murray
(Publishers) Ltd.

**Routledge and
Kegan Paul**: Excerpt
from Nov. 10, 1822,
letter from Washington
Irving to his sister from
The Travellers'
Dictionary of Quotation,
edited by Peter Yapp
(1983). Reprinted by
permission.

Vanguard Press:
Excerpt from Sigmund
Freud: Father and Man
by Martin Freud,
copyright © 1958 by
Vanguard Press, Inc.
Reprinted by
permission of Vanguard
Press, a division of
Random House, Inc.

**W.W. Norton & Co.,
Inc**: Excerpts from
letters of August 22,
1781, and May 3, 1783,
from Mozart to his
father, and excerpt from
letter of December 5,
1791, from Sophie
Haibel to Georg
Nikolaus von Nissen
from The Letters of
Mozart and His Family,
3rd Edition, edited by
Emily Anderson,
copyright © 1966, 1985,
1989 by The Executors
of the late Miss Emily
Anderson. Reprinted by
permission of W. W.
Norton & Co., Inc.

LIST OF ILLUSTRATIONS ◆

◆ LIST OF ILLUSTRATIONS

◆ LIST OF ILLUSTRATIONS

◆ INDEX

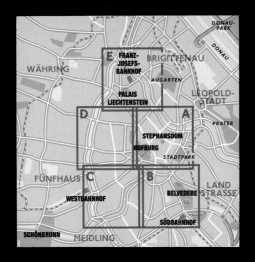

Map section

Key

▦	Freeway
▦	Freeway under construction
▬	Expressway
▤	Main road
▭	Railroad
Ⓤ	Subway line
⚡	Railraod
✚	Hospital
✈	Airport

A

1 2

AUGA
BRÜ

FUNDAMT

SIGMUND-FREUD-
HAUS

ROSSAUER KASERNE

SCHOTTE

WASA
GASSE

BERGGASSE

LIECHTENSTEIN-

TÜRKENSTRASSE

HÖRLGASSE

Schlick-
platz

Deutsch-
meister-
platz

FRAN-

RINGTURM

WÄHRINGERSTRASSE

HÖRLGASSE

KOLINGASSE

STR.

MARIA-THERESIEN-STRASSE

SCHOTTENRING

GONZAGAGASSE

ESSLING GASSE

NEUTORGASSE

VOTIVKIRCHE

BÖRSE

BÖRSEGASSE

SIGMUND-FREUD-
PARK

SCHOTTENTOR-
-UNIVERSITÄT

WIPPLINGERSTRASSE

Börse-
platz

A

UNIVERSITÄTSSTR.

JURISTISCHE
FAKULTÄT

BÖRSEGASSE

HELFERSTORFERSTRASSE

GASSE

Concordia-
platz

HEINR

REICHSRATSSTRASSE

UNIVERSITÄT

SCHOTTENGASSE

RENN-

SAL

MÖLKER
BASTEI

WIPPLINGERSTRA

PASQUALATI-
HAUS

MARIA
AM GEST

RATHAUS-

SCHOTTEN-
KIRCHE

PALAIS
SCHÖNBORN-
BATTHYÁNY

TEINFALTSTRASSE

TIEFER GRABEN

BÜRGERLICHES
ZEUGHAUS

BÖHMI
HOFKA

LÖWELSTRASSE

PALAIS
KINSKY

PALAIS
HARRACH

FREYUNG

AM HOF

Rathaus-
platz

BANKGASSE

HERRENGASSE

PALAIS
FERSTEL

NAGLERGASSE

BOGNERGASSE

KIRCHE
AM HOF

KURRENT

TUCHLAU

BURGTHEATER

PALAIS
STARHEMBERG

WALLNERSTRASSE

BR

B

DR.-KARL-LUEGERRING

NIEDERÖSTERR.
LANDHAUS

PALAIS
ESTERHÁZY

Peters-
platz

PARK

STADTPALAIS
LIECHTENSTEIN

MINORITENKIRCHE

HERRENGASSE

PETERS-
KIRCHE

GRABEN

LÖWELSTRASSE

BUNDESKANZLERAMT

LOOSHAUS

KOHLMARKT

STEPHAN

PARLAMENT

Ballhaus-
platz

Michaeler-
platz

MICHAELER-
KIRCHE

HABSBURGERGASSE

BRÄUNERSTRASSE

ANKERHAUS

DR.-K.-RENNERRING

VOLKSGARTEN

HOFBURG

STALLBURG

SPIEGELGASSE

SEILERGASSE

DOROTHEERGASSE

ERZHERZOG-KARL-
-DENKMAL

Hel/denplatz

Josefs-
platz

DOROTHEUM

Neue
Mark

BELLARIASTR.

BURGRING

PRINZ-EUGEN-
-DENKMAL

BURGTOR

NATIONAL
BIBLIOTHEK

AUGUSTINER-
KIRCHE

AUGUSTINERSTRASSE

PALAIS
LOBKOWITZ

KAPUZINER-
KIRCHE

C

NATURHISTORISCHES
MUSEUMS

NEUE HOLFBURG

ALBERTINA

STRASSE

KI

Maria-Theresien-
-Platz

PALMENHAUS

Albertinaplatz

PHILHARMO WA

Museums-
platz

KUNSTHISTORISCHES
MUSEUM

BURGGARTEN

NIKERSTR

BABENBERGERSTR.

STAATSOPER

MA

MUSEUMS-
QUARTIER

BABENBERGERSTR.

OPERNRING

OPERNGASSE

Opern-
Passage

GETREIDEMARKT

ESCHENBACHG.

ELISABETHSTRASSE

Schiller-
platz

AKADEMIE
DER BILDENDEN
KÜNSTE

OPERNGASSE

KÄRNTNER-

KÄRN

D

1 2

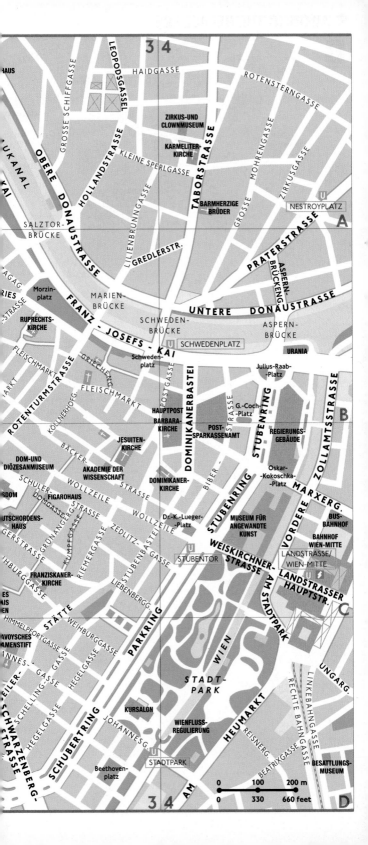

B

1 2

GETREIDEMARKT

Schiller-platz

AKADEMIE DER BILDENDEN KÜNSTE

OPERN-GASSE

KÄRNTNER STRASSE

KÄRNTNERR

SECESSION

FRIEDRICHSTR.

AKADEMIE-STRASSE

HANDELS-AKADEMIE

KÜNSTLER-HAUS

MUSIK-VEREINSGEBÄ

LEHÁRGASSE

MILLÖCKER-GASSE

THEATER AN DER WIEN

U
KARLSPLATZ

LOTHRINGERSTRAS

GRABDIGASSE

LINKE WIENZEILE

RECHTE WIENZEILE

Kühn-platz

BIBLIOTHEK DER TECHN. UNIV.

HAUPTSTRASSE

Karlsplatz

HISTORISCHES MUSEUM DER STADT WIEN

A

OPERNGASSE

WIEDNER

Rilke-platz

PANIGLGASSE

TECHNISCHE UNIVERSITÄT

KARLS-GASSE

KARLSKIRCHE

FRAN BO

SCHIKGASSE

SCHLEIFMÜHLGASSE

FRANKENBERG-GASSE

GUSSHAUSSTRASSE

SCHWIN

MÜHL-GASSE

SCHIKANEDERG.

PRESSGASSE

PAULANERGASSE

TECHNISCHE UNIVERSITÄT

WOHLL

ARGENTINIERS

HEUMÜHLG.

WAAGGASSE

MOZARTGASSE

MARGARETENSTRASSE

SCHÄFFERGASSE

RIENÖSSLGASSE

FLORAGASSE

TAUBSTUMMENG.

FUNKHAUS

B

KLEINE NEUGASSE

GROSSE NEUGASSE

FLEISCHMANN-GASSE

WIEDNER HAUPTSTRASSE

U
TAUBSTUMMENGASSE

Brahms-platz

SCHLÜSSELG.

FAVORITENSTRASSE

KRONGASSE

KLAGBAUMGASSE

MAYERHOFGASSE

THERESIANUM

MITTERSTEIG

LAMBRECHTG.

SCHAUMBURGERGASSE

GRAF-WALTERGASSE

THERESIANU

PHORUSGASSE

WIEDEN

BELVE

ZIEGELOFENG.

SCHÖNBURG.

STARHEMBERGGASSE

FAVORITENSTRASSE

KARO

C

HARTMANNGASSE

ST.-THEKLA--KIRCHE

JOHANN-

REINERGASSE

HARTMANN-SPITAL

HARTMANN-PARK

WIEDNER HAUPTSTRASSE

TRAPPELG.

STRASSE

SCHÖNBURGSTRASSE

PALAIS SCHÖNBURG--HARTENSTEIN

WE

RAINERGASSE

STRAUSS-

KOLSCHITZKY-GASSE

SCHELLEIN-

Süd P

SÜDTIROLE

BLECHTURM-GASSE

SCHÖNBURG-GASSE

SCHELLEINGASSE

ANZENGRUBERG.

KRIEHUBERGASSE

WIEDNER GÜRTEL

D

1 2

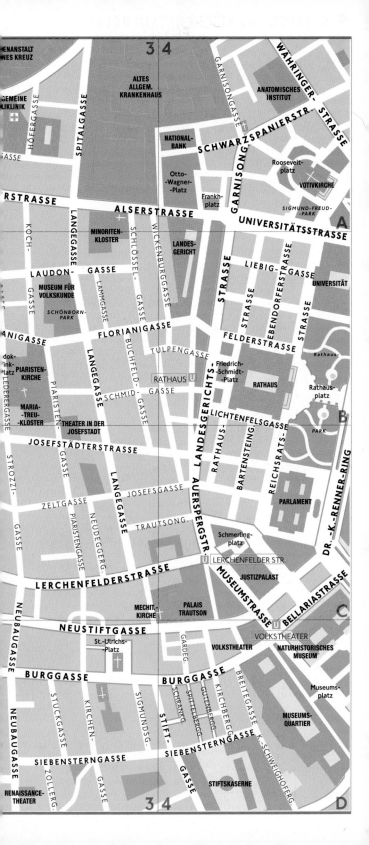

◆ AROUND THE LIECHENSTEIN PALACE

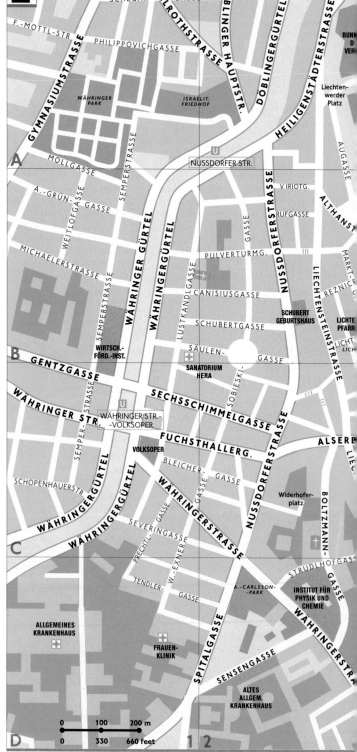

E

SCHEGAR- GASSE 1 2 DÖBLINGER SOMMERG. SPIT

F.-MOTTL-STR

PHILIPPOVICHGASSE

BILLROTHSTRASSE DÖBLINGER HAUPTSTR.

DÖBLINGERGÜRTEL

HEILIGENSTÄDTERSTRASSE

BUNN
D
VER

GYMNASIUMSTRASSE

WÄHRINGER
PARK

ISRAELIT.
FRIEDHOF

Liechten-
werder
Platz

AUGASSE

MOLLGASSE

A NUSSDORFER STR.

ALTHANST

A.-GRÜN- GASSE

WEITLOFGASSE

SEMPERSTRASSE

V.IRIOTG.

RUFGASSE

NUSSDORFERSTRASSE

LIECHTENSTEINSTRASSE

MICHAELERSTRASSE

WÄHRINGER GÜRTEL

WÄHRINGERGÜRTEL

GASSE

PULVERTURMG.

MARKT-

REZNICE

CANISIUSGASSE

LUSTKANDLGASSE

SCHUBERTGASSE

SCHUBERT
GEBURTSHAUS

LICHTE
PFARR

LICHT
LICH

SEMPERSTRASSE

WIRTSCH.-
FÖRD.-INST.

SÄULEN-

GASSE

SOBIESKI-

B GENTZGASSE

SANATORIUM
HERA

WÄHRINGER STR.

SECHSSCHIMMELGASSE

WÄHRINGER STR.
-VOLKSOPER

SEMPER- STRASSE

FUCHSTHALLERG.

VOLKSOPER

ALSERP

SCHOPENHAUERSTR

WÄHRINGERGÜRTEL

WÄHRINGERGÜRTEL

WÄHRINGERSTRASSE

BLEICHER- GASSE

NUSSDORFERSTRASSE

Widerhofer-
platz

BOLTZMANN-

LIE

C WÄHRINGERGÜRTEL

WÄHRINGERGÜRTEL

SEVERINGASSE

PRECHTL- GASSE

W.-EXNER- GASSE

STRUDLHOFGAS

TENDLER- GASSE

A.-CARLSSON-
PARK

INSTITUT FÜR
PHYSIK UND
CHEMIE

WÄHRINGERSTRA

ALLGEMEINES
KRANKENHAUS

FRAUEN-
KLINIK

SPITALGASSE

SENSENGASSE

ALTES
ALLGEM.
KRANKENHAUS

0   100   200 m
0   330   660 feet

D 1 2

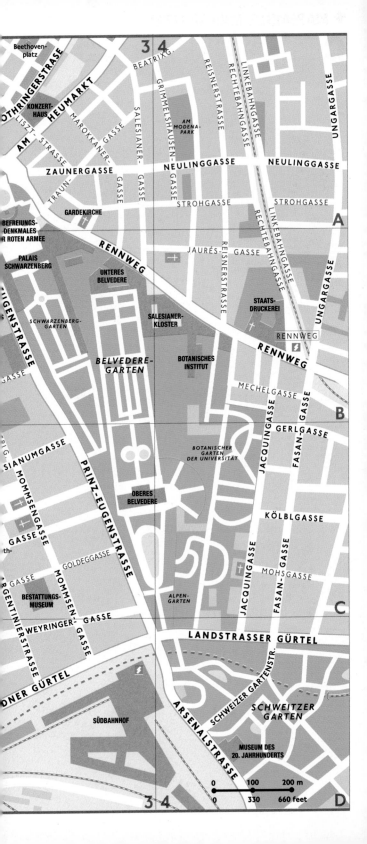

C

1 2

WESTBAHNSTRASSE

WESTBAHNSTRASSE

ST.-LAURENZ-KIRCHE

REN

KENYONGASSE

NEUBAUGÜRTEL

KAISERSTRASSE

SEIDEN-GASSE

SCHOTTENFELDGASSE

ZIEGLERGASSE

SEIDEN-GASSE

HERMANNGASSE

LINDENGASSE

ANDREASGASSE

RICHTERGASS

NEUBAUGÜRTEL

KENYONGASSE

STOLLGASSE

KAISERSTRASSE

SCHOTTENFELDGASSE

APOLLO-GASSE

ZIEGLERGASSE

A

NEUBAUGÜRTEL

Europaplatz

SOPHIEN-SPITAL

LAZARISTEN-KIRCHE

MARIAHILFERST

ZIEGLERGASSE

OTTO-BA

WEST-BAHNHOF

MARIAHILFERSTRASSE

WEBGASSE

HUGO-WO

WESTBAHNHOF

STUMPERGASSE

SCHMALZHOFGASSE

HIRSCHEN-

LINIENGASS

Loquai-platz

DINGELSTEDTG.

MARIAHILFERGÜRTEL

BÜRGERSPITAL-GASSE

MILLERGASSE

HAYDNGASSE

HAYDN-MUSEUM

WEBGASSE

B

MARIAHILFERGÜRTEL

AEGIDI-GASSE

MITTELGASSE

MARIAHILF

STUMPERGASSE

GUMP

RAIMUND-THEATER

MILLERGASSE

GRAB

WALLGASSE

LINIENGASSE

KRANKENHAUS DER BARMHERZIGEN SCHWESTERN

STUMPERGASSE

BRÜCKENGASSE

GUMPENDORFER STR.

GUMPENDORFERSTRASSE

ST.-AEGID-KIRCHE

SECHSHAUSER GÜRTEL

GUMPENDORFER GÜRTEL

WALLGASSE

EISVOGELG.

GUSTAV-ADOLF-KIRCHE

MOLLARDGASSE

BRÜCKENGASSE

C

MOLLARDGASSE

LINKE WIENZEILE

NEVIL

LINKE WIENZEILE

WACKENRODER-BRÜCKE

BRÜC

FR.-SCHWARZ-PARK

ST. JOHANN-PARK

SCHÖNBRUN

MARGARETENGÜRTEL

BÄRENGA

DUNKLERGASSE

FR.-SCHWARZ-PARK

GAUDENZDORFER-

LUFTGASSE

BRÄUHAUSGASSE

Am Hunds-Turm

BRÄU

SCHÖNBRUNNERSTRASSE

STEINHAGE

KOLLMAYERGASSE

MARGARETEN-

KONGRESS-HAUS

MARGARETENSTRA

EINSIEDLE

J.-SCHWARZ-GASSE

JOHANNAGASSE

DIEHL-GASSE

GIESS-

D

ARNDTSTRASSE

GÜRTEL

ARBEITERG

1 2

3 4
STIFTSKASERNE
RAHLG.

KIRCHEN-

STIFTGASSE

LINDENGASSE

GASSE

ST.-JOSEF-
-KIRCHE

STIFTSKIRCHE

LEHÁRG.

WINDMÜHLGASSE

FILLGRADERGASSE

GIRARDIG.

MARIAHILFERSTRASSE

MARIA-
-HILF-KLOSTER

GUMPENDORFERSTRASSE

LAIMGRUBENGASSE

KÖSTLERGASSE

ASSE

BARNABITENG.

MARIA-HILF-
-KIRCHE

STIEGENG.

A

CHADEKGASSE

ESTERHÁZY-
PARK

LUFTBADGASSE

JOANELLIG.

DÜRERGASSE

LINKE WIENZEILE

KETTENBRÜCKENG.
U

RECHTE WIENZEILE

MÜHLG.

PRESSG.

TR

KAUNITZGASSE

CORNELIUSG.

HAMBURGERSTRASSE

WEHRGASSE

KETTENBRÜCKEN-

FRANZENS-

GASSE

GASSE

HEUMÜHLG.

KLEINE NEUG.

B

MÜHLGASSE

GASSE

STURMBURGG.

PILGRAM-
BRÜCKE

PILGRAMGASSE
U

RECHTE WIENZEILE

GRÜN-

RÜDIGERGASSE

GASSE

SCHÖNBRUNNERSTRASSE

STROBACHG.

WEHRGASSE

KRONGASSE

STRAUSSENGASSE

GASSE

PILGRAMGASSE

LINKE WIENZEILE

WIEN

ST.-
-JOSEF-
-KIRCHE

GROHGASSE

MARGARETENSTRASSE

Margareten-
platz

ZIEGELOFENG.

MITTERSTEIG

HARTMANNG.

ECHTS-
CKE

RAMPERSTORFFERGASSE

GARTEN-

GASSE

SCHLOSSGASSE

C

SSE

SPENGER-
GASSE

MARGARETENSTRASSE

CASTELLIGASSE

ZENTAGASSE

HARTMANN-
SPITAL

HARTMANN-
PARK

REINPRECHTSDORFERSTRASSE

MARGARETENSTRASSE

SCHWARZHORNGASSE

Bacher-
platz

ARBEITERGASSE

SPENGER-
GASSE

SIEBENBRUNNENGASSE

RAMPERSTORFFERG.

MARGARETEN

Zenta-
platz

ZENTAGASSE

KOHLGASSE

SIEBENBRUNNENGASSE

WIMMERGASSE

MAYERGASSE

STÖBERGASSE

3 4   STOLBERGGASSE

0   100   200 m
0   330   660 feet

D

D

JÖRGERSTRASSE

BORSCHKEGASSE

HERNALSER HAUPTSTRASSE

THERESIENGASSE

ZIMMERMANNG.

MEYNERTG.

LAZARETT

ALSER STRASSE
U

GEBLERGASSE

Zimmermann-platz

KINDERSPITAL

KINDERSPITALG.

MA

OTTAKRINGERSTRASSE

HERNALSERGÜRTEL

HERNALSERGÜRTEL

ALSERSTRASSE

GASSE

FELDGASSE

DO

A

PAYER- GASSE

VERONIKAGASSE

FIAKER-MUSEUM

BREITENFELDER

Albert-platz

GASSE

BENNO-

GASSE

ALBERT-

Yppen-platz

SCHELLHAMMERGASSE

BLINDENGASSE

LAUDONGASSE

BRUNNEN- G.

Benno-platz

GAULLACHERGASSE

U

Uhlplatz

SKODAGASSE

Hamerling-platz

NEULERCHENFELDERSTR.

LERCHENFELDERGÜRTEL

LERCHENFELDERGÜRTEL

JOSEFSTÄDTER STR.

JOSEFSTADT

BRUNNEN- G.

JOSEFSTÄDTERSTRASSE

B GRUNDSTEINGASSE

BLINDENGASSE

STOLZENTHALERGASSE

TIGER-

LERCHEN-

GASSE

THALIASTRASSE

BLINDEN-INSTITUT

PFEIL-

GASSE

ALBERTGASSE

GASSE

GASSE

BRUNNENGASSE

THALIASTR.
U

HASNERSTRASSE

LERCHENFELDERGÜRTEL

LERCHENFELDERGÜRTEL

KAISERSTRASSE

JOS.-STRAUSS-PARK

ALTLERCHENFELDER KIRCHE

LERCHENFELDERSTRASSE

HIPPGASSE

WIM-

MENTERG.

BERNARD-

GASSE

NEUSTIFT- GASSE

NEUSTIFT

C HERBST.

BERGER-

HALBGASSE

ZIEGLER-

K.-FA-P-

GABLENZG.

BURGGASSE-STADTHALLE
U

GASSE

BURGGASSE

HALBGASSE

SCHOTTENFELDGASSE

BURG

GASSE

NEUBAUGÜRTEL

NEUBAUGÜRTEL

WURZBACH-GASSE

KAISER-STRASSE

NEUBAU

ZIEGLER-

BAND-

KANDL-

GASSE

KANDL-

GASSE

GASSE

SORBAITG.

MÄRZ-PARK

0   100   200 m
0   330   660 feet

WESTBAHNSTRASSE

ST.-LAURENZ--KIRCHE

ZIEGLER-

D

1   2

◆ PUBLIC TRANSPORT SYSTEM

- U1 Subway line (U-Bahn)
- S1 Schnellbahn line (S-Bahn)
- Vienna–Baden railway
- Bus station
- i Information point
- ✈ Airport

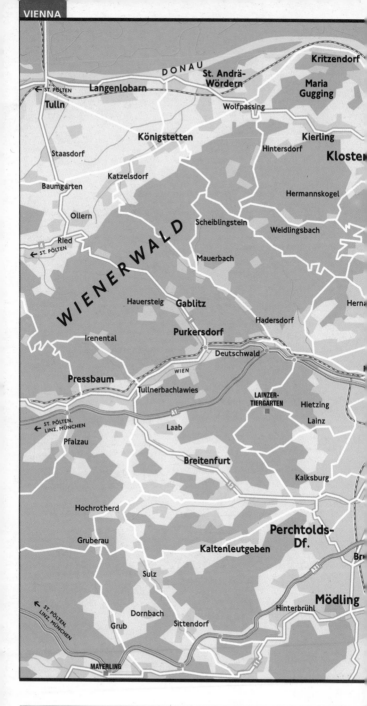

VIENNA

DONAU
Kritzendorf
St. Andrä-Wördern
Maria Gugging
← ST. PÖLTEN Langenlobarn
Tulln
Wolfpassing
Königstetten
Kierling
Hintersdorf
Staasdorf
Kloster
Katzelsdorf
Baumgarten
Hermannskogel
Ollern
Scheiblingstein
Weidlingsbach
Ried
← ST. PÖLTEN
Mauerbach
WIENERWALD
Hauersteig Gablitz
Herna
Hadersdorf
Irenental
Purkersdorf
Deutschwald
WIEN
Pressbaum
Tullnerbachlawies
LAINZER-TIERGARTEN
Hietzing
← ST. PÖLTEN, LINZ, MÜNCHEN
Laab
Lainz
Pfalzau
Breitenfurt
Kalksburg
Hochrotherd
Perchtolds-Df.
Gruberau
Kaltenleutgeben
Br
Sulz
Mödling
Dornbach
Hinterbrühl
← ST. PÖLTEN, LINZ, MÜNCHEN
Grub Sittendorf
MAYERLING

VIENNA FACTS AND FIGURES
Capital city and province of Austria, Vienna is the hub of Austrian political and economic life. It is also the country's cultural and artistic center.

AREA
160 square miles; 83 miles circumference; 23 districts (from under 1 square mile to 39 square miles)
Ist Innere Stadt
2nd Leopoldstadt
3rd Landstrasse
4th Wieden

5th Margareten
6th Mariahilf
7th Neubau
8th Josefstadt
9th Alsergrund
10th Favoriten
11th Simmering
12th Meidling
13th Hietzing
14th Penzig

15th Rudolfsheim Fünfhaus
16th Ottokring
17th Hernals
18th Währing
19th Döbling
20th Brigittenau
21st Floridsdorf
22nd Donaustadt
23rd Liesing